THE AUTHOR.

OUR SISTER REPUBLIC:

A GALA TRIP

THROUGH

TROPICAL MEXICO

IN 1869—70.

ADVENTURE AND SIGHT-SEEING IN THE LAND OF THE AZTECS,
WITH PICTURESQUE DESCRIPTIONS OF THE
COUNTRY AND THE PEOPLE,

AND

REMINISCENCES OF THE EMPIRE AND ITS DOWNFALL.

BY

COL. ALBERT S. EVANS.

WITH NUMEROUS ENGRAVINGS.

HARTFORD, CONN.:
COLUMBIAN BOOK COMPANY.
LONDON:
TRÜBNER & CO., 8 & 60, PATERNOSTER ROW.
1871.

TO HER

WHO THROUGH ALL MY WANDERINGS HAS EVER BEEN PRESENT IN MY MIND, AND WHOSE LOVE HAS BEEN THE GUIDING STAR OF MY LIFE,

THIS VOLUME IS DEDICATED, IN TESTIMONY OF UNCHANGING AFFECTION.

INTRODUCTORY LETTER

FROM HONORABLE WILLIAM H. SEWARD.

AUBURN, August 6th, 1870.

MY DEAR COLONEL EVANS :—

Your book on Mexico contains the observations which you made while a member of the party with which I traveled through that magnificent and interesting Country. Received and entertained there as a guest of the Republic, I have practiced in regard to Mexico, since my return to the United States, the same delicacy which I expect a friend whom I have been entertaining to practice when he has left my house. For this reason I cannot sanction either your observations or your deductions.

I am at liberty, however, to say that your details of our travels are full and accurate; your account of the resources and capacities of the country is not exaggerated; your pictures of Mexican society will be thought by the public too highly colored: I think that your error lies on the other side. The Statesmen of the country deserve all the praise you have bestowed upon them. Your style is attractive, the book is spirited, and I think it calculated to be useful.

Sincerely,

your friend and well-wisher,

WILLIAM H. SEWARD.

COLONEL ALBERT S. EVANS,
San Francisco, Cal.

PREFATORY.

THIS work embodies the observations of the Author on Mexico and her people, made while traveling as one of the party of the Hon. Wm. H. Seward, in 1869–70.

Through the kind partiality of Mr. Seward, and the liberality of the Government and Citizens of Mexico, the Author undoubtedly enjoyed greater facilities for seeing the country and its inhabitants, than have been accorded to any other traveler for many years.

I have endeavored to give an impartial description of what I saw and heard in that land of wonder and romance, avoiding neither the lights nor the shadows of the picture.

I had been familiar with the people of Mexico, a portion of their country, and much of their history, for many years; had sympathized with them in their noble struggle against invasion, and the infamous attempt of European rulers to subvert free government and plant despotic institutions on the soil of America; against the bigoted, superstitious and intolerant party of conservatism, which steadfastly opposed the education of the masses and all progress; against slavery, and the remnants of monarchical institutions handed down to them as a part of the curse of Old Spain, and was prepared to make many allowances for errors and short-comings, in view of the obstacles in the way of the country's progress, and the trials through which the nation had been called upon to pass.

The journey was in many respects the most remarkable one on record. No private citizen—whatever might have been his former station in life—ever received such an ovation as was given to Mr. Seward, by the people and Government of Mexico. From the Pacific to the Atlantic,—over a journey of some twelve hundred miles,—it was one grand triumphal march, and all classes and parties joined in the demonstration.

Seeing much to praise, something to blame, and much to excuse as the inevitable result of the acts of those who administered the Government and shaped the destinies of Mexico before the present generation came upon the field of action, I can safely say that the balance was decidedly on the right side and that I came away with more respect for the people, more sympathy for a nationality struggling—sometimes blindly, but always earnestly and persistently—along the path of progress, and more hope for the future of that much misunderstood and much misrepresented Republic, than I had when I entered it.

The journey was one of the most pleasing episodes of my life, and the memory of the friendships established, and the unceasing kindness and consideration received at the hands of Mr. Seward and the other members of his party, and the people of the country through which we traveled, will be a source of heartfelt enjoyment through all coming years.

I have not aimed at writing a comprehensive, statistical, and historical work on Mexico, but have left that task to other and abler pens, giving only what came under our personal observation, and endeavoring to show the reader, the country and the people as we saw them.

In a land where nature has lavished all her wealth with tropical prodigality, where the scenery is grand and beautiful beyond description, and every step is over historic ground, and amid scenes around which the romance of centuries has accumulated, I could not fail to see much to interest the reader and make the story of such a journey worthy of perusal, whatever my abilities as a writer might be.

The relations between Mexico and the United States must become more intimate as years elapse. The interests of the two Republics are growing, every day, more nearly identical. Nature and republican institutions have made us allies, and an injury inflicted upon one must be felt by the other, as well, in the end. If what I have written shall assist my countrymen in forming a more just and favorable idea of Mexico than they have hitherto entertained, I shall have every reason to be more than satisfied with the result of my labors.

List of Illustrations
Engraved by
FAY & COX
105 NASSAU ST. N.Y.

CONTENTS.

CHAPTER I.

CHAPTER II.

CHAPTER III.

CHAPTER IV.

CHAPTER V.

CHAPTER VI.

CHAPTER VII.

CHAPTER VIII.

CHAPTER IX.

CHAPTER X.

CHAPTER XI.

CHAPTER XII.

CHAPTER XIII.

CHAPTER XIV.

CHAPTER XV.

CHAPTER XVI.

CHAPTER XVII.

CHAPTER XVIII.

CHAPTER XIX.

CHAPTER XX.

CHAPTER XXI.

CHAPTER XXII.

HON. WILLIAM H. SEWARD TRAVELING IN MEXICO.

A GALA TRIP THROUGH MEXICO.

CHAPTER I.

FROM SAN FRANCISCO TO COLIMA.

GLORIOUSLY beautiful was that bright morning of the 30th day of September, 1869, when I reluctantly left the darkened chamber in which lay the mortal remains of a brave man, and true champion of freedom, my friend of many years, Señor Don Jose A. Godoy. the Consul of Mexico, who had fallen dead while attending the last reception of Mr. Seward on the evening previous, and bidding farewell to his stricken family, hurried on board the Pacific Mail Steamship Co's magnificent steamer Golden City, which was lying at her berth in San Francisco, with steam up, ready to bear us away to the tropics.

Blue and clear was the sky above us, calm and mirror like the surface of the broad Bay of San Francisco, soft as velvet in all their outlines, the brown, grey, and mauve-tinted mountains which surround it, when seen through the purple haze of Autumn which enveloped city and village, hill, mountain, island, fortress, and inland sea, alike in its tender and loving embrace. When I come again from beyond the snowy mountains, and the shores of another ocean, a change will have come over all the fair scene, and hill and valley, mountain and plain, will rejoice in the verdure and flowers of the spring-time. "Good-Bye!" "Good-Bye!" "Good-Bye!" The last friendly hand is shaken, the last affectionate embrace is given, and the plank hauled in, the crash of the great gun on the forward deck startles the echoes of all the hills around the bay, the great steamer moves slowly away from the wharf, swings around with the tide in the harbor, and gliding swiftly past the city front, the shipping from many

THE GOLDEN GATE.

ports, Alcatraz, Point San Jose, Fort Point, and the Presidio de San Francisco, passes through the Golden Gate, and heads out into the blue, illimitable Pacific.

The sea is calm, and the sky is clear, and everything promises a quiet, pleasant voyage. Capt. Lapidge, is an old and thorough seaman, Purser Mattoon understands making everybody comfortable, and is disposed to do it in an off-hand, unobtrusive way, and Dr. Miller, U. S. A. is on hand to attend to all who need his professional services; so that all our wants, and all contingencies are provided for. From one end of the steamer to the other, everything goes on like clockwork,—no noise, no loud talking, no confusion; Chinese sailors spread the awnings which are to shelter the passengers from the sun of the tropics, and Chinese waiters, clean, quiet, and orderly, with their list-soled slippers, move quietly about the cabin and state-rooms, keeping everything in order, and seeing that no wants of the passengers are left unattended to. On the whole, I think it must be conceded that John is the "coming man," and take him all in all, he is a pretty good fellow; it is well for us that no worse man is to come in his place.

On the afternoon of the second day—Friday—we were passing the islands off the Santa Barbara Coast, having made two hundred and thirty-five miles during the first twenty-four hours. On Saturday we were out of sight of land all day, and the register showed a progress of two hundred and twenty-two miles for the last twenty-four hours. On Sunday afternoon we came in sight of the large barren island of Cerros, and its outlying rocks and lesser islands, and the whole of the afternoon and evening skirted along the treeless, red mountain shores of Mexican Lower California. No living thing was to be seen on these verdureless mountains. Sitting back far enough from the rail to hide the blue stretch of water, you might fancy yourself upon the Colorado or Mojave Desert, without any serious stretch of the imagination; the same saffron-hued horizon, pale blue sky, red, brown, and yellow, jagged, naked mountains; the same eternal silence of utter desolation. "Mother," said a little prattling child upon the steamer, "mother, do anybody live in that land?" "No my darling, I hope not," was the earnest reply. God is merciful, and I trust she was right.

Sunday service at sea, of the Episcopal Church, was read by Capt. Lapidge, the few cabin passengers all joining in the responses, and then we went out on deck to watch the changes in the dreary, barren shore. A single little sail came in sight, and passed near enough for us to see that the craft was a sloop, of perhaps, twenty tons burthen, flying no flag, and carrying some half dozen dark-hued men—Italians, or other southern Europeans—who made no signals, and evidently did not care to court attention to the business in which they were engaged, whatever that might be; there is a little smuggling carried on, even upon this barren coast.

Monday morning found us plowing through a glassy sea, with no land, no sail, no bird in sight; only the great, glaring sun in the unclouded sky, and the deep, blue, glittering sea below. At 2 P. M. we were in sight of land once more—as desolate and uninhabited as the last. Had any one told us that day, that the noble steamer which was bearing us so safely and swiftly over the sea, would in less than six months more be lying an utter wreck on that terrible shore, with what increased interest would we have gazed on both! Passing Santa Margarita Island and Magdalena Bay, at sunset we were well toward Cape St. Lucas, or within one hundred miles thereof. At 5 P. M. we were a thousand miles from home.

At 8 P. M. a light was seen before us; then blue and red signal lights were sent up, and answered, and soon, out of the darkness emerged the great hull of the steamship Montana. Both steamers stopped, boats were sent off to exchange the latest papers from either side of the continent and carry letters and messages for the dear ones far away. Then a stream of flame shot far out across the waters from either steamer's deck, the loud roar of the signal guns filled the startled air, and the two great black masses moved away swiftly into the darkness again, and each was lost to the sight of those on board the other.

I know of no scene which one may witness in all one's life, more full of unwritten poetry, unenacted romance, more dreamily suggestive of "what might have been," than this meeting and parting of two great steamers on the pathless sea. Who were they who crowded the decks and wonderingly watched us as we watched them? In what mysterious way were their lives linked with ours? Were there any there who might have loved us, any we might have loved? What stories of love and hatred, and all the thousand emotions which distract the human mind, and affect for good or ill a human life, were spoiled, when the thousand souls which those two steamers bore, came thus near together, almost within touching distance, as it were, and then parted again, and for the most part forever? Had we met and mingled, how the whole story of this life, or that, might have been affected, and changed it may be for all time. There is food for conjecture and speculation without end in all this, but it is only vague unsatisfying speculation after all, and the questions suggested to each of us, must remain unanswered to all, forever.

Daybreak on Tuesday, October 5th, found us passing Cape St. Lucas, and within the tropics. Still the same dreary, barren, mountain shore; not a sign of human life have we seen while skirting along the Lower California coast for nearly a thousand miles; not a tree, not a flower, not a blade of grass, no living thing of any kind—only rocks and sand and loneliness, eternal silence and utter desolation. All the settlements—and they are few at best—are on the inner or Gulf side of the peninsula, and completely hidden from the passing vessel. The sun poured down all day from an unclouded sky, and no breeze ruffled the face of the ocean, which was smooth as a mirror, save where, at regular intervals, the long, heavy ground swells came rolling in from the south-westward, and pitched and tossed about the great steamer like an egg-shell.

The poet says:

> "There is no crowd however slight
> But one cockney is there."

We had ours. He stood looking over the rail, eye-glass in place, watching the tumbling of two great monster blackfish, which rose and disappeared like porpoises. "Aw! what kind of a whale might that be?" he demanded. The venerable looking McElroy, who represents the U. S. Custom-House Department on board, promptly replied, "That, my *dear* friend, is the Castor oil whale," a broad, genial smile of true benevolence spreading far and wide over his fine open countenance. "Haw, yes; that's what I thought. We 'ave hoceans on 'em in the Hinglish Channel!" was the prompt return of the true son of old Albion.

As the day died out and the sun went down in a blaze of glory, all hands assembled on deck to witness a sunset in the tropics. We often hear the remark, "That sky is unnatural; it is far too gaudy!" as we stand in some art gallery in the cold North before a picture in which the artist has faithfully labored to depict the glories of a tropical sunset. The paint sufficiently brilliant to do justice to the scene before us that evening has yet to be made. A smooth blue sea for a base, a soft blue sky above; along the western horizon a row of solid purple clouds standing up like jagged volcanic rocks from the bosom of the ocean, for which, indeed, they would have been unhesitatingly taken but for the constant alteration in their outlines. Every moment they

> "Suffered a sea change
> Into something new and strange."

A sea-lion, a land-lion, a sphynx, a castle, a walled city, a mighty volcano, an Orizaba or a Shasta, grew each in turn, before our wondering eyes. Soon the whole long line was cut off from its base, as if by a knife, and lifted high into air, and from the bosom of the sea rose up another, almost a duplicate of the first. Then the intervening sky, from brilliant orange, took on the hue of the inner surface of the sea-shell, deepened into the brightest vermilion, which glowed like a flame, and seemed to give off light and heat of its own, filling all the air. As the shadow of evening fell, the horizon grew by contrast brighter and brighter, the clouds became inky black, while the vermilion sky spread out like a valley between the two great Sierras—mountains of iron in a land of fire. We stood like the wondering denizens of another planet in the hour of this earth's last agony, and saw "the elements dissolve with fervent heat," and mountains undermined go crashing down into the hungry sea of flame. Then the black curtain of night fell over all, and, almost in the twinkling of an eye, that strange, wild, weird, enchanting scene, passed like a dream away.

Wednesday morning found us crossing the mouth of the Gulf of California, or the *Mar de Cortez*, as the Spaniards termed it, rain pouring down, the sea rough, and many on board sick, the writer among the number. Accursed be the memory of the man who found the ocean first! At 2 P. M., we passed Cape Corrientes, and when night came down with an almost impenetrable pall of darkness on the heaving waste of waters, we were within seventy-five miles of the entrance of the Bay of Manzanillo.

Slowly the great steamer crept along the rock-bound, dangerous coast, feeling her way cautiously as she went, and at 2 o'clock on Thursday morning, almost a week from our leaving San Francisco, we felt that we were once more in smooth water, and the loud report of the steamer's gun conveyed to us the glad tidings that we had entered the harbor of Manzanillo, and finished that portion of our journey comprised in the voyage down the Pacific. The Custom-House officials, Governor Cuerva and staff, and other officers and citizens, came on board at once to receive Mr. Seward, congratulated him on his arrival, and tendered him in behalf of the Republic and its citizens, the hospitalities of the country.

At day-break our baggage was sent ashore and passed at once, unopened, through the Custom House, and the party were then conveyed to the beach in boats carried through the surf to the shore on men's backs to the solid land. We stood at last on the soil of Mexico, saw the steamer sail away through the storm and disappear in the distance, then turned our faces eastward and looked about upon the strange land to which we had come, and the strange scenes and strange faces which surrounded us.

Nothing can be more thoroughly tropical and attractive in its appearance than Manzanillo as seen from the harbor at this season of the year. A bay, five miles across and nearly round with an entrance half as wide

BEACH AND HOUSES AT MANZANILLO.

as the bay on the southern side, surrounded by high conical hills, covered with dense foliaged trees, and bright and flowering shrubs, forms the harbor, one of the finest in the world for its size. The town itself is not much to speak of. Half-a-dozen long one-story houses with thick adobe walls, white-washed, with large court-yards, and surrounded by outhouses, all with broad verandahs, are used as general store-houses, offices and dwellings, by the proprietors of the American and European importing houses, while they have their principal places of business at Colima, Guadalajara, and other cities in the interior. A dozen or two tule thatched huts or *jacals* inhabited by natives, and scattered irregularly along the beach and on the hills above, constitute, with the barn-like Custom-House, or "*aduana maritima*," the remainder of the town, the whole being a mere *embarcadero* or depot, for the trade of the interior.

The Americans and Europeans, dress and live much as they do at home in their own countries, and appear to enjoy life pretty well, "considering." Society must of course be limited and select. The natives live *a la Mejicana*, wear a costume consisting of a white cotton shirt and drawers, and broad-brimmed *sombrero*. Those in good circumstances add a *poncho*, or Mexican woolen blanket of fine texture, and those who are out of luck content themselves with a shirt or pair of drawers alone: if particularly unblessed by fortune they contrive to get along without either, a *sombrero* and breech-clout of coarse cotton answering every purpose tolerably well. They are excellent boatmen, and generally willing to work, if employment is offered, at very moderate wages. The women dress as lightly as the men, and are in nowise charry of their personal charms. The people greeted our party with cordiality, but manifested little curiosity.

The Governor and his friends were all dressed in European costume, and though generally ignorant of our language contrived to anticipate every want, and show all possible hospitality. The merchants took possession of our party, furnished us with beds, and spread hospitable tables for us. Capital cigars and *cigarritos* we found here in abundance, and extremely cheap.

Thirty-two bunches of cigarritos, each containing thirty-six, are sold for one dollar, or about two per cent. of their retail price in New York or San Francisco. Let it rain! Matches, and all similar trifles made in the country, sell at correspondingly low prices, and imported goods are generally lower than in the United States, the duty being about the same, and rates nominal.

From Manzanillo to Colima, about ninety miles, there is no wagon-road though one could be easily built. Just back of the first range of hills, behind the town, there is a fresh-water lake, thirty miles in length, which would float a small steamer. By this lake, people are carried by native canoes toward Colima for its entire length, and from its farther end there is a tolerable wagon-road most of the way to that city.

The Government some time ago commenced to cut a canal, a fourth of a mile in length, through the hill back of the town, to connect the lake with the harbor, and make it possible for small steamers to pass through, thus opening up the country to commerce. The work was about half finished and then suspended for want of funds, about thirty thousand dollars having been expended. One hundred Chinamen working at one dollar per day, would finish the work in sixty days at most. The merchants seem to be doing well. They say that the duties are collected regularly and fairly now, the old custom of knocking off half or two-thirds of the amount on a full cargo, to the ruin of the smaller importers, having been abolished by the Juarez administration. They have not been subjected to "forced loans" since the mushroom "Empire" collapsed, the last squeeze having been made in January, 1866, by the French, when they levied $300,000 on the City of Colima, a town of 20,000 to 30,000 people, but were forced to decamp by the arrival of the Liberal army under Gen. Ramon Corona, when only $100,000 had been collected. There are still many French families residing in the country, and considering the provocations which the Mexicans have suffered, they are remarkably well treated everywhere.

The verdure on the hills is magnificent, and wonderfully soothing to the eye grown wearied with the sight of the bare, red hills of Lower California, and blinking under the rays of the fierce sun of the tropics. All the freighting between vessels and the shore, is done by lighters; there is only one miserable old rickety disused wharf, and everything has to be carried through the surf to the dry land on men's backs. The bay swarms with sharks, and the lake with alligators. Two years ago a sudden freshet drove the alligators out of the lake into the bay, and a fight, long, bloody, and terrible to witness, took place between them and the sharks. The inhabitants looked on with calm indifference—it was none of their funeral anyhow—and finally saw the alligators "cleaned out bag and baggage" by the sharks. This fact is well attested by numerous eye-witnesses still living here. On the beach is found the machinery for a large sugar-mill, imported six years ago at a cost of $30,000, and now lying rusting away in the sand. The want of a wagon-road, and the then disturbed condition of the country, prevented its reaching the plantation for which it was intended, near Guadalajara, and may now be left there for as many years to come, before the owners will take a new start and get it up into the interior, and put it in operation.

The forests all around abound with game, quail, deer, wild turkeys, pheasants, partridges of two varieties, &c., &c. It is a paradise for a hunter, and the waters of the bay abound with fish of all kinds.

The rain came pouring down in torrents for two days in succession, so that leaving for Colima was out of the question. Meantime we had nothing to do but go around and see the sights, such as they are. The beautiful white coffee of Colima, which is superior to the best Mocha, and sells here for a little less than thirty-three cents per pound, was carefully examined. Then the delicate-flavored and almost pure white sugar of Jalisco, which sells at ten cents per pound, was duly sampled and pronounced excellent and cheap. Tropical fruits, oranges, lemons, limes, sweet lemons, pomegranates, melons, bananas, and various others, nuts, etc., are abundant and cheap. In the court-yard of one of our hosts, Mr. Dieckman, we found trees loaded with oranges and *zapotes*, and at the lower end of the town, a cocoa palm tree, covered with nuts of all sizes.

We found cigars equal to a fair Havana, made at Tepic, selling for two dollars per one hundred, neatly put up in boxes. The temptation to smuggle a few of them into San Francisco, if we had been going that way, would have been almost irresistible. Half a million of silver dollars came down here from Guadalajara, in September, by one train or conducta, and were sent to San Francisco by the Golden City, which steamer brought them immediately back, on the way to New York or Europe, via Panama. They were on board when we came down the coast. Even the poorest people appear to have some small change, and there is far more money in the country, apparently, than our people, who form their opinion from letters written for publication abroad by European correspondents residing here, generally suppose.

A few years ago a vessel was loading Mexican dollars in the harbor of Manzanillo, when a box or two fell overboard, and the divers failed to recover them. The boxes at last rotted and went to pieces, and since that, from time to time, the waves during great storms wash the dollars ashore. When we arrived the waves had been immense, and the shore all along the front of the town, was lined with the poorer natives, hunting for the precious *pesos*. As these men earn their living by hunting, and loading and unloading vessels, having perhaps two or three days work in a month, a dollar is quite a fortune to them, and the finding of two or three is an event of their lives. The dollars are stained to an inky blackness by long immersion in the sea-water, but are still worth their face, and no discount is charged on them by the merchants, who get them all in the end. The people are small eaters in this hot climate, and beef is ten cents per pound, and beans fifteen cents, while fish can be obtained for the taking from the water, and fruit costs next to nothing; so that every time a native finds one of these dollars, he has secured the means of a comfortable living for a month, and may consider himself a gentleman for that time if he is of economical habits, and not given to gambling.

We heard much apparently well grounded complaint about the management of postal matters in this part of the Republic. The Government charges twenty-five cents on each letter, but, singularly enough, while there are no Government mails between here and the interior, there is a Post-Office, and the postage is rigidly exacted.

Thus a merchant makes up his correspondence and takes his letters to the Post-Office, where he pays twenty-five cents on each. There are stamps provided for by law, but none are for sale here, and the letters receive no mark from the Postmaster to show that the postage has been paid. Then the merchant dispatches a mail carrier to Colima, and pays him ten dollars for carrying the same batch of letters on which he has just paid the Government twenty-five cents each. At Colima the letters are delivered to the Post-Office, and twenty-five cents each collected again for simply passing them out over the counter, as there is nothing to show that they have paid the legal dues. Letters come from Mazatlan by steamers, prepaid, and twenty-five cents each is collected on them on their arrival here. Then they are sent to Colima as stated, and pay again before starting, and also on their arrival there, or three times in all. Letters from San Francisco, by steamer, for persons here, must be delivered to the Postmaster by the purser on his arrival, and twenty-five cents each is charged at once before they can go into the hands of the persons to whom they are directed. If the entire postal system of the country was thus managed, the Post-Office Department ought to be a paying institution, but I was told that the abuses complained of are exceptional and local, and that the Federal Government does not reap the benefit of the imposition. However, the tax is a heavy one on the merchants. I was told that one house having a depot here and a large store at Colima, paid last year $6,000 in postage and courier charges.

Despite the incessant rains, our time in Manzanillo passed not unpleasantly away, we were elegantly lodged, and fed, and cared for kindly every way. Gov. Cueva, Señor Rendon, the Administrador of Customs, and Mr. Morrill, the American Consul from Colima, all of whom had come down from Colima to meet Mr. Seward, staid with us until the storm at last cleared away on the night of the 8th of October, and we made ready for departure.

Gov. Cueva is a tall, dark, finely-formed, and intelligent young man. He is a physician by profession, but has been "acting Governor" for some years, and appears to be quite popular. He has taken a great interest in the establishment of free schools in Colima and other towns in the State, and a decided advance has been made within the last two years in general education. He appears to be fully aware of the importance of public improvements and the development of the great natural resources of the country. This little State of Colima—The smallest, or one of the smallest in the Union—contains a population of sixty thousand, of which three-fifths are pure Indian blood, and two-thirds of the remainder have but little European blood, a few only being of pure Castilian descent. Singularly enough, this Indian element appears to be the most liberty-loving and progressive portion of the population, and foreigners generally concede that it is less corruptible and changeable than the pure European. Whatever may be its faults, bull-dog tenacity, courage, and love of country are among its virtues and most hopeful characteristics. It has capacities which, developed by education, may yet prove the salvation of this beautiful country.

Señor Luis Rendon, a small, spare, sharp-featured, dark-hued man, appears to be a thorough gentleman.

He has effected great reforms in the Custom House and is called a "a square man" by the importing merchants who, however, dislike him because he exacts full and complete obedience to the law, which has put a stop to the old system of reductions on imports, in favor of the great merchants, to the ruin of the small ones. Under his administration, Manzanillo, from yielding five hundred thousand dollars per annum in revenue to the Federal Government, has come to yield $1,500,000. and all without a single wagon-road into the interior in any direction. When roads already commenced are finished, a wharf built, and some other improvements made, this place will grow into a thriving port, and have a grand commerce.

SEÑOR LUIS RENDON.

Give Mexico ten years of uninterrupted peace, and Manzanillo, with its natural advantages and the expediture of a small sum for improvements, would become an important seaport. The town is somewhat unhealthy because the lake gets low and breeds fever and ague during the dry season, but the Europeans and Americans appear to suffer but little, while the natives, being poorly housed and exposed to all sorts of weather, are sick half of the time. We saw many of them lying around under the verandah, apparently half dead with ague. Everything here comes down from the interior on mule-back, and it takes six days for a train to make the ninety miles from Colima to Manzanillo. Some time this will be all different. Already, a telegraph line is in operation from the City of Mexico to this place, and Mr. Seward was met by congratulatory dispatches direct from President Juarez and Cabinet. Stage-coaches and steamboats will come next, and then railroads and a higher civilization.

After two days' waiting at Manzanillo the rain suddenly ceased, and a clear sunset gave promise of fine weather to follow. At day-break on the 9th of October, all Manzanillo was astir, and our party prepared to leave for Colima. By arrangement, the entire company, "bag and baggage," was to be transported by boats up the Laguna de Cayutlan thirty miles, then across the divide of three leagues, between the end of the lake and the Rio Maria, in Concord coaches sent down by Don Juan Firmin Huarte, the hospitable proprietor of the immense estate formerly known as "Los Chinos," now as "La Calera," and thence over the river and the succeeding three leagues to that place, as could be best arranged under the circumstances.

As the party left the house and walked out through the straggling, crooked street, lined with low, thatched huts half of which were flooded from the rains and vacated by the owners, the people stood hats in hands all along the way, to give Mr. Seward a kindly parting salutation. All was bustle and confusion at the landing. Men were wading back and forth in the muddy water, carrying packages, or altering and arranging the boats. Five light, strong boats, each painted white, red and green—the national colors of Mexico—had been provided. Two boats carried the "Seward Party," Gov. Cueva and Señor Rendon; a third the promiscuous escort, and the fourth and fifth were loaded down with our luggage, provisions, etc., etc.

Despite the many delays all the party was safely on board the boats just after sunrise. The air was still and the sky clear, and in a short time the heat became almost insupportable. Then, little black-eyed Mexican boys, spry and agile as cats, crept around each boat hanging out gaily striped awnings, and rich colored blankets, to shield us from the blazing rays of the tropic sun, and we lay down in the boats, at full length, and watched with a wondering interest, the shifting of the glorious panorama before us. The great mountain chain, which forms a semi-circle around the inland side of the Laguna de Cayutlan, is clothed in magnificent vegetation, from the waters edge to its summit; all the wealth of the tropics is lavished on the picture. The long lines of palm trees on the heights, cutting sharply against the blue sky, seem to have been set there by some cunning hand, to make it perfect in all its artistic details.

The Laguna de Cayutlan runs nearly east and west for thirty miles, parallel with and but a short distance from the sea, and at this season is from four to ten feet in depth, and one to six miles wide. It would float a steamer the year round.

Within the charmed circle in which we floated, all was peaceful and still; there was hardly breeze enough to puff out the sails which our boatmen spread to lighten their labors, and the surface of the Laguna was like glass, while at the same time we could hear the hollow booming of the ocean waves, and the dull incessant roar of the surf, breaking on the beach just beyond the line of palm- trees, which bounded the view upon the south.

Our rowers, five in each boat, nearly naked, or entirely so, worked well. I never saw better rowers. They appeared to be all of pure Indian blood—the working element of the country. Their oars all struck the water at once, and they sent the boats through the water at a high speed. Had they been selected instead of the Harvard crew, to row against the Oxfords, I would have staked my money on the American side, if I chanced to have any to risk.

On our arrival at Manzanillo from the steamer, at the house of Mr. Bartling, who most hospitably entertained our party during our stay, we were provided with six excellent camp bedsteads, with beautiful gilded frames and canopies, lace mosquito bars, and lace-covered pillows, rich crimson counterpanes, and fine soft matresses complete in every detail. While going up the lake we noticed, among the baggage, six neatly wrapped packages covered with matting and securely corded, and learned with surprise that each contained one of these beds packed for transportation, and that they had been purchased expressly for us at Colima, and were to be transported for our especial use from one side of Mexico to the other.

At one point we landed on the rocky shore of the Laguna, and gathered beautiful wild flowers, but the chaparral was so matted together with tangled vines and parasitic and climbing plants, that we could not travel ten rods in any direction, and after vainly endeavoring to get a shot at the flocks of gaudy parrots which filled the larger trees, we returned to the Laguna and were carried pick-a-back, to the boats again. The alligators, who fill the Laguna, are very cautious and shy, and it was only now and then that one would show the point of his dark snout above the surface. A volley of ill-directed pistol balls would send him down in an instant every time. On the whole I don't think the alligator crop of Cayutlan, will be to any serious extent the smaller next season, on account of our visit.

When we had gone about twelve miles up the lake, the flotilla came to a halt opposite a beautiful rocky island covered with giant cacti. All the boats came together, and in a few minutes the entire party was engaged in discussing; with keen relish, a bountiful lunch. When the repast was finished, Gov. Cueva proposed, as a sentiment, "Welcome to our distinguished guest; peace, and a better understanding, and more perfect friendly relation between the people and Government of the great Republic of the United States, and the people and Government of the Republic of Mexico." The toast was drank with the honors, and duly responded to, and the flotilla again moved up the Laguna.

At 2 P. M., we reached the landing at the eastern end of the lake, and found two light, Concord spring coaches, sent down from the interior for our use, and a multitude of attendants waiting to receive us. They had a full pack-train of mules ready to carry the baggage up to Colima, but the piles on piles of plunder which came on shore from our boats until the whole beach was strewn with it, startled them not a little, and made some of the mules drop their ears in utter dejection. The mules in common use all over the country are the smallest I have ever seen. Some of them do not weigh more than two hundred pounds, and it is a large sized one which will weigh three hundred and fifty or four hundred pounds: but like the little horses of the country, they are "lightning" when it comes to traveling or pulling.

Three leagues—about seven and a half or at most eight English miles—across a flat sandy country, entirely covered with impenetrable thickets of small thorny shrubs, trees of the acacia species, cacti, creeping plants, and climbing vines, over a road heavy with the rains, and poor at best, brought us to the Rio de Santa Maria, a small stream in ordinary times, but now a tremendous torrent, thick with mud. It looked wholly impassable. On the opposite shore there is a village of palm-thatched bamboo huts, inhabited, with one exception, by families of the civilized and Christian Indians of the country—once peons, but now all enfranchised. The rocky banks were lined with dark-skinned men in loose, white cotton drawers and shirts, immense broad-brimmed hats, and with rawhide sandals on their feet. We signaled the boats on the opposite shore, and a party of the natives immediately put off into the raging torrent, some wading as far as possible and pulling the boat by main strength, others handling the paddles.

It looked like certain death, to attempt the passage of the torrent in those little boats, but we could not stay there for it to fall, and cross we must, or drown in the attempt. I essayed the passage first, and though we went bounding up and down like an india rubber ball, and took water several times, we made the riffle in safety, and soon after, Mr. Seward and the entire party were across, and proceeded to the house of the great landholder of the vicinity, Don Ignacio Largos. His house is of bamboo or cane, like the others, and has a mud floor, but everything is as clean and neat as the parlor of the most thrifty New England housewife, and his young wife—a comely woman of the Spanish blood and type—made us at home at once.

Don Ignacio, a man of about seventy years, but stout, and well preserved, with hardly a gray hair in his head, came in to inform Mr. Seward, that the stream was too high to allow of the passage of the stages, but that during the night it would subside. They would then put the wheels of one side of the stage in one boat, and those of the other side in a second, and so row the cumbersome vehicles across. Meantime, he and all he had was "at His Excellency's service." He had two coaches in tolerable repair, which he was ready to hitch up to convey us on three leagues more to the "Hacienda Calera," the residence of Don Juan Firmin Huarte, where we were to pass the night. The old gentleman told us that he had about four thousand five hundred acres of the best sugar, cotton, and Indian corn land in America, and, he did not know exactly how many, though quite a number of square miles of good pasture lands in this rancho, which he would sell me [some one had wickedly represented me as the rich man of the party] for $8,000 in gold. He had a few thousand cattle, all good stock, though diminutive, which he would also dispose of cheap. There might be 2,000 or 10,000, but he would not be particular about a few hundred head any way. He wanted to move upon a larger rancho somewhere up in the interior. I agreed to think it over until I came back, and give him my answer then. I trust that he will not get tired out, and die waiting to hear from me.

Dinner, consisting of a variety of meats, vegetables, fruits, sweetmeats, and wines, was placed on the table, and I take occasion to say that a cleaner, better cooked, and better served dinner could not be obtained at any hotel in the United States, though there was not a sign of a stove, carpet, or even floor about the premises.

At sunset, we saw our baggage train of pack mules

arrive on the other shore, and the boats commence to take it over. We started at night-fall for La Calera, three leagues further on, and were whirled along over the heavy road at good speed, by the smart little mules furnished us by Don Ignacio. Up to this point the country, except for the densely wooded mountains in the background, might have been mistaken for the Bayou Teche country in Louisiana, though the vegetation was more abundant, and the soil richer and softer—a fine country for cultivation. Now, we crossed the Llano de San Bartolo, a more open country, with occasional Indian villages. On this plain, the Spaniards were defeated with great loss, and driven back to their ships, in the time of the conquest by Cortez; but a second battle resulted in their favor, and the Indian power in Colima was forever broken. Passing in the moonlight an immense hacienda, with solid stone walls on all sides, now partially deserted, we arrived at La Calera at 10 o'clock, and were warmly welcomed.

When we arose at day-break on Sunday and walked out upon the broad verandah, which surrounds the great house at the hacienda of Don Juan Firmin Huarte, the scene before us was entrancingly beautiful. The estate occupies a broad valley, through which runs a small river, and is surrounded on all sides by mountains as high as the highest peaks of the Coast Range of California These mountains are covered from base to summit with low timber, as thick as it can stand on the ground, and all covered with a brilliant green foliage, save where the beautiful *primavera*, which bears great loads of white, red, pink, and blue blossoms, gives variety to the scene. This wood is all crooked, and mainly worthless for building purposes, though the amount of fuel on an acre is enormous The valley itself is one grand garden, run to wild. In one place, rows of tall graceful cocoa palm-trees, loaded with fruit in all stages of growth, lift their feathery heads in air, and call up visions of the gardens of Damascus. Then wide fields of sugar-cane, ripe, and ready for cutting, then corn-fields, where the corn is equal in size to that of Illinois, rice-fields, and great patches of banana plants, fifteen or twenty feet in height, each leaf being of the size of a counterpane on a double bed at home.

Turning our eyes from this scene to that more immediately at hand, we saw life in the tropics in all its lazy luxuriousness. Upon this grand hacienda, which is exactly as large as the District of Columbia, reside three hundred to four hundred natives of pure, or nearly pure, Indian blood, who are employed as laborers in the fields and around the mills. The men receive thirty-seven and-a-half cents per day, and board themselves. They are not very cheap laborers even at that price. For their accommodation, a meat-market is kept under a large open shed in front of the "*casa grande.*" This market is supplied with beef from cattle killed during the night—we had been disturbed in our sleep by the bellowing of the poor beasts—and the market was in full operation when we saw it at day-break. The women by dozens, tall, slender, and dark, dressed in light-colored cotton gowns, without hoops, and barefooted, with black *rebosas* wrapped around their shoulders and heads, half hiding their faces, were buying the day's supply of meat for the family, while the men lounged about in every variety of dilapidated garments, smoking cigarritos. A few wore brilliant-hued *serapes* closely wrapped around them, or thrown with negligent grace over one shoulder. This hacienda has the name of being very unhealthy, and many of the men appeared ill from malarious diseases. The meat was cut in irregular pieces with rude knives and axes, and sold at from six and a half, to ten cents per pound. Each purchaser took but a small piece, about enough for a "square meal" for three persons in a cold climate. The fat was being tried out for candles in a large kettle in front of the market, and the offal was lying in a corner. Swarms of long-nosed wolfish-looking dogs hung around, snapping up every scrap of meat left within reach, or thrown to them.

Beyond the market stands an immense half-finished sugar-house, and all around the place was scattered machinery therefor, hardly two pieces, belonging together, being within hearing distance of each other. The walls were of brick made on the place and poorly laid in cement. The roof is to be of tiles, but it is not yet finished. A vat for water, intended to hold at least two million gallons, built of brick and cemented, is built along-side. The three great boilers for this mill were being towed through the Laguna of Cayutlan—having been closed and cemented water-tight to insure their floating—as we came up on the previous day. The mill cannot be finished in less than six months, and meantime a superb crop of cane goes to waste. Opposite the sugar-mill is a huge building containing a rice mill, saw-mill, &c. The sugar machinery and distilling apparatus are from Hamburg, the steam-engines and boilers from England, and the rice and saw-mills from Boston and San Francisco. Everything consumed on the place is raised on it. Between the two mills is an enormous ditch or race for carrying the water to a great turbine wheel which is to run some of the machinery and assist in irrigation. The grounds all around are filled with carts and other agricultural implements, exposed to sun and rain, and a great part of the work done on the buildings and ditch, &c., has been wasted, because not half done,—a set of incompetent theoretical European engineers, having botched everything from the start. The proprietor, Señor Huarte, now sees how he has been imposed upon, and when we were there, was endeavoring to secure the services of a clear-headed practical American, then at Colima, to take charge of the work and carry it on to completion. He has already expended $200,000 on improvements on his estate and from appearances, it will cost fully half as much more before he will derive an income from it. The fields are rudely fenced with round poles, and cultivated in a very primitive manner with clumsy agricultural implements. When in full operation with proper management, the estate ought to pay interest on a million dollars.

Señor Huarte is a native of old Spain, short, dark, rotund, polished in manner, courteous and hospitable, and fond of doing everything on a princely scale. His grand house is at Colima, where his children reside—he is a widower—and this is only his country residence. During our stay, he entertained us on a scale of magnificence which puts the hospitalities showered on our visitors to California completely to shame. His kitchen swarms with domestics, male and female, and at his table, course after course of meats, fowls, vegetables and fruits follow each other with rapidity, for hours at a time, and are washed down with wines from every grape growing country from Ay and Malaga, to Sonoma.

When we arose on Sunday morning we, found a fat, round-bellied, jolly-looking priest, in black, sitting in the door-way, while his assistants were hanging a bright, large-patterned chintz curtain up along the wall under the lower verandah, and preparing for mass. Donning his rich embroidered white satin robes, he opened the service. The native women and children came stealing quietly in, and knelt on the pavement, in the great walled area by themselves, while the men in lesser numbers came in, and knelt or sat carelessly about in the verandah. The priest read his prayers in an inaudible voice in Latin, then, seated in a chair, read indifferently a very good, sound, practical, moral sermon in Spanish, then concluded the services "with bell and candle," and then proceeded to pack up his traps. I observed that Señor Huarte stood by as "patron" during the services, but the congregation, consisting of perhaps one hundred, all told, contained no other men of intelligence or education. Gov. Cueva, Señor Rendon, and the other educated men who were with the Seward party, regarded the priest and his proceedings with apparent indifference. When the service was over the priest packed up his things, mounted his little mule, took his umbrella in his hand, and galloped away to hold service somewhere else. His figure as he galloped off was so strikingly Spanish and picturesque that it might answer for an illustration of Gil Blas or one of Cervantes works.

All that morning mounted men were galloping back and forth, receiving orders from Señor Huarte, hat in hand, or detailing the latest news from the river. At 2 p. m. the stages arrived, and the baggage, which had come up meantime, was packed and started off. Having done the honors of his country house to the party, Señor Huarte announced his intention of accompanying us to Colima, and acting the host there. As we left La Calera, the party consisted of Mr. Seward, Fred Seward and wife, Abijah Fitch, Señor Don Francisco, Javier Cueva, Governor of Colima, Señor Francisco Gomez Palencia, his Secretary, who is also "*Diputado Suplente al Congreso de la Union*," from Colima, Señor Damiar Garcia, "*Capitan de buque y Director Politico de Manzanillo*;" Señor don Luis Rendon, "*Administrador del Aduana Maritima del Departamento de Colima*;" Señor Jacinto Cañedo, "*Oficial 2º de la Aduana Maritima del Manzanillo*;" Dr. Augustus Morrill, Consul of the United Sates at Colima, the writer, and about fifty followers of all classes, not forgetting to mention Mr. Seward's colored servant, John Butler, who condescendingly taught our language to the Mexican servitors down stairs, while Mr. Fitch did the same to our host above. If "Pigeon-English" did not break out as an epidemic at La Calera immediately after our departure. I can only account for the fact by assigning it to a special interposition of an All-Merciful Providence, in behalf of an afflicted people.

To each coach, four little mules were harnessed abreast at the lead, and two a trifle larger at the wheel. Half a dozen men held the six mules until ready to run, then we "cast off;" the "*cochero* yelled," the "*postillion*" cursed, and cracked his whip, and we went off like a railroad train. When we came to a particularly heavy place in the road the cochero hissed," *ist*, i-s-a-h, i-i-i-s-s-s-t-a-a-a!" and shouted, "Aha, ha-ha-ha-ha, ha, h-a-a-a-a!" incessantly, while the postillion lashed the poor little panting mules furiously, and occasionally jumped off and varied the performance by stoning them, then jumping back to the seat while the coach was in full motion. These postillions carry matting sacks holding about half a peck, which they fill with stones about the size of a hen's egg, and keep in reserve for emergencies. If the team balks, or is stalled for a moment, they will send a steady stream of these stones through the air, hitting each mule on the head in turn, with the accuracy of a Western sharp-shooter.

Some places which those little mules took our heavy coaches through, hardly seemed passable, but they did it. The old simile of the "rat running off with a haystack" loses all point when applied to these little Colima mules, but it is death on the rats, nevertheless. Four "police of the road," mounted on little agile horses, with costly saddles and rich trappings, each man carrying a *machete*, or straight, short sword, Henry rifle, and a Colt's revolver of the finest pattern, rode in advance, and four fine, tall, intelligent-looking men of the Custom-House Guard, still more splendidly equipped and armed, rode behind us. One of these last men was

SEÑOR HUARTE'S HOUSE AT COLIMA.

about twenty-five years of age, of olive complexion, classic features, six feet three inches in height, and slim and straight as a young palm tree. I never saw a finer rider—all these men ride like Centaurs—or a handsomer man. His belt buckle was of finely wrought silver, and his pistol holster and pistol, marvels of rich ornamentation in the same metal.

At Tecolapa, twelve miles from La Calera, we saw long rows of Indian women going to the well with water-jars poised on their shoulders, exactly as has been done in Palestine from the days of Jacob and Rebecca to our own day.

It is thirty-six miles from La Calera to Colima. The Government is spending a large sum in grading a wagon-road over the mountains from Colima to the sea, and the thirty miles nearest Colima are finished. But the storm had torn it up fearfully, and in many places it was almost impassable. Rain came on, and when the moon went down behind the mountains, the darkness added to the difficulty of the trip, and we went on at a snail's pace. We changed teams three times in the thirty-six miles, but it was 2 o'clock in the morning before we emerged from the long "Via de Colima" upon the well-paved streets of that fine old city, and our coach, with a rattle and uproar which awakened all the sleeping watchmen, rolled up to the door of the truly palatial mansion of Señor Huarte.

CHAPTER II.

COLIMA.

IT was 2 o'clock in the morning,on Monday, October 11th, when we entered Colima. We swallowed a hasty lunch, and retired to bed just as the watchmen, whom we had noticed sitting along the sidewalk, with muskets in their hands, and great oil-fed lanterns by their sides, blew all their whistles, and, as with one voice, drawled out the hour, "3 o'clock in the morning, and all quiet," (in Spanish,) a proceeding totally unnecessary, as the Cathedral and different church bells all strike the hours, and in fact give the cue to the watchmen, none of whom have anything like a time-piece of their own. It seemed as if we had just closed our eyes in welcome sleep, when the air was filled with shrill and piercing music, the sharp rattle of the kettle-drum, and the blare of trumpets.

Awake in an instant, I listened in doubt, and for some minutes I tried vainly, to decide where I was and to what I listened. The music was such as enlivened the march of Cortez and Pizarro, and their companions, when they came to spread desolation and the religion of the cross, through peaceful and unoffending lands, but the air must have been centuries older: if it resembled anything originating since the flood, it was "The White Cockade."

I looked down at the bed, with its crimson and fringed

counterpane and gilt canopy, and from that to the walls, painted in pale blue, and frescoed, and the cream-colored ceiling, with cross-beams of a soft, chocolate color, and then went to the iron-latticed window and looked down on a neatly-paved court, around which the house was built, and the great staircase with its wealth of brilliant-hued tropical flowers and climbing delicate-foliaged plants, and its Moorish dome painted in fresco. Where was I? Opening the door of my bedroom, I looked into the grand saloon, about sixty or seventy feet square, with its walls and ceiling painted like those just described, its glazed tile floor, double rows of Moorish arches and pillars supporting the roof, and chandeliers suspended with iron chains from the ceiling, and the long table with its crimson damask covering, and at last the truth of the situation flashed upon me. I was not in the Alhambra at Grenada, in 1469—I might have been, for everything was as thoroughly Moorish—but in Colima, in October, 1869.

"Is it a revolution?" I asked of the obsequious servant in white, who came at once to attend upon me. "Oh no,Señor; only the troops changing guard at the State Prison on the Plaza!"

Going out on the balcony, I looked across the way, and saw the band in front of the prison and the white-clad soldiers—all of Indian blood—with red plumes in their hats, and Springfield muskets of the year 1862 in their hands, going through the form of guard mounting. I saw those muskets in San Francisco, during the late war with France, if I mistake not. The ruinous old cathedral, dating far back into the 1600 and something, adjoins the prison, and all around the Plaza runs a row of shops, for the most part but one story high. All the buildings are of brick, with immensely thick walls, iron-latticed windows, and heavy wooden doors with curious antique iron locks, and flat, red-tiled roofs. Beyond the buildings, in all directions, towered the feathery cocoa palms and giant-leaved banana trees—or plants—of the rich gardens of Colima. Still back of them were the green, wooded mountains which surround this lovely Valley of Colima, with the great "Volcan de Colima," with a crown of dark smoke hanging over its crater, towering above all else, in the north-east. It was a scene worth half a life to look upon but once.

On the street the scene was less beautiful, but very picturesque and peculiar; not a carriage in sight. Little asses, loaded with green corn fodder, or carrying frames, in which were set on either side two large red earthen water jars, trotted along the long, straight, narrow streets. Men in broad hats and light Summer costume of white cotton or linen, trotted along on small, but spirited and richly saddled horses, and the common men and women of the country, on foot, filled the streets and sidewalks. All the marketing, except on Sunday when the great market is held, is done at an early hour, before the heat becomes annoying, and at sunrise the scene on the streets of Colima and all other Mexican towns, is most interesting. In the middle of the day the streets are almost deserted, and toward evening the visiting and fashionable promenading commences.

The principle dry goods and fancy stores are situated in the large buildings, with the portals fronting on the plazas, and the sidewalks are, during a considerably portion of the day, given up to small traders, who spread their little stock of cheap jewelry, slippers, watches, cigaritos, knives, swords, and a thousand minor articles such as are usually found in a "notion store" at "Cheap John's" in the United States, on mats, and squat beside them on the pavement. The main market is held in an open square, where the more common articles of coarse food, green corn, fruit, etc., and the light, strong, red earthen ware of the country are exposed for sale in the morning. Colima has 35,000 or 40,000 inhabitants, and at morning or evening they are all on the streets. As our party passed along, people always civilly made room, and the better class generally bowed politely. In passing the prison, the guard invariably presented arms to me, and I found after a time, this was all owing to the fact that I wore a vest of blue cloth, with brass buttons bearing the coat of arms of the State of California, and for my own convenience I was forced to change it, and by donning a plain white vest retire to private life.

They make the change here, when you buy anything at a store, down to the smallest fraction of a cent; there is nothing like the Californian contempt for the odd bit in Mexico. Being in want of a pair of light pantaloons, I learned to my surprise that there was no ready-made clothing store in Colima, and a tailor was sent for at once to wait upon me. My order and measure taken down, the "artist" departed, and at night returned with the garment finished. "How much?" He at once rendered me a bill for cloth, buttons, thread, labor, etc., amounting to seven dollars and twelve and one-half cents, and he would neither take seven dollars, nor seven dollars and twenty-five cents, but must have the exact change. The barber, boot-maker, shoemaker, and other tradesmen wait on you in the same manner, and exact the same minute change.

The servants receive $5 to $8 per month, in extreme cases $10, and are exceedingly respectful and attentive. They come at the clapping of the hands instead of the bell-call, as with us, and always stand bare-headed when addressed, even though the rain be pouring, or the sun scorching hot.

At the invitation of Señor Huarte, the party one evening rode out to the suburbs, and went through his private garden, one of many such in the vicinity. The grounds, enclosed with a high stone wall in front, and a stake and pole fence elsewhere, probably comprise, all told, about ten acres. Trees and plants fill the whole inclosure, the paths only excepted, and the variety and richness of the fruit and foliage are beyond description. Tall cocoa palms, covered with fruit, tower high in air in all parts of the grounds, and the bananas, of which there are four varieties, fill in beneath as an undergrowth, though fifteen to twenty feet in height. Then there are red-berried coffee trees, with bright green leaves; *aguacates*, or alligator pears; *zapotes*; *cacao*, or the chocolate tree; oranges, lemons, peaches, sweet lemons, limes, mangoes, *cheremoyas*, pineapples, citrons, and an almost endless variety of minor tropical fruits. It would require the space of a full page to name them all. Of flowers, there are many, large and brilliant-hued, but generally devoid of pleasant odor. It was curious to see the common "lady's-slipper" of the North, here cultivated beside the gaudy flowers of the tropics, and regarded as something very rare and choice. Of creeping plants, there are hundreds. One of these has foliage like the cypress tree, as delicate as lace, and beautiful red blossoms.

In the corner of the garden stands a large brick house

with a wide brick-paved verandah: this is the lounging place. Adjoining is a brick-walled tank, thirty-five feet long and fifteen broad, filled with water kept fresh by constant running; this is the proprietor's bathing place. It is shaded by the palm trees and banana plants, and the coolness makes it a delightful resort at morning and evening in this fervid climate. There is no "fruit season" here; it is fruit all the year around. The cocoanut is never eaten here as with us. The nuts are picked when just two-thirds grown and while the fluid inside is as clear and limpid as the finest spring water. This is called "*Agua de Cocoa,*" and is a favorite and very healthy and palatable beverage. The Indian servants who attend to the garden, had many of the cocoanuts already prepared with one end chipped off with a *machete*, to allow the water to be turned out as from a jug, and as we took seats in the verandah they served it around in large glasses. When the water is turned out there remains a white mucilaginous substance like thin custard, which is scraped out and eaten with a slip of the green husk for a spoon. It is highly flavored but not agreeable to the uninitiated.

From these gardens, fruit is sold to all who desire it. Cocoanuts are sold for twenty-five cents per dozen at retail, bananas for twelve and a half to fifteen cents a bunch of one hundred or more, and other fruit in proportion. One hundred square yards of ground in bananas, will afford sustenance for an entire family the year round; why then should people kill themselves with hard work? Señor Huarte paid $2,000 for the garden, and expended $2,000 more in building the house and bath, or $4,000 in all. He thinks that the income from this garden may be two per cent per month on the money invested, but as he has no guard upon the Indian servants he cannot tell how much they receive, and is probably cheated out of four-fifths of the actual proceeds of the sales.

Señor Canedo, who has traveled in the United States, and has some excellent practical ideas, coupled with a degree of patriotism which led him to fight valiantly against the French, coming out of the war with numerous honorable wounds, accompanied us, and gave us much valuable information in regard to the country and its products. He told us that the coffee we saw was of the finest variety grown in Colima. This coffee readily finds sale at home, and except as a curiosity, is seldom sent abroad. The choicest berries picked out by hand, sell at the fancy price of one dollar and twenty-five cents in coin, and the ordinary berries, really quite as good for family use, at twenty-five cents. If he could be sure of getting even twenty cents per pound net, in San Francisco, he would undertake to furnish any amount in a few years. The berry is round and white, and the flavor equal if not actually superior to that of Mocha. Only about 40,000 or 50,000 pounds are produced in Colima annually, but the amount could be increased indefinitely. Cocoa-nut oil, produced from the small round cocoa-nut, called "*Cochita*," about the size of a hickory-nut, not the ordinary cocoa-nut, is also produced in considerable quantity. At Manzanillo it is worth about seventeen dollars, coin, per barrel.

Of tropical fruit, Colima—the State at large—is able to raise unlimited amounts, and with good roads to Manzanillo, and a foreign market, an immense trade might soon be built up. Cacao—pronounced ka-kow, not cocoa—or the chocolate bean is produced all over the Tierra Caliente of Mexico, and its product could be increased indefinitely. The chocolate made from this, in Mexican style, is the most delicious warm drink I have ever tasted. It is no more like the coarse compound made and sold under that name in the United States and Europe, than champagne is like lager-beer. If our people knew how to prepare it in the manner in which it come upon the table in Mexico, I think that it would supersede coffee and tea to a very great extent.

There is a bright yellow wood called "linoloe" growing all over these mountains, which, for cabinet-work, the lining of bureau-drawers, etc., would be invaluable. It is similar in color to the California laurel, but somewhat softer, and exceedingly fragrant, the odor being like that of the nutmeg and moss-rose combined, and where it is desired to keep furs or other articles free from moths, it has no equal. A delightfully fragrant oil for toilet purposes, superior to sandal-wood oil, is obtained from the berry which the tree produces. Samples of this were shown me at the extensive drug store of Mr. Augustus Morrill, the American Consul in the city. This article ought to become of commercial importance. There are other equally valuable woods in abundance here. Nature has done more for Colima, and man less, than for any other country on earth I think.

The people of Colima had heard of the hospitalities showered upon Mr. Seward in California, and the other Pacific States and Territories of the "United States of the North," and they were determined not to be behind hand for a moment; to do them justice I must here admit, in spite of my pride as a Californian, that they were very far ahead. Upon Mr. Seward's arrival, the officials called at once and offered the hospitalities of the city and State, as Señor Huarte did those of his house.

We had hardly time to finish breakfast on the morning after our arrival, when two elegantly-dressed gentlemen, Señors Firmin Gonzalez Castro, and Francisco Santa Cruz, were introduced; they informed Mr. Seward that they came in behalf of the officers Aduana Maritima and the Governor and people of Colima, to invite the party to attend a ball and banquet at the palace, on the evening of the 12th of October, to be given in honor of his visit. The address being duly translated, Mr. Seward replied as follows:

"GENTLEMEN: I have received only hospitalities, undeserved, since I landed in Mexico. I thank you sincerely for the hospitalities you have now tendered me. Desirous of extending my acquaintance with the citizens of this ancient and respected city of Colima, I will attend the entertainment you tender me this evening with much pleasure."

When evening came, the party entered the carriages in attendance at 10 o'clock, and were driven to the palace. Arriving there, all were surprised beyond measure at the oriental magnificence of the decorations and preparations for the occasion. Outside, the building, which is of pure Moorish style, was one blaze of light A crowd of the common people standing in respectful silence blocked the way, and were kept back from the portal by the bayonets of a company of regular troops, under command of Capt. Reyes. The sidewalks on either side were lined with rows of feathery palm-leaves fastened upright and decorated with lamps, and the whole front of the building was similarly decorated. Entering the portal, the soldiers presenting arms as we passed, we found a numerous and brilliant company in attendance, and arranged near the door to allow the party to pass through into the main saloon.

The scene presented as the party entered was brilliant, and wonderfully beautiful. The main hall is in the form of a square, surrounded by wide corridors, separated by pillars and Moorish arches, with wide galleries corresponding above. The floors were covered with cloth, and sprinkled with gilt paper-clippings. The pillars, the arches, the walls, and the ceilings were loaded with the richest vegetation of the tropics; palm-leaves in all their varieties; the rich, cream-colored blossoms of the cocoa, looking like gigantic heads of wheat done in wax-work, the green fruit and flowers of the banana, and all the indescribable wealth of the tropical flora, in variety and brilliance beyond description. Mr. Seward exclaimed, "It is a tropical forest, with an oriental illumination." Rich Chinese lamps and glasses, filled with perfume and brilliant colored cocoa oil, with burning tapers, were on all sides.

The roof was hidden by a canopy of green, white and red gauze, and all around the hall were the flags of Mexico and the United States side by side. At one end of the hall, "Don Benito Juarez, Salvator de la Patria," looked down in grim silence from the canvas, and at the other, a handsome portrait of Mr. Seward, painted within two days by a native artist, was enwreathed with laurel and the flags of the two Republics. Around the corridor hung the portraits of Gen. Ramon Corona, commander of the Army of the West, and his compatriots, and the heroes of the Mexican War of Independence. On one side of the gallery was the illuminated legend "Al. H. W. H. Seward," formed from glasses of red, green, and blue cocoa-nut oil, with tapers hanging against a bank of tropical verdure. The committee of arrangements must have expended a very large sum in the preparations, and all to the best advantage. Better taste was never exhibited in any ball-room in America.

Introductions over, the band seated in an alcove struck up a lively air and the dance commenced, Gov. Cueva leading off with Mrs. Frederick Seward, and Mr. F. Seward with the beautiful and accomplished wife of Mr. Oetling, the Consul of the North German Confederation, the most perfect type of the pure Spanish beauty I had seen thus far in Mexico. The ladies, wore little jewelry, but were dressed richly and in excellent taste, and the gentlemen were all in black, with white vests and white kid gloves.

After midnight the banquet was served in the gallery; the tables which were loaded with every fruit, fowl and vegetable of this wonderfully prolific tropical clime, and with flowers and wines *ad libitum*, extended entirely around the gallery. After the substantials of the feast were disposed of, Acting Gov. Cueva arose and addressed the assembled guests and Mr. Seward in the following language, as nearly as I am able to translate it:

Señores: The State of Colima, of which I have the honor to be the representative, in order to celebrate the brief visit to this city, of this illustrious guest, who humbled the proud diplomats of the Cabinet of Napoleon III., desires through me to manifest its appreciation of his friendship and admiration of his conduct. Undoubtedly thou (apostrophetic) art the Genius of that Democracy who marked the line "Thus far!" to the aggressions of Monarchy! The wrinkled forehead, and wintry hair of Europe, cannot marry with the tropical ardor of Young

America. The world has contemplated with awe-struck astonishment this struggle of giants; the darkness of the Past wrestling furiously with the light of the Future, whose lesson has been taught us by Progress, and once more the crowned heads have trembled before the irresistible power of Fraternity, which, invoked by all people must become universal. Mexico, whose misfortunes have been such as to place her within the reach of French intervention, has, before all free and independent nations, demonstrated that she is worthy to be ranked in their catalogues, and now, feeling the proud consciousness of sovereign power, celebrates, full of joy, and the enthusiasm inspired by patriotic sentiments, the fact of the presence among us, of the eminent statesman, who from the *Casa Blanca* at Washington, presented a barrier to the irruption of the barbarians who presumed to sow in our fertile fields the noxious and rotten weeds which have paralyzed the sons of the Old Continent. The prouder world of Colon, which was imprudently attacked and wounded, answered unanimously with defiance to the piratical threat promulgated to her, and then shone with redoubled effulgence the sun of the *Cinco de Mayo*, and blinded with its radiance the eyes of the enemies of Republican institutions. Señor: The glories of my country fraternized with yours in the struggle of the past. I salute thee in the name of the Mexican people, and offer you its friendship as sincerely as thou hast been a true and sincere friend to the Government and people of this nation, who applaud and bless thee!

When he concluded his address, the company applauded loudly, by the clapping of hands and a "hurrah" *a la Americano*, in special compliment to the guests. Don Firmin Gonzales Castro, and Don Francisco E Trejo, followed in short but fervent addresses, in similar spirit, and Mr. Seward then arose and addressed the audience, amid profound silence, as follows:

Señor Governor and Gentlemen: I thank you with a full heart for these most undeserved hospitalities and honors. The experience of the eighteenth century indicated to mankind two important changes of society and government on the Continent of America. First, that all American States must thereafter be not dependent European colonies, but independent American nations. Second, that all independent American nations must thereafter have, not imperial or monarchical governments, but republican governments, constituted and carried on by the voluntary agency of the people themselves. During a large part of my own political life, these great changes of society and government have been, more or less, in logical debate contested in Europe, and on the battle-field throughout America. While they have often involved the American States in civil and international wars, they have more than once provoked European intervention. A third improvement was easily found necessary to guarantee full success to the two principal changes which I have already mentioned. This third improvement consists in the continuation of the many, or several contiguous nations or States, which are weak of themselves, into United States distinct nations. My own country, the United States, has taken the lead in these changes, so essential in the American hemisphere. The Mexican Republic has early, and bravely and persistently, adopted a similar system. Central America, and nearly all the South American States, have followed the example thus set by the United States and the Mexican Republic. One additional principle remains to be adopted, to secure the success of the republican system throughout the continent. If it shall become universal on the American continent, we have reason to expect that the same great system may be accepted by other nations throughout the world. That additional principle is simply this: That the several American Republics, just as they constitute themselves, while mutually abstaining from intervention with each other, shall become more, than ever heretofore, political friends through the force of moral alliance. This, in short is the policy which I have inculcated at home, and which, with your leave, and the leave of others interested, I shall commend, as far as possible, to the Republics of Mexico, Central America and South America. I sincerely trust that the severest trials of the republican system are already passed in Mexico, and I shall never cease to pray God for her continued independence, unity, prosperity, and happiness.

When Mr. Seward ceased speaking, the applause was hearty and enthusiastic, and the last shade of doubt and distrust that seemed to have been lingering in the public mind as to the motives of his visit, appeared to have vanished. The banquet over, the party again returned to the ball-room, and the dancing re-commenced. The German merchants of Colima mingled with the dark-eyed beauties of the country, side by side with the American guests, and an era of good feeling and brotherly regard seemed to have been inaugurated. At 4 A. M., a grand "fandango," by dancers and musicians specially sent for, was given. The dance is not unlike the can-can in its voluptuous abandon, and though curious, I do not recommend its adoption by the sons and daughters of my native land. At day-break the first grand party given in Mexico in honor of the distinguished American visitor broke up. It was a magnificent success.

On the following morning, at 7 o'clock, a few friends. and myself—kindly accompanied by W. H. Broadbent and Mr. John Bulkley, late Superintendent of the San Cuyatano Cotton Mills—started off on horses sent for our use by Señor Luis Rendon and Consul Morrill, to visit the cotton mills of Colima. A two mile ride through the narrow, straight streets of Colima, and out along the woods overhung with the garden verdure of this land of fruit and flowers, along the banks of the Rio de Colima, brought us to the San Cuyatano mill. This establishment, like everything here, surrounds a wide court-yard, each building being but one story in height, of brick, and tile-roofed. The motive power is furnished by a huge overshot wheel, forty-two feet in diameter, which runs two thousand spindles, and the mill employs two hundred and fifty men and women when in operation.

It is now idle, owing to the overstock of domestic cottons, and the high price of the raw material. It has large quarters, consisting of long rows of tenements, each with a front and rear room, and a verandah and small back yard, which, when the mills are running, are rented to the families of the operatives at one dollar and fifty cents per month; not a high rent. The women, all young and clean, and some quite pretty, were sitting around in the verandahs doing some small work, and on our passing, all arose and greeted us with a pleasant smile, and "Buenas dias, Señors!"

We went on to the Armonia Mill, which is of similar character, and now running. It has one thousand spindles, and employs eighty operatives. Then we went to the Atrevida Mill, which has twenty-five looms and eight hundred spindles, and employs eighty people. The machinery of the Atrevida and San Cuyatano is from Fall River—"Estados Unidos Del Norte"—and that of the Armonia from England. The Armonia was built in 1845, and paid from thirty thousand to forty thousand dollars per annum dividends until 1864, when the business fell off in consequence of the civil war. The cloth is all of coarse sheetings or muslin, known here as *manta*, and sells at six dollars and twenty-five cents per piece of thirty-two varas (a vara is two and three-fourths feet, English) for the best, which weighs eleven pounds per piece. The second quality, weighing nine pounds, sells for five dollars and twenty-five cents per piece. The women get two and one-half rials—thirty-one and one-fourth cents—per piece for weaving the cloth, and the other operatives thirty-seven and a half cents per day, they boarding themselves. The cotton costs thirty-four cents per pound cleaned, at present, and two dollars and twenty-five cents per *arroba* of twenty-five pounds unginned.

The present cotton product of the State of Colima is two million, five hundred thousand pounds, and there are many thousands of acres of uncultivated land available for cotton raising if required. The women work faithfully and quietly, but with downcast and generally hopeless look. They are of all colors from red to white, a mild lemon color being the leading and fashionable hue. I have been told that a number of these girls recently went to California to better their condition, and that their letters from San Francisco, to their friends in Colima, have created a general desire among their sister operatives to follow in their footsteps, and seek a home in the Golden State.

From the roofs of the mills we looked down on gardens filled with tropical fruits, oranges, bananas, cocoanuts, coffee, vanilla, and a thousand, to us, rare things, growing in rank and neglected luxuriance, then mounted our animals, and galloped back along ruined bridges and shattered walls, in part the effect of the cannon-balls rained upon Miramon's forces by the Liberal artillery under Col. George M. Green, when Juarez was advancing on Guadalajara from the West; in part to the contest between the French and Liberals, when the latter were defeated and the city taken, and in part the effect of a great flood in 1864, and were soon at the door of Señor Huarte's hospitable *casa*.

At the invitation of Gov. Cueva, who is acting Governor in place of Gov. Ramon de la Vega, the latter having been absent for a long time on leave from President Juarez, I visited the public schools in Colima, in which he takes a very commendable interest. I found them well attended, and the pupils exceedingly well-behaved and intelligent. The schools are free to all, and seem to be appreciated. This is an evidence of actual progress in Mexico, very pleasant to witness, and must convince the most skeptical that the world does move, even here.

From the schools we went to the State Prison, the Prefect of the State or municipality, Don Sebastian Fajerdo, kindly accompanying us and showing us all the points of interest. The prison is guarded by the garrison of Colima, comprising one hundred regular troops, and is used in part as a jail or calaboose, as well as a State Prison. It is of great age, and exceedingly defective in construction, so far as ventilation is concerned. Each ward is separated by an open-work iron door, of great strength, from the next, and one is locked before the second is unlocked on every occasion. I found one hundred and fifty-seven prisoners all told. Of these, half were common drunkards, or perpetrators of light offenses, sentenced to chain-gang duty for a brief time. Many of the others have the word "*perpetua*" entered opposite their names; and one poor, cowering wretch in irons, was pointed out as under sentence of death for a horrible and cruel murder. Gov. Cueva, who seems to be a thoroughly mild, kind-hearted, and merciful man, explained to me that he had not yet signed the death-warrant, and he disliked to do so always, putting it off as long as possible, and then ordering the shooting to take place at day-break as quietly and privately as possible, it being his opinion that such exhibitions had no good effect on the public mind.

After a conviction for a capital offense, the transcript of the records of the trial, evidence, etc., must be sent to Mexico to be reviewed by the Supreme Court. If that tribunal decides that the trial has been fair, and the finding is according to law and the evidence, then an order for the execution of the sentence is sent back, the Governor must sign the death-warrant within a given number of days, and the shooting must take place within twenty-four hours thereafter.

Pardons can only be issued by the Legislature (Congresso) of the State. The records appeared regularly and neatly kept, and the prisoners as well and humanely treated as possible with the present prison accommodations. Each prisoner had a mat to sleep and sit upon, but other furniture there was none, and in some of the wards the air, for the want of proper ventilation, was very oppressive. All were naked to the waist, or nearly all, and with the single exception of one demoralized Swiss—probably one of Maximilian's mercenaries—in for stealing, of native birth and Indian blood. The precautions against revolt or escape would be considered extraordinary in any other country. Nearly all are engaged in braiding fine palm-leaf hats, worth about two dollars each, or making fancy worsted work-baskets, etc., which they are allowed to have sold for their private account. As we entered each room the prisoners arose and bowed respectfully, at a nod from the turnkey, and remained standing until we left. If Gov. Vega, or acting Gov. Cueva, had the means at command, they would soon have a better prison erected, and change the entire system to that of New-York, which they highly approve.

At 2 P. M., of our last day in Colima, the party repaired to an old Spanish church to assist at the christening of the two youngest children of Consul Morrill. Mr. Seward, the elder, acted with Mr. Buckley as godfathers for one, and Mr. Fred Seward, wife, and Mr. Buckley, as godfathers and godmother for the other. The ceremony was soon over, and as we reached the portal, there came a rush of men, woman and children of the poorer class to receive bright, clean *rials* called "*bolos*," as mementoes of the christening. The term comes from the response of the godfather during the ceremony "Yo bolo!" (I consent!) It is the custom for each of the godfathers and godmothers to give every person present a *bolo*, and it took about a quart to go around. Then, at the residence of Señor Huarte, trays filled with these pieces—twelve and a-half cents each—punched and adorned with red, green and white ribbons, were brought out, and were presented by the "Compadres," to each of the army of servants and children in the place. It is an odd and peculiar custom.

Having been left out in the cold, as it were, personally at the christening, I got even by distributing some dollars worth of American dimes among the highly appreciative audience, on behalf of the next candidate for ordinance, whether it should be a girl or boy, Mr. Buckley kindly promising to act as my proxy at the ceremony, as a few thousand miles, more or less, would be pretty certain to intervene between us before that interesting event could take place.

On the afternoon of Wednesday the 13th of October Colonel Sabas Lomeli, commander of the State Guard of Jalisco, a richly dressed, and fine, soldierly-looking officer, with one hundred cavalry, detailed by the Governor of Jalisco to act as an escort to Mr. Seward and party, as far as Guadalajara, arrived from that city, and immediately presented himself, with his aids, for orders. Colima, the beloved of the Sun, had won all our hearts, and it was with not a little regret, that we made preparations for departure next morning, at day-break. Colima! Colima! shall I ever look upon you again?

CHAPTER III.

FROM COLIMA TO ZAPOTLAN.

ON the evening of Oct. 13th, we made our final preparations for departing from Colima, and at 4 o'clock next morning all was bustle and excitement in the grand house of Señor Huarte, and in the streets and Plaza in front. The long roll of the drum, and the shrill notes of the trumpet, announced the assembling of the military guard before day-break, and when the dawn came, the scene as viewed from the balcony was magnificent. The squadron of the Guard of Jalisco, one hundred strong, lined one side of the Plaza, with their horses saddled and caparisoned for the road. In front of our house, a long train of pack-mules was being loaded for the journey by a swarm of servants; two coaches, each with six mules, four in the lead and two at the wheel, stood ready for the party, and the police of Colima, finely mounted, with Señor Cañedo, Don Luis Rendon, Gov. Cueva, our worthy Consul Dr. Augustus Morrill, and other officials and private citizens, were galloping about on horseback, all handsomely mounted, and each with servants, spare horses, and camp equipage, ready for the road.

At last all was ready, the trumpets of the advance-guard sounded "to the saddle," and they filed away at a gallop down the streets. The crowd in front was forced back by the police, and Mr. Seward entered his coach with the members of his party, the other coach was filled by our friends, and the people bared their heads and bowed respectfully as a last salutation, as the coaches rattled away over the cobble-paved streets.

The rear-guard and the long pack-train fell in behind, and the police and other officials and friends galloped alongside. *Vamos! ah-ha-ha-ha-ha-ha-h-a-a-a!* yelled the *cocheros;* the *postillons* cracked their whips, and so, with clatter and uproar, and strange music indescribable, we dashed past the Plaza Nuevo, with its triumphal arches, its orange groves and seats for summer-evening loungers, out through the long, straight, narrow streets, into the garden-lined roads of the suburbs, and Colima the Beautiful was behind us.

In the last chapter, mention was made of a prisoner in irons in the State Prison awaiting death for a brutal murder. The order for his execution had been signed by Gov. Cueva on the day previous to our departure, and he was to be shot at day-break on that morning. While standing in Consul Morrill's office on the evening before our departure, I heard a terrible outcry in the corridor, and saw the poor old mother of the condemned criminal on her knees before the Consul, begging him in the name of God and all the saints to interfere in her son's behalf. "You represent the great *Estados Unidos del Norte*, and are all-powerful. Save him, Señor, and all the saints of heaven will bless you!" He told her as mildly as possible, that he had no power to interfere, and that the young man—a bad youth, who had committed murder before, and on this occasion butchered, in cold blood, a merchant's clerk, who had, under orders from his employer, refused him credit for four dollars—deserved his fate. Then she fell insensible to the pavement.

When the sympathizing women had restored her to consciousness, she rushed to the house of Señor Huarte, and fell on her knees before one of our party, mistaking him for Mr. Seward. She was taken away by the police before she could see him, and so he was saved the useless pain of meeting her. Gov. Cueva, being told that the prisoner was apparently insane, sent two physicians to examine him, but they reported him thoroughly sound in mind; and as he had no power to pardon him, that being reserved to the State Legislature and the President, while a reprieve would be no mercy, he ordered, as a mark of respect to Mr. Seward, that the execution be delayed until we were out of the city. Our coaches had hardly rolled off the last pavement of Colima, before there was a sharp rattle of musketry from the river's bank, a puff of blue smoke curled up above the house-tops, and drifted away in the clear morning air, and the story of a life was told.

A few miles out of Colima the character of the country begins to change from ultra-tropical to semi-tropical. We drove over execrable roads, between wide fields of rice, now half-grown and richly green, beautiful castor-beans, and Indian corn. The cocoa-palms decreased in number, and finally, at twenty miles north-east of Colima, entirely disappeared, while the bananas grew less thriftily and abundant. The land, where not cultivated, was everywhere covered with rich, nutritious grasses, and cattle and sheep abounded. We have no grass, properly speaking, in California, the wild oat out there taking its place, and these green, grassy fields appeared more beautiful to me from the fact that I had not looked upon their like for many years. The country is well populated, and though the people—mostly of Indian descent—live in poor huts of cane, with rice straw-thatched roofs, open all around the sides to wind and rain, and are miserably clad, they appear to have abundance to eat, and are quite well behaved, and apparently contented with their lot.

Twenty-five miles from Colima, we reached the first "Barranca," a branch of the great "Barranca de Beltran," the insurmountable obstacle to the construction of a passable wagon road from the coast to Guadalajara. These Barrancas, some five or six in number, three very large, are minor Yosemites in appearance, having been formed by the action of water in a stratum of sand, bowlders, and loose gravel. They are many miles in length, uniting finally like the various branches of a great river as they approach the sea-coast, and are from five hundred to fifteen hundred feet in depth, with steep precipitous sides.

The amount of labor required to construct even passable mule roads up and down their sides, is almost incredible. The road has been laid out—it was done a century ago—with great engineering skill, and the zig-zags, with acute angles, are beautifully constructed. The road-bed is from eight to thirty feet in width, the sides inclining to the center, and neatly paved with cobble-stones, the large and small stones being arranged in lines in regular order. Each year, the water cuts the bed of the Barranca deeper and deeper, and the work must be extended, while the heavy rains gullying out the pavement, make constant repairs necessary. The lower side of the road is usually fenced in, or lined with a substantial stone wall neatly plastered, and in one of the smaller Barrancas a solid stone bridge with a single arch, evidently of great age, spans the stream.

Señor Huarte had provided a large palanquin to convey Mr. Seward through the Barranca country, as his injuries, received some years ago, rendered it impossible for him to guide a horse, or hold on to a saddle for a long time. The palanquin, or litter, consisted of two stout poles, three feet apart, bolted together with cross beams, supporting in the center a platform on which was fastened a large, cushioned arm-chair, above which was a canopy of brilliant green merino stuff with curtains of the same material. When going up and down the Barrancas, and in particularly dangerous places, the palanquin was borne on the shoulders of four stalwart men in white cotton pantaloons, and broad plam-leaf hats, with rough sandals on their feet. When the procession came to a good place on the road, the palanquin was transferred to the backs of two mules, who carried it along at a swinging trot. The men were relieved at intervals of a few minutes, and despite the heat and bad roads, they would get along nearly as fast as a man on horseback, riding at an ordinary gait.

At the first Barranca we left Señor Huarte's excellent coaches, and took to mule and horseback. Descending the first Barranca and climbing its precipitous sides again, we crossed a small plateau, and came to the first arm of the great Barranca de Beltran, probably eight hundred feet deep. Looking up this Barranca we saw, on the opposite side, the old red-tile-roofed town of Tornila, embowered in tropical foliage and flowers, with banana fields and trees, each bearing a profusion of brilliant flowers, on either side, and the great Volcano of Colima towering into the heavens in awful majesty, his head crowned with a turban of sulphurous smoke, in the background. Surely, I mused, I must have been here before, the scene is so wonderfully familiar.

At last it occurred to me, this is the perfect counterpart of "the Heart of the Andes," as Church painted it. Even the trees covered with parrots, and the rushing waters, were all there. On that day, and again the next day, we saw the picture repeated in a thousand varied forms, and each more beautiful and wonderful than the last.

At noon, we reached Tornila, and were warmly received at the hospitable residence of Señor Don Ramon de la Vega, the elected Governor of Colima. Tornila is just over the line, in the State of Jalisco, and Señor Vega is residing there by permission of President Juarez, while Gov. Cueva acts in his place. He was driven out by the French, and was compelled to flee to San Francisco, but immediately returned on the restoration of the republic. He has served several years, and will decline another re-election, as he is old, and desires to devote himself to his private affairs. His mansion overlooks on one side, a broad and beautifully irregular valley, with ranges of low hills, and the Sierra del Tigre, rising to the clouds in the southern background. Nearer, are gardens filled with fruits and flowers in endless profusion.

From the northern front of Gov. Vega's residence a magnificent view of the great Volcano of Colima may be obtained. The western peak of this great mountain is a perfect truncated cone, very beautiful, and majestic in proportions. It is estimated to be from twelve thousand to fourteen thousand feet above the sea—no two estimates agree by hundreds of feet—and is wooded to the very summit. This peak, though formerly in eruption, had been silent for forty years. Now, we can see small jets of smoke or steam issuing from crevices near the summit, but in no considerable quantity, and there is no rumbling or other indications of an eruption. Back of this first peak to the eastward some miles, is a second peak, called the Snowy (Nevada) Peak, or Old Crater. This is now wholly silent.

Between these, but further to the northward than either, and lower down, is the crater formed in August, 1869, from which the smoke now pours in dense volume, but not a sound of any kind nor any trembling accompanies the eruption. In fact, this whole affair is an unexplainable mystery. The former eruptions sent forth immense rivers of lava, and were accompanied by frightful earthquakes and rumblings. This, commenced in the night, with a shock so slight that it was hardly noticed in the City of Colima, and continued in the same manner from the 12th of July 1869 up to the time of our visit. No lava is poured out, but there is a constant discharge of red-hot rocks, some of which weigh hundreds of tons, which are merely vomited out and rolled down the side of the mountain: not hurled into the air.

The engineer who was sent up to examine it, made a full report, and through the kindness of Gov. Cueva, I was furnished with a copy. I am inclined to the opinion that the present demonstration is only preliminary, and that the actual eruption, attended with lava discharges and wide-spread devastation, is yet to come. At present, the Volcano of Colima is the best-behaved volcano in the world—mild-mannered, but wonderfully beautiful and awe-inspiring to the beholder.

The dinner-table was spread in the corridor overlooking all the scene, and the party sat down to a sumptuous entertainment prepared on the shortest notice. Señor Huarte had provided an unlimited supply of wines and liquors of every description, and poured them out like water all the way to Zapotlan, to which place he accompanied us. He is a perfect prince of hosts, and his kindness and unceasing care for the comfort of our party will not soon be forgotten. These Mexican people "beat the world" in the number and excellence of the dishes they prepare for the table at short notice. Chicken, turkey, and beef may be had at every little hamlet in abundance, and they serve them up in a variety of styles, always well-cooked and palatable. They also contrive to produce *dulces*—literally "sweets"—from almost every conceivable fruit and vegetable, and also pastes and jams in endless variety. On this occasion the *dulces* were prepared by the hand of Señora de la Vega herself. Their three bright-eyed daughters, handsome young ladies, with light olive complexions, their cheeks tinged with a rosy hue, sat at the table with the party.

When the dinner was dispatched and wines brought on, Gov. Cueva arose, and in feeling terms thanked Mr. Seward for his visit, and for the good services he had rendered to Mexico. On behalf of the State of Colima he desired to bid him good-bye, wish him God-speed, and a safe return to his home in the far North, and give him a hearty embrace. The Governor then embraced him with great fervor, bade each of the party an affectionate adieu, and started on his return to Colima.

The rainy season in this country commences in June, and according to the almanac, ought to conclude in September, but this year it did not. It was now the middle of October, and still the clouds poured down showers every evening and during most of the night, making traveling, which ought to have been better than at any other season, almost impossible and slow at best. It was raining when we left Tornila, and we hardly saw the sun that day. The country from Colima to Zapotlan is quite populous, and in the middle part nearly all the arable land is cultivated.

The road is very wide, but poor, and inclosed between very high and substantial stone walls. The crops are corn, beans, pumpkins, rice, sugar-cane, &c., &c., and all are very good. From Tornila we ascended rapidly, and were soon among the foot-hills of the Sierra Madre of Mexico. The country is not unlike Central Arizona in formation, but the vegetation is rank and luxuriant to a degree beyond comparison. At all the houses along the road there are little open windows, in which are exposed for sale fruit and bread, cakes, tortillas and cheese. For a *medio*—half a *rial*, or six and one-fourth cents—you can buy a milk-pan full of bananas or other fruit, and bread, etc., is very cheap.

Women, lightly dressed in loose cotton *camesas* and skirts, are seen in every house, squatted before the hollowed block of lava, on which they grind to a paste the half-boiled hulled corn, from which they make tortillas. Placing a handful of the corn on the stone, they take hold, with both hands, of a stone about a foot in length and three inches square, which they rub back and forth over the corn until it is reduced to a pulp, then taking up a little mass, pat it with both hands until they have spread it out to the thickness of common paste-board, and bake it on a hot stone. This is the *tortilla*, which with the dark red beans known as *frijoles*, form the leading articles of diet of the humbler class. The *tortilla* is also used as a spoon, when they eat beans or soup, and the spoon is eaten up at the close of the feast.

A MEXICAN COOK.

Our military guard was an object of no little curiosity and admiration They belong to a force of eight hundred picked men, armed, equipped, and put into the field by the State of Jalisco, to free the roads from robbers and maintain public order. Col. Sabas Lomeli, their commander, is a splendid-looking man, tall, stout built, quite fair complexioned, with long whiskers and mustaches, *a la Americano*, and is not only remarkably good looking, but has the air and carriage of a soldier. He is said to be a very brave and accomplished officer, and the fact that within a few months his command has practically cleared the roads of the great State of Jalisco of robbers, and captured or killed nearly two hundred of the banditti, who had made traveling very dangerous, speaks well for his energy. He is accompanied by a major, captain, and the company lieutenants, all of whom are uniformed with dark-blue jackets, trimmed with broad silver bullion and large silver buttons, bright scarlet pantaloons, with silver lace, and top-boots of enameled leather. Their caps are nearly the same in form as the regular United States fatigue cap, but with green trimmings, and with a white linen cover having a cape, which when let down, protects the shoulders from sun and rain.

COL. SABAS LOMELI.

The soldiers have caps, blue coats and pantaloons with green trimmings, and the pantaloons are foxed with dark leather. They carry swords, Colt's revolvers, and Springfield muskets, and are mounted on small, but very spirited and quick-traveling horses, of which they take excellent care. The officers carry swords and Colt's revolvers, and wear broad, red sashes thrown carelessly over their shoulders. Their uniform is very brilliant and picturesque. The force of one hundred men have only three pack-mules to carry all their baggage. They take no tents or cooking utensils, and can get over the ground with twice or thrice the speed attained by our troops in the United States. One hundred miles within thirty hours is no great march for them, and the infantry can keep up with them. The common soldiers are all of Indian blood, small in size, but active, and admirably fitted for rapid marches and the guerilla style of warfare. I never saw so well-behaved, quiet, and orderly men. They receive thirty-seven and one-half cents per day in coin. Of this twelve and one-half cents is paid them daily, and the remainder at, or near, the end of the month. They get no rations, but live easily on the twelve and one-half cents. They will gallop up to a road-side shop, and with three cents purchase a dozen *tortillas*, and a piece of the sour-milk cheese of the country, which serves them for lunch. For breakfast, an ear of soft-boiled corn will serve them admirably, and for supper a few *frijoles* and *tortillas* are sufficient. In camp or at garrison duty, they get rations, and are charged for them. Col. Lomeli wears a magnificent diamond ring and gold watch, and is splendidly mounted, a silver-ornamented saddle setting off to great advantage the fine black horse which he rides.

Leaving the party just before night-fall, I galloped on alone to the great hacienda of San Marcos, where we were to pass the night, meeting by the way the proprietor who had started out to meet Mr. Seward and welcome him to his house.

This great hacienda cost a million dollars, and for many years prior to the French invasion paid $60,000 net profits annually. The war ruined its old proprietor, and its present one bought it for $200,000. The buildings surround a large square, in the center of which there is a fountain constantly playing, to which all the workmen and women resort for water. On one side of the square are the workshops where the casks, boxes, etc., are made. On the opposite, is the immense sugar-mill, with splendid machinery of the best pattern. At the entrance, on one side, is the office and counting-room; on the other, the pyre or altar-like pile of mason-work, on which a fire is kindled with pitch-pine wood at night, to light up the entire place. At the opposite end is the extensive distillery in which the cane, (after the greater part of the juice has been expressed,) is permeated with the molasses, to make a villainous kind of rum called *aguardiente del cana*, which is as much like boiled lightning as can be imagined, and the very smell of which will cause a very fair sample of the Christian gentleman to commit murder. Above this, rises a small hill of solid rock about seventy feet in height, surmounted by the *casa grande*, or great house of the estate. This house is one story in height, with a vast corridor all around it, and a hollow square in the center. It is painted white outside, and inside it is like all the better houses in this country, elaborately frescoed in blue and chocolate colors.

The view, from the corridor, of the great volcano—the base of which is but ten miles distant—and of the Sierra Madre in the east, the Sierra del Tigre, and intervening plains on the other side, is wonderfully beautiful. The business of the hacienda is now but moderately profitable, since the fine, almost pure, and richly flavored sugar is worth but two dollars and fifty cents per arroba of twenty-five pounds, and the aguardiente only realizes three dollars per barrel of eighteen gallons, after being packed on mules to Zapotlan and Guadalajara, the barrel itself being returned.

Night came on while I was sitting on the broad verandah waiting for the arrival of the party, and drinking in the glory of the scene before me. The darkness was almost palpable to the touch, and I began to fear that the party must encamp on the mountains for the night. Suddenly, the notes of the bugle came floating through the air, and a long line of brilliant lights, moving with a steady motion which showed that they were carried by marching men, came out upon the hill-side some miles away.

Like a great fiery serpent the column, with its hundred torches unfolded itself, and crept steadily toward the hacienda. On it came, winding and turning with the sinuosities of the road, until I could discern the outlines of the horsemen who bore the flaming torches, and see the great-leaved trees come in and out of the panorama of ever-shifting lights and shadows, as the column moved along. It was a scene of enchantment which seems too much like the work of imagination to be real, even now, as I look back upon it through memory's gateway.

At last the procession entered the patio, and all was bustle and confusion for an hour or more before the troops were finally quartered for the night, the baggage disposed of, and the party quietly provided for in the various rooms of the great house. The family of the proprietor, Mauricio Gomez, reside most of the time at Zapotlan, and were not at the hacienda when we were there. We supped royally, slept soundly—there are no musquitoes, and very few flies in all this country—and at 6 A. M., on the 15th were off for Zapotlan, our road leading for miles between the rice-fields, sugar-cane and corn-fields which covered the whole country.

Soon after leaving San Marcos we came to the main branch of the great Barranca de Beltran, which is about two thousand feet wide and fifteen hundred feet deep, with almost perpendicular sides, down which the road has been cut with infinite labor and paved at an immense expense. The descent into this Barranca on horseback is no trifling feat, and the beauty of the views at every turn is really wonderful. At places, the whole road is over-arched with trees and climbing vines, and on every hill-side the wealth of flowers is beyond imagination. Parrots in great flocks yelled at us from the trees, and little parroquets and other brilliant-hued birds, swarmed in the thickets all around. Mules, loaded with the produce of the country, met us at every angle of the road.

BARRANCA DE BELTRAN.

The scene, as the procession wound down the defiles into the bed of the Barranca and up the other side, the green palanquin swaying back and forth at the head, the brilliant uniforms of the officers and soldiers of the guard coming in and out among the trees in vivid contrast to the deep green of the vegetation, and the scarlet and blue and orange of the flowers, the sabres and muskets flashing in the sun, with the hundred minor but still picturesque details of the march was one, once witnessed, not soon to be forgotten.

It was high noon when we reached the *Mesa* on the eastern side, and crossed over to the Barranca Atenquiqui, beyond which we expected to meet the stages from Zapotlan. Looking back, I noticed two projections or points between divided branches of the Barranca; these might serve for points on which to erect piers for a suspension bridge, which might be constructed so that each span would not exceed eight hundred feet in length. On the highest point, Gen. Arteaga, at the commencement of the French invasion, erected earth-works defended by artillery, but finding his troops, who were poorly armed and thoroughly demoralized, could not hold the position, he pitched his cannon down the Barranca, and retreated to the interior. He was subsequently taken by surprise, and murdered in cold blood by the French, under the orders of Maximilian. Gen. Arteaga's remains, with those of Gen. Salazar, who met a like fate, have recently been removed to the Pantheon, at the city of Mexico, and interred in great state.

Take the Yosemite Valley, diminished in depth one-half and narrowed in like manner, cover all its sides and bottom with the luxuriant vegetation of the tropics, and you have the great Barranca de Beltran as we looked back into it for the last time.

At 1 o'clock P. M., we paused for a rest in the last of the Barrancas, that of Atenquiqui, in which the forces of Miramon were bush-whacked and completely routed, with almost total loss, by the Liberals under Gen.

Cheeseman, immediately commanded by Col. Geo. M. Green, if I remember correctly, toward the close of the war.

The stages were not forth-coming, and people who came over the road told us that it was impassable for vehicles for the greater part of the way from Zapotlan to the Barranca owing to the damage done by the recent storm.

An Indian messenger was sent off, on foot, with a promise that if he returned before 4 P. M., with news of the stage-coach, he should have two dollars. It was then 2 P. M., and we laid down to rest. At five minutes before 4 P. M., the barefooted messenger returned with the news that the coach would meet us nine miles down the road, at a point where a great gully had made it impossible to get the vehicle farther. He had made eighteen miles at a run, within the two hours, as was subsequently demonstrated, and well earned his two dollars.

We mounted at once and pushed on, Mr. Seward on a mule led by a half-naked native and holding on by both hands, and met at last the fine, large stage, made by the American pattern in Mexico, sent out from Zapotlan for our accommodation. Here, we were near the summit of the pass through the Sierra Madre, and the country looked not unlike the foot-hills of the Sierra Nevada about Grass Valley and Colfax, in California. The chaparral had mostly disappeared, and the country was sparsely covered with stumpy, yellow pines, with long leaves hanging down, so as to give them a weeping-willow aspect. The air at this elevation was quite comfortably cool, and we discarded the thin apparel in which we had sweltered in the Terra Caliente, which we were now passing out of, and put on such as is worn in San Francisco.

At every turn on the road we met trains of pack-mules laden with the produce of the country, going down to the coast, or were, for hours, mixed up with similar trains going up from the coast to the interior.

INDIANS FROM MICHOACAN GOING UP TO GUADALAJARA.

The down trains were loaded with the hard soap of Zapotlan, coarse earthen ware, fruit, sugar, etc., but principally, soap. The up trains were loaded with sugar, rice, and *aguardiente*, of which there seemed to be no end. One train must have numbered at least two hundred and fifty mules, each loaded with two barrels of the accursed aguardiente, eighteen or twenty gallons in each cask. The poor little mules were utterly exhausted with climbing and descending the barrancas, and were dropping down at intervals of a few rods all along the road. It is estimated that not less than twenty thousand mules are constantly employed transporting goods over the road between Colima and Guadalajara and intermediate points, and as each carries at least two hundred and fifty or three hundred pounds, the aggregate amount must be enormous. Many of the smaller trains which we met were loaded with coarse rush matting, used for covering floors, or earthern jars, and were driven by Indian families, men, women, and children, on foot, who appeared to be doing business on their own account. In many cases a mule would have goods worth not more than three dollars on his back, and the family must be poor indeed to go so far for so little money. We must have met or passed at least fifteen hundred or two thousand mules during the day.

We passed also several Mexican families of the better class, traveling on horseback and attended by numerous servants, all well armed. The women, invariably, had their heads covered with *rebosas*, or large handkerchiefs under their broad-brimmed hats, hiding all their hair and most of their faces, so fearful do they seem to be of any exposure to the air when traveling, though when at home, they go, bare headed, in the hottest sun, or coldest breeze to church, theater or promenade, all the year around.

Passing at a distance the magnificent hacienda of Huescalapa, which appeared like an immense white palace, we saw soon after night-fall, the long rows of paper lanterns which adorned every house, and were strung across every street in Zapotlan, giving to the tumble-down old city an air of enchantment. The illumination was in honor of the feast of San Jose of which saint this was the anniversary.

Driving up to the door of the residence of Don Trinidad Viszcayno, we alighted, and were soon provided for, for the night. The City Council of Zapotlan called immediately to pay their respects, and a band commenced playing in front of the house. The crowd was dense, but well-behaved and respectful, and during our stay, nothing but kind treatment was experienced. Among those who paid us most attention was Señor Don Manuel F. Alatorre of Guadalajara, cousin of Gen. Alatorre, a popular republican commander, then in the City of Mexico.

Zapotlan contains from eighteen thousand to twenty thousand people. There are more Indians in proportion to the whole population than at Colima, and fewer well-dressed people on the streets. This is one of the oldest cities in America, and is situated in one of the richest regions of Mexico; but, two hundred and fifty years' experience have only brought the people up to manufacturing soap and sugar. There are ten or twelve large soap factories in Zapotlan, and the trade is enormous. One of them we visited. There are no iron kettles or utensils in it, and all the heating is done in vats made of brick, while the ladling is done with immense calabashes fastened to long poles. And yet, the work is well done, and the soap much superior to the common brown soap in general use in the United States. The alkali is obtained from soda-earth in immense quantities on the margin of a lake ten leagues from Zapotlan, and the hogs are thrown into the vats whole, bristles and all, as we had an opportunity to see. This is emphatically "going the whole hog." In some parts of Mexico cakes of soap are used as small change, and hence the expression so common in the

United States, "How are you off for soap?" I charge nothing extra for this explanation.

The town is full of churches of ancient date, and there are the ruins of an immense cathedral which was thrown down in 1806, when many people were killed. They are just erecting a new one, from lava taken from a field of great extent near the town, and which flowed from the great volcano centuries ago. It will probably be finished in another century.

Above the door of one of the churches, we noticed an inscription, announcing that there were thirteen stations in the church at which one could deposit money, and have any friend he might name, prayed out of purgatory, or helped along on his way. Willing to lend a helping hand, I deposited twenty-five cents on behalf of a friend in San Francisco. I forgot to mention the fact that he is not yet dead, but presume that will make no difference, as he is sure to need it sooner or later, and the longer he waits the greater call he will have for all the assistance his friends can give him.

BRIDE AND GROOM ENTERING THE CHURCH.

While at Zapotlan we saw a wedding party enter the church. Bride and bridegroom were of pure Mexican blood, the common people of the country, and the whole party were of the same class. The costumes of the bride and bridegroom, and their floral decorations, were of such a remarkable character, that nothing but the engraving can give a good idea of them.

The city, though dull, is growing and slowly improving. It contains a number of beautiful residences, and about twelve first-class families.

When the infamous robber and patriotic cut-throat "General Rojas" took Zapotlan on one occasion, his men reported that the bell-tower of one of the churches was full of the enemy, who had surrendered, and were ready to come down and deliver up their arms. "What shall we do with them, your Excellency?" Rojas considered a moment, and then replied, "Oh, these poor men are not to blame; they must not be killed, but sent home, as they only acted under orders." His men could not understand such unusual clemency, as it was his custom to kill all who, by any misfortune fell into his hands. Seeing the officer who had made the inquiry standing irresolute, as if in doubt of understanding correctly what Rojas had said, the latter added, "I say sent home; of course you will not take any extra trouble with them, but send them home *by the shortest road.* The officer understood the infernal monster's hint, and returning to his command, gave such orders that in a few moments a well-directed fire from below forced all the soldiers in the tower to jump to the street, and of course they perished to a man. This anecdote was related to me by a gentleman who knew Rojas well, and belonged to the political party with which he was acting at the time. As we advanced into the interior we heard many similar anecdotes of this atrocious criminal. It is a satisfaction to know that the brute got his deserts, and was killed like a wild beast at Seyula, at last.

Rojas came from the district of Tepic, where he was employed for many years by one foreign importing house, to oppose by fraud, violence, and blood-shed, Manuel Lozada, who was in the pay of a rival house. Lozada finally triumphed, and has for years carried on a sort of independent monarchy, with Tepic for its capital, in the Northern corner of the State of Jalisco. He styles himself "Manuel Lozada, Natural Chief of the district of Tepic," permitting no one to share the cares and responsibilities of office with him. San Blas serves as an importing or smuggling port for his kingdom, and as he has a mountain district which is impenetrable to an opposing force if defended at all, his army, of devoted followers like those of Lopez in Paraguay, which can be swelled to eight thousand or ten thousand in a few days, enables him to bid defiance to the Federal Government, and carry things all in his own way. He was originally a muleteer, and is too ignorant to write his own name, but has much capacity for governing, with an energetic, cruel, and unforgiving nature. Skinning the feet of his enemies and forcing them to walk over live coals, is one of the mildest of the practical jokes in which he sometimes indulges. To do him justice, he keeps excellent order in the district of Tepic, allowing no one else to murder or rob within his jurisdiction. The republic has been forced to tolerate him for many years, because unable at any time to send a sufficient force against him to crush him at a blow. Should a period of entire peace in all other parts of the Republic come within his time, the Government would make short work of him at any cost; but how soon such an opportunity may occur, is a question for unreliable speculation only.

In 1868–9, an expedition against him, to be under the command of General Ramon Corona, was planned and nearly ready to start, but never got marching orders, disturbances requiring the presence of the troops arising elsewhere.

It is a noticeable fact, that nearly all the local revolutions or *pronunciamentos* in Mexico,—especially in the states bordering onthe sea-coast—are fomented and sustained for the moment by foreign houses, who desire to profit, pecuniarily, by the misfortunes of the country and its inhabitants. When several cargoes of goods from Europe, on which duties ranging from fifty to one hundred and fifty per cent *ad valorum* are payable by law, are about due at some port, the parties in interest look up some ambitious chief, who will consent to be used by them, provide him with the means to raise the first body of troops at hand in a *pronunciamento.* He then seizes the Custom-House, and if possible, the nearest mint, lets in the cargoes for twenty or twenty-five per cent. of the legal duties, and levies a forced loan or two, on the merchants within his reach. Of course, he takes good care to give receipts for the amount of the *prestimo* due from the houses in whose interest he is acting. By the time the Government troops arrive to attack him, he is ready to decamp with what funds he has raised, and seek an asylum in the United States, or some other country. The legitimate Government authorities, on being restored to power, find it always difficult, and generally impossible, to collect the duties on the goods which have thus been smuggled into the country, and so the Republic is not only swindled out of hundreds of thousands of dollars in the time of its most urgent necessity generally, but is put to a heavy expense to suppress the rebellion. The only parties who profit by the *pronunciamento* are those who get up the scheme and the leader of the forces in rebellion. The men forced into the army of the *pronunciados*, and the regular troops of the Republic, are the victims who meet death every time these outbreaks occur. This game has been played over and over, year after year, at the expense of every administration, legitimate or otherwise, which has held power at the time. It is not to be wondered at that the rich grow richer, and the poor poorer, year by year, under such a state of things, and that legitimate trade and industry are finally crushed out and disappear.

CHAPTER IV.

FROM ZAPOTLAN TO GUADALAJARA.

WE were under a cloud, as it were, in Zapotlan, where we arrived somewhat unexpectedly, in advance of the time which had been fixed upon by the population, and the reception of Mr. Seward, though hospitable, lacked the warmth and enthusiasm we had noticed elsewhere on our trip. We left Zapotlan on the 17th of October, therefore, with no feelings of regret, even in view of the fact, that by prolonging our stay a few days we might have been enabled to "assist" at the bull-fights, which were to last a full week, and for which a large amphitheatre was being erected, and extensive preparations making. The bull-fights were to be followed by cock-fights, on a grand scale. It is a little singular that the people of the towns where the festivals of the Saints are celebrated with the greatest furore, take the most delight in the cruel and demoralizing amusements of the bull-ring and the cock-pit, but it is true nevertheless. Zapotlan is a good illustration of the union of piety and brutality. Zacatecas and several other States have by legislative enactment abolished bull-fights. but in Jalisco they are still the popular amusement.

As we advanced into the interior we continued to ascend the spurs of the Sierre Madre, until we had reached a point twenty miles north-eastward from Zapotlan, when we found ourselves upon the summit of a range of broken mountains, in a locality famous for its brigandage. The bandits, who have been so relentlessly pursued and are now being exterminated, formerly, rarely allowed a traveler to pass this point unrobbed. All along the road from Zapotlan, we had noticed large wooden crosses by the roadside. Each of these crosses bore an inscription giving the date of the murder of some traveler by the brigands, and such facts as might be known concerning him, with a request for travelers to pray for the repose of his soul. These crosses were, in nearly every case, adorned with fresh flowers, though they were often of great age, judging by their weather-stained and moss-grown condition.

From passages in Byron's Childe Harold, we learn that this custom is observed all over Spain, and I know, from personal observation, that it is common in all Spanish America. In the Apache Country of Arizona, I have many times seen the poor Mexican miners stay for hours, to erect a rude cross of stone over the remains of some victim of the relentless savages, although they were personally unacquainted with him, and knew naught of his history, only judging by his appearance that he was a Christian.

These gentlemen of the road are still numerous and daring. Only quite recently they kidnapped a gentleman at night in the streets of Zapotlan, and run him off to the mountains, where they kept him prisoner until his friends raised and forwarded to them one thousand dollars in coin; and a few days before, they attacked and routed the guard accompanying the brother of Mr. Oetling, North German Consul at Colima, within a few miles of Seyula, and he only saved himself by the fleetness of his horse. The members of the fraternity who have been made prisoners and executed, acknowledged their guilt, and admitted that they were connected with a band which had ramifications throughout the Central States of the Republic, and kept regular accounts of their profits and losses, and made dividends to the stockholders on the best and most liberal commercial system. But the Republic and the several States are

HACIENDA IN THE MOUNTAINS OF JALISCO.

now actively at work in conjunction, and it is "short shrift and a long rope" whenever they catch any of the precious rascals.

From the summit of the range which we had been ascending all the morning, we looked down at 11 A. M., on a scene of infinite beauty, and almost unlimited extent. Spreading out from the base of the hills on which we stood, to the very limit of the vision in the eastward, was a magnificent valley, divided into farms with neat hedges and fences, and dotted with mesquite and other trees, giving it the appearance of one vast orchard and garden. Fields of tall corn, now almost ripe for the harvest, waved through all the valley, and here and there the white walls and red roofs of large haciendas and village churches were seen through the embowering foliage. Far away, in the north-east, were the mountains which cut off the valley from Lake Chapala, and northward rose a range of magnificent mountains—a spur of the great Sierra Madre—green to the summit, and checkered, here and there, with lighter green fields of corn. The long Laguna de Seyula stretched through the valley on its north-eastward side, and villages could be seen all along its banks. The bright sun shone down on all this peaceful scene, as it does in June in the United States, and the dark shadows of the flying clouds drifted like the moving figures of a panorama over valley, village, and mountain. But for brigands, and revolutions, and foreign invasions, this would be an earthly paradise—

> "A right good land to live in,
> And a pleasant land to see."

We descended, at a gallop, into the valley of Seyula, the long line of our military escort, with their dashy uniforms and glistening muskets, stretching far out in the rear, and passed through a small village, inhabited mostly by people of Indian descent, who regarded us with unrestrained curiosity, but great respect, doffing their hats and saluting us with the pleasant compliments of the country, as we passed.

At a second village, we came unexpectedly upon a collection of eight or ten elegant carriages—regular New York turn-outs—drawn up in a line, and fifty horsemen, magnificently mounted, their saddles being of the costliest pattern and glittering all over with silver, formed in double column. Instantly, the bells of a little church rang out a joyous peal, unusual on a Sabbath-day, and as the coach stopped, the horsemen advanced and sat with uncovered heads, while their spokesman informed Mr. Seward, that they came on behalf of the Government and people of the State of Jalisco, and the authorities and residents of Seyula, to welcome him to their State and town, offer him an humble dinner, and the hospitalities of the place for as long a time as he chose to abide with them. Mr. Seward replied as briefly and heartily as possible, and leaving the stage and entering the carriages, the party started off with the double escort at full speed for Seyula, five miles distant.

Arriving at the town, we found all the population out to meet us, and from every door and window, and every accessible spot on the sidewalks, respectful salutations greeted the strangers from the North. Dark eyes and red lips, such as we saw but seldom in the "Tierra Caliente," smiled welcome upon us, and as the carriages rolled into the Plaza de Armas, the ringing of bells, firing of cannon, strains of martial music, and vivas of the populace, added emphasis to the greeting. Through a double file of well-dressed and intelligent-looking citizens, then through the portal lined with swarthy soldiers presenting arms, the party passed into the great paved court-yard of the *Casa Grande* of Seyula, and entering the parlor of the house were made at home, at once.

The presentations over, we were invited into the hall, where breakfast—it was a grand dinner in fact—was spread, and the tables were speedily filled, all the places not occupied by our party being taken by the citizens and accompanying ladies, while a swarm of servants and citizens waited upon them. It is the fashion, in Mexico, to change the plates of the guests with every dish, and plate followed plate in rapid succession, until we were surfeited. Wines, too, were there in abundance, and the best of all was the dark, rich, fruity, and oily product of the grape of Seyula, resembling Malaga of the finest quality, which it fully equals, if it does not actually excel.

We were now, for the first time, in the grape-producing region of Mexico, and our first introduction to its wines was an agreeable one, indeed. Fraternity and good feeling were the order of the day. What surprised us most, was the fact, that these people had only heard of the coming of the party six hours previously, and that this whole demonstration was thoroughly impromptu. I doubt if any town in the United States of the same, or even twice the population, could, or would do as much in thrice the time, for the President himself; and all this was for merely a distinguished citizen of the United States, and friend of Mexico.

When the solid viands had been removed, Enfraus Carison, Political Prefect of Seyula, arose and read a warm address of welcome. José G. Arroyo, a young representative of the press of Guadalajara, followed in an impassioned and truly eloquent and patriotic address, and others followed in like manner. Mr. Seward made a brief reply, in terms similar to those of his speech at Colima, and his remarks being interpreted to the audience by Señor Cañedo, were enthusiastically applauded.

It was then announced that the annual conferring of rewards in one of the public schools in Seyula, which was going on when we arrived, had been suspended for the time, in order that Mr. Seward might be present. Repairing to the school-house—there are four in this old town of eight thousand inhabitants—we found about one hundred and twenty-five boys and two hundred girls, arranged in the two wings of the building, the sexes being seated separately. All arose at our entrance and bowed politely, remaining standing until requested to be seated. The furniture of the school-room was scant, and of the plainest kind, and the children, mostly, very plainly dressed; but they looked cheerful and intelligent, and all were perfectly neat and clean. There were all colors and shades of colors among the pupils, but there was no distinction of class or condition, so far as their treatment and conduct toward each other went.

A bright, manly little fellow, Lorenzo Villalbazo, aged twelve years, came forward, and read in a loud, clear voice, an address which had been delivered at Guadalajara by an eminent friend of education; and Amanda Ron, Reymunda Villalbazo, and Geronima Ortega, aged eleven, twelve, and thirteen years respectively, followed with readings of selections copied by themselves. Their reading was equally faultless, and could not well be improved. I noticed that in each selection, special reference was made to the public schools of the "great and powerful Estados Unidos del Norte" as the source of our strength and glory, but was told that the selections had not been made with reference to our being present, as we had not been expected.

The distribution of prizes, silver coins with tri-colored—green, white and red—ribbons, followed. I noticed that a majority of the prizes were carried off by children of full Indian blood, and one of the highest was taken by a young Indian woman of seventeen years, whose scant, but scrupulously neat apparel indicated, unmistakably, that she was the daughter of people in very poor circumstances.

I am surprised at the excellence of the public schools of Mexico, when I remember how recently they were called into existence, and, even more so, at the bright intelligence and excellent deportment of the pupils. On the streets, the children of Mexico are patterns of good behavior, and the rowdy element, so painfully apparent among the youth of our Northern cities, is wholly absent here.

Seyula is one of the oldest cities of Mexico, and boasts of a number of churches quite out of proportion to its population. Some of these we visited. We found one of them, though plain outside, a magnificent structure inside, with long rows of pillars and vaulted ceiling, painted in rich fresco designs beautifully executed.

The inhabitants of Seyula, not to be outdone by those of more pretentious towns, got up a select dancing party in the evening, in honor of their visitors, and among the dancers I noticed an unusual number of fine-looking men and beautiful women, of the pure, or nearly pure, Spanish type. One of these, Dolores Mora, daughter of the paymaster of the State Guard of Jalisco, then in the field against the bandits, was a perfect beauty, and would have been a belle in any ball-room in Christendom. A full, round face, soft, dark-brown hair, large, lustrous, black eyes, complexion just tinged with the hue of the olive, cheeks like the ripe, red peach, bright red lips, contrasting with the pearly teeth, and a slender, petite figure, moving with a willowy grace through the dreamily voluptuous mazes of the *danza*; in all the store-house of my memory there is not a sweeter picture than that.

At midnight we retired to rest, and all night long, heard the strains of soft music from harp, and guitar, and violin, which told us that the festivities still went on.

At day-break, as usual, we were off again on our journey. Our road all day—about thirty miles—lay along the margin of the Laguna de Seyula, and between fields of tall corn, sugar-cane, beans, red pepper, &c., &c., surrounded by high fences of solid stone, mostly of lava formation. The roads were heavy with mud from the recent rains, and our progress very slow. The lake, swollen by the storm—was from three to six miles wide and thirty long. Geese, and little white cranes, curlew, plover, ducks, &c., abounded along the shores, and great flocks of pink-hued birds, resembling flamingoes, were seen from time to time. We saw two bright red birds, called "cardinals," perched on the tops of the great "pitilla," Cactus, which here forms a prominent feature in the vegetation; the castor-bean, which here becomes a permanent and beautiful tree, was seen all along the road, and the tree-cotton—a cotton-plant entirely unlike that of our Southern States, really a tree—abounded. The mountain sides were everywhere patched with fields of corn and barley—the first ripe and the latter two-thirds grown—far up towards their summits.

Villages, inhabited by working-people of Indian descent were frequent. At one of these, called Techa-luta, we were met by a company with a fine brass-band —every little hamlet in the country has one—and men with rockets, who played, and fired rockets as long as we were in sight. They had no flags, but had stretched every handkerchief and piece of bright-colored goods in the town, on lines across the street; and a horseman, dashing up to the carriage, threw in an address of the most progressive republican fraternity type, addressed to Mr. Seward and signed by the principal men of the municipality. At another Indian village, Guamacate, we obtained a breakfast of tortillas, chicken, and frijoles in abundance for fourteen persons, all for one dollar and a half. The same fare would have cost us in New York two dollars each.

At 2 1-2 o'clock P. M. we reached the end of our day's journey at the village of Zacoalco, and were met outside of the town by thirty finely mounted men, as at Seyula, and escorted to our lodgings in a large, cool, roomy house, surrounding a square area filled with tropical trees and flowers. The military guard of the town were drawn up at the gate-way to receive us, and the entire population was gathered in the vicinity. We were now at the head of the Laguna de Seyula, and at the commencement of the Laguna de Zacoalco. From the shores of the lake at Seyula, is taken the soda-earth used in making soap all over this part of Mexico. From its waters, salt of a fair quality for mining purposes is manufactured; and the owner of the lake, Señor Escandon of the city of Mexico, derives from it a revenue of sixty thousand dollars per annum, though it is but carelessly administered.

The valley is dotted all over with the bean-bearing

mesquite trees, and on them grows a variety of parasites—the misletoe and a similar parasite plant—bearing bright scarlet blossoms in wonderful profusion. The variety and beauty of the flowers are so great as to be beyond the power of description. Even the best educated residents of the country do not know the names of half the flowers we saw by the roadside. Twenty leagues is the distance from Zacoalco to the great city of Guadalajara, where we were to rest on our journey for a week or more.

We left Seyula, under the impression that at Zacoalco we should rest in peace, with no serious demonstrations, the place being represented as extremely dull. We were therefore much surprised to find the town of some fifteen thousand people, wide-awake, and determined not to be behind the other little cities of the State of Jalisco, in its hospitalities. We were invited at 8 P. M. to participate in a dinner, which for completeness and sumptuousness in all its details, could not be excelled at the finest hotel in New-York with every preparation, and found a number of prominent citizens of the place in attendance, anxious to do the honors of the table in the most creditable manner. They did it. After dinner, the company returned to the parlor, where addresses, fervid, eloquent, and patriotic, were delivered by the Political Prefect and other leading citizens. Mr. Seward responded, in terms similar to those of his previous speeches, and his remarks being translated by Señor Cañedo, were warmly applauded. Music and singing followed, and it was midnight before one of the most pleasant reunions we attended in Mexico finally broke up.

At 6 A. M. on Tuesday, the bugles of the military escort sounded the advance, and the long train was off for Guadalajara; just as the first rays of the warm Autumn sun of the tropics gilded the tall towers of the grand old Church of Zacoalco—towers which have looked down on the gray-walled town unchanged for three hundred years—kissed the placid waters of the Laguna de Zacoalco, and crowned with glory the grand, old, green-clad mountains which surround the ever-beautiful valley.

Half-a-dozen miles from Zacoalco, we ascended a steep hill of volcanic origin, and came upon the battle-field of La Coronea. Here, the Imperialists sent out by Maximilian, to prevent the Republican Army of the West commanded by Gen. Ramon Corona advancing from Sinaloa, from uniting with those of Escobedo who commanded the Army of the North before Queretaro, were strongly intrenched on the summit of the broken, irregular hills, with stone walls in front. The position commanded the road on both sides and is naturally a strong one; but the tide of war had turned; the ragged Chinacos, who at first were demoralized in presence of the better drilled and better armed French, Belgian and Austrian mercenaries, had learned from experience how to fight them, and the foreign invaders were themselves demoralized and disheartened. Corona's forces carried the position at the point of the bayonet, and the Imperialists were utterly routed, the entire force being killed or made prisoners. Escobedo had already routed and scattered like chaff the Imperialist Army of the North under Miramon, at Zacatecas, and was laying siege to Queretaro. Corona arrived before the doomed city just in time to participate in the most desperate portion of the contest.

When the last desperate sortie was made by Maximilian with the hope of cutting his way out and escaping to the Pacific coast, *via* Morelia, Corona's division caught the full weight of the blow, and was savagely handled and cut to pieces; but the delay was fatal, though the sortie had become an almost insured success, for it enabled the Republicans to rally to the rescue just in time. Escobedo's victorious army came up, and, falling upon the Imperialist forces, rolled them back in utter rout within their intrenchments, and from that time forth, the fate of the Empire and of Maximilian was sealed.

Among the most daring, active, and determined of the officers in General Corona's command, was General Angel Martinez, a native of Sinaloa, and commander of a brigade noted for its rough style of fighting and defective outfit. This dashing officer, with the most inadequate means, accomplished important results and contributed much to the overthrow of the Imperial cause in the North-west. His enemies nicknamed him "*El Machetero*," from the *machete* or short sword—the favorite weapon of his followers—a weapon which he himself wielded with terrible effect on more than one occasion. When Corona was holding the French in Mazatlan, after the terrible defeats he gave them at the Presidio of Mazatlan and Palos Prietos, Martinez entered Sonora, and swept it like a whirlwind; nothing escaped him in the field, and the hurried evacuation of Guaymas by the French at his approach, alone saved a remnant of the force from utter extermination.

In one of the battles, near Hermosillo, the forces of the Imperialist butcher, General Lanberg, who was the perpetrator of the wholesale massacre of La Noria, were cut to pieces, and Lanberg, himself, lassoed and pulled out of the saddle, with a jerk which broke his neck, by one of Martinez's subalterns. War to the death had been proclaimed on both sides, and no quarter was given or asked.

One day in 1869, the writer was standing on Montgomery street in San Francisco, conversing with General Martinez and others, when the subject turned on the languages which each spoke, or did not speak. One could speak Spanish, English and French; another German, English and French, and so on. One of the party deprecatingly remarked that his Spanish was deficient, but added, "I have managed to wade through a good deal of French in my life-time." "What does he say?" asked the General quickly. The remark was translated to him literally, when he instantly lifted his hat with a polite bow, and responded, "*Yo tambien* Señor!" (I also Sir!) It was, all things considered, the most terrible pun I ever heard uttered.

For twenty miles, our road led us along the shores of the Laguna de Zacoalco, a part of the time with the Laguna de Seyúla on the opposite side of the tongue of land on which we traveled. The soil was for the most part coarse and gravelly, and the country little cultivated. The mountains, though covered with dense verdure, were composed almost wholly of old lava, and all the fences along the roadside were built of the same material, in fact, this entire country is of comparatively recent volcanic origin. At the upper end of the Laguna de Zacoalco, we passed near the water-side for miles. Great cane-brakes came up to the road in many places, and, growing by the edge of the water, we saw thousands of beautiful pink and spotted lilies, richly fragrant, and much like the Japanese lily in appearance.

Many species of birds, unlike those of the United States, were seen all along the shores of the lake. Among them were flocks of large pink birds, which in the distance appeared to me like the ibis. I also noticed the "wandering ibis" of Audubon, and the "Great Whooping Crane," snow white, except two bars of black on the wings, with black legs, red spots on the top of the head, and black bill. This crane is occasionally killed in Illinois and other western states, and was confounded by Audubon with the sand-hill Crane of the west, he supposing it to be the old bird of that species. There was also a large crane with snow white body and jet-black wings, of which I once killed a single specimen north of the Rio Grande, in Texas, the small white crane of the west, and swarms of birds of the curlew and plover species, quite new to me, though I am familiar with the birds of all parts of the United States.

At 10 o'clock, we arrived at the village of Santa Anna Acatlan, where we breakfasted at a Mexican fonda, or hotel, the first we had visited in Mexico. Our table was set in the corridor, opening on the square area, or patio, in the center of the establishment, and adjoining the kitchen. Everything came upon the table in excellent order, clean and well cooked. It is a singular fact that in Mexico one never sees a badly-cooked dish. Such a thing as a joint of meat coming upon the table half-raw, is wholly unknown here. There are many people who adhere to the belief, that when modern "improved" cooking-stoves came into use in the United States, and the old-fashioned bake-ovens disappeared, good cookery vanished with them, and I am more than half inclined to admit that they are right. These Mexicans who have only earthern ovens and stoves, utterly unlike anything ever seen in our country, and not a single iron dish, all being of the light glazed, brown earthernware of the country, contrive to cook twenty times as great a variety of dishes as we are able to compound, and what is more, cook them all to perfection. On the whole, I don't think we know anything about cooking in the United States.

The charges at these Mexican "fondas" are quite reasonable; say twelve and a half to twenty-five cents, at the outside, for a "square meal," and lodgings, such as they are, at a nominal cost. They do not usually provide beds, the travelers carrying blankets, or mattresses, with them; and as the beds are not unlikely to be a little too much crowded for comfort when they are furnished, it is better to carry your own sleeping outfit with you.

From the hill above Santa Anna Acatlan, we had a fine view of the immense Hacienda del Plan, the largest and finest sugar estate in the State of Jalisco. The house stands upon a hill overlooking the Laguna de Zacoalco, and is surrounded by the sugar-works and other buildings, with vast fields of sugar-cane, now two-thirds grown—it requires from one year to fourteen months to come to full maturity—in all directions. The house is like a great square castle in appearance, with columns and verandah all around, and looks like a fit place for the residence of a prince.

From this estate, a large part of the great State of Jalisco, which has nine hundred thousand inhabitants, or more than any other in Mexico, derives its supply of sugar, and its products are sent even as far north as the Rio Grande. It belongs to Señor Ramos, one of the wealthiest land owners in Mexico. The grand canal, miles in length, and of solid masonry, through which the water is carried for irrigating this estate, cost in itself a colossal fortune, and the sugar-mills and other improvements must have required an outlay of a million dollars, at least. As it was a little distance from our road, we did not visit it.

After leaving Santa Anna Acatlan, we passed through a better cultivated country for some miles, and then entered a pass through the mountains to the north-eastward, which led us into the Valley of Guadalajara. Passing through one Indian village, we saw a number of men and women kneeling in groups by the roadside and looking imploringly at the carriage, but they did not speak or hold out their hands like beggars, and we were unable to form any idea of their object. They remained kneeling and regarding us in silence as long as we were in sight. There was something unnatural and painful to me in the spectacle of those men and women thus kneeling on the earth, in silent supplications, as if they had mistaken the party for visitors from heaven instead of another country, and I would be sorry to see it repeated.

We saw another strange sight next day. Indian men and women, walking by the roadside, carrying great burthens on their backs, three hundred or four hundred pounds weight of coarse earthernware or other articles, in long wicker baskets, and braiding straw hats, or knitting fine embroidery as they moved along, bending beneath their loads. Of this embrcidery I shall speak again hereafter.

Our road continued to be fearfully cut up, and heavy from the recent rains, and our progress slow. We were now in a country where the freighting business is carried on, mostly, with heavy wagons and heavier ox-carts with enormous wheels of wood, with wooden axles and no felloes, the whole middle of the wheel being filled with a solid block of heavy wood. The oxen are yoked by the head instead of the neck, and driven, half a dozen yokes to a single cart, like mules before a wagon. The wives, and often the children, of the cart-drivers accompany them on their long journeys from city to city, and one of their camps by the roadside is a little village in itself. The poor people of the villages along the route live, to a considerable extent, by supplying these teamsters and other travelers with articles of food, cheese, fruit, cigarritos, matches, and ardent spirits. A bottle of the fiery liquid distilled from the mescal plant, otherwise called the "American aloe," or "century plant," which blossoms in this latitude in five to seven years from planting, instead of once in a hundred, as is commonly believed at the North—called "*mescal*,"—is sold at the little wayside stands for six and one-fourth cents, and will produce as much drunkenness as a barrel of North American whisky.

There is a superior variety of the mescal produced near Guadalajara, and called after the village in which it is made "Tequila," (pronounced Tekela.) This costs more, and is sent to the City of Mexico and elsewhere, as something very choice for a present to one's friends. I took one drink of it under the supposition that it was *annisette*, or some other light liquor, swallowing possibly about an ounce, druggist's measure, before I smelled the burning flesh as the lightning descended my throat. As I sat down the glass my head began to increase in size so rapidly, that I saw at once, that unless I got outside immediately, the door would be too small to admit of my passing through it. Seizing my hat which appeared to have become of about the size of an ordinary umbrella, I turned it up edgewise, and succeeded by a tight squeeze in passing it through the door; the street then appeared funnel-shaped, and I remember an odd fancy that I was to resemble the man who "went in the big and came out at the little end of the horn." Curiously enough my legs decreased in size, as my head enlarged, and my last recollection of the affair is that my person resembled a sugar hogshead walking off on two straws: body I had none. No more tequila for me, please!

A SWELL-HEAD.

The teamsters and muleteers drink this clear, colorless, harmless-looking concentrated lightning with apparent impunity; but a single bottle of it will cause a rebellion among an entire regiment of soldiers, and very likely result in a *pronunciamento* on the spot. Nevertheless, the ox drivers, like the muleteers, are a quiet, well-behaved, and generally honest and trustworthy class of men, quite equal in these particulars to any class in the same walks of life in any country.

When we were in the pass through the hills, between the Valleys of Zacoalco and Guadalajara, our team went down in a mud-hole of unusual depth and enormity, and stayed there for nearly two hours before it could be extricated. When, at last, we passed across to rolling and but sparsely grassed and wooded plains, resembling those of Southern California in appearance, with numerous villages, each with its great house and white-walled church, and came upon the edge of the table-land overlooking the proud City of Guadalajara, the sun was just going down in the west, and the full round moon coming above the eastern horizon. What a glorious scene! The city, white-walled and red-roofed, with its numerous churches, and immense and magnificent Cathedral overtopping all, stood out grandly beautiful in the double light, a sight to look upon and admire, and to exult over in memory henceforth through all our lives.

At a little town three or four miles outside the walls of Guadalajara, we met a line of light carriages, with an escort of about one hundred citizens, splendidly mounted, on horseback, with the Municipal Council and the Secretary of Gov. Cuervo, and others, coming to offer the hospitalities of the city, and a hearty welcome to the Capital of Jalisco.

Entering the carriages, we were driven rapidly toward the city, the military escort, civil police in uniform, and mounted citizens forming a magnificent cavalcade nearly half a mile in length, galloping on either side. As we neared the walls, the roadside was lined with private carriages, filled with the beauty and fashion of the city; and when we passed through the barrier and dashed down the narrow, well-paved streets, the sidewalks were crowded, and every window and house-top occupied. Beautiful women waved their handkerchiefs, and gave a smiling welcome on all sides. All Guadalajara seemed to be abroad in the cool, bright evening, all pleased, all happy, and all anxious to welcome the strangers from the North.

We were driven directly to a house, in elegance of appointment the counterpart of that of Señor Huarte at Colima, but on a much grander scale, and as soon as we were in doors, the keys were presented to Mr. Seward, and the whole establishment was placed at his disposal; he was told to consider it his own, and each member of the party requested to order what he desired, from a drink of water to a carriage, during our stay. With the exception of the servants, the party were the sole occupants of the entire premises, and we were most emphatically "at home" for the week. Gov. Cuervo, with much consideration, sent word that as we had traveled so far, and must be very weary, he would postpone his call until morning, and we were left alone for the night! And such a night!

Dinner over, I wandered alone out into the streets, visited the grand plaza, and saw the people of the city, old and young, rich and poor, proud and lowly, sitting on the seats beneath the orange trees, conversing and passing the time happily and innocently away, myself alone, of all the crowd, unknowing and unknown. I heard the visit of Mr. Seward and party frequently mentioned, and some curiosity as to its object and full purport expressed; but no unkind sentiments, no harsh suspicions were uttered in my hearing, and there seemed to be but one feeling toward the visitors.

In this proud old city, the source of unnumbered revolutions and pronunciamentos in times gone by, I heard more whisperings of love than talk of war on that delicious evening; and when I retired to rest, the soft, fragrant air, heavy and sensuous with the breath of flowers, coming in through the open window, was accompanied by the music of the light guitar, and the sweet voice of woman, singing the old, old song, from the blossom-wreathed balcony on the opposite side of the street.

CHAPTER V.

GUADALAJARA.

THE strange, ancient, aristocratic, and haughty City of Guadalajara, held us a full week from the prosecution of our journey, and after seeing its sights from morning till night, during all that time, we were as loth to leave it as ever. Every morning we went out to see some one of the dozens of beautiful ancient churches with which the City is adorned, attend early mass, and examine the quaint old pictures with which each abounds. One of the finest of these, perhaps the finest excepting the great Cathedral, is the Church of Our Lady of Guadaloupe, which is half convent, as well as church. There is attached to this church a "Retreat," with two hundred cells. To this place the pious citizens of the City, repair to spend nine days of Lent, in monastic retirement, for the good of their souls. Each cell has a table, chair, and cot-bed, and meals are served to the temporary occupants by servants, thus enabling them to pass their time in absolute seclusion from the world. For the nine days' board and lodging, and spiritual comfort, those able, pay four or five dollars, the others nothing. More women than men resort here and the cells are filled every year.

All these churches have beautiful chimes of bells, cast in the city centuries ago, and the air is at times filled with their music. By the municipal laws, they are now allowed to ring only two or three minutes at any one time, but they contrive to make the intervals between the ringing nearly as brief as those between the drinks in San Francisco. The services are similarly brief and frequent, and the churches appear to be nearly always open.

The great Cathedral of Guadalajara is one of the most beautiful and costly temples of worship on the Continent; ranking in Mexico only second to those of Puebla and the City in point of wealth, and for beauty far in advance of the latter. I cannot describe a Cathedral, though I try never so hard. Suffice it to say, that the roof is supported by ten combined or quadruple columns, of immense size, painted in pure white

THE GREAT CATHEDRAL AT GUADALAJARA.

and gold. From above the huge capital of each rises a beautiful arch, which seems so light and airy, as to make it impossible to believe that it is built of solid stone, and weighs hundreds on hundreds of tons. The grand dome, which without is covered with beautiful glazed tiles of different colors, laid in mosaic, is painted within in fresco, in the most florid but highly artistic style. A narrow gallery of bronze metal richly gilded, runs around the entire building, on a level with the capitals of the pillars which support the roof. Under the great dome is the grand organ, and arranged in a semi-circle behind the choir, the twenty-four seats for the Bishop and Canons. The choir is as superb as gilding and carving can make it.

A few years since, this Cathedral was struck by lightning, and two of the organists were killed. In a vault below the pavement of the Cathedral, the dead Bishops and Priests have been accumulating for centuries. Under the great dome, in front of the choir, they are now erecting a magnificent altar, some thirty feet in height, of white marble and metal, gilded and burnished, which was imported from Rome at a cost of fifty-thousand dollars, and hauled—Heaven knows how—over the terrible, and, as we found them, almost impassable roads, all the way from Vera Cruz to Guadalajara. Several of the blocks are immensely heavy, one I should judge, weighing from ten to twenty tons, and the task of transporting them must have been, indeed, herculean.

Around the walls hang pictures of great age; and in one of the rooms back of the altar we saw a collection of life-sized statues of saints, apostles, and martyrs, done in wood, and covered with some kind of flesh colored lacquer work, by native artists. Physical torture, mental suffering, unmurmuring and glad obedience to the behests of an all-powerful faith, or the beatific delight of the dying martyr, beamed on the face of each. A more distorted, frightful and painful collection to look at was never seen together. The skill of the artists in depicting physical and mental suffering, with such materials, is beyond praise for its perfection.

On either side of the altar, next to the wall, are old, plain, square, wooden boxes, each about six feet in length, covered with red cloth. In these two boxes, are enclosed the mummified remains of the first two bishops of Guadalajara. One of them has been lying there for three hundred years, and the other some forty years less. Both are said to be in a good state of preservation. Above the coffins, on the wall, hang the broad brimmed hats worn by these worthy men in their lives, and we were gravely informed by our guide, that when the coffins are opened for any reason, the hats will immediately swing from side to side of their own volition, as if doing reverence to the holy dust below. We did not see the coffins opened.

But the charitable institutions and schools of Guadalajara claimed more of our time and attention, and are worthy of mention, even before the grand cathedral, which is one of its especial wonders.

The great hospital of San Miguel de Belan, generally known as "the Belan," is near the center of the city, and encloses within its walls about eight acres of land. It was founded, as the inscription over the inner gateway shows, in 1787, by Bishop Alcalde, whose first name I do not remember, and with whom, I presume, the people of the United States of the present day had no personal acquaintance. Its revenues were once immense, they say one million dollars per annum; but each succeeding revolution has impoverished it, and six or seven years ago, the late Bishop Portugal found it almost wholly in ruins and without funds to support patients. His office was worth a large sum per annum, and he had a large private property. He set himself earnestly to work to rebuild and endow this great hospital, and lived to see it once more in the full tide of prosperity, after having devoted his entire fortune and all the voluntary contributions he could secure to the institution.

The amount expended in building and repairing, and the property bestowed upon the institution, from the rents of which it is now sustained, was estimated, all told, at six million dollars. The first thing a revolutionist did in past times, was to enlist all the prisoners in the Jails and State-Prisons, then seize the moneys in the custom-houses, mints, and charitable institutions, then force into his ranks all the able-bodied men in the community, and levy *prestimos* on the merchants and wealthy men In this manner, society has regained from time to time all the thieves, robbers, and vagabonds which had been lost to it through the criminal laws, and the public funds and charitable institutions have suffered in proportion. The Liberal Government, during the late war, was compelled much against its will, but from sheer necessity, to use a million dollars of the property of the Belan Hospital; what amount the French and Austrians got I am not informed. The hospital now has about five hundred thousand dollars worth of property, from which it receives twenty thousand dollars in rents, all of which it expends upon its patients, and through a commission of citizens it is most admirably administered.

The Sisters of charity attend upon the patients, but do not control the management of the institution. The number of patients now in the hospital is three hundred, and this is about the average in seasons of peace, but at times during the last war, it was nearly trebled. Bishop Portugal died poor, but left behind him in the hospital, a monument which will cause his name to be honored and revered for centuries.

The building is admirably constructed for the purpose. It is but one story in height, and there are, of course, no stairs to climb up and down. Then the rooms are twenty-five feet from floor to ceiling, insuring perfect ventilation, and all of immense size. The walls, of brick or adobe, are very thick, and the thick roof, with red tiles above, keeps out effectually the heat of the sun, so that there is no very perceptible change in the temperature in summer or winter, and no artificial heating is necessary. No dirt, no noise, no blinding light, no musquitoes, flies, or vermin, are there.

Entering the portal, near the center of the building, the visitor finds himself in a gallery, from which radiate, in fan form, six wards of immense length, three on either side. These wards are designated by the inscriptions over the doors, "God the Father," "God the Son," and "God the Holy Ghost," on one side, and on the other, "St. Vincent de Paul," "The Sacred Heart of Jesus," and "St. John of God." The patients are allowed to see their friends as often as they desire, and appear to be well waited upon and cared for. The kitchen, dispensary, bath-house, &c., all appear to be remarkably well-arranged and supplied.

Passing one of the large rooms I noticed the sign "Operating Room" over the door, and looking in through the open grating, saw a party of surgeons and students busily engaged in dissecting a corpse, so thoroughly occupied in fact that they paid no attention to our presence. This part of the work was carried on much more openly than with us, and seemed to be regarded quite as a matter of course by all present.

Grander in proportions and conception than even the Belan Hospital, is the great Hospicio de Guadalajara, the equal of which cannot be found on the American Continent. This was founded a century ago by Bishop Juan Cruz Ruis Cabanais, a man of great wealth and piety, who endowed it magnificently. His full length portrait, in which he is represented standing, in full Canonicals, before a table, on which rests a diagram of the complete structure, just as we see it to-day, and holding in his hands the purse containing the endowment of the institution, hangs in the chapel of the establishment now. What it cost to erect a structure covering six or eight acres of ground, with walls from three to eight feet in thickness, inclosing no less than twenty-two court-yards, each surrounded by magnificent corridors or portals, and furnish it throughout, I cannot tell, but it must have been millions of dollars, even in a country where labor costs next to nothing.

This establishment was greatly run down a few years ago, but through the efforts of the late Señor Matute, and other patriotic and public-spirited citizens, it has been regenerated, and now holds within its walls sixteen-hundred human beings, from the foundling just brought in from the street, to the young woman or man ready to go forth into the world as a teacher, artizan, house-servant, husband or wife. It is superintended by the Sisters of Charity, of whom there are some twenty in the establishment, and managed with an amount of economy and skill wonderful to witness. In its sixteen different departments it is at once, a foundling hospital, reform school, juvenile school, orphan asylum, asylum for the aged and indigent, boy's and girl's high school, school of arts, workshop, college and hospital.

In one department we saw thirty foundlings, two of which had just been brought in, all white, and most of them presenting an effeminate delicacy of feature, indicating "blue blood." The Indians, and people of part Indian blood, do not throw their children into the streets, to be eaten by dogs and hogs, whether born in or out of lawful wedlock. They are neatly dressed, nursed by Indian women, and well cared for. In another ward were one hundred and five boys, arrested by the police, as vagabonds on the streets, and sent here to be reformed. They were drilling as soldiers when we came in. The City pays six and one quarter cents each, per day, for the support of these boys, and they all have to learn useful trades before leaving the institution. I noticed among the children many who had lost one or both eyes, and was told that in the Indian villages it is not uncommon for the parents to thus mutilate their children in infancy, to fit them for begging, or to enable them to avoid military duty.

In another ward we saw the old women, some of them from eighty to one hundred years of age, and girls of weak intellect, sitting in the sun and doing some little plain sewing or knitting, and in an adjoining room a number of blind girls busily engaged in grinding half-hulled corn, with the *metate* into *tortillas*, a sweet smile on their faces indicating their knowledge of our presence. In another, boys were at work making shoes, tailoring, carpentering, and setting type in a regular printing office, and printing with one of Hoe's Washington presses, just such as I "rolled" upon twenty-four years ago, in a country printing office in the then "Far West." In another, girls were sewing, embroidering in silk and bullion, making lace, knitting, etc. In another, young ladies of the first families, who reside with their parents, were learning painting and the highest styles of embroidery.

BLIND GIRL IN THE HOSPICIO.

In another ward, two hundred children, between two and five years of age, one hundred boys and one hundred girls, belonging to parents too poor even to dress them, were being taught orally, as at the school of San Felipe. All the cloth for the clothing of the pupils, is made within its walls, and all the clothing, and boots and shoes required, are made up by the boys and girls.

The kitchen, as large as an ordinary school-house with us, is floored with glazed tiles of beautiful pattern, and the old Spanish ranges have recently been replaced by English iron ranges, which cost twenty-four hundred dollars, but save fifty dollars per month on the charcoal bill, and are considered a good investment. Soup, meat, and beans are cooked here for sixteen hundred persons at once, and they are now erecting an enormous kitchen in which the entire cooking for the State-Prison, containing from seven hundred to one thousand prisoners, is to be done. It now costs the State five cents per day, to board the State prisoners, and the Sisters expect to do it better, and make a profit on that figure, for the benefit of the Hospicio.

The Chapel is really a grand Church, magnificently decorated with paintings, with a great dome, beautifully frescoed. The founder gave forty blocks of buildings in Guadalajara, all under rent, as an endowment for this establishment; but most of the property is now gone. It costs only sixty thousand dollars per annum to support the Hospicio and Belan Hospital together and their resources being but forty-four thousand dollars, the State and City pay the rest. We spent four hours wandering through this great establishment, and, after partaking of a collation, listened to a brass band of thirty pieces, played by boys instructed in the place, and operatic music by the young ladies, and then left because night had come and we could wait no longer.

The schools of Guadalajara, new as they are—some of them but a year or two established—astonished us more than anything else we saw in this ancient City. The municipality of Guadalajara now supports eighteen primary day schools, nine for girls, and nine for boys, free to all, and five evening schools, beside contributing to the support of several more advanced schools, accommodating in all seven thousand pupils, and all at an expense, as I was informed by Señor Juan Ignacio Matute, a member of the Municipal Council, whose father may be called the father of the Common School system of Jalisco, of only twenty-five thousand dollars per annum.

Then, the State provides two High Schools, or "*lycees*," one for boys and one for girls, which are free to all who are unable to pay ten dollars per month for board and tuition—no scholar who can pass the examination can be refused, however humble or poor—where the youth are taught all the higher branches of mathematics, the languages, vocal and instrumental music, and many arts by which they can gain an honest livelihood; a school of Arts, in which four hundred boys are taught all the useful arts and trades, such as tailoring, saddlery, blacksmithing, boot-making, carpentering, etc., etc., and an Institute or college of higher grade, for the instruction of boys intended for the learned professions. In addition to this, the State contributes a comparatively liberal sum towards the support of the Hospicio and other institutions of learning.

We first visited the Girl's High School. This is the school provided by the State of Jalisco for graduates of her Grammar schools. It is situated in the old Convent of San Diego, which was closed and confiscated to the Nation by order of President Juarez, and is now wholly devoted to the purposes of free education. The building, like nearly all similar structures here, surrounds an entire square, and incloses a large court-yard filled with orange-trees and tropical flowers. It is two stories in height, and the rooms are all of great size, light, clean, and well ventilated. When the nuns were turned forth, the Government gave the use of the property to the State of Jalisco, for educational purposes. We found here two hundred and thirty girls from the age of twelve to twenty years, all bright, intelligent and happy looking. Those able to do so pay ten dollars per month, or one hundred and twenty dollars per year, and those who are not, (they comprise a majority of the pupils) pay nothing. For this they receive instruction in all the studies usually pursued in the higher schools in the United States, vocal and instrumental music, object drawing, all the fine arts, embroidery, lace-making, and, better still, cooking, washing, ironing, and other household duties. They all board in the building—board being included in the ten dollars per month—and take turns in doing the work in each department, that all may know how to do such work well. Brighter and happier faces I never saw around me.

We visited all the departments, from kitchen to fine art gallery, and found that all of the teachers were native Mexicans, male and female, mostly young, and educated in the country. The pupils usually belong to the best Republican families of the State; but the highest and lowest, richest and poorest, fairest and darkest, are all admitted on the same terms of equality. When they graduate they are fitted for teachers in the public schools, or for housekeeping, or the various trades.

We saw in the embroidery room, lace-work and embroidery in silk, cotton and bullion of the most exquisite fineness and delicacy. Some of the linen handkerchiefs, worked with portraits of Lincoln, Juarez and Zarragosa, in black silk floss, were equal in delicacy and accuracy to the best steel engravings, and the copies of oil paintings in silk embroidery, were perfect fac-similes of the originals. In the Music Hall, the pupils gave us the opera of Ernani in as grand style as it is usually given by the regular opera companies of the United States, the part of Ernani being sung by a little Miss fourteen years of age, with a wonderfully powerful and highly cultivated voice.

On leaving this beautiful retreat, once the shade of darkness and superstition and bigotry, now so justly the pride and the hope of the State, Mr. Seward remarked, "Why, in Heaven's name, do people talk of 'Protectorate' for a country capable of such things as these."

Next, we visited the Boy's High School. This establishment, originally built by Bishop Parades, but now under civil control, contains nearly four hundred students, and will soon have five hundred. It is almost a counterpart of the girl's High School, the system of tuition, cost to those able to pay—board, &c., &c.—being the same. It is admirably conducted, and is as creditable to the town as the other. The professors teach gratuitously, or for very small salaries. One teacher of four classes gets but eighty dollars per month, and Señor Matute and others teach classes gratuitously. We saw a gymnasium, art gallery, considerable scientific apparatus, and other adjuncts of a first-class school of this grade, in the building. One great feature of this school is its library of thirty thousand volumes, mainly the spoils of the confiscated monasteries. This, in New York, Boston, or England would be an immense feature. There are thousands on thousands of volumes three centuries old and more, printed or illuminated by hand, and as perfect in their parchment coverings as on the day they issued from the press. Most of them, are in Spanish, but there are many in French and some in English.

I saw a dictionary in Spanish and Aztec, printed in Mexico in 1571, and another, equally perfect, printed in Michoacan in 1559, long enough before we had printing offices in English America. There are many works printed years earlier in Spain and France. A large number of these books are in duplicate, and five thousand volumes of the most rare, carefully selected and exposed for sale in New York or Boston, would attract all the old book-fanciers on the Continent, and bring money enough to provide this school with what it most needs; viz: a large and complete modern library in Spanish, English and French. An antiquarian book-dealer might make a fortune, and benefit mankind, by coming to Guadalajara and purchasing such of these works as the authorities would be willing to sell.

The last institution of learning which we visited was the School of Useful Arts. This School is unique, and deserves more extended notice than I can give it. It is located in the old monastery of San Augustine, which, like the other establishments of the kind, now belongs to the Federal Government. We found four hundred boys, from eight to eighteen years of age, learning every trade from shoemaking to blacksmithing, carpentering, weaving, tailoring, etc., etc. There is a great desire to enter this school among the youth of Jalisco, and if there were accommodations and funds provided for them, there would be one thousand students instead of four hundred. The boys are first taught to read, write and keep accounts, and then go into the workshops.

All the clothing and boots and shoes worn in the establishment are made by the boys, the cloth being made up from the raw cotton, spun, woven and colored. The boys do the cooking and other menial duties in turn. No work is paid for out of the place. It costs nine cents per day to board, dress, and educate each boy, or a total of thirty-six dollars per day for four hundred boys. The Municipality pays six and one quarter cents per day—when it has the funds—for the support of each, or twenty-five dollars per day, and the remainder is made up from rents of the property belonging to the School, which bring in two hundred dollars per month, and from voluntary contributions. All the earnings of each boy at any kind of work are paid over to him, and he deposits what he can, if his family do not need it for their support, in a savings box belonging to himself, kept in a common depository. When he has grown to manhood and has his trade well learned, he goes out with the little capital he has laid by, and enters business for himself. Sometimes he has twenty dollars only, and sometimes two hundred or three hundred dollars.

The wonderful musical talent of this people is shown in the band of one hundred musicians, all boys in the school, who have earned their own instruments and have a fund in advance. A band of fifty played before us. One bright little fellow, Pedro Gallardo, twelve years of age, played the key-bugle in a style which would render him an acquisition to any military band in the United States. This band, by playing at public meetings, balls, &c., had earned six hundred dollars clear that year already. At the end of the year this fund is fairly divided.

A fine old gentleman, Señor Dionisio Rodriguez, has managed this school for twenty years, giving all his time to it, the year round, free of charge, and when revolution or other causes cut off the sources of supply, has from his own pocket made good the deficiency, his total gifts amounting to many thousands of dollars. God bless and prosper him ; he is a true benefactor of mankind.

Some of the work done by these boys is very beautiful. We were shown a *rebosa* or lady's scarf-shawl, eight feet in length, and twenty-eight inches in breadth, made from the silk and cotton spun in the establishment, and woven in a common hand-loom of the oldest and rudest pattern, which was as beautiful in its changeable colors as the finest product of the looms of Lyons. It could be drawn through a small sized finger-ring, and was offered for eight dollars.

The primary schools of the city contain five thousand pupils, and the schools for the two sexes are separate. The children are bright, intelligent, and ready to learn, and the schools absolutely free to all. There are one hundred and four Municipalities in the State of Jalisco, outside of the City of Guadalajara, and each of them supports one or more of these schools. The girls in addition to the usual lessons with us, are taught sewing, knitting, and other useful and necessary accomplishments.

Say what you may, this is progress ! Give Mexico fifteen years of uninterrupted peace, in which to spread these schools throughout all the States, and she will astonish the world with her material advance, and make the dream of establishing a monarchy on the ruins of Republicanism in the New World, idleness and vanity. God grant that she may have the opportunity to make good my prediction.

After visiting the schools we went into the great

cemetery of Bethlem. It is curious that the dead of the different families, Republican and plebeian, or Imperialist and aristocratic, cannot forget their differences and rest quietly side by side, even in death; but such is the case in Guadalajara. Here, in the cemetery of Bethlem, the Republicans are buried, and in another sleep the Imperialists. There are but few graves in the open ground, as we see them in our American and European cemeteries, and none of them are decorated with shade trees and flowers, or even marked with tall monuments and tomb-stones.

The greater number of interments are in niches or alcoves in the walls, which run in three tiers, one above another, all around the cemetery, which must cover from four to six acres. These alcoves are each about three feet square by six and one-half feet deep, and when a coffin is placed in one, the entrance is closed with cement, and the name, date of birth, death, etc., etc., of the deceased, placed over the stone fitted into the opening. It costs twenty-five dollars for the use of one of these alcoves five years, paid in advance. If at the end of that time another twenty-five dollars is

THE CEMETERY OF BETHLEM.

not forthcoming, the place is again for rent. In the open ground you can buy a lot six feet by eight, but the alcoves are only rented for five years at a time.

In the center of the grounds there is a large chapel with vault beneath, in which rest many of the early church dignitaries of the diocese of Guadalajara.

The roads are so unsafe all around Guadalajara, that the inhabitants never ride many miles beyond its walls without a strong, armed escort. The great, and almost only, place of public resort beyond the Plaza, is the *Paseo de San Pedro*, a broad, double, tree-lined avenue or alameda, with carriage-drives on either side, and

A MEXICAN CART.

banks of green turf-covered earth, or plain stone between, for seats. This is about a mile in length, and just outside the gates on the road to Mexico. Thither, all the carriages in the city repair every pleasant evening, just before night-fall. Some of the fair occupants drive up and down in carriages, while others dismount, and, seated on the banquettes, pass their time in chatting with their friends, male and female, saluting each acquaintance who passes.

The young men ride around upon gaily caparisoned horses, and the young ladies frequently exhibit their love of odd adventure, by hiring one of the clumsy ox-carts of the country, and, a dozen of them together, riding up and down the *paseo*, singing light songs and playing on the guitar, their gallants riding near them on horseback and keeping up a running fire of chaffing and pleasant conversation, or bending from their saddles to whisper the story we have all heard and told, into willing ears as occasion offers. This is one of the oddest customs of the country.

Leaving my seat in the carriage in which we visited the *paseo*, to take one beside a fair young country-woman of mine, to ride back to the city, I noticed a full-loaded Colt's revolver lying on the cushion by her side. "Oh! that is nothing; I always bring one out here when I come, as this is a noted place for robbers, who sometimes jump out of the cane-brake, and rob a carriage before assistance can arrive," she said nonchalantly in reply to my look of inquiry. "Pleasant place to visit and enjoy one's self in! I think I hear you say. Well, all that may be, but when you have nowhere else to go, what can you do; one must have some recreation you know!" I said "Please pass me," and we rode home.

Notwithstanding the slaughter of brigands by the State troops acting under the authority of the civil tribunals, the business of kidnapping citizens and carrying them off into the mountains to be held for ransom, is carried on with astonishing audacity in various parts of the country, and even in the immediate vicinity of the city of Guadalajara. Some pretty tough stories concerning the standing and social position of the parties engaged in the business, are related by the victims. These stories are, perhaps, not always reliable, but I gathered enough from people who had been *plagiared*, to satisfy me that an organization, as strict and effective as that of the Thugs of India, has for some time existed, and still exists, though more limited in number than formerly, in Guadalajara, and numbers among its members some of the most prominent men and women of the old Imperial regime. Men, who have been rich, but who are now absolutely without legitimate income and unable to earn an honest livelihood, direct the movements of the bands, and map out the work for the lower order of cut-throats to carry out. Sometimes revelations made were of a startling character. I was one day conversing with a gentleman of high standing in Guadalajara, who had been carried off from the immediate vicinity of the city, and only released upon the payment of five thousand dollars, in coin. I asked him if he could not identify the men who kidnapped him, and received a ransom. "I know every one of them!" was the reply. Then why do you not prosecute them and have them shot? I asked. "I will tell you why: Every member of the gang has friends who would be apprised at once of the facts, and instructed to avenge their deaths in case I lived until the trial was ended. Governor Cuervo and his subordinates would do their duty without fear or favor, and the men would be shot; but I should be assassinated within a week thereafter, or possibly, kidnapped again and carried off, to be tortured with every atrocity which Apaches are capable of, and die a lingering death; even my family would be persecuted, and perhaps meet a fate as terrible as my own."

"But are the leaders of the band so highly connected as I have been told?" I asked.

"You may be your own judge in that matter. *I saw you introduced to one of them yesterday, and holding a long conversation with him!"*

"But you did not put me on my guard," I said.

"Not I; I have even visited at his house and dined with his family since my release, and his daughter is a warm friend of my own. *That man received the money from my brother, and he knows that I know him to be the regular financial agent and broker for the band!"* It is hardly possible for a stranger to understand how such a state of affairs can exist without the direct connivance of the authorities; but it does so exist, nevertheless; and the rigor with which Gov. Cuervo and his associates execute the laws, leaves no room for doubting that they are in earnest in the work.

INDIAN EMBROIDERERS AND THEIR WORK.

Guadalajara boasts of two Indian specialties, viz: the wonderfully elaborate embroidery in cotton and linen, on lace formed by the drawing out of part of the threads in fine white goods, of which, you can buy enough for a lady's skirt, six inches wide, for five to ten dollars; worth from fifty to one hundred dollars in the United States; and statuettes, vases, and similar goods in earthenware, molded from common clay, with the hands alone, by men and women who cannot read or write, and have, in fact, no education whatever. This work is executed in a small village called Tonila, the seat of the Aztec Kings of Jalisco in the days of Cortez, fifteen miles distant, and sold around the streets. There is a place on the *Plaza de Toros* where they have cart-loads of every description of this earthenware, from a toy-cup to a flower-vase three feet high, for sale. They ask more for it than they do at the village where it is made, but still sell it astonishingly cheap. They have statuettes of every noted man in the country and of the world, ancient and modern, from an inch in height to two feet, all elaborately worked and colored, and many of them handsomely gilded. They will make you a statuette, a perfect fac-simile of yourself in miniature, on two day's notice. Of burlesque statuary they have hundreds of specimens, and their figures representing local characters, once the celebrities of the country, are wonderful. During our civil war, an American artist produced in clay, groups representing scenes in the war, the dying sentinel, wounded to the death, the attack, etc., all of which were fine; and he gained great credit thereby; but these poor illiterate Indians can show thousands of such statuettes and groups, all fully equal or superior in execution and vivid expression. A noted and infamous character is generally represented as being carried off, bodily, by the devil. Gen. Rojas, the bandit, formerly of Tepic, one of the most bloodthirsty cut-throats and murderers who ever cursed the earth with his presence, and who was shot some years ago at Seyula, is a common subject for this style of art. I purchased a group representing him, in full costume, being thus carried off on a grotesque devil's shoulders, the figures being each twelve inches in height, for one dollar and a quarter, and, I was told, that I paid more than double the usual price. For a pair of black enameled and artistically gilded water jugs of Japanese pattern, holding two quarts each, very handsome, seventy-five cents. Statuettes of water-carriers, peddlers, etc., one foot in height, twenty-five cents each, and smaller figures from a half cent to six and one-quarter cents each. My purchases filled a box containing about four cubic feet, and the whole, cost only three dollars and a half.

INDIAN STATUARY MAKERS.

There are four cotton-factories near the City of Guadalajara, viz: El Escoba, thirty-three hundred spindles; Atamepac, five thousand; Salto, five hundred, and Experience, one thousand. The last belongs to the five brothers Lowery, who, though they have resided there twenty-five years, are still Americans. All were in operation on the same plan as those at Colima, and none making much more than expenses, owing to the high price of cotton, and the excess of manufactured goods in the market. Atamepac, we found to be, in appearance, a great college building, of cut stone, standing back about thirty rods from the road, with a double row of orange-trees, in full bearing, on either side of the wide, grassy lawn leading up to it. The others are on a similar plan, but on a smaller scale. Two more cotton-mills are being erected in the vicinity.

The paper mill, the only one in the State, belonging to Señor Palama, is an immense structure with fourteen grinding or pulp engines; a Foudrinier machine, which makes fair, white printing and telegraph paper six feet in width, and a smaller one which makes manilla paper. The process followed is the same as with us.

They have an opera-house and theater in Guadalajara on the Plaza fronting the Palace; it was erected by the city, but is not yet finished. It has already cost three hundred and fifty thousand dollars in coin, and will require fifty thousand dollars more to finish it. It is now occupied, but has very little scenery—only a white cloth drop-curtain, and white-washed walls. The proportions are magnificent, and when finished it will seat four thousand persons, comfortably, and become one of the finest on the continent. It has five tiers of boxes, each with twenty-five separate apartments running around the entire wall. Each box, or apartment, is divided from the next by a low iron railing, and has its own distinct entrance and dressing and refreshment rooms. There are seats for eight persons in each box. Below, the parquette covers the whole floor of the building, and is provided with cheap arm-chairs. Admission to the boxes is one dollar, and to the parquette seventy-five cents each.

We attended one evening by invitation, and found a well-dressed and elegant, but not large audience. A company from Cuba gave the "Domino Azul," in good style, and as effectively as the circumstances would admit. The singing and dialogue was in Spanish, and the music of a national character. The audience, men and women, left the boxes and lounged in the galleries, chatting, and smoking cigarritos and sipping fruit-syrup flavored drinks between the acts. The old—always treated with great respect here—and the middle aged and young, occupied seats in the same boxes, and there seemed to be no distinction on account of wealth and dress. The opera house is badly lighted with oil lamps suspended over each box, and the general effect is much marred in consequence. The house yields but six thousand dollars per annum to the city, and of course when money is loaned at five per cent per month, does not pay as a pecuniary investment.

On another evening we attended again, by special invitation, the "Valley of Andorra," being given in honor of Mr. Seward. The boxes, which are usually occupied by the wealthy classes who lean toward Imperialism, were only partially filled, but there was a large array of beauty, and the galleries were crowded with the Republican element. The "Mochos," evidently hate the men of the North, while the common people welcome them. There are no low melodeons in Guadalajara as with us, and with the exception of the bull arena, there are no other places of in-door public amusement in the city.

The cruel and thoroughly demoralizing amusement of bull-fighting, once the national sport of Mexico, has been prohibited in the capital and various States, but is still maintained in Guadalajara. Determined to see all that was to be seen of the manners and customs of the people at this out-of-the-way corner of the world, we naturally inquired after the bull-fight, and were gratified.(?) On Saturday, a long bill, magnificently printed in gold, on blue satin with a lace border, was sent to our house. As a curiosity, and a memento of a custom now, thank Heaven, fast passing away, I translated the bill as nearly literally as possible:

BULLS (*i. e., bull-fight*) IN THE PLAZA OF PROGRESS.

GRAND PERFORMANCE ON SUNDAY, OCTOBER 24, 1869.

The company have arranged for this afternoon a selected and varied performance, which will proceed in the following order:

PROGRAMME.

1. The music of the First Light Battalion, wisely directed by Prof. Santos Hernandez, will begin to play from 3 P. M., the best airs of his repertoire.
2. Five valiant bulls will be fought, from the well-known hacienda of Cuisillos, four of which will be done to the death.
3. After the death of the fourth bull, a young bull will undergo the Novillo de Cola, which exercise will be performed by the intelligent and agile coleador, Francisco Rodriguez.
4. Immediately thereafter another Novillo de Cola, will be performed, and the bull be ridden by the celebrated bull-rider, Francisco Moya, and both the other coleadors. These exercises will be done at the fullest speed, and the coleador will throw down a bull and mount him with rapidity.
5. Other bulls will be fought by the company if the time will permit.

PRICES.—A box with six chairs, four dollars; seats in the

shade, fifty cents; seats in the sun, twelve and a half cents; seats in chairs, twelve and a half cents extra.

Performance begins at 4 P. M., precisely.

RULES.—It is not allowed to pay money at the inner doors, and patrons of the performance will carry their own tickets to avoid confusion and crowding at the entrance, which would create annoyance. The soldiers at the garrison of Guadalajara will pay six and a quarter cents each, and will occupy the roof.

Whenever the judge shall graciously grant the bull to the fighters, the company shall be allowed the usual gratuity in place of the animal.

All the morning, a party of *matadores*, *picadores*, and their assistants, on horseback and on foot, with a band of music at their head, were parading the streets, the clowns in grotesque costumes yelling at the top of their voices, the praises of the "*gran funcion*," which was to come off at the Plaza de Progresso, in the afternoon. Two of the mounted men carried a pole, on which was arranged the *banderillas*, or light frame-works of wire, in the form of palm-trees, Chinese lanterns, lyres, cornucopias, and other objects, each about three feet in length, covered with long, waving strips of gilt and tissue paper, which were to be attached to the bulls by sharp iron barbs to drive them to madness. At the hour announced we drove to the Plaza of Progress, and found an immense amphitheater of stone, not less than five hundred feet in diameter, open toward the sky, and provided with seats arranged in five tiers, running around the entire structure, receding toward the top, until they reached the corridor beneath which were the boxes of the aristocratic and wealthy portion of the audience. Soldiers guard every public place in Guadalajara, and we saw their bayonets everywhere among the crowd which surged around the entrance and within the gates.

The roof above the grand corridor was covered with the soldiers of the garrison, and the State Guards, in their picturesque uniforms, and the tiers of seats "in the sun and in the shade" presented a sea of heads, the common and poorer people fairly packing them. The corridor was fairly filled—many ladies being present—but I noticed that the more refined and educated portion of the community did not appear, generally, to be there. There were, at a rough estimate, at least three thousand people in the amphitheatre. The band, of about fifty pieces, struck up a grand march, and at the sound of the trumpet, the company came into the arena. They were twelve or fourteen in number. The two matadors, men of advanced age, stout and agile, were in ordinary *vaqueros* costume, with broad hats, mounted on poor horses, and carried their spears, with short, blunt ends, in their hands. The two *matadores* and their assistants were all dressed in the full, old Spanish costumes, brilliant with gold and scarlet, knee breeches and shoes, short jackets, and black jaunty caps.

Halting before the judges' box, the party sent two of their number up over the barriers and tiers of seats—as agile as cats they seemed—to exhibit to them the *banderillas*, and ask their high permission for the fighting to commence, which was of course given.

In rushed from a side door, a tawny brown bull, with wide spreading horns, the points of which had already been sawed off about four inches, and, throwing his head high in the air, he gave one glance around the arena within, like a dog in play, and dashed at the nearest man with a red mantle. The mantle was whirled quickly over the head of the wearer as the bull just reached him, and, with a bound to one side, the youth was out of his reach.

This bull was too young and quiet for the sport, (?) and the *banderillas* were fixed in either side of his neck by a very clever and active assistant, who bounded out of the way as he threw them, just in time to

THE SUNDAY BULL-FIGHT.

escape the horns of the animal. Still, the bull, though throwing his head from side to side, whirling the *banderillas* around as if in sport, did not half fight, and the red mantles flaunted in his face, and thrown at times over his horns, only provoked him to momentary madness. So a *matadore* advanced with a sharp, straight sword, and as the bull dashed at him, made a thrust just forward of the shoulder to pierce his heart, the crowd yelling to him to kill him at the first blow. The sword bent almost double by striking a bone, and went wide of the mark. The *matadore* stopped to bend it straight again, and meantime the now bleeding bull dashed at one of the *picadores* on horseback. The *picadore* dropped his lance so as to catch the bull on the shoulder, and the moment the barb pierced the skin the poor animal, as is his wont, wheeled away. This was repeated again and again, and then the *matadore* gave him half a dozen thrusts, finally reaching a vital spot, and bowed to the judges; the mob in the galleries on the opposite side, rewarding his courage and skill (?) by hurling banana-peel, oranges, and stale vegetables at his head whenever he came within their reach. An assistant now struck the dying bull in the neck with a double-edged knife, and the creature dropped dead as if stricken by lightning. Then, three old horses, harnessed abreast, were driven in and hitched to the bleeding carcass, but it required the united strength of the whole company of "artists" to assist in pulling it out.

The band played, and the second bull came dashing in. The fight, if such it could be called, was simply a repetition of the first. The third bull ran away from the horses, and would only fight in self-defence, running around the arena with his head raised as if appealing for mercy, and the now enraged audience shouted loud and long to "Turn him out," which was finally done by order of the judges,

The fourth bull was a game fellow, and made things lively. He dashed at everything within reach, and drove the assistants again and again behind the barriers. The populace, excited to the highest pitch of enthusiasm, reached over the wall, and yelled, and shook their great hats and ragged blankets in his face to madden him to the utmost. He dashed at one of the *picadores*, got the horse under the belly, and shook him on his horns as he would toss a blanket. The crowd were frantic with delight. Then he made another dash at the same horse, and despite the vigorous prodding of the *picadore*, caught the poor, wretched animal in the same place, and held him on his horns until one of them penetrated his abdomen and fatally injured him. Notwithstanding this, the wounded horse was ridden until the entire performance was ended. The populace were happy. Then the bull "went for" the other horse, caught him, and rolled horse and rider over and over in the dirt—and the crowd roared with delight. To tell the truth, I felt a little satisfaction myself, until I saw the dismounted *picadore* unroll himself and spring to his feet uninjured. The horse was stricken to the death and taken away to die.

The *picadores* have their right legs incased in a shield made of leather with bars of steel inside, similar to those worn on the arms by the Chinese short-swordsmen. They invariably present that side to the bull, and so escape injury, except in very rare cases. The *matadore* gave this bull a thrust to the very heart at the first pass of his sword, and the stricken animal staggering half around the ring, fell to his knees, and was dispatched in an instant. This ended the killing, though the crowd furiously demanded another bull in place of the third, who had proven unfit for fighting.

Then the *coleadores*, mounted on fine spirited horses, dashed in, and a young bull was let out at them. They rode at full speed along side of him, and endeavored to spring from their horses upon his back, but failed on every occasion. Once, one of the *coleadores* (i. e. tail-pullers) went down between horse and bull, and was trampled upon by both, but not killed. This bull was turned out and a second and more lively one let in. He was run around and around the arena, and finally caught by the tail and thrown to the earth by one of the *coleadores*, and tied by the assistants, who held him until a cord—or, as a Californian would say, "a cinch"—was tied around him. Francisco Mayo then sprang upon his back, and he was allowed to regain his feet. The bull dashed around and around the arena, bucking and jumping, to rid himself of his rider, but in vain; and so the performance ended, just as night set in.

And all this time delicate, beautiful women and little children had been sitting in the corridors, sipping cool drinks and looking placidly on, while they chatted on familiar subjects with their friends around them. Worse than that, as I looked up at the walls of the great Hospicio, that wonder of practical charity and benevolence, I saw several of the pious Sisters of Charity, whose holy work and holy lives we had so much admired when we visited the institution, standing on the battlements and looking down upon us. They could not see the slaughter, but could hear and enjoy the shouts of the populace, the music, and the moans of the tortured animals.

This was the first bull-fight I had ever witnessed; it will be my last. I believe I can say, that I never flinched from duty, however painful, and in the course of my journalistic life, I have been called on to witness many things of a cruel and horrible character; but I have never yet been guilty of wantonly torturing any living creature, and I should loathe and despise myself beyond measure if I felt that I could be guilty of again witnessing such a scene. The entertainment was given in good faith as a compliment, and accepted as such; but such scenes can but brutalize and demoralize a community which tolerates them, and I thank God that enlightened public sentiment is now setting so strongly against them, that the day is not far distant when they will be prohibited by law in this State, as well as in all other parts of Mexico. I have had just enough of bull-fights for the measure of my life, be it large or small.

Every day I staid in Guadalajara, I saw something more to remind me of the fact that I stood among the dry bones of the past—that the world around me was a strange mixture and confusion of the fifteenth and nineteenth centuries, the ideas of each struggling for the mastery. Utopian dreams of the future, and the savage faith and despotism of the past, jostle and crowd each other, day by day, and the end of the conflict is not yet. One day, I went out to see the Indian recruits for the Army of the Republic of Mexico, drilling on the plaza, and, returning, saw in the distance the tower of the ancient place of worship in the Indian village of Tonila, in which the curious earthen structures of which I have spoken are made. This Tonila was the capital of the Kingdom of Jalisco, when Cortez landed in Mexico, and there, the descendants of the fierce Aztec warriors still reside—making clay images, while their sons and brothers fight for the maintenance of Republicanism, side by side with the descendants of the *conquistadors*.

Reaching our sumptuous quarters I found on the

table, as a present to Mr. Seward, a time-yellowed document, written in quaint old Spanish, dated at Madrid in 1676, and signed in a bold, round hand, with ink which might have been made but a week ago, "*Yoe el Rey*" ("I, the king.") This is a royal proclamation of Charles, King of Spain, commanding that, thereafter, the officers of his army and civil administration should abstain from the practice of compelling the Indians in the Spanish-American colonies to carry their baggage, and furnish them with provisions on their journey without charge, and ordering regular payments at fair rates to be made for their services thenceforth.

Attached to this is a decree of Pope Clement Xth, addressed to his "Beloved Son in Christ, Carlos, Catholic King of the Spains," commanding and ordering the enforcement of the decree by the aid of the clergy. This document was filed in the Custom-house of Guadalajara, in which, at this day, the officers are sitting, collecting the customs duties on every article of goods carried from one state to another in the republic, as they did in 1676. At the same time came a certificate of honorary membership in the Academy of Sciences of Guadalajara, in which Mr. Seward is styled "Defender of the liberty of the Americas."

The citizens of Guadalajara, without distinction of party, united on Saturday night in a grand farewell ball, at the "Institutio de Ciencias," in honor of Mr. Seward's visit, it being understood that the party were to leave on the following Tuesday for Guanajuato. The building, of one story, surrounding a fine large smoothly paved court-yard, was beautifully and very tastefully decorated for the occasion, and the illumination was very brilliant. The tables were set in the corridors, and the dancing took place in the beautiful hall of the State Congress of Jalisco—a Legislature, by-the-by, composed of but eleven members, a dangerously convenient number for the formation of a "ring"—which is hung with the portraits of all the early patriots of Mexico, and paintings and engravings of rare merit.

The hall and corridors were filled with as fine a company as could be gathered on the Continent, and with all due respect to my fair countrywomen, I must admit, that I never saw so many beautiful ladies at a ball of the same size in the United States. The ladies here usually make their own dresses—there is but one French milliner in this city of ninety thousand people—and exhibit a taste in the selection of materials and colors very rare with us. Light gauzes, green and white, blue and white, or red, green and white, contrasted, appear to be the favorite, and the dresses are cut low at the neck and with short sleeves. The temptation to bring out their brilliant black hair and lustrous eyes in strong contrast by the use of pearl powder and rouge, is often too strong for resistance with the belles of Guadalajara, but this feature is not more noticeable in one of their ball rooms than in one of our own. They all dance well, but their parties on public occasions are less enjoyable from the fact that introductions off-hand, are not in vogue as with us, and a stranger may roam around all the evening without making an acquaintance, save by chance.

When the guests had cleared the tables of the well-arranged collation, at 2 A. M., Señor Don Antonio Gomez Cuervo, Governor of Jalisco, a plain, honest, outspoken, and energetic man, whose vigorous and unceremonious shooting of brigands last winter got him "impeached" before the National Congress, (though he came out triumphant in the end, and returned to the work with more vim than ever,) arose and introduced Señor Don Juan Ignacio Matute, who read a brief address of welcome which I translate as follows:

Hon. Wm. H. Seward: He who has given his blood, and after forty years continued effort succeeded in abolishing Slavery in his country, deserves well of humanity. He who aided Mexico to conquer her independence a second time, deserves our most cordial thanks! He, who, full of a spirit of conciliation, after a Titanic war, contributed to his utmost ability to the recommendation of the humbled South, deserves well of his country! The people of Jalisco, filled with the love of liberty, salute with the greatest respect and honor, the distinguished American citizen, William H. Seward! May Mexico, my adored country, following his noble example, yield a frank and prudent amnesty, and so conserve her future prosperity and welfare. On that day Hidalgo and Washington, rising above the shadows of the tomb, shall join hands together, and joy shall fill the hearts of a free people. Honor to the abolitionist of Slavery!

Alfonso Lancaster Jones, a Mexican citizen, grandson of the founder of the Lancasterian school system, next addressed the audience in Spanish, very eloquently and in a scholarly manner.

Mr. Seward then spoke as follows:

Señors y Señoras: We all are well aware, that the occupation and settlement of the southern part of the American continent anticipated, by a period of more than a century, the occupation and settlement of the northern portion of the continent—that the former fell to the lot chiefly of the Latin nations of Europe, and was conducted upon the priciple of an implicit faith and confidence in the ecclesiastical and civil ideas and institutions which prevailed throughout Europe in the fifteenth century—that the occupation and settlement of the northern portion of the continent fell to the lot of the German and Sclavonic races, who were deeply moved by ideas of political and ecclesiastical reforms. The result has been, that at the beginning of the nineteenth century, two different, and in many respects, antagonistical systems came face to face with each other; the one extending along the Atlantic coast, from the banks of the Mississippi to the inclement regions of the north, the other extending, unbroken and undivided, from the Mississippi over the southern and western portions of the continent. The ideas of the North have continually gained strength everywhere, and have culminated there in republican institutions, which are based upon the sovereignty of the people, and which guarantee, in their highest perfection, civil and religious liberty. The southern nations of the continent have accepted the same broad and noble ideas, but the perfect establishment of them in a system of republican government has encountered the resistance of a long-cherished and powerful conservatism, animated and sustained by European influence and intervention. The southern nations, by the fidelity with which they have adhered to the republican system through so many and such serious obstacles, have given abundant evidence that they will ultimately and entirely acquiesce and coöperate with the republican nations of the north, so far as their institutions and laws are founded in natural justice and equality. What remains, and all that remains now necessary, is the establishment of entire tolerance between the North American States and the Spanish American Republics, and the creation of a policy of mutual moral alliance, to the end that all external aggression may be prevented, and that internal peace, law and order, and progress may be secured throughout the whole continent. The people of Mexico have not misunderstood me in my past political career: and since my visit to Mexico, I feel encouraged more than ever, in the hope that the intimate relations which have been already secured, will become permanent and perpetual. It is a satisfaction to have learned, on my way to the Capital, that the policy and sentiments which I expect to find prevailing there have been fully sanctioned already by the people of the great, important, and leading State of Jalisco. I ask you to indulge me, gentlemen, in the sentiment:

Peace, prosperity, and honor to the Governor and State of Jalisco.

To these remarks, and the toast, Gov. Cuervo responded as follows:

As a citizen of Jalisco, as a Mexican, as an American, more so as a free man, I cordially appreciate the splendid initiative of the illustrious guest of Jalisco, Mr. Seward, for the creation of the great continental American policy, so well defined by him in the toast I have the honor to answer. As a patriot, I will devote to the realization of that noble idea all that the influence of an honest man may ever be worth, with all the faith inspired in me by the remembrance of its having been the golden dream of one of the most eminent martyrs of our liberty, the great Degollado. May the sisterhood of all the American republics transform the world of Columbus into what it must be: the home of every free man, with no other distinctions but those imposed on all true hearted men by the services lent to humanity. Among the citizens of that glorious future country, our noble guest will be one of the first; not for the eminent service he rendered to his country in a career as long as honorable, as a lawyer, a legislator, senator, governor, and finally, as Secretary of State with the glorious martyr Lincoln; not for having been a faithful and loyal friend of Mexico in her days of painful trial, but for a whole life, devoted to the most noble of all causes: the absolute and unconditional emancipation of millions of slaves. God preserved him from the assassin's weapon to reward him with the complete triumph of his holy idea. Join me, gentlemen, in this sentiment: To that citizen, whose name is his greatest pride—Mr. Seward. [Enthusiastic applause.]

I have given these speeches, at length, as an illustration of the spirit and aspirations prevailing in this community, at this time, and as a part of the history of the day. That these aspirations will ever be fully realized may well be doubted; but surely every right thinking friend of humanity will pray that they may be. We left the hall at 3 A. M., and on awaking at 6 o'clock A. M. found the dancing still going on.

On the following Tuesday morning, at day-break, our luggage was packed, the escort ready, and the stage at the door, and a host of warm-hearted friends of both sexes, came to say farewell—kiss, and bid us God-speed on our journey.

CHAPTER VI.

FROM GUADALAJARA TO GUANAJUATO.

WE left Guadalajara at 10:30 A. M., Tuesday, Oct. 26th, in the customary style—a large guard of the regular cavalry of the Mexican Army in advance, and another following in the rear. Our vehicle was a capital thorough-brace coach, sent out from the City of Mexico for our especial use, drawn by eight fine mules, and driven by George Elmore, a veteran stage-driver, who is said to be the best in Mexico. Elmore was born about forty-five years ago, at No. 187 Broadway, New-York, but has lost, in outward appearance, all indications of his nationality. When addressed in English, however, his hearty "You bet!" betrays his Californian education at once.

Gov. Cuervo, Señor Don Juan Ignacio Matute, Señor Don Luis Rendon, and Señor Cañedo, accompanied us as far on the way as the old, half-ruined suburban town of San Pedro, and there took leave of us in the most affectionate manner.

Col. Lomeli, Commander of the Guard of Jalisco, came also to bid us adieu, and told us that on the previous evening his men had shot, and mortally wounded, another robber, just outside the gates of the city on the road over which we had lately passed, and that the poor wretch was then dying. He also informed us that the confirmation of the sentence of death upon two robers then in prison at Guadalajara had arrived, and that they would be shot immediately. Mr. Seward had been appealed to by their father, to intercede for them at the city of Mexico, but they were in their graves long before we reached Guanajuato. They deserved no sympathy.

We took leave of our old friends, who had accompanied us all the way from Manzanillo, with much regret, and shall not soon forget their kindness and constant care for our welfare. Henceforth, we were under the care of Señor Don Luis G. Bossero, the special commissioner sent out from the City of Mexico to meet us at Guadalajara and escort us to the capital. He is a large, fine-looking gentleman, exceedingly courteous and polite in his manners, and speaks English with just enough foreign accent to make his droll stories more amusing and enjoyable.

Our baggage was loaded upon a cart drawn by four mules, abreast, which were managed by about a dozen retainers and servants of different degrees. Our road, all day for thirty miles, led us over a broken, hilly country, something like Central New York in appearance, and almost entirely devoted to cattle raising. The few small villages through which we passed were all inhabited by very poor people, of Indian descent, and the country generally seemed to be in keeping. The whole country is underlaid with ancient and partially decomposed lava, and the roads, though hard enough at the bottom, were fearfully rough. Our baggage-cart was repeatedly stalled or overturned, and one of the mules had his leg broken, and was turned out to die by the roadside.

A few miles out from Guadalajara, we crossed the

Riō Grande de Santiago, the outlet of Lake Chapala, upon a stone bridge of some nineteen arches. This bridge is one of the remarkable structures erected by the old Spaniards, and looks as if it might stand for many centuries more. At either end of the bridge are statues of the king and queen of Spain who were reigning when the bridge was erected, but so worn and defaced by time as to be unrecognizable. The stone tablets on which the records of the erection and other facts about the bridge were engraved, have all been plastered over with cement to deface and destroy them, for some reason not apparent. The only date I could decipher was 1718, and that appeared to refer to a repair instead of the erection of the structure. No one living in the vicinity could give us any data concerning it.

The falls of this river, a few miles below where we crossed, are said to compare, not unfavorably, with those of Niagara, but we did not see them.

We staid at Zapotlanejo, a curious old town of four or five thousand inhabitants, on our first night out from Guadalajara. A deputation of the citizens, on horseback, met us outside the town, and escorted us in. They are very poor, but wonderfully hospitable people. The houses have in many cases barricades upon the roofs, reminders of the former revolutions and invasions; and the remarkable number of fair-haired and fair-skinned children to be seen on the streets, tell the same story. A fine band welcomed us, the citizens made speeches in the evening, and were answered by Mr. Seward; and a concert by native Mexicans, all excellent players, the harper being blind, closed the evening's entertainment. The town has a fine old church, at present under repair, and stands in a small but fertile valley, surrounded by cane, corn, and rice fields. We left Zapotlanejo on the morning of Oct. 27th, to ride thirty-two miles to Tepotitlan, a town of from five to eight thousand people. Our roads had been bad enough in all conscience before, but they grew worse and worse as we advanced, and the night rains grew heavier. This day's travel was the hardest we had yet experienced.

Nine miles beyond Zapotlanejo we crossed the Bridge of Calderon, a stone structure, spanning a deep but narrow *arroyo*. It was here that the Padre Hidalgo, the Washington of Mexico, with eighty thousand men, all Indians, armed with bows and arrows, and a few wooden cannon which burst at the first fire, attacked the Spaniards, in January 1811. The Spaniards were not a tenth as strong, numerically, but they were well armed, and all the desperate valor and enthusiasm of the Indians went for naught. The poor fellows rushed up to the Spanish cannons and pushed their hats into them to prevent their going off. So little did they know of the use and power of artillery. They were mowed down by thousands, and broke and fled at last in utter rout, leaving Hidalgo to make his way to Chihuahua, where he was betrayed into the hands of his enemies, sent to Guanajuato, tried, condemned, and executed.

The soil in this vicinity is a dark red earth, which resembles that of the gold belt of the Sierra Nevada, and is tenacious to the last degree when wet up by the rains, and worked into brick material by the wheels of vehicles. We passed during this day, a poor little village at which the butcher Rojas captured eighty men—all the able-bodied male population of the vicinity—and murdered them all in cold blood, some years since.

One of the most fearful brutes who ever infested the roads of Jalisco, was Simon Gutierrez, whose band was exterminated by the State troops in the Spring of 1869. Gutierrez took refuge in the city of Guadalajara, and when his hiding place was discovered, (beneath a floor,) jumped into the middle of the troops, with a revolver, and fought until they riddled him. His body was propped up in a chair and exhibited three days in front of the prison on the Plaza, as shown in the picture, and crowds went to see it and make sure that the terror of Jalisco, for so many years, was dead, indeed, at last.

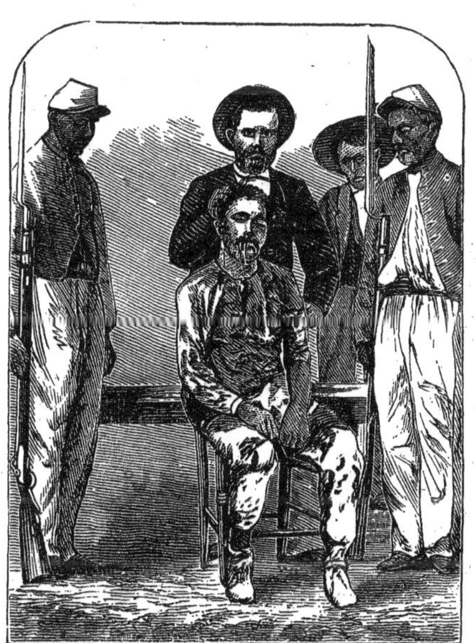
THE TERROR OF JALISCO.

The poor people, all along the road, eke out a miserable living by selling a few small fruits, frijoles, tortillas, etc. etc., to travelers. I found one old fellow sitting on a stone by the roadside, miles from any habitation, with about a half-bushel of the nasty, little fruit resembling our northern "mandrake," or May-apple, called the guava—pronounced "guyava"—from which the guava jelly of commerce is made. I asked him how much he would take for his whole establishment, stock in trade, basket, plates, and all. After a nice calculation, he decided that it was worth all together fully twenty-five cents, I paid him the money and made him distribute the fruit among the escort which just then came up; there was about enough to give them all the cholic for a week. Suddenly, an idea, suggested by my reckless liberality, struck him with great force. Was I not the *grande hombre* from the *Estados Unidos del Norte?* I had not the heart to deny it; then he fell on his knees, kissed my hand, and said that he had heard of me often, and now thanked God that he had been permitted to live to see me face to face. I had intended to break the plates and basket, and "bust up" the shop; but his devotion saved him, and I gave them back to him and made him a friend of the Americans for life. It is pleasant to do good at so small an expense.

THE GRATEFUL GUAVA MERCHANT.

On our second night out from Guadalajara, we staid

at Tepotitlan. It was 9 o'clock in the evening when we entered this ancient town, escorted by the citizens with torches, while bells rang a tremendous peal, and a brass band played the national airs. We had a good dinner at the house of the curate of the town, and though our baggage did not arrive until two in the morning, we were provided with good beds and comfortable quarters, furnished by these kind-hearted people. The city contains from five to six thousand people and four churches. They repair the churches, and let everything else go to ruin. The people are mostly farmers, in a small way, and very poor. This year their crops were nearly an utter failure, and they appeared down-hearted.

We found here an American physician, Dr. John Rush, nephew of the famous Philadelphia physician of that name, and R. E. Armstrong, a resident of San Francisco, traveling with his family for their health. Dr. Rush served as surgeon in the 1st West Tennessee (colored) Volunteers, during the Rebellion, under Gen. Thomas. The town has its plaza, with public fountains in the center, and all towns in this country have. The streets, once well paved, are going to ruin.

Next morning, we drove until the middle of the day, over a poor, open, hilly, and mostly barren and uncultivated country, and then came in sight of the quaint, old city of Jalos, far below us in a tree-embowered valley.

This is a well-built little city of six thousand inhabitants, standing in a narrow *cañada*, wholly hidden until you come upon the brow of the hill from which we first saw it. It has a magnificent old church, in fine repair, and many beautiful private residences, painted outside and inside in brilliant fresco. How the people all live I cannot imagine. As we entered the city the bells were ringing a joyous peal, and a band playing as usual. A fine house had been prepared for us upon the plaza, but as we did not propose to remain over night, we drove on, and lunched privately at the residence of a friend of Señor Bossero. As we passed through the streets a large party of school-boys met us, and at a sign from one of their number, all went down on their knees, on the cobbles, holding their hats in their hands.

The people, as we advanced eastward, became more white, and blue eyes and fair hair were not uncommon. The number of women was vastly in excess of the men, and, of course, lawful marriage is out of the question with the great number of the poor girls of the towns. They are human, and, as they cannot marry, is it a wonder that they sin? Nearly every girl among the lower orders, from fourteen years old upward, whom we saw as we passed along, had a child in her arms. I never saw so little corn, and so many children to the acre.

That night, we staid at Venta de Los Pagarros, twenty-four miles from Tepotitlan. Señor Perez, the owner of this great *hacienda*, which is twenty miles long, and has forty thousand head of stock upon it, has owned the property two years He bought it when nobody else dared occupy it on account of the robbers. His house is literally a fortress, impregnable to all but heavy artillery. He organized his neighbors at once into a military corps, and commenced a war of extermination against the robbers. In an hour, he can rally two hundred well-armed men, and as soon as a band is heard of, they start for them, hunt them down, and shoot them all like dogs, making no prisoners. In this way he has restored peace to the neighborhood,

VENTA DE LOS PAGARROS.

and is building up a town around him, already. He and his band have killed about eighty robbers within two years.

From this point the country grows still more broken, being cut up with deep *arroyos*, *cañons* and *barrancas*. The mountains in the distance are nearly all bare of timber, save a few mesquite trees, and the country has the general appearance of Western Texas along the southern edge of the great Llano Estacado. We were now ascending all the time, and had reached an altitude of about six thousand feet above the sea. We had left the orange, palm, banana, and other fruits, and all the flowers of the tropics behind us, and were upon the Great Central Plateau of Mexico. The scenery is mostly tame, and the country poor, and comparatively uninteresting.

Just as a heavy shower came upon us, we met the deputation of mounted citizens from San Juan de Los Lagos or "St. John of the Lakes," and dashing down a long, winding, well-paved grade, into a deep cañada, and over a high, well-built stone bridge, entered that substantial-looking city. A splendid house was provided for the company, and, as usual, we found that the family, having placed it at our disposal, had left it entirely themselves.

The District Judge, a young man, apparently of twenty-five years, who has the power of life and death over forty thousand people—there is no jury system here, and no appeal in criminal cases, though sentence of death passed by him must be confirmed by the Supreme Court of Mexico before it is finally executed—with the Political Prefect, and others, was in attendance to welcome Mr. Seward, and to see that the party wanted nothing. They told us that they had shot many robbers of late, but that there were still a number of very skillful ones in the vicinity.

Here and at Jalos, for the first time, we saw fences made on the simplest possible plan, from the great *organo* cactus. This cactus is eight-sided, and shoots up straight as an arrow, from ten to twenty-five feet in height, and five to eight inches in thickness. They cut the cactus into sections of the right length, stick the cut end into a trench, cover the dirt around it to the depth of a foot, and the fence is made. The pieces are set as closely together as possible, and, as they take root and grow for centuries, the fence improves with age, instead of going to decay like other fences. The *nopal* or prickly pear grows to perfection here, and the aloe or century plant, as well, or better, than in the *tierra caliente.* The town stands in a deep cañada, and a few inferior orange trees grow in the court-yards on the sunny side. Wheat grows well in this vicinity, and the flour, too, is excellent, almost equal to that of California, and much superior to that of the Atlantic States.

Looking up from the plaza, I gazed in silent admiration at the magnificent cathedral finished within one week of one hundred years before—they were making the most extensive preparations for celebrating the centennial anniversary—and the finest I had seen in Mexico, not even excepting that of Guadalajara. Its two graceful towers, wrought and carved with elaborate richness, to the very summit, from the beautiful pink lava rock of which the whole structure is built, are each two hundred and ten feet in height, and the main building is two hundred and ten feet long. The grand dome is covered with brilliant tiles in mosaic, and the vaulted roof, of solid masonry, is at least seventy-five feet above the floor.

CHURCH OF SAN JUAN.

In the basement, I descended eight wide stone steps, all cut from a single piece of stone, and in the sacristy saw the tomb of the projector of the cathedral, who died four years before its completion, and numerous magnificent and valuable old paintings. One is a picture of the Virgin, which performs miracles daily. Around this picture are hundreds of votive offerings, in the shape of others, illustrating the miracles performed by the Virgin in behalf of the persons offering them. Some of these were ludicrous in the extreme.

Entering the main building, I saw graceful columns in pale green and gold, supporting the fretted arched roof in the same colors, a magnificent altar in marble and silver, a chapel with a shrine of silver, and countless pictures and images, and decorations of barbaric richness. The rich notes of a superb organ resounded through the building, priests in gorgeous vestments mumbled the morning services, and incense filled the air. Gold and silver, satin and gilding, met the eye on every side, and the scene at first glance was one of bewildering beauty.

But I looked around me and saw men and women, barefooted and in rags, come creeping over the wet flagging of the wide yard, and down the long aisle upon their knees, some of them carrying lighted candles to offer at the shrine in fulfillment of vows made when the assistance of the Virgin was greatly needed, or groveling on the flagging at the doors; and I glanced from the sleek priests, who take in sixty thousand dollars per annum from votive offerings, to the poor wretches who toil for it and give it, and I went out with more of bitterness than satisfaction in my heart.

At the door I saw a conspicuously posted list of

the names of those who had during the month offered wax-candles at the shrine. Four-fifths of those who offered these candles and paid the price, had *tortillas* plain, or an ear of boiled corn for their dinner, dirty rags for clothing, and the earth for a bed. God be thanked, the last great temple of any faith has been built on earth from the sweat and blood of the toiling millions, and these things shall not be for all time.

From San Juan de los Lagos we proceeded, on the 30th of October, to Lagos, thirty-six miles eastward toward Guanajuato, arriving at 5 P. M. Here we had intended to remain all night and go on at sunrise; but of the three carts conveying our bedding and extra luggage, only one got through before morning, the others being out all night in a driving rain, and stuck fast, in the mud and darkness. This delayed us so that we were compelled to pass the day in the handsome house which the citizens, who met us in carriages outside the city, had placed at the disposal of the party.

The city of Lagos has a population of all hues and ages, estimated at eighteen thousand, and of course supports half a dozen churches, whose bells keep up an incessant ding-donging from morning to night. The finest of these is the Parochial Church, an immense structure, larger even than the cathedral at San Juan de los Lagos, built on the same plan, and only second to it in costliness and elegance. It was founded in 1784, and the spires of cut stone, like those at San Juan, are as yet only two-thirds finished; they are still at work upon them. The interior is exquisitely beautiful, with pale blue and gold ceilings, carvings and statuary, tiled floor, and vaulted fretwork roof. The congregation, assembled at the early morning mass, are even more ragged and devout than that at San Juan; hardly a single representative of the richer and better educated classes being present.

The specialty of this church is its Saint. I forget his name, but the record posted on the walls shows that he was a Roman soldier who suffered martyrdom for his faith (Christian, of course, though that is not stated,) in Rome, so the record affirms. His body was found by miracle, A. D., 901, preserved as if he were but just defunct, and he was canonized as a saint.

From Rome the body was carried to Spain, and from thence brought to Lagos and placed on the altar with the Bishop's own hands eighty years ago. The body is inclosed in a magnificent casket about five feet long, by three broad, and four high, with sides of glass, and corners and top of richly gilded metal. As a special favor to Mr. Seward, the doors before the casket, as it stands in the wall, were opened, and we went up and looked into it, while hundreds of awe-stricken worshipers knelt and crossed themselves in silent adoration.

From a close inspection of this remarkably well-preserved specimen, I am able to draw the following conclusions: First, that the ancient Roman soldiers were about four feet, eight or nine inches in height—not over five feet—allowing a fair margin for shrinkage; second, that they had no beard, and their faces were as delicate as that of a girl; third, that they had wax teeth, finger and toe-nails, and cuticle on hands, face, and shins, and wore gilt pasteboard tunics, and coats of mail, silk stockings, and fancy bootees. I respect every man's religion, and mean no disrespect for this illustrious deceased as a saint, but as a soldier I cannot refrain from the remark, that if he was in life a fair specimen of the

Roman troops, I would back the National Guard, Capt. Ben Pratt, of San Francisco, or the MacMahon Guard, Gen. Cazneau, of the same place, to give odds and knock the starch out of the entire phalanx. Of course such men could as bravely die for their faith as if they weighed three hundred pounds, and measured six feet two inches in their stocking-feet, each; nevertheless, I am no longer surprised at the overthrow of Rome by the Goths and Vandals, since I have seen what kind of fighting stock they had.

One thing is apparent in these churches of Central Mexico, at the first glance, viz,: that the people who come there to worship are in earnest, and not hypocrites or doubters. They accept the whole faith as it is taught them, without hesitation or mental reservation, and never seek to evade its responsibilities, or hide the fact of their faith when in the presence of unbelievers. For that I honor them above many of my own countrymen and countrywomen.

Sunday is the great market-day in Lagos, and no sooner is morning service over than the two plazas and the streets between them swarm with buyers and sellers. Venders of peanuts, peppers, yams, vegetables, bread, tortillas, and fruits of all descriptions, raise enormous umbrellas, in shape exactly like those of the Chinese, covered with matting, and ten or twelve feet across, upon stout poles, spread out their little stocks on the pavement, and hour after hour cry their wares, announcing in a loud voice how much of any given thing they sell for a *claquo* or *quartilla*, a cent or three cents. Earthenware, charcoal, sugar, salt, and other goods are sold in one plaza, dry goods in another, and beef in little shops on a street between the two. Men with piles of *rebosas* on their shoulders, walk up and down among the crowd, and others, with brilliant-hued *serapes* and *ponchos*, hang their goods against the walls, while young girls and old women, nearly all with infants at their breasts, sit on the curb-stones and sell hot soups, etc., from jars, for half a cent a bowl.

We left Lagos Nov. 1, for a thirty-six mile ride to Leon, being led to expect a fine ride and easy trip. To cut off three or four blocks, the driver avoided the fine, new bridge and drove directly into the river, which came up to the body of the stage and was quite rapid and broad. The mules, suspicious of the security of the bottom, baulked in the middle of the stream, and not all the lashing by a half-dozen volunteer *cocheros* and postilions, and curses and blasphemy enough to sink a ship, would start them a foot. We were taken off in boats, and no sooner were we landed than we saw the pig-headed mules start up of their own free will and walk majestically ashore. Perhaps their hides did not suffer for that freak.

Then we entered a broad alameda lined with immense trees of the variety known farther north as the California pepper tree, but here as the Peruvian, which has drooping limbs and foliage, giving it the graceful appearance of the weeping willow, and is at this season covered with long clusters of bright red berries which inclose the pungent black pepper grains. This alameda is flanked by ditches inclosing cultivated fields, which are higher than the road. Of course we found it a river of mud and water, and almost impassable.

We had not gone a mile before we found our three luggage cars which had started before daylight all down in the mud and unloaded. Pleasant prospect indeed!

After more than three miles of floundering in the mud, running along the embankments, and climbing in and out of the stage, we reached higher ground at noon, and went on more comfortably, over an open, rolling country wholly devoted to stock raising, until we reached the boundary of the State of Jalisco, and entered the State of Guanajuato, nine miles from Leon.

Just at this point, we saw a body of troops moving along the road in advance of us. When they discovered us, they made off at full speed and disappeared. A mile further on, I saw some of them peeping at us from behind a stone wall, and we subsequently learned that in order to give an appearance of perfect safety, to the road—our regular escort left us at Lagos, and returned to Guadalajara—they had been instructed to keep out of our sight entirely, and we were to travel through the State of Guanajuato without any apparent escort.

Seven miles from Leon we came out upon the summit of a range of broken hills, and looked down into a lovely valley, highly cultivated, filled with fields of green, growing grain, and tall ripe maize, and dotted here and there with rich and beautiful, white-walled haciendas.

Entering the city, we found, for the first time in our journey, no deputation with carriages waiting to receive the party, and drove directly to the magnificent house just finished and beautifully furnished for the occasion—fronting on the grand plaza—which had been prepared for us. The *Prefecto Politico* of Leon, Col. Rosado, and a deputation of the *ayuntamiento*, called at once to say that they had not received the telegram announcing the departure of Mr. Seward from Lagos, and that we had arrived many hours sooner than expected, which accounted for the apparent neglect to send out carriages to meet the coach.

This city, during the war, under the wise administration of Gen. Doblado who tolerated all classes who obeyed the laws, irrespective of Republican or Imperialist tendencies, gained largely in population, and is now one of the most prosperous, or least unprosperous towns in the country. The population of the city proper is eighty-two thousand, or two thousand more than that of Guadalajara, and the smaller towns in the suburbs swell the population of the municipality to one hundred thousand or more. There are very few rich families, most of the people being tradesmen, boot-makers, saddlers, hat-makers, rebosa aud serape weavers, workers in metal, etc., etc. There are many pure white families, and the average complexion of the population is much lighter than in the towns nearer the Pacific coast.

The country around has been much afflicted with robbers, but Col. Rosado, acting vigorously in conjunction with other State and Federal authorities, is fast thinning them out. Only a month or two since he discovered the existence of a band of seventy of these gentry in a cave near the road to Guanajuato, telegraphed to the three principal towns in the vicinity, organized a simultaneous attack upon them, and captured them all at a blow. He took his share of the captives to Leon, and tried and shot them; but those taken to some of the other towns were, after some ceremony, set free, probably to resume the practice of their profession.

The town appears very orderly, and is well and compactly built. It has some old convent buildings, now converted into free schools, and one immense church, and several minor ones. I was disappointed in these churches. The largest has beautiful colored glass memorial windows, the pictures being of the highest grade of merit, and many rich paintings, but otherwise it does not equal that at San Juan de los Lagos, and the others are comparatively poor affairs, very old, and not in the best of repair.

Apropos of churches, I must relate an incident which recently occurred here. Two robbers had been arrested by the authorities, and they—the robbers—threw themselves upon the protection of the new saint of the place, for whose canonization sixty thousand dollars in coin, wrung from the hard and stinted earnings of the laboring poor had just been forwarded by the Bishop of Leon to Rome, who, probably from a fellow-feeling, and possibly old association, so interested himself in their behalf, that the hearts of the authorities were moved and they were discharged without trial. The priests at once seized upon this fact as a miracle, and played for all there was on the board. They issued a pamphlet or tract, setting forth the details of the miracle, and rudely illustrated for the edification of the faithful. But, alas, they had crowed before they were fairly out of the woods, and the result was discouraging. Col. Rosado, who is an educated man, and appears to have a prejudice against saints and highway robbers being allowed to work together, immediately re-arrested the two robbers, tried, convicted, and shot them, thus spoiling the miracle, and causing the impression to go abroad in the community that even sixty thousand dollar saints will not always do to gamble on.

When we entered Leon, the Feast of All-Saints was

in full blast. The plaza is large and very beautiful, being surrounded by a handsome iron railing, flanked with tall, heavy-foliaged *fresno* trees, and paved with little cobbles in a beautiful mosaic, filled with beautiful flowers, and has a very large and elegant fountain in the center. The municipal palace, the handsomest building of the kind, exteriorly, which we had seen in Mexico, and other public buildings, and rows of stores with broad-arched portals, front this plaza. During the feast the broad sidewalk around the plaza is wholly given up to the sale of articles peculiar to the occasion. It is the custom of the country to distribute bon-bons, confectionery made into every conceivable form in imitation of birds, beasts, fishes, men, angels, devils, &c., &c., richly gilded and elaborately ornamented, among all one's friends, and especially among the children. Around the entire plaza was a row of stalls constructed of light matting and cloth, tastefully decorated with colored curtains and flowers, devoted exclusively to the sale of this confectionery and *dulces*, and attended by women old and young. Beyond the sidewalk was another row of stalls devoted to the sale of wax-candles of all lengths from six inches to six feet for offerings at the church altars.

When evening set in, the crowd which surged around the plaza became so dense that it was almost impossible to pass through it, and when the lamps were lighted, and the military band played its most inspiring airs, the scene, as we looked down upon it from the balcony of our house, was the most animated and brilliant we had ever seen in Mexico. At about 9½ P. M. the common and partly-dressed people began to thin out, and the richer and more pretentious came in to make their purchases, sit on the benches, or promenade up and down. In company with Mr. Burgess, an American photographer resident here, Mr. Fitch and myself walked around in the crowd for some time. The booth-keepers cried their wares—fair women, old men and women, and children in rags or tastefully dressed, walked up and down, young men in broad *sombreros* and gorgeous *serapes* lounged around in groups, beggars, blind, ragged, filthy, and hideous, groveled on the pavement of the street and yelled forth their wants, and incessantly discoursed on the blessedness of giving in charity; while the church bells sent forth their clangor until the whole air was filled with a surging ocean of sound.

We were lost in the crowd, and admiration of the scene. Just then a party of tall young men, hustled us, and I, having had doubt, from the start, of the safety of money and valuables, which to a considerable extent I carried on my person, got on the outside. Unsuspecting Mr. Fitch, conscious of his own rectitude, and suspecting no one else, kept on a few seconds, and then suddenly discovered that the pocket in the skirt of his coat behind had been cut out, and he was minus a handkerchief, two pair of old kid gloves, and a pocket guide to Spanish conversation, which, if it proves as great a curse to the thief as it had been to the owner, will have a tendency to cause him to abstain from stealing for the remainder of his life. Our party adjourned at once to the house, determined to retire for the night in the best order possible.

Next morning I went out alone, and found the churches, as usual, filled with devout worshipers—even the pavement outside was covered with kneeling devotees. At one of them the janitor was just passing around a deep copper plate, in which he had collected about a quart of *claquos* and *quartillas;* there was not a single silver or gold coin in the lot. As he looked significantly at me, I dropped an American dime into the plate. Looking back a few minutes later, I saw him standing by the corner of the church, outside, biting the dime, and regarding me with evident suspicion. He undoubtedly thought that I had been palming counterfeit coin on the Church. I do not allow any man to misinterpret my motives, and henceforth I give nothing but copper.

The city of Leon is compactly built, and in all the central part of the town the inhabitants cultivate flowers in the *patios* or court-yards, and more especially upon terraces and on the roofs of their houses. From the observatory upon our house I looked down upon the city, and saw one vast garden of brilliant flowers, thus cultivated in tall urns of fancifully fashioned earthenware. Such, on a larger scale, were the famous "Hanging Gardens" of Nineveh. The custom is a pleasant one, and greatly contributes to the enjoyment of life in a crowded city. Leon has about the climate of San Francisco at this season—the first of November—and the average temperature here is said to be from sixty to eighty degrees all the year round. The finest tropical fruits do not flourish here, but oranges, and some other fruits, such as are cultivated with success in the vicinity of Los Angelos, California, grow in great luxuriance.

As I have previously stated, we had left our military escort behind at Lagos, in the State of Jalisco, Señor Bossero having been assured by telegraph that the road was perfectly secure. Eighteen miles from Leon we stopped to change mules, and Mr. Seward, Mr. Fitch, and Mr. Burgess, who had accompanied us from Leon, were walking a mile or thereabouts in advance, not suspecting any danger, while I rode forward upon a saddle-horse loaned me by Mr. Burgess. The stage had been delayed by our first upset, which had no more serious consequences than the landing of Mr. Seward's colored servant in a nice, healthy *nopal*, or prickly-pear plant, the spines of which will stay with him long after his return to the United States, and we were some fifteen or twenty minutes behind time.

Just then we saw a detachment of Mexican cavalry, some twenty-five in number, coming toward us. When they saw the party they ranged themselves in double line to salute. We had almost reached them when one of their number, who had been scouting along in a corn-field, some distance from the road, raised a shout, and in an instant the whole party dashed off into the corn at full gallop, unslinging their carbines ready for action as they went. I rode after them, anxious to find out the cause of this sudden stampede, and saw one of them rise up like a circus-rider and stand upright on his saddle. He descried something in another direction, and with a yell, the squad changed its course and dashed off with redoubled speed. A few minutes later I saw a party of men in dark clothing, running over a high ridge a mile away beyond a ravine, making for a timbered mountain in the south-west, and in five minutes more the white caps of the troops could be seen darting in and out among the mesquite trees in close pursuit.

We watched them until they disappeared in the distance, and then rode on, saying little, but each "thinking a heap." Had the stage not been delayed by the upset, or had the soldiers arrived fifteen minutes later —well, I will not pursue the subject further, as it is unprofitable; but if we did not have a narrow escape from falling into the hands of the party of high-toned gentlemen who were laying for us in that corn-field, I am a sinner. I am always grateful for hospitalities, but in this case, am more than willing to take the will for the deed. As I saw the flying *bandito* and the pursuing troops disappear, I, for the first time, fully appreciated the force of the quotation:

"Tis distance lends enchantment to the view."

All day we were in sight of the range of treeless mountains, on the summit of which are situated the famous mines of La Luz, which occupy a position not unlike that of those on the the top of Treasure Hill, at Treasure City, in the White Pine district, Nevada. We could see vast piles of quartz, probably low grade ores, upon the mountain side. These ores, hundreds of thousands of tons in amount, cannot now be worked to advantage, owing to the heavy taxes on bullion, and to the cost of *beneficiating* them; but in time they will yield a vast amount of treasure under more favorable circumstances. The mountains in which the silver mines of Guanajuato are situated, resemble those in which the famous Comstock Lead of Nevada is found, and the situation of the City of Guanajuato is not unlike that of Virginia City, and Gold Hill, the elevation being not less than five or six thousand feet, apparently, above the level of the sea.

On our road to Siloa, and when still some miles from the town, we saw a party of laborers from some of the little hamlets which dot the country around, carrying a sick and dying man in a litter to the town that he might receive spiritual consolation in his last moments. They were all evidently of the humbler class, but neatly and cleanly dressed, and the delicate care with which they bore their dying companion along the rough and toilsome road was touching to observe. The day was very hot, and the labor of carrying the heavy litter by no means a trifling one; but each quietly took his place and assisted to bear the burden when his turn came without a word, and while a part were sustaining the load upon their shoulders, the others fanned the sufferer or held water to his parched and feverish lips. Probably each man in the party had lost a day's labor which he was ill able to spare, and contributed something from his scanty means besides, towards defraying the expenses of making the last hours of their friend and companion as comfortable as possible.

This kindness and consideration for the sick and unfortunate is characteristic of the people of Mexico, and notably so of the humbler classes. The poorest family in the land will share its last meal with the sick or the stranger, and when there is not a mouthful of food in the house—as is too often the case—will still give you "a cup of cold water in the name of Jesus," and some kind words of regret and apology for not being able to do more.

Passing through the dilapidated old town of Salado, or Siloa (pronounced Salow,) where we saw a church bearing an inscription which shows that it was erected in 1739, when New York contained fifteen thousand people, we entered the foot-hills of the mountains of Guanajuato.

CHAPTER VII.

GUANAJUATO, AND BENEATH IT.

FROM a height three miles from the City of Guanajuato, just as the sun was sinking behind the mountains in the west, we looked down on what appeared to be three separate towns situated in a deep ravine or cañon. The tall spires of the Cathedral of Guanajuato, glowing like gold in the red sunlight, were the conspicuous feature of the main and central city. Entering the cañon, we rode for two miles along the narrow bed of a tortuous little stream, whose waters, having done duty in all the silver reduction or *beneficiating* haciendas of the district, were clogged and thick with the residuum of the pulverized quartz which they were bearing away into the valley.

The town of Marfil, which is wholly supported by the beneficiating works which constitute its sole industry, lines the banks of this stream on either side, and the different haciendas, each of which is surrounded by a high wall, and capable of being defended against attack by a strong force, give it the appearance of one vast fortress. The houses are all hidden by the walls, which come down to the bed of the stream, and we hardly saw a human being in all this ride.

Passing, at last, an ancient tower, of a quaint pattern, constructed by the Spaniards for raising water, looking like a relic of the days of the Crusaders, we arrived at the lower portion of the city of Guanajuato, and found a delegation of officers waiting, with carriages, to escort Mr. Seward to the magnificent new house, completely furnished throughout, which had been prepared for the reception of the party. The keys were handed to him as soon as we had entered, and the committee then, considerately, bid us good-night, and left us to dine and retire to rest.

Guanajuato impressed us with an idea of permanence and comparative prosperity rather unusual in this part of the country, in spite of its greatly reduced population, its languishing industries, and its suburban mining towns deserted and tumbling into ruins. It has many beautiful private residences, which cannot be excelled in comfort, extent, and elegance, in any part of the United States, and many still wealthy and aristocratic families of pure, or nearly pure, Castilian descent. The city, proper, runs along on the steep hill-sides on either side of a very narrow and tortuous ravine or cañon over a mile in length; and the streets are narrow, crooked, and very steep. There are only two streets at the bottom of the cañon which admit of a carriage being driven over them at any speed, although all of them are most beautifully paved with small cobbles, generally in mosaic. The houses on the back streets, of course, rise above each other in successive terraces, like stairs, and each, in turn, affords a fine view of the back-yards and private portions of the residences next below.

At the upper end of the cañon, Señor Rocha, one of the oldest residents of Guanajuato, a few years since, built three large dams of solid masonry, beautifully constructed and tastefully ornamented, to collect the waters of the little stream which trickles down there from the mountain side; and from the reservoirs thus created, the people of the entire city, and mills below are supplied. At the commencement of the rainy season, in June, the flood-gates are opened, and the pent up waters which have been accumulating for a year, are allowed to flow out in a rushing river, which surges through the cañon, and washes everything clean, before it; the reservoirs are then cleansed and repaired. Here for the first time in Mexico, we missed the women at the plaza fountains, and the donkey-driving water-carriers, and drew fresh water from the hydrants.

THE RESERVOIRS AND PROMENADE.

Señor Rocha has a concession for the supplying of the city with water for twenty years, and will be able to repay himself for his vast outlay. He has also built terraced promenades and seats all around the reservoirs, and thus furnished Guanajuato with one of the great requisites of a Mexican city, a place of social public resort for its population at evening and-morning; he has fine natural taste, and has made the peculiar architecture best fitted for this country and climate, a thorough study; and whenever he sees a man about to build a house of any pretension, he at once offers to superintend its entire construction, free of charge.

Above the city, not far from the reservoirs, is a peculiar, high mountain, crowned with a curious perpendicular rock, which, from its fancied resemblance to the outlines of a giant buffalo, has been christened "El Buffa." From this mountain is procured, in unlimited quantities, a species of lined, and beautifully variegated sandstone, of all the colors of the rainbow—blue, pale green, and chocolate predominating. The sandstone cuts readily, has a fine grain, and is the best material for private residences and public buildings imaginable. With this, and in this way, Señor Rocha has lined the sides of the cañon all the way up to the reservoirs, with residences of the most beautiful style. Graceful pillars in long colonnades, arched portals, and corridors and *patos* decorated with all the flowers of this prolific climate, are seen by the delighted traveler on every side. Surely, this fine, old, Mexican gentleman is a public benefactor in the largest sense of the term.

For three centuries, Guanajuato furnished the world with an almost uninterrupted stream of silver, and in spite of wars and dissensions, crude and primitive systems of mining and reduction, oppressive taxes and general mismanagement, her mines of incredible wealth still pour out millions annually.

Early in the present century, Humboldt visited this city, and described the mines of the district more fully and scientifically than I am capable of doing; his description will still hold good in the main, and I refer the reader to it. I was told, that the mine owners—as is somewhat customary in all countries and all ages—imposed upon him in many particulars—and that the figures which he gave, are not to be trusted; but for reasons, which can only be guessed, I find that it is still impossible to obtain any more exact data concerning the yield of particular mines, even at this day. The records are usually imperfect at best, and there is a natural desire not to allow the public a full insight into the workings and value of particular mines. If a mine is paying well, it is always popularly supposed that it is really paying much better than reported; and if not paying at all, it is probably for sale, and the best possible showing is made.

In 1852, the annual yield of the mines of this district was estimated at nine million dollars, of which one-tenth was gold and the remainder silver. It is now only a little more than four million dollars; but with peace, and a judicious investment of capital, it could be doubled, or even trebled, very speedily. The population meantime has fallen off probably fifty per cent, and the city now contains only forty-five or fifty thousand people at the outside estimate.

General Florencio Antillon, Governor of Guanajuato, to whom I am indebted for many courtesies, furnished me with some interesting statistics. From them I learned that the present population of the state is seven hundred and twenty-nine thousand, nine hundred and eighty-eight. This is, in proportion to its size, the most densely populated state of the Repulic. There are six hundred prisoners in the state-prison, at Salamanca, or one hundred and fifty less than in the California state-prison, with a population fifty per cent. greater. The state forces, under pay, consist of one battalion of the line of four hundred and seventy-nine men, and four squadrons of mounted *gendarmes*—in all nine hundred and eighty-eight men. These belong to the National Guard, and are always on duty on the road or in the Municipalities. There are also four hundred members of the National Guard not on active duty and pay, and three hundred and ninety-four more doing duty at intervals, and liable to be called out at a moment's notice. The guard of the Department of Guanajuato, is now being armed with Henry rifles from the United States, but the others still have the old English Tower, and the Springfield muskets of 1860–63.

There are two hundred and eight students in the free college. The free schools cost ninety-four thousand dollars per annum, and are well attended. They have day and evening schools connected with the primary department for boys and girls separately, and High Schools intermediate between them and the colleges. The old debt of the state, January 1st, 1868, was fifty-eight thousand eight hundred and three dollars and ten cents. The income of the state in 1868, from all sources, was seven hundred and fifty-nine thousand one hundred and seventy-two dollars and nineteen cents, and the expenses, seven hundred and forty-eight thousand thirty-six dollars and fifty-five cents.

The condition of the state, in spite of the depression of its leading interest, silver mining, seems to be comparatively good, and its credit well maintained.

A substantial, well macadamized, carriage-road is now being built from Queretaro to Leon, running entirely through the State of Guanajuato, from South-east to North-west, under the direction of Gilberto Torres, a native Mexican Engineer, formerly in the United States Coast Survey, on the California Coast. This road is to be 216 miles long, and will cost the incredibly small sum of $316 per mile, including the erection of several substantial stone bridges already completed.

Governor Antillon, who is a man of splendid personal appearance, tall, handsome and intelligent, was a commander in the Republican army during the war. His reputation as an executive officer is excellent, and the State is said to be one of the best governed in Mexico. He is vigorously shooting the "road-agents or highwaymen, and already the roads in all parts of the State are comparatively safe for travelers, and will soon be quite so. If the duties on the production of silver could be reduced fifty per cent. on what they now are, the quantity would very largely increase, and the State and Federal Governments would both be largely benefited by it. The climate, generally, throughout the State is about that of Southern California, and as healthy as the climate of any part of the United States.

GENERAL FLORENCIO ANTILLON.

We visited the Mint of Guanajuato, said to be the best in the Republic, and the only one which is worked by steam. Its machinery is on the English plan, and English made, and the mint is run, under contract, by an English company. The Treasurer of the mint, Señor Don Juan B. Castelazo, an intelligent and highly educated Mexican, who speaks English well, showed us through the establishment. From him we learned that the annual coinage of the mint is $4,000,000, of which $500,000 is gold and the remainder silver. The old silver coinage was dollars, half-dollars, quarters, *reals*, (12 1-2 cts.) *medios*, (6 1-4 cts.) and *quartillas*, (3 1-8 cts.) and this is the common currency of the country, though the old copper or brass *claquos* and *quartillas* still circulate extensively. The Governor has now prepared dies for a new half-dollar similar to the American, and ten and five cent pieces of our pattern. These coins are already being struck off, but are not yet put in circulation. By the courtesy of Mr. Frederic Meyer, I obtained the first of these new half-dollars coined at the Guanajuato Mint; and for American gold, I obtained a handful of the smaller coins to take home as curiosities to my friends. The gold coined is in *onzas* or sixteen-dollar pieces, corresponding to the Spanish doubloon. Gold dollars will be coined hereafter, and the old silver, 12 1-2 cents, 6 1-4 cents, and 3 1-8 cents coinage, wil lbe abandoned. In other words, the American decimal system has finally been adopted for all the mints in Mexico.

Señor Castelazo gave me the following list of the taxes which silver producers in Mexico now pay: State tax, three and one-eighth per ct.; melting and assay of bars, one-half of one per ct.; coinage and Government tax, four and three-eighths per ct.; total eight per cent. If the coin is exported—as it generally is—it pays an additional export duty of eight per cent. or sixteen per cent. all told. This is a reduction of at least seven per cent. on the old rates; but farther reductions must be made before the silver interest can become again thoroughly prosperous.

One of the greatest objects of interest in Guanajuato, is the ancient Castillo del Grenaditas, a square, two story, stone structure of immense size, flat roof of stone slabs, cemented water-tight, and walls from five to ten feet in thickness, built early in the last century, and originally intended to be used as a granary in which to store surplus corn for the public protection against seasons of scarcity. There is a large court-yard in the center of the structure, surrounded with cornices and graceful pillars.

When Hidalgo, after his pronunciamento with eleven men at Dolores in the State of Guanajuato, in 1810, arrived here, the whole Indian and native-born Spanish-American population flocked to his banner. They were hardly armed at all, but were brave and determined. The Spaniards, two thousand strong, fled into this Castle of Grenaditas, and defended themselves through a long siege, with obstinate courage and determination. The patriots sought in vain to carry the place, as the Spaniards were constantly on the watch, and gave them no opportunity to approach the gates. At night, the Spaniards burned great torches, and by their light, shot all who came within reach.

At last, an Indian placed a great flat stone upon his back, and thus shielded from the bullets which the Spaniards rained down upon it, crawled up to the gates and burned them down. The stone which he used as armor, is still shown. The besiegers followed up their advantage, and, after a part of the garrison had perished from suffocation, carried the castle. It is said that not a Spaniard escaped.

In the following year, when Hidalgo, defeated at the Bridge of Calderon, fled to Chihuahua, and was betrayed,

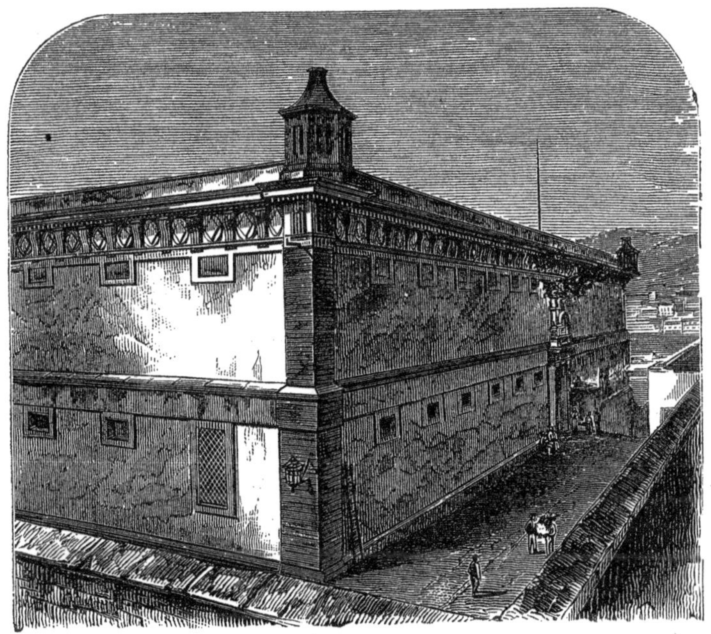

CASTLE OF GRENADITAS.

tried, and shot, his head and those of his three companions, were brought here, and placed on four hooks still projecting from the four corners of the building near the roof; and there they remained until 1823, when the successful revolutionists took them down, and buried them, with the honors due to the memory of the first martyrs of Mexican Liberty.

Visiting this Castle, alone, I found it occupied as a *Carcel* or municipal prison, Police Judges' offices, etc., etc. The troops of the State, all of Indian blood, but fine, stout, hardy, and well-disciplined men, stand guard at this prison, and among the prisoners were many white men, descendants of those who suspended the heads of Hidalgo and his companions, on the hooks. A young man, who informed me that he was one of the three judges of the minor criminal court, politely showed me through the building. There were about three hundred men and boys, and thirty-six women in the *Carcel.* They were in apartments containing from twelve to twenty-five each, all opening on the great court-yard, and light and well ventilated. They were working at boot and shoe making, hat-making, weaving *serapes* and coarse blankets, making tallow candles, etc., etc., or attending school. The white blood appeared to predominate among the prisoners, all of whom looked cheerful, clean, well-fed, and comfortable.

All kinds of manufactured goods are hawked about the city on men's shoulders, and you must be careful how you look at anything, or you will be surrounded in a moment with anxious sellers. I asked the price of a pair of blue-steel spurs handsomely inlaid with sterling silver.

"Six dollars, Señor but what will you be pleased to give?"

The same spurs, in California, would bring at least twenty dollars, and I have seen not much finer ones sold at fifty dollars.

I looked at some *rebosas,* merely to ascertain the price, and was offered good ones for three dollars, and finer ones for six dollars. Remarking, by way of getting rid of the dealer, that they were not fine enough, as my family wore only silk—Heaven forgive me!—I left, and an hour later the dealer was waiting for me at the door of our house, with a dozen costly silk ones in boxes, for my inspection. I gave him fifty cents for his trouble, not feeling able to buy, and he went off pro testing that I was a Republican Prince and a *Cabellero grande.*

I wanted a pair of boots and could find none in the shops to fit me. Seeing a boot-peddler in the crowd I called him up, and looked at a pair with short legs faced with buff, and soles fancifully shaped and fastened with small metalic nails; they were made at Leon, he told me.

"Too small; I wear number eight!"

He passed his hand carefully over my foot and without another question thanked me, bowed low, and hurried off. When I got back to the house and entered my room, a servant brought me a pair the exact counterpart of those I had looked at, except in size, saying that the owner was in the ante-room. I tried them on, and found them the nicest fit I had ever seen; if they had been made for me in New York they would not have fitted me half so well.

"How much?" I asked of the servant.

"Four dollars Señor!"

"Tell him I will give him three dollars and a half!"

He came back in a minute: "*Esta bien*, Señor!" He would have taken three dollars, had I offered it, but they were cheap at twice or three times the money, according to our American ideas. How he found out who I was and where to find me, is a mystery I am unable to explain.

The scenes in the market-place or plaza of Guanajuato are beyond description. The poor people of this great mining district cannot afford to waste anything, and they literally eat up an entire animal "from the tip of his nose to the end of his tail." All the meat not sold fresh is dried, and sold in that shape. You see men and women squatted on the ground before a pile of sheep and goats heads and necks, dried with the horns on, and the hair or wool still adhering to them in patches, and notice, not without a rising of the gorge, that the poor customers crowd around, and after haggling for one of them, purchase it for perhaps a cent or two, and walk off, gnawing at it as a dog would gnaw at his bone. Boiled pumpkins or *calobassas* are also among the staple articles of food among these poor people, and the principal article of their diet is a kind of gruel or soup made from ground corn; and they think themselves vastly fortunate if they can add to this a dried goats-head, sheeps-neck, or the nose or tail of a bullock on Sunday. How they can live and work as they do on such a diet Heaven only knows.

As a rule the people of the lower order are not dishonest, but there are many petty thieves among them. To show how far they will go in the stealing line I will mention a single fact. In a hardware store on the plaza, I noticed several grindstones fastened to the wall by chains, passed through the hole in the center, and padlocks; on inquiry, I learned that this was done to prevent their being stolen and carried off bodily by men who did not even know the use of them, but would take them in preference to almost anything else on which they could lay their hands, because they were heavier, and as they supposed, consequently more valuable.

The priests have given the authorities much trouble, but appear now to have become pretty thoroughly humbled. This was once one of their strongholds, and it would hardly have been believed by a visitor twenty years ago, that at this time the holy fathers would be forbidden by law to walk the streets of Guanajuato in their clerical robes and broad hats; but such is the case. About the time we were there, some of them, becoming over-confident, ventured to disobey the law, and appeared in their black robes on the streets. Thereupon, General Antillon issued an order requiring the police to arrest all such offenders, and gave notice that they would be punished with a fine of five hundred dollars, and thirty days in the chain-gang, with double the penalty for each repetition of the offence. Next day there was not a black gown or shovel-hat to be seen in the streets of Guanajuato: and this was the city in which the Church condemned the Padre Hidalgo to death.

Education is by no means neglected or despised by the people of Guanajuato at this time. While there, we attended the annual examination and distribution of prizes at the State College. Governor Antillon presided and distributed the premiums. The College has nearly three hundred students, and is, partly, self-sustaining. It appears to be well managed, and a model institution in its way. The graduating class, with few exceptions, were in full dress black suits, with white kid gloves; but I noticed with not a little pleasure, that some of the highest prizes were carried off by young men of almost unmixed Indian blood, in clean but coarse leather pantaloons and roundabout jackets, who were, apparently, treated with as much consideration by the faculty and their fellow-students as any one there. There was an abundance of exceedingly fine operatic music, some superior declamations, and when all the prizes, consisting of elegantly bound books of practical value—not merely parlor ornaments—and diplomas had been distributed the hall, which was beautifully decorated, was cleared and an array of brilliant loveliness, such as I have seldom if ever seen elsewhere, was soon mingling with the student-throng in the mazy dances of this land of music and of flowers. As we were to leave for Celaya at 4 o'clock next morning, I was reluctantly compelled to leave the ball-room and return home to get some sleep, and so missed the conclusion of the festivities.

The reduction works, or beneficiating haciendas of Guanajuato and Marfil are worthy of especial attention. One of the best establishments of this character in the district, that of Mr. Parkman—an American long resident in Mexico—was visited by our party who spent some hours in inspecting it. The "mill," or crushing apparatus, is run partly by steam, and partly by water power. It is rude and primitive to the last degree. The stamps work on wooden shafts, and the quartz must be constantly shoveled under them by hand, as there is no provision for self-feeding as with us. There are twenty-nine arastras worked by mule-power to reduce the crushed quartz to pulp. All the rock is "dry crushed," and the process is slow and clumsy in the extreme. But the "amalgamation," as we term it, or "beneficiating," as it is termed here, is the most interesting part of the work. We finish the whole operation in a day, but lose on an average twenty-five to forty per cent. of the silver. In White Pine, where the ores are chlorides and oxides, they lose only four to eight per cent. —or a little less than is lost here. The cost of fuel is eight dollars per cord, and steam machinery could be run—if it were not for the difficulty of making repairs—for less than it costs in Washoe, as labor is cheaper; but in *beneficiating* they would probably lose as much as they saved on the crushing, if the American system of reduction and amalgamation was fully adopted here.

Mr. Parkman's *tortas* are an improvement. He has seven of them, each sixty feet in diameter, and holding one hundred and twelve tons of pulp. The mules—only two in number—travel around the outside, and draw a shaft which works on a pinion in the center, on which there is a pair of heavy wagon wheels, which, by an adjustable scale, are made to run in a smaller or larger circle, thus working over all the pulp in time. As the pulp works outward toward the side of the *torta*, it is shoveled back towards the center, by hand, and is thus well mixed. The time required in beneficiating is twenty-five days in Mr. Parkman's hacienda, and the work is always well done. The ore is not of a very refractory character, being mainly pure black and bronze sulphites, and the *patio* process appears to save more of the silver than any other. I am told that there are occasionally small deposits of chlorides found here, but that by the *patio* process none of it is saved.

The great mine of San José de Valenciano, which is said to have produced in its day eight hundred million dollars, was not visited by Mr. Seward, but I had the good fortune to see it.

This mine is situated on the mountain, high above the city on the North-east, and occupies a large and rich portion of the *Veta Madre* or "Mother Vein," of Guanajuato. It was discovered immediately after the conquest by the Spaniards, and for many years was a wonder of wonders. For forty years in succession it was "in *bonanza*," paying enormous dividends to its owners; and when Humboldt visited it, he estimated that it then produced one-fifth of all the silver in the world. It passed after his time into the hands of the "Anglo Mexican Company," which commenced with a capital of five million pounds sterling, (say $25,000,000 in American coin,) with a board of directors sitting in London, who sent out officers of the army and navy who had never seen a mine in their lives, to superintend its workings at fabulous salaries, erected an immense engine, and run it at constant disadvantage and loss; and finally, after sinking in this and other mines, nearly their original capital, learned wisdom from experience, and changed the programme. They employed a competent director, Mr. Charles Furber, working some other mines here at a profit, and in time their stock would have been once more in demand, but a fearful tragedy which I shall presently relate, put an end to all operations again, for a time, at least.

Accompanied by Messrs. Anthony Burgess, Thomas Abrams, Frederick Meyer, Smith, and Dr. Harris, all American residents, who with Governor Antillon, and Alfred Jeanotat had been unceasing in their attentions to us, I started out to visit this famous mine at day-break, Thursday, November 4th. Mounted on the beautifully fleet and easy riding horses of the country—which have an artificial gait, trotting with the hind legs and galloping with the fore legs at the same time—with revolvers at our waists, and swords hung at the pommel of the saddle and run through under the stirrup-strap so as to be held under the left knee of the rider—when will our American cavalry learn this neat trick and dispense with the knocking and rattling sabres hung at the belt and always a nuisance?—we started off, at sunrise, up the winding streets and alleys, and over the rugged hillsides to the mine and town around it.

At the crossing of a deep, dry *arroyo* we crossed over a bridge, which bore an inscription, "For more than three centuries the people of Guanajuato crossed here without a bridge. Behold progress!" In another part of our journey we passed a bridge on which there was this inscription: "This bridge was built here, etc., etc.;" as it is of solid stone, I don't wonder at its having been built there instead of having been built somewhere else, and sent there ready made by express.

An immense church with an elaborately carved and sculptured front, worn and defaced by the storms and convulsions of centuries, but still with unshaken walls of massive stone, stands in the center of a town, which must once have contained from ten to twenty thousand people, all dependent on the working of the great Valenciano mine. The church is unfrequented, save by a few squalid and destitute devotees; the town is in ruins; and desolation reigns sole mistress of the scene. We galloped through the deserted streets, and entered the gate-way of the enclosure out of which have been borne, in times past, enough mule-loads of treasure to sink the largest ship now afloat on the seas. Little boys received our horses, and walked them up and down, while we went through the vast enclosures, where men and animals by thousands, once toiled and suffered, but where now the grass grows and silence reigns.

The extent of these works above ground cannot be adequately described. They cover acres on acres of ground, and cost millions of dollars. All around, you see walls from three to eight feet in thickness and solid as the rocks of the mountains, radiating in every direction. There are many shafts sunk deep into the bowels of the earth, each with its separate enclosure and outworks, and the chambers and drifts underground, now filled with water, measure miles in extent. At the main shaft the works resemble a vast fortress, and are on a scale of extent unprecedented in the history of mining in America. The mule-yard surrounded by a high wall, with mangers of cut stone running all around it, must contain, at least, three or four acres of ground, and all the other enclosures and out-buildings are on a proportionate scale.

The extent of the works under ground cannot be seen at this time, as they are filled with water; but it is affirmed by engineers, that the galleries, chambers, and drifts, are longer in the aggregate than all the streets of the city of Guanajuato, and incredible as the statement looks, it is probably correct. We went to the mouth of the "*tiro general*" or great perpendicular shaft, out of which so many millions of tons of ore have been hoisted in years gone by, and laying down upon our faces, looked into the yawning depths below. This shaft is the largest on the American Continent, and nothing in the mining line to be seen in the United States, will bear a comparison with it. It is 687 varas deep, —say 1939 1-4 feet of our measurement—thirty-six feet wide, and eight-sided. The walls of this shaft are exactly perpendicular, and for the protection of the work, men below, laid up in cement, as smooth as the ceiling of an ordinary dwelling-house in the United States. The water now comes up to within 125 varas or about 344 feet of the surface of the ground.

We dropped stones into the abyss, and when they struck the water the report and echoes which followed, lasted fifteen seconds, and were perfectly deafening. We then fired a pistol down the *tiro*, and the report which came back to us was like that of a twenty-four pounder cannon, causing our ears to ring for hours thereafter.

The enclosure around the great *tiro* is circular and of immense extent. Radiating from the tiro to the outer wall, like the sections of an opened fan, are eight sub-enclosures corresponding to the eight sides of the *tiro*: in each of these enclosures stood, formerly, a great upright drum wheel, or winze, called a *malacate*, on which were the cables which hauled up and let down the buckets filled with water and ore, or men and supplies. The rope was always winding up on one end and down on the other end of the *malacate* when it was in motion. These eight great *malacates* were all worked by mule power for centuries, but the English company introduced an immense hoisting engine to do the work. The engine was found to require more feed than the mules, and so was put out of use and the mules substituted again. There is another, but smaller *tiro* lower down the hill. Humboldt estimated that it would require a tunnel seven or eight miles in length to drain this immense mine; but it seems to me that a much shorter one would do the work effectually; and the chance of striking "feeders" or "blind veins" of ore in the course of the work sufficient to pay the whole or a considerable portion of the cost of its construction, would, apparently, justify the adoption of the plan, by a company having an adequate capital. As the mine now stands, it is estimated, that it would require two million dollars, in coin, to put the requisite machinery on the ground, drain the mine by pumping, and commence work. It is generally believed that countless millions of treasure yet remain in this mine, and will some day be exhausted.

In the chapel near the *tiro*, we saw the votive offerings and pictures presented by grateful miners in commemoration of some miraculous escape from death. One of these was a rude painting representing a miner falling into the great *tiro*, and being miraculously caught and stayed in mid-air by the Virgin, as he pronounced her name. If any man will convince me that a human being ever fell into that shaft, and escaped with a whole bone in his body, I will swallow all the stories you may tell me about ancient and modern miracles henceforth, without a doubt or question. We saw a number of men sorting over and sifting a great pile of waste ores, the accumulation of years, and this was all the work going on at this great mine when we were there. On every wall, and over every gate-way was the sign of the cross, and ruin and desolation overshadowed all.

Near the church we saw a cross, erected on the spot where a man was waylaid and murdered by bandits only a few months before. Near this, and on the direct road to Guanajuato, a priest was stopped only a short time before our visit, "put up" and "gone through," by the bandits who took every dollar he had, kicked him, and told him to travel. After they had let him go he felt in his pockets, and finding a *rial* which they had overlooked, called them back, and with a grim humor said to them, "Here my poor friends, there is still 12 1-2 cents coming to you!" They took the money, and kicked him again for joking under such serious circumstances.

I have alluded to the new Superintendent of the English Company, Mr. John Furber, who was in charge of these works when we were there. He was a fine, intelligent young man, for whom we all conceived a great liking. A long and useful life appeared to be before him. On Sunday, the 19th of December, a month after we saw him he left his brother's house at 5 o'clock in the afternoon, accompanied by a servant, to return to his residence at Marfil, distant about a league. After passing the *Cerro Trozado*, he was attacked a little in advance of the junction of the old and new roads to Marfil, by four men on horseback, supposed to have been *plagiaros*, belonging to the band of the notorious Juan Duran. A struggle took place in which Mr. Furber was wounded by a pistol-shot in the stomach, after which he was carried off, along with the servant (who was blindfolded) in the direction of the hacienda of Burburron, and, after many turnings and windings, the party crossed the high road to Siloa, (not many miles from where we saw the supposed robbers being chased by the soldiers,) and the river Santa Anna, and entered on the territory of the hacienda of Santa Teresa. At this place the unfortunate gentleman was hung up to a tree, whether dead or alive will probably never be known, and the servant, after having been stripped, was set at liberty and returned to his late master's residence with the news of his murder.

The authorities at once dispatched a party to bring in the body, which was found suspended to a tree without coat or waistcoat, with a paper affixed to the braces, on which was written in ink, the following: "This has befallen me because I did not give five thousand dollars."

In justice to the "gentleman of the road" in Mexico, I must say that as a rule they are the most polite people on earth, and even in taking a man's money and watch, do it with a certain courtesy and grace that makes the operation comparatively easy to bear on the part of the victim. They always apologize for the act, regretting that necessity compels them to do it, and in parting with the traveler, devoutly commend him to the protecting care of Divine Providence. When not too sharply pressed by the Government, the different gangs in any one state usually have a sort of business connection, and, if you desire it, the leader of the first band into whose hands you fall will very courteously, write out a pass for you to take along to save you from further molestation. I have one of these passes in my possession. It was given by the leader of a band in the State of Guerraro, to a friend of mine, who was "put up" in the most approved manner. He went through the party in the highest style of the art; and then, sitting on his horse, wrote with a pencil on a slip of paper, on the pommel of his saddle, a pass as follows:

"Dear Gomez: This party has been done according to our regulations. Please let them pass without molestation. Manuel."

The gentleman who received the pass then said:

"But, my dear sir, you have not left me a dollar to buy meals on the road!"

The brigand replied, "Pardon Señor? How much do you require?"

"Well, about five dollars will take me to Acapulco, I think!" said my friend.

The brigand chieftain, thereupon, not only gave him back that amount but added to it a nice porte-monnaie which he had just taken, with others of the same sort, from a German peddler, saying that he would find it useful to prevent his losing the small change out of his pocket while sleeping at night. He then told the party that near a certain barranca they would be stopped by the band who had control of that end of the road, to the leader of which this pass was directed. In due time they met the other band, presented the pass, and not only were allowed to proceed without molestation, but were actually furnished with a fresh horse to replace a lame one which had given out on the road, no "boot" being demanded. It is true that the horse, probably, did not cost the bandits anything, and they could afford to be liberal; still, it was an act of courtesy on their part, for which the party felt duly grateful. I have a prejudice against being robbed by anybody, but if I must be robbed, let it be by a Mexican robber, by all means.

The business of kidnaping or carrying off travelers into the mountains and holding them for ransom, and murdering them if the amount demanded is not forthcoming, now so active in Mexico, is of modern origin and a foreign innovation. A few years since the Mexican Government paid a large sum for the importation of an Italian Colony of two hundred men, who were to introduce the culture of silk, and stimulate industry in many branches new to Mexico. These two hundred Italians each brought a hand-organ with them, and took to the business of grinding out "mooshic" on the streets, at once. When that lead was worked out they took to other occupations. Some of them had formerly been in the brigand business in their dear, native land; and finding, much to their astonishment, that the trick of kidnaping or *plagiaring* had not been brought into general practice in Mexico, proceeded to introduce it in all its purity at once. They soon made the roads of Mexico as unsafe as those of any part of Italy; and by the practice of frugality and economy, and strict attention to business, were in a little time enabled to sell out their "stock and good will" to native artists, who now carry on the trade in all its branches at the old stands. The penalty for carrying on this business is death by shooting, and the Juarez Administration, whenever it is backed up with a will by the local authorities, execute it with a relentless vigor which promises to end the practice, or depopulate the country in the end. This is the popular version of the origin of the practice of *plagiaring*, but I cannot vouch for its being correct in all its details. It is quite certain however that it is not a native institution, and it is a fact, that all the bands engaged in it have more or less of the natives of Southern Europe among them as leading spirits. Of the remnants of Maximilian's army, dispersed widely through the land, there are very few of any nationality, now engaged in an honest occupation. Some are plain robbers on the highway; some merely petty thieves in the cities; and many are *plagiaros.* Those not in either of the above branches of trade are quite likely to be in sympathy with, if not actually engaged in the various *pronunciamentos.* There are a few Turcos, some Frenchmen, and now and then a Belgian or Austrian, once soldiers, following some honest trade, and unmolested and respected in the principal cities; but the bulk of the foreign mercenaries brought over by Maximilian, were thieves and ex-convicts in their own land, and it is not surprising that they fall back into their old occupation, when set free in a new country. The road from Manzanillo to Mexico, via Colima, Guadalajara, Guanajuato and Queretaro, is but little traveled by foreigners visiting the country, and the few who do go over it, generally carry no valuables and ride in the stage, trusting to luck to get through without being robbed, or in any event losing but little The rural guards keep the road in tolerable safety for the *diligencias*, and by law the owners of property in the immediate vicinity of a point where a robbery has been committed are pecuniarily responsible to the victims for damages, though few suits of recovery are brought, I imagine. On the road from Acapulco to the the city of Mexico, travelers always secure a guard of six to twenty *macheteros* and usually pass through the worst districts in safety.

On our return to the city, we passed within sight of the second great mine of the district of Guanajuato, "El Reyes," situated, like the Valenciano, on a hill, with a large town around it, but we did not have time to visit it.

After dinner we went to the *Serrano* mine, which is being worked at a profit at this time. This is situated in the hill below the Buffa at the upper end of the city. Five hundred men, women, and children are employed at this mine, getting out the ore, breaking it up, and sorting, it. The men generally work in small gangs for a share of the sales of the ore they take out. The amount of silver mined weekly is about five thousand dollars, and the expenses one thousand dollars, leaving a net profit of four thousand dollars. The great *tiro* is about 950 feet, in depth.

A horizontal tunnel penetrates the hill from a level with the hacienda, cutting the *tiro* or perpendicular shaft at four hundred feet from the surface. This tunnel may be about fifteen hundred feet in length. A railroad track runs through it, and lying down in the cars we were carried in to the edge of the *tiro*. This *tiro* is thirty feet in diameter, and six-sided, laid up in cement like that at the Valenciano. The necessity for this is seen in the fact that a rock, weighing many tons, was displaced from a station near the bottom of the shaft, a few days previous to our visit, and falling upon the miners beneath, killed and maimed a large number of them.

Standing here, four hundred feet below the surface of the earth, and six hundred feet above the bottom of the shaft, with a patch of pale blue sky far above us, and inky darkness almost palpable to the touch around us and filling all the depths below, we witnessed the most wonderful scene on which we gazed in Mexico. Men were sent up to the top of the *tiro* at the surface of the ground, and told to discharge rockets down it. This they did; and the hissing and explosions of the fiery messengers caused the most deafening echoes and re-echoes, while the sides of the shaft, dripping with ooze and slime, were revealed with startling distinctness by the momentary glare.

But this was nothing to what followed: balls of the fibre of the maguey or aloe plant, three feet in diameter and steeped in pine pitch, or resin, were swung out over the mouth of the shaft and set on fire. When the first was in full blaze it was detached and allowed to fall into the abyss. Like a great comet, with body of molten metal and long tail of flame, rushing on a doomed planet, the monster projectile came down from the dizzy height above us, and passing the mouth of the tunnel in which we stood, with a roar more deafening than the loudest thunder, went bounding and crashing into the depths below, illuminating everything for a moment with its blinding, lurid glare, followed by a darkness and silence more profound than before. As soon as the tremendous echoes which were awakened by the first had died away, a second was sent down, and others followed in quick succession.

Most of our party were unable to control their nerves sufficiently to enable them to approach the edge, and look up and down the *tiro*, holding by ropes to prevent them from becoming dizzy, and falling headlong into the depths; but those who could do so, beheld a scene, the awful sublimity and grandeur of which beggars all the powers of language.

The remainder of the party now left, and I, in company with the superintendent, clothing myself in a miner's suit to keep off the water and mud, descended to the bottom of the mine, one thousand feet and more from the surface. We went down ladder after ladder, along gallery after gallery, through chambers like great churches in size, and others in which we could not stand erect, down steps cut in the rock and so slippery, with dripping water and soft clay, as to compel us to use an iron-shod staff to support ourselves, and through many a winding turning, until we stood at the bottom of the *tiro*, wet through with perspiration, and trembling with exhaustion.

At the bottom of the *tiro* is a great pond of water, the reservoir into which all the drainings of the mine are gathered, and the buckets on the great cables worked by the *Malacates* at the surface, were constantly coming and going between it and the end of the tunnel, six hundred feet above. These buckets will hold three to four hogsheads of water, and are made of raw-hide in the form of an ordinary Mexican water-jar. An iron ring distends the mouth of the bucket, and when the vessel descends, the wet hide flattening down allows the water to rush in, and as the lifting commences, it falls back into its original form, filled to the brim with the dirty fluid. When the bucket reaches the level of the tunnel, it is hauled into the opening, and as the cable is slackened up it flattens down again, and the water escaping over the rim, runs off down the side of the tunnel.

But there are still lower depths. We went down nearly two hundred feet more, and at the bottom of the last level found men at work taking out ore. The dripping of the water at this point is very considerable, and two plans are made use of to get rid of it. A part of the water is carried up to the reservoir, in pig-skins, on the backs of naked and sweating Indians; and a part—the larger part—is pumped up to that point by hand. The pumps are mere straight logs, thirty feet long, with a bore of three inches, and a piston and bucket, pulled and pushed back and forth by two stalwart Indians, sitting on either side, working by main strength without even a lever purchase to help them along. There are stations or reservoirs at the end of each pump, and all must be kept going continually night and day. The Indian pumpers sit down to their work upon the wet rock, and are as naked as when born; the great heat and want of ventilation, at this depth, rendering clothing, if they had it, a superfluity. They get fifty cents each per day, and work twelve

14

hours at a shift. In all my mining experience, I have never seen such a waste of power and such thoroughly primitive appliances for mining.

I went through many of the galleries and drifts, and examined the vein carefully. The main vein is five to twelve feet wide, quite irregular, and runs in a generally south-western and north-eastern direction, dipping to the south-westward as it descends. It carries metal in a very unequal degree, in different portions, and though presenting rich specimens and bunches of almost pure silver in spots, is not generally very rich.

A HUMAN TARANTULA.

In one chamber I saw a number of mules and horses feeding, a thousand feet below the surface. These poor creatures are let down in slings from the surface, through the *tiro*, and never go out again alive. They turned their glazing eyes upon us, with evident pain, as we passed with lighted torches, and appeared to regard us with mournful interest, as in some way connected with the world above, of which they still retained some dim recollection, but which they were never to look upon again. In another chamber I saw women and children cooking food for their husbands and parents; they appeared to live here altogether, probably returning to the light of day only at long intervals. Utterly worn out, at last, we climbed our way back to the tunnel, emerging into daylight just as the sun was setting, swallowed a liberal allowance of brandy to protect ourselves against taking cold, mounted our horses and galloped back to the city.

The weekly sale of ores at the several mines is called the "*rescata.*" One at the Serrano I attended. The ore is placed on the ground, each miner's work in a separate lot, and the buyers sample it before the sale. It is sold in the lump, by guess, not by weight, the buyer taking his chances on the amount. The auctioneer stands silent, under an umbrella, while the miners who have a small interest in the sales over and above their wages, volubly shout the praises of the lot in turn. As each lot is put up, the buyers, singly, whisper their bids in the ear of the auctioneer, and when all have bid, he announces who bid the highest; the other bids are not named. The chance for collusion seem to me to be very great. Some lots brought as high as five hundred dollars, and the aggregate sales exceeded six thousand five hundred dollars, at this *rescata.* This ended our sight-seeing in Guanajuato.

CHAPTER VIII.

FROM GUANAJUATO TO QUERETARO.

WE left Guanajuato at 4 A. M., Monday, Nov. 8th, without a guard, and preceeded by postilions running on foot, and carrying torches, drove at a gallop down the long *arroyo*, between the fortress-like haciendas of the suburbs and Marfil, and out into the open country below the mountains. When day-break came we were crossing a broad "sand-river," near a little town. Many women were carrying water in jars upon their shoulders from shallow wells scooped out of the sand in the bed of the stream, which is not a stream at all, save during the floods of the rainy season.

We had the choice of the "Empressa General de Diligencias" teams at every station, and as the road was excellent went along at a glorious pace. This was the best part of Mexico, which we had yet seen. The plain is broad and extremely fertile, and generally pretty well cultivated. We saw many fields of corn which would be called No. 1, and something over, in Illinois, and broad belts of wheat already well up and brilliantly green. The farms or ranches are of immense size, separated only by pillars of masonry, some fifteen feet in height, to mark the boundaries, and each hacienda or head farm-house is a fortress in itself, surrounded by a small village, occupied by the former *peons*, but now enfranchised laborers.

High walls with stout gates surround most of these great haciendas, and on the roofs of some we noticed breastworks of adobe, with loop-holes for musketry, carried up above the battlements. These tell the story of the times of civil war and brigandage so happily passing away I trust, from Mexico forever. One of these great haciendas, if resolutely defended by its occupant and his retainers, could only be taken by means of artillery. The villages are all surrounded by square lots, each containing half-an-acre to two-and-a-half acres, fenced with the *organo* cactus, and each cultivated by a separate family.

At 12 o'clock M., we were in the ancient city of Salamanca, the penal capital of Guanajuato, having meantime passed through the old market-town of Irapuato, which has some five thousand inhabitants, and two very old churches with elaborately carved stone fronts, now in a dilapidated condition. The State-Prison at Salamanca is located in what was once a convent, which had a church attached, and thieves and desperadoes come to work where nuns had droned away their lives in pious idleness. The convicts, five hundred in number, are engaged in various kinds of labor, as at Guadalajara, and in spite of the clamor raised by the Church party and press, about the despoiling of the Lord, and desecration of the property by substituting a penal colony for a nunnery, the buildings are being improved and extended, and it is evident that the property will never again be used as a place of religious seclusion.

The Government of Mexico seems to be thoroughly aware of the necessity of maintaining its attitude towards the church in all firmness, and the indignant protest of Bishop or priest, and the anathemas of the

Church herself, are treated with equal contempt. A few days since, the remains of the patriot General Doblado, were exhumed at Guanajuató, and laid in state in the College building in great pomp, before being taken to Mexico to be interred in the Pantheon, as the Nation's honored dead. He had aided in carrying out the orders for the secularization of the real estate of the Church, and of course was excommunicated. The Church refused to allow his remains to lie in the Cathedral or any of the minor Church buildings, but the people attended the ceremonies all the same, and the funeral cortege, as it moved through the streets on its way to Mexico, presented a spectacle impressive and suggestive to the last degree.

There was not much else to see in Salamanca, and we drove on towards Celaya, through a valley at least twenty miles broad, and almost an unbroken corn-field. In one field we counted thirty-four ploughs drawn by oxen, at work at once, and in another, quite as many. We saw many orange-orchards around the little villages, and at one hacienda a very extensive olive plantation in full bearing. The soil is in many places six to ten feet in depth, clear black loam like that of the prairies, and exceedingly rich.

It is singular how little wild game you see here. After leaving Santa Anna Acatlan, near Seyula for the south-west of Guadalajara, we saw nothing in that line save a few sand-hill cranes, pied cranes, and two species of doves—the common "mourning dove" or "turtle dove" of the West, and a little fellow with mottled silver-gray plumage, and pink and yellow under the wings like a "yellow-hammer"—a very pretty creature. It is true that the inhabitants can occasionally indulge in a snap-shot or two at a brigand band, but this must be a poor substitute, after all, for the manly sports of the field, such as we enjoy in most parts of the United States.

We reached Celaya soon after noon. This city contains at this time not more than nineteen thousand inhabitants, and, yet, has twelve churches, four of which are immense. We visited several of these, in succession, and found them much alike; and all built of solid stone and in magnificent proportions.

In one of them I saw a case containing three hundred and sixty-five relics of Saints and Martyrs, pieces of the true Cross, the Manger in which Christ was born, the column at which he was scourged, the Holy Sepulchre, etc., etc., if there has been no mistake in the record, and I have no reason to suppose that there has been any.

While coming out from one of the churches we heard a steam-whistle sound, for the first time in Mexico, and went to a large woolen-factory from which the whistle was calling to the workmen. This establishment employs six hundred men and women and young boys, and supports half the town. The wool used is all of the coarse, common article, costing twelve cents per pound, raised in the country, and all the dyewoods come from the vicinity of Guadalajara. The master-dyer gets seventy dollars per week, and the common hands from two dollars for the boys, to three and four dollars for the women and men. Most of the employes are men, and among them are thirty officers of the Imperial Army of the late General Mejia, who appear to find woolen-spinning and weaving a better paying business than fighting, in the nineteenth century, in the vain effort to found new empires when old ones are crumbling and tottering to their fall. During the war in the United States the factory made immense profits; cargo after cargo of coarse woolen goods being smuggled into the Southern Confederacy and sold. Only one cargo worth sixty thousand dollars, was seized and confiscated, and the owner could well afford the loss. The goods made are common *serapes*, worth two to five dollars each, blankets, and stout, striped cassimeres of all colors, of which last, a pattern for a pair of pantaloons is sold at two or three dollars. The machinery is from the United States. The building and machinery cost four hundred thousand dollars, and the business employs an active capital of five hundred thousand more, and is very profitable. The principal owner, Señor Carosse, is a native of the Basque Provinces, and one of the richest men in Mexico. He came here without a dollar thirty years ago, and now counts his wealth by thousands.

The City of Celaya is now supplied with pure water, of blood heat, from an artesian well four hundred feet in depth, sunk at his own expense by Col. Saria. This well throws out ten jets, of one inch each, and the water is free to all. I can testify that a bath in it is among the luxuries of the world. For his liberality and public spirit in this matter, Col. Saria was thanked by a resolution of the State Congress of Guanajuato, signed by every member. Opposite the enclosure in which this magnificent well is situated, in the center of a handsome plaza with orange trees in full bearing and a thousand beautiful flowers, is a large fountain, and a tall and exceedingly graceful column, surmounted with the arms of Mexico, boldly sculptured and painted in the proper colors. This was erected in the year 1822, in commemoration of Mexican Independence.

Twenty-four miles from Celaya, is a town called Salvatierra, which is said to be the most prosperous one in Mexico. There is unlimited water-power in that place. In the district of Guanajuato, within a circuit of fifteen miles, there is estimated to be, at this time, forty million dollars worth of silver ore, which will yield twenty-five dollars to the ton; but owing to the expense of reducing it there, it will not pay for working at all, and is now lying valueless on the surface of the ground.

A railroad of about one hundred miles, through a wonderfully rich valley, offering no engineering obstacles of any moment, would connect the two cities, and enable the builder to bag $20,000,000 in profits on this ore already out; to say nothing of the future. With water power unlimited, and American stamp-mills, enormous profits could be made by working this ore. The Jaurez Administration will grant no more franchises, for railroads to be hawked about by speculators; but if anybody in the United States, or Europe, desires to build a railroad in good faith, here is a chance to do it, and win fame and fortune. The people are extremely anxious to have some one take hold of the enterprise.

We left Celaya early on the 10th of December, and drove at a rattling pace, over a road which was then being re-turnpiked and placed in perfect repair, a distance of about twelve leagues, or thirty English miles, to Queretaro. Our road took us through a broad and beautiful valley, filled with little towns—nobody thinks of living alone in this country, but all the people crowd into towns for self-protection—and covered with ripe corn and green wheat-fields.

One of these haciendas which we passed was beautiful, indeed. The rancho contains some fifty thousand acres. It is in the highest state of cultivation, and is valued by its owner, Justo L. Carresse, at $300,000 in gold. His wheat crop from this rancho, and a smaller one which we passed, is worth annually, fifty thousand dollars, and he also produces twenty thousand sacks of Indian corn of fine quality.

The laborers get only twenty-five or thirty-seven and a half cents per day, own no land, have no vested interest anywhere, and are half-clad in ragged cotton goods, and eat *calabossas* and *tortillas* and *frijoles* the year round. Were they born to be merely hewers of wood and drawers of water to the end of time? Is that all which is in store for them? What Spanish despotism, peon slavery, and religious superstition begun, poverty and civil war have perpetuated; and they are still but little advanced beyond the old state of slavery. They stand, hat in hand, in the blazing sun, so long as you are addressing them, and appear, on all occasions, to be thoroughly respectful, orderly, patient, and good dispositioned, though their poverty is something painful to behold. There is money enough sunk in the twelve great churches of Celaya—three would hold all the population—to build railroads through all this great valley, and decent houses for every family, and clothe and educate every child in the State; and these poor, patient, people and their ancestors paid it all.

Some day, not far distant, will, I hope, see these people becoming small land-owners, and fully informed of the rights with which the Republic has invested them;

and it will be well, for all, if they acquire the knowledge gradually, instead of being taught it, and errors with it, suddenly, by some loud-mouthed demagogue, who may incite them into inaugurating a new reign of disorder and terror.

In justice to the Republic and State authorities, I must say, that they do all in their power to educate the youth, and ameliorate the condition of the people; but while the million poor are so very, very poor, and the few rich are so very, very rich; commerce depressed, public improvements few, and the Government impoverished by foreign and domestic war, and its long struggle with the church, progress is necessarily very slow indeed: nevertheless there is progress. A better time will come; but will it be in our day and generation?

We met and passed many country people, going to market, with great wicker baskets of *camotes*, fruit, sweet-potatoes, etc., etc., on their backs, and many of them were braiding palm-leaf hats as they trotted rapidly along, bending beneath their heavy burdens, in the full blaze of the tropical sun. It is useless to say that these people are idle and dissolute from nature, and will not work. They will work all the year round if the work is offered them, and fairly kiss the hand that gives it to them. A railroad across the Continent, by the route we followed from Manzanillo, would put an end, forever, to revolutions and civil wars—I think the end is almost reached already—enrich the whole country and the road-owners at the same time, and confer on humanity a boon, greater than all the bequests of the philanthropic Peabody.

Some fifteen miles from Celaya, we entered the State of Queretaro, the towers of that historic city looming up grandly in the distance across the plain. Our road led through a wide avenue lined with immense pepper trees in full green foliage, contrasting vividly with the brilliant red berries which loaded down every bough.

All was quiet and peaceful as a New England Sabbath in the olden time. But three years since, this same tree-embowered road presented a far different scene. The usurping "Emperor" and his foreign mercenaries and domestic traitors, brought to bay, at last, and rendered desperate by the hopelessness of their position were making a sortie, for the purpose of cutting their way out towards Morelia and the Pacific Coast, when they saw, streaming down through the wide avenue, the victorious "Army of the West," under Ramon Corona, from Sinaloa, who, with wild yells rushed directly into the thickest of the fight, and closed the last avenue of escape to them forever.

CHAPTER IX.

QUERETARO.

WE had been told that we should find a revolution in full blast at Queretaro, and everything in confusion. Instead, we found every thing going on in clock work order, peace, apparent contentment, and comparative prosperity. The Governor, it is true, having quarreled with the Legislature or State Congress, had been impeached, and was then in the city of Mexico, awaiting trial before Congress; but the Gefe Politico, Señor Angel Dueñas, and other officers, were conducting business with regularity in his absence.

We found the City and State officials, ready with carriages at the gates to receive the party. The city contains forty thousand people, and though far less important, commercially, than it once was, is still reckoned a wealthy one. It has schools, churches, and historic localities enough to occupy one's attention for a week; but as we had only a day and a half to devote to it, we decided to spend the first half-day in visiting the great factory which, in fact, supports the town; then devote all the following day to the scenes of interest connected with the siege, and the capture and death of Maximilian.

We rode at once out of the City to the north-west, past a long aqueduct carried across the valley on high stone arches, the whole work having cost a million dollars. It was the work of a rich Mexican who offered, by way of a banter, to do it free of cost to Queretaro, if a friend of like wealth would build a saint and shrine of solid silver. The bantering offer was accepted, and both parties carried out their agreement. The city is still supplied with water through this aqueduct.

The first factory which we saw was the small one known as *La Purisiana Conception*—*i. e.* The Immaculate Conception—which is run by water, and employs only three hundred operatives. It is owned by Señor Don Cuyatano Rubio, an aged, and very wealthy and enterprising Mexican, whose sons carry on all his immense business. It stands in a beautifully arranged enclosure, with high walls, fountains, orange-trees, and flowers around it, and is guarded all the time by watchmen in full military uniform, armed and drilled in the best modern style. It is lighted with gas, and the fine machinery is of the most improved pattern. Only *manta* or common cotton-cloth, such as is used by the poorest class and the common people, is made at this factory.

We passed on to the next and largest factory, not only in Queretaro, but in Mexico. This is situated just outside the city limits, and is known as the "Hercules." This is one of the largest establishments of the kind in America, and is a model in its way. It was founded twenty-five years ago by Señor Rubio, who then employed fifty workmen. Since then he has added to the capacity of the works until he has now the largest establishment in Mexico, and his income from it is immense. The buildings, mostly of but one story, cover a large extent of ground, and are enclosed by a high wall and guarded by watch-men in uniform, armed and drilled as soldiers. The motive power is furnished by two double oscillating engines of English manufacture and one hundred horse-power each, and the largest over-shot water-wheel in the world, sixty-five feet in diameter, and of iron, wholly. The factory employs at present eighteen hundred men, women and boys, directly, and has eighteen thousand spindles in operation. The buildings are erected, already, for five thousand spindles more, and the number of operatives will be increased to three thousand. This mill produces six thousand pieces of common cotton goods, each thirty-two varas—say thirty yards English—in length, weekly. The women and men who do the weaving, receive thirty-one and one-fourth cents per piece, or about one cent per yard for their work, and are paid weekly. They earn two and one-half to five dollars per week, and are furnished with comfortable quarters near the factory at a nominal rental. But they work from 6 A. M. to 9 1-2 P. M., with only an intermission of half an hour, for breakfast, and an hour for dinner. Among the employes are many small boys from seven to ten years of age.

The Government provides a day-school on Sunday for these poor, little unfortunates; but what can they be expected to learn, when they have worked fifteen hours out of the twenty-four during the entire week, and can only have, at best, one brief day of liberty and enjoyment of the sunlight in seven? The buildings are all well-lighted and ventilated, and were as well-calculated for the purpose as any I have ever seen, and the office and residence of the superintendent are on a scale of extent and magnificence to be found in no similar establishment, elsewhere. The factory was working at the time, on orders largely in advance, and literally "coining money." The universal testimony of the employers in all these factories, is that the workmen and work-women are patient, laborious, and reliable; and that no better class of operatives could be procured in the world. A beautiful statue of Hercules and the lions, the latter spouting water, stands in the center of the court-yard, and the entire surroundings of the place give evidence of a cultivated taste, and unbounded wealth on the part of the proprietor.

Queretaro was once famous for the bigotry and fanaticism of its people. The appearance of the procession carrying the Host, on the public streets, was the signal for everybody in sight falling on his knees at once; and if any heretic dared to remain standing, or with his hat on, he was sure to receive violent handling even if he escaped with his life.

A few years since, an Englishman who was employed at one of the mills, chanced to be on the streets when the procession with the Host hove in sight. Not being posted on the customs of the country he remained standing until he was knocked down and nearly killed. Some time after, he heard a small bell ringing on the streets, and as this was the signal for the appearance of the Host, supposed it was time to kneel. Down he went on his knees and remained there with his face buried deep in his *sombrero* until somebody came along, and recognizing him, demanded an explanation of his conduct. It turned out that the bell which he had supposed headed the procession of the Host, was being rung by the official dustman, as a warning to the inhabitants to have their refuse dust and garbage ready for him to remove.

He was of course quickly on his feet upon making this discovery, but the joke on him was too good to be kept, and he was almost driven out of the country by the wags, who never tired of going after him, on the subject. The carrying of the Host through the streets of Mexican towns is no longer permitted, and the mistake is not likely to be ever repeated.

I believe all countries and all languages have the same stories, only slightly varied to suit the locality. A man told me in Queretaro, with all possible gravity, that a few years since, an American bought a rancho in the vicinity of that city, and took a large drove of mules to pasture for a year, for one-half of the increase As the mules did not breed as rapidly as he had anticipated, he lost money, and finally bursted up in business. This story has been told me in every country I have ever visited, at the expense of the next door neighbors, and I am half satisfied that, spite of the Mosaic account of the affair, the real cause or origin of the difficulty between Cain and Abel was the telling of this very anecdote by the former to the latter. Abel replied, "that is an old story, you had better start something fresh!" and the brutal row began.

On the evening of our arrival a number of gentlemen assembled at the parlor of the house occupied by Mr. Seward and party, and Señor Angel Dueñas, Political Chief, made an address, to which Mr. Seward replied, briefly; and on his leaving, presented him with a letter of thanks for the address and the efforts made by the people of Queretaro and the authorities, to make his stay in the state and city, a pleasant one.

Señor Manuel Gomez then advanced and pronounced a "felicitation", to which Mr. Seward replied in writing, as follows:

"SEÑOR GOMEZ: I pray you, my dear sir, to accept in this form my grateful acknowledgment for the generous words of welcome, which on my arrival at this place you addressed to me, on behalf of the officers and agents of the Federal Government residing in the city of Queretaro. Repulicanism on this continent, my dear sir, is not the cause of the United States of America, or of the United States of Mexico, only, but it is the common cause of both countries, and, as I believe, of all the nations which now exist on the American Continent. It will be a happy consequence of my present travel in Mexico, if it shall enable me, in any degree, to cultivate and mature this sentiment, either in your interesting country, or in my own".

The legislature of the state of Queretaro, presented by one of its members, an address of welcome, of which the following is a translation:

The Legislature of the State has the honor to felicitate Mr. W. H. Seward, giving him the welcome. It is the true interpreter of the people of Queretaro with regard to the expressions of its gratitude. Meanwhile, history does not efface off its pages the unjustified invasion of France in Mexico; likewise, will not be effaced the important services which Mexico received of the Hon. Minister of America, in 1866.

Queretaro, Nov. 11th 1869.

(Signed,) B. GANDARILLA,
President.

In reply Mr. Seward wrote a letter, concluding:

"The Legislature will scarcely need to be assured that I appreciate the legendary and historical character of the state of Queretaro. While its capital will be forever celebrated, as the scene of the earliest and most pious labors of the humble founders of Christianity in Mexico, it will be even more distinguished, as the scene of those mighty events, which concluded the last and most desperate attempt of all, to establish European monarchial domination on the American Continent. Peace, harmony, and sympathy among the several American Nations, is now the common interest of all of them, and it is soon to be perceived that it is equally the interest of all mankind. With most profound respect, etc."

A similar reply was addressed by Mr. Seward, to a letter of welcome from Governor Varquez, which closed the felicitations.

We spent all one day riding around Queretaro, visiting the scenes of the last act in the bloody farce of the "Empire of Mexico," and hearing the story from the lips of men who witnessed it all, and participated in it, or were familiar with all the details.

It is the common belief in the United States and Europe, that the execution of Maximilian and his associates, Miramon and Mejia, was in defiance of the will of the majority of the people of Mexico, and that Maximilian's memory is greatly revered by all classes of society. Certain newspaper correspondents, whose motives may well be questioned, have represented that every relic and trace of him, is regarded with superstitious reverence by the people of Mexico; and that the men who sent him to his death, are everywhere dedetested and abhorred. I could see no trace of such a feeling, and must be allowed to express a personal unbelief of the whole story. Imperialists, belonging to the wealthy and, former, "ruling classes," who might be expected to speak reverentially of him, so far as my observation, at least, goes, all hold his memory in contempt, and regard him as the author, not only of his own misfortunes, but of those who adhered to his cause. They often say of him that he was, personally, a gentleman, in his carriage and demeanor, but vain to the last degree, cold-blooded, fond of idle pomp and show, and devoid of all the qualities of heart and head to fit him for personal popularity, and enable him to succeed in such an enterprise as founding an empire on the ruins of a republic.

Queretaro is situated on the north-eastern edge of a wide plain, around which, on the north-east, north, and west, runs a range of low hills commanding the city. In April, and the early part of May, 1867, the position of the contending armies was about as follows: Gen. Escobedo, the Commander-in-Chief of the Republican forces, had his head-quarters on the heights east of the city, and held undisturbed possession of the north-east and south-east, and debated with the Imperialists the possession of the lower part of the city nearest his head-quarters. The Imperialists held the west, south-west, and south-east, and the main portion of the city; while Gen. Corona on the south, and Regules and the American Legion on the west, hemmed them in, and prevented their escape toward the Pacific.

The old Convent and Church of Las Cruces, is an immense structure, with walls of great strength, and is situated on a hill sufficiently high to command the city, but is commanded in turn by the heights beyond the town occupied by General Escobedo. The Alameda is on low ground, overlooked by the heights occupied by Corona, but is surrounded by a stout, stone wall, and was well defended by artillery and the Casa Blanca. Between it and the Cerro de Las Campanas is an old hacienda, with immense walls, invulnerable to everything but the fire of the heaviest ordnance. From Las Cruces to the Cerro, in a direct line, is a mile and a half, and the line of defences was nearly two miles—twice too long for the force that held it, or rather, tried to hold it.

The story of the siege of Queretaro and the deeds of daring on both sides is now tolerably familiar to the reading public. Maximilian sent out Miramon with the flower of his army to attack, and if possible, capture Juarez at Zacatecas. He captured the city, Juarez barely escaping, but next day was attacked and routed by Escobedo, and on the following day, having retreated thirty miles and united his forces to those of Castillo, was again overtaken and routed completely, by Escobedo, his whole army being killed or dispersed, and himself escaping wounded, and with but a handful of men remaining.

On the fourteenth of April, Corona made a daring and desperate attack upon the strong-hold of Las Cruces, and scaling the high walls of the cemetery on the north-east side, occupied a position under the very walls of the Convent for an hour, but was driven out at last by the besieged, after a hand-to-hand conflict. Later in the siege, Corona, while resting his forces in the plain, in the rear of the Casa Blanca, was surprised in the early morning by the forces under Miramon, who marched under the cover of the night from the Casa Blanca to the Alameda, and suddenly flanking his position, routed him, and compelled him to retreat to the hills, a few hundred yards in the rear. This, however, gained him no permanent advantage, and he was in turn flanked by Escobedo, and compelled to retire within the intrenchments.

The sortie made with a view of escaping to Morelia, had been made by Maximilian's forces previous to this surprise of Corona, and had failed. Now for the final catastrophe. The story, I heard from one of the officers of the court-martial which condemned Maximilian, Miramon, and Mejia to death; and from other parties who were eye-witnesses, some of whom evidently sympathized with the Imperialists.

On the night of the 14th of May, 1867, the Imperialists were defeated at all points; exhausted and dispirited. They had lived on mule-meat and bean-bread for weeks, and even that was gone. Maximilian, despairing, at last, of assistance from abroad, saw that all was lost, and at 11 P. M. he sent Lopez, who was then the "officer of the day," to the head-quarters of General Escobedo, with instructions, to say to him, that he proposed to take fifty picked horsemen, escape across the Sierra Gordo to Tampico or Tuxpan, and embark for Europe, leaving the place to surrender at once, if his own life was guaranteed him. Escobedo repelled the proposition with contempt, telling Lopez that he had strict orders to refuse all terms to Maximilian, as an outlaw, and violator of the laws of war, and that he would carry the city by assault at the next attempt. Lopez returned to Maximilian, told him of his utter want of success, and then returned to the advanced post occupied by him, just below Las Cruces, on the north-western side, and in the outskirts of Queretaro.

Escobedo, reasoning that the proposition could only come from a man in the last extremity, at once called a council of war, and the general assault which had been previously ordered for the following day at 8 A. M., was directed to be made immediately. The Republican troops reached the out-post held byLopez in front of Las Cruces at 4 A. M., and as soon as Lopez saw them, he told his men that further resistance was useless. Some say, that he said that the Republicans were deserters who came to join the Imperialists, but this is denied by Lopez and his friends. At any rate, he ran directly to the head-quarters of Maximilian at La Cruces, told him all was lost, and urged him to fly to Las Campanas, and escape if he could. Maximilian, who appeared to have completely lost his senses, ran down from his room in the second story of the convent to the basement, and demanded his horses, but was told that the Republicans already had possession of the stables. He then ran out toward the north, but was caught by the shoulder, by an officer who pushed him back, telling him that he was running directly into the jaws of death. He then ran on foot through Queretaro in a south-westerly direction toward the Cerro de Las Campanas. On his way through the city he was seen in uniform by some of the soldiers of the regiment of Col. Rincon of the Republican forces, who had already made their way to the heart of the city. They cried out to stay him, but Col. Rincon, either because he did not recognize him, or because his father had been under great obligations to Maximilian, replied, "No; he is only a private citizen, and a countryman of ours; let him go!" He then ran on to Las Campanas uninterrupted, and, demanding horses, was told that it was useless, as all the country in front was already occupied by General Regules.

Thus cut off, and surrounded at all points, he took a white flag in his hand, and started down the slope of one hundred feet toward the city, and before reaching the bottom met Col. Geo. M. Green, the accomplished officer in command of the American Legion of Honor from San Francisco, whom he recognized. Shots had by this time been fired at Maximilian, repeatedly, by the advancing Republicans, and he was in a pitiable condition; exhausted, disheartened, and with his great, weak lips trembling so that he could hardly command his speech, he asked Col. Green not to let him fall into the hands of General Escobedo, of whom he stood in mortal terror, but to point out General Corona and allow him to surrender to him. Col. Green said to him:

"Calm yourself; the Emperor of Austria has sent a commission to ask the American Government to intercede for your life!"

Maximilian apparently greatly relieved by the information, replied:

"And my brother has done this?"

By this time—all had passed in a few seconds—General Corona had reached the spot, and going straight up to him, Maximilian said:

"I am Maximilian, Emperor of Mexico." (drawing his sword and presenting it;) "I am the Emperor no longer, but a Mexican citizen, and your prisoner?"

Corona replied:

"No, Maximilian, you are not now Emperor, and never were!"

He then motioned to a subordinate to receive his sword, refusing himself to accept it, or make any terms of surrender, and referring him, altogether, to General Escobedo, his superior in command. Lopez now ordered the Austrians and others in his command, to disarm, and the work was complete.

The story that Lopez sold out to Escobedo for seventy thousand dollars, in coin, is in a measure rebutted by the facts that the Republicans had not a dollar to pay him; that he has not been known to have a dollar since; and that there was no need of such a bribe, as all chance for successful resistance was gone, and the

Republicans already, had the city, practically, in their power; the City of Mexico was certain to fall, for it could not be defended long by the forces within it. There was no point on the continent from which succor could possibly come. It is a fact against him, that he was not imprisoned, for a time, like his brother officers; but may not that be explained on the hypothesis, that although detested (as were all those who had gone over to the Empire,) by the Republicans, they still felt that he was entitled to some consideration for having stopped the effusion of blood, when the proper time arrived, and it was just and proper that he should do so. Strict military disciplinarians might urge that his duty was to have died at his post; not to presume to judge of the exigencies of a situation when his superior officer was in command, and on the ground; but civilians will ask, to what good would such self-sacrifice conduce, and it will be hard to answer. I do not propose to offer an apology for a man whose former life had been regarded infamous by his most intimate acquaintances; but something is due to the truth of history; and it really seems to me, from all the evidence which I gathered at the time, and that which I found on the spot, that Maximilian was not betrayed by Lopez; and that he (Maximilian). on the other hand, did, on the night of the 14th of May, offer to abandon his companions to their fate, and escape, personally, to the coast of the Gulf of Mexico, and from thence to Europe, is beyond a doubt.

We found the room occupied by Maximilian at Las Cruces, unroofed, and filled with rubbish, from a pile of which, small trees had grown up; from one of them, as much as twelve feet in height, I plucked a handful of flowers. Some one had written in bold letters, on the wall, with charcoal, "Mexico es Libre!" but I saw no other inscription. In the rooms below, all was just as it was when the imperial horses were taken out, after the fall. We went up and stood in the bell-tower in which Maximilian stood when a cannon-ball from Escobedo's batteries cut down his aid by his side. All the buildings around the Convent were tenantless, roofless, and in ruins, having been dismantled by the Imperialists, or leveled by the Republican batteries, and never repaired.

From Las Campañas, Maximilian, with Miramon, Mejia, Prince Salm Salm, and others, was taken back to the city and imprisoned for six or seven days in the old Convent of Theresite. From thence he, with Miramon and Mejia, went to the old monastery of Los Capuchinos, and there they remained under guard (while the court-martial decided their case) until the 19th of June, thirty-four days after their capture, when they went out to die. Maximilian persisted until the last hour in the belief that the barefooted and ragged Republicans of Mexico would not dare to shoot a Prince of the house of Hapsburg-Lorraine, and one of the "Lord's Anointed." But they did!

When at Los Capuchinos, I was shown by a friend who accompanied me, the window at which Maximilian was looking out, when he visited the place during the pseudo Emperor's confinement after the court-martial had sentenced him to death. It faces the *patio*, and in the room adjoining, on the other angle, Miramon and Mejia were confined. By looking diagonally across the corner of this *patio*, they could see each other when standing at their windows. When my friend entered they were conversing. Miramon called out to Maximilian:

"Emperor: I beg you to prepare for death; I tell you that they will certainly shoot us!"

Maximilian replied confidently:

"No, they dare not do it: they may shoot you possibly, but Don Benito will not let me be killed. He will send me either to the United States or to Europe!"

Miramon shrugged his shoulders and replied:

"I assure you that you are deceiving yourself; they will certainly shoot us all!"

In Maximilian's room I saw a hole in the floor where the pavement had been taken up, as if to effect an escape into the room below; but could not learn whether this was made during the time that he was there confined or subsequently.

In company with Señor Dueñas, I rode out to see the spot where the three met their death. On the northeastern slope of the low, rocky hill-side, facing the city, a rude barrier of adobes had been thrown up to stop the bullets, and here the carriage halted. Gen. Escobedo, with a motion of the hand, directed Maximilian to come down. The puppet Emperor, unaccustomed to such treatment from those he regarded as the dust of the earth, gave him a look of doubt which finally changed to a scowl, descended hesitatingly, and walked mechanically toward the summit of the hill. Miramon arrived next, and, seeing that Maximilian was going wrong, called him back. They stood at first with Maximilian in the center, but the position was changed, and when the troops drew up on the hill below to fire upon them, Maximilian stood on the west, Miramon next, and Mejia on the east. Maximilian, from a repugnance to touching the hands of common men, had contracted the habit in Mexico of standing with his hands behind him, and in this position he stood, and said something inaudible to the spectators, to Mejia and to Miramon. Then he commenced a bitter, rambling, and incoherent speech to Escobedo—not the words, at all, which have since been put in his mouth—about being willing to die for the good of Mexico, but was stopped and told to face the muskets. Mejia stood with his arms folded, Miramon holding his written defense; and

THE EXECUTION OF MAXIMILIAN.

Maximilian with a cross elevated in his right hand, when the sharp crash of the volley came, and all three rolled upon the ground. Mejia and Miramon died instantly, but Maximilian repeatedly clapped his hand on his head as if in agony, and expired with a struggle, as the echoes of the muskets died away among the cañons of the distant Sierra.

Died away did I say? No; not there, nor then! Those echoes rolled across the broad Atlantic and shook every throne in Europe. The royal plotter against the liberties of men heard them in his palace by the Seine, and grew pale as he listened. They rolled over the Pyrenees, and the throne of Isabella began to crumble; over the Alps, and every monarch from Italy to the farthest East heard in them the rumblings of the coming earthquake—the prelude of the fall of empires. They will roll on, and on, through the coming ages, and be answered by the uprising millions of future generations, until "Kingly Prerogatives" and "Divine Right" are things of the past. The world had waited long for these echoes, and was better when it heard them at last.

The ground, which but a few short months ago was torn by cannon-shot, trampled by contending armies, and drenched with the blood of Europe and America, is now covered with corn-fields; and three plain, wooden crosses, painted black, without inscription of any kind, and mounted on a rude pile of stones, alone mark the spot whereon was enacted the last scene of one of the most tremendous dramas of our time.

The laborers were engaged in gathering the corn, when our carriages drove up, and they stopped a moment and looked on with silent interest, as Mr. Seward stood beside the rude mound, while the uncle of Miramon told the story of the execution, and the two sisters of the most ambitious, bigoted and unscrupulous of Mexico's celebraties, clad in black, stood weeping silently behind them. Some there may be, who will think that

I am hardly human, in my want of sympathy for the men who expiated their crimes against liberty and the rights of men, at the Cerro de Las Campanas; but let them see the widows and orphans, the ruined towns, depopulated districts, poverty, misery and woe, which they brought upon this lovely land, as I have seen them, and then sympathise with dead royalty and its supporters if they can. I have as much sympathy for human misery as any man living, but it is with the innocent victims of this crime against all that is holy,—the starving, poor and helpless,—that I sympathize; not with those who staked their all on the dice,—trusting to gain the wages of crime, be worshiped for their success, and feared for their power,—lost, and paid the penalty. I would have doubted the justice of God, had Maximilian lived, and the thousands of brave men whom he sent to death through his black flag decree slept unavenged in their bloody graves. I have stood on the Cerro de Las Campanas, and I know that God is just!

> "The mills of the Gods grind slowly,
> But they grind exceeding small."

They never ground a grist finer than that which Napoleon III. sent to their mill, marked "Empire of Mexico."

THE END OF THE EMPIRE.

CHAPTER X.

FROM QUERETARO TO MEXICO.

WE left Queretaro early on the morning of Nov. 12th, and, passing through the battle-field of El Cemetario, around La Cruces, and San Francisquito, with their loop-holed and shattered walls, ruined outworks, and surrounding hamlets, deserted and desolate, ascended a long hill, from the summit of which, we obtained a glorious view of the white-walled city and the lovely valley around it. Our road led us, nearly all day, through a very broad and rich valley, covered with corn-fields stretching out to the very horizon, well cultivated and very productive. The haciendas of the proprietors of these vast estates, each a strong-walled fortress surrounded by the hovels of the laborers like ancient feudal castles, formed a very picturesque feature of the scene.

At 2 P. M., we had made forty-two Mexican miles, and reached the fine old Mexican town of San Juan del Rio, where we were received and entertained in the most hospitable manner, by Señor Don Antonio Diaz y Torres and his amiable and accomplished wife, at their beautiful city residence. The municipal authorities welcomed Mr. Seward with addresses and music, and Señor Don Ramon de Ybarrola, a young civil engineer, proprietor of the great estate of Galindo, in the vicinity, made a brief "felicitation" in English.

The town has numerous churches and old convent buildings—the latter now confiscated and converted into public schools—but not much else worth seeing. The population numbers ten thousand.

Next day, the 13th of Nov., we drove the same distance over a wide, prairie-like, uncultivated plain, and a lava-field of twenty miles in width, the road through which was fearfully rough. This old lava underlies the soil—the rich, black loam, of the country—at a depth of three to six feet, for many square leagues. We had been passing over such beds, or "flows," from time to time, on all the journey from Colima. Where so much of this material could have come from, is a mystery, at this day.

We were now at an elevation of forty-five hundred feet above the sea, and steadily ascending. Here, the American Aloe, Maguey, Century, Mescal, or Pulque plant, as it is termed in different localities, grows to an immense size—much larger than in the *tierre caliente*—and is planted out in regular order, in extensive fields, all along the road. Many of the plants were sending out their blossom stalks, ten to twenty feet in height, looking, for all the world, like telegraph poles at a distance, and like gigantic asparagus sprouts when near at hand; and a few were bursting into blossom. This is the "Century plant," which, Northern people have so long believed blooms but once in a hundred years, but, which matures here, in from five to ten years. It blooms but once, the stalk being cut out to form a reservoir for the milky sap which accumulates therein, and is drawn out to be converted into *pulque* and *mescal.* From each old plant, five or six "suckers"—each of which will produce a new plant—spring up, and are cut off and planted separately to keep the plantation good. The plant requires but little cultivation, and costs, on an average, about fifty cents from first to last. Each plant yields about a barrel of pulque, and a large amount of fibre for ropes and matting, and is worth, altogether, about five dollars. The owner of a plantation of one hundred thousand magueys considers himself worth five hundred thousand dollars.

At night we stopped at a fonda at Arroyo Zarco, a large old hacienda, rich in pictures of great age and merit, and other curious things. The owner long since abandoned it as a residence, on account of the state of the of the country, moving his family for safety and comfort to the city of Mexico.

As the Governor of Queretaro, who had started for the capital on three hours notice, to stand his trial before Congress, had been stopped and robbed, just outside the gates of Mexico, in the week previous to our arrival, it was not deemed prudent for us to go over the road alone. The authorities, accordingly, furnished us with a detachment of regular cavalry, and from village to village we were further escorted by detachments of the rural guard, a very well mounted, and reliable body of men, armed with the Maynard rifle, revolvers, and sabres. These rural guards furnish themselves with everything, pay all their own expenses, and receive one dollar each per day from the municipalities.

Next day, Nov. 14th, we rode forty-five miles—Spanish—over the roughest kind of a road, soft lime-rock and lava, mixed in about equal proportions, through a country mostly unfitted for cultivation, and inhabited only by a few poor people, scattered at wide intervals. We staid at night at Tepeji del Rio, at the residence of

16

Mr. Archibald Hope, an Englishman forty-five years resident in Mexico, who is erecting a cotton and woolen factory and flour-mill, at this point, which were to be ready for operation in a few days. This mill is furnished with the best of machinery from England and the United States, and will employ three hundred workmen, and is in all its departments, one of the most complete in Mexico.

Wood is sold every where in Central Mexico, by the *arroba* of twenty-five pounds weight. Here it costs only five or six cents per *arroba;* at Celaya it costs seven to eight cents, and at Queretaro ten cents. As we approach the Capital and ascend to greater altitude, the country become less well-wooded, the hills—save in a few places—are bare of trees, and only on the highest mountains could we see any large timber. The oak—of a species resembling the live oak of California—fresno, willow, water-beech and mesquite are the principal trees to be seen.

The *nopal*, or prickly pear, grows in great luxuriance, and the maguey increases in size and value, but the peculiar vegetation of the tropics has mainly disappeared. The nights at this time were cool, though there was no frost, and the thermometer during the day stood at sixty to seventy degrees.

We left Tepeji del Rio, early on the 15th of Nov., for our last days' ride towards Mexico. For thirty-eight days we had been "swinging around a circle," as it were, having advanced northward from Manzanillo to Guadalajara, thence eastward to Guanajuato, thence southeasterly and south to Queretaro and Mexico, traveling in all a distance of about eight hundred Spanish miles, and halting some days at each of the principal cities.

THE BLIND MEXICAN AND HIS DAUGHTER.

During all this time we had heard not a word from home, and knew nothing of the passing events in the United States; as a matter of course, we were anxious enough to finish our journey and be once more in communication with the outside world.

As we were passing along the road I observed an incident which my readers may think hardly worth recording, but which struck me at the moment as very affecting. In a narrow part of the road we met a little Indian girl of perhaps twelve years, carrying a large basket filled with some country produce upon her back, and guiding her father at the same time. The father was old and blind, but still strong, and carried a heavy burden, likewise, on his shoulders. To guide himself he kept one hand resting lightly upon the basket carried by his daughter, and when our coach came suddenly upon them, and she sprang out of the track to give it room, he followed, keeping exact pace with her, evidently, reposing in perfect confidence upon her judgment and discretion. Something which she may have said in an undertone, or more probably her start of surprise and attitude of attention, led him to think that there was something unusual in the spectacle presented to her eyes, and with a blind man's instinct he laid his other hand gently and with a loving caress against her cheek, as if he sought to divine her thoughts from the changes which passed over her features, as fear, wonder, or animated curiosity affected them. Of all the scenes which I witnessed in Mexico, grand, beautiful, or painful, none impressed itself more vividly on my memory than that of this timid, shrinking child, bearing life's burden in all its fullness thus prematurely, and her blind old father, bending beneath the load of years and poverty, standing there by the dusty roadside, on the lonely highway, in such attitude as could not fail to strike the eye of the painter or the poet—I am neither—on the instant; a picture unpainted, a poem unwritten, but a picture and a poem filled with tender sentiment and touching pathos, nevertheless.

After a ride of ten miles, over a rough, hard mountain road, through a poor, barren country, we emerged at last, upon the summit of a divide, and looked down for the first time upon the valley of Mexico.

The day was bright and beautiful. Lake Zupango lay off to our left, on the south-eastward, and beyond it the little city of that name, with its tall old church tower peeping out from among the embowering trees. The valley immediately before us was broken up with small hills which interrupted the view, somewhat, at first. Numerous small lakes, natural or artificially formed for irrigating purposes, were scattered here and there among the hills, and on the right, on the left, and all around, were little hamlets, often half in ruins, with dilapidated old stone churches and abandoned convents and monasteries, in endless profusion. The valley grows richer as you advance towards the Capital. The vegetation is more luxuriant—and the villages larger and more thrifty in appearance. The corn-fields on either side of the road were large, and the ripe crop heavy, and the maguey plantations grew more extensive at every mile. The road is bordered with tall trees—beeches, willows, fresnos, and pepper trees, in full bearing. At the little towns we noticed the potteries at which the delicate, red earthenware of Mexico is made and kept for sale, and numerous "*pulqueries*," with the *pulque*-drinkers standing around them leaning against the walls in a state of stupid intoxication, with an expression of utter vacuity or idiocy upon their faces.

The liquor is exposed to the sun in the skins of pigs, sheep, and goats, denuded of the hair and bristles, which appear to have been taken off whole. After much diligent inquiry, Mr. Fitch elicited the statement, that the

MANEUVERING FOR A PIG-SKIN.

skins are taken off by allowing the pigs to fast twenty four hours, then tying them by their tails to posts, and coaxing them out of their coverings by holding ears of corn just in front of their noses.

The statement went down in his book, at once, and was added, unhesitatingly, to the, already, large stock of useless knowledge he had accumulated on the trip. The fact is that the animal is beaten with a club until all the bones are smashed, and the flesh reduced to a pulp, and the mass is then drawn out, little by little, at the neck.

Walking on down the road in advance, as the coach was ascending a hill, I saw an officer riding toward me, and was so startled by a resemblance to an American friend whom I left in White Pine Mining District, Nevada, that I accosted him at once. To my great relief and surprise, as well, I found that he could not speak a word of English. There was a slightly unpleasant episode recalled to my mind by that resemblance. When the rush, in mid-winter, into the airy and inclement mountain region of White-Pine, was at its height, a party had gathered one cold, stormy night in our cabin on the summit of Treasure Mountain, and was whiling away the hours—in the absence of theaters, churches, lecture-rooms, and choice female society,—imbibing hot fluids, and filling in the odd minutes at the elevating and ennobling occupation of playing draw-poker. (I would here observe that draw-poker is played with five cards, dealt, one at a time, all around—not two first and three next, as in *euchre.* I make this explanation as a matter of necessity, the second and third propositions having been advanced in my hearing not long since, by no less an authority, than an United States Minister, who, in spite of his professed knowledge of the game, has been known to lay down two large pairs, when his opponent, who only held ace high, raised him with six hundred dollars already on the board. I make this explanation in the interest of the heirs of Hoyle—not that I care anything about it myself.)

Among the party were two of the tallest men in the camp—Messrs. Downton and Gerry—who had been introduced to each other for the first time that evening.

As the night advanced, their conversation became more and more affectionate and affectingly personal. Each was over six feet in his stockings, each blue-eyed, light-haired, a little inclined to stoop in the shoulders, and possessed of a decidedly camel-like hump, or protuberance on the bridge of the nose, and a very considerable deflection of that organ from the line of the perpendicular. These facts had not attracted the attention of the rest of the party to any considerable extent; but as the drinking and playing went on, the worthies noticed them of themselves, and commented upon them freely. The more they thought of it and talked about it, the more thoroughly they became convinced that the resemblance was something more than accidental, and that in some mysterious and undefined way, they must be blood-relations of a very near degree of kindred.

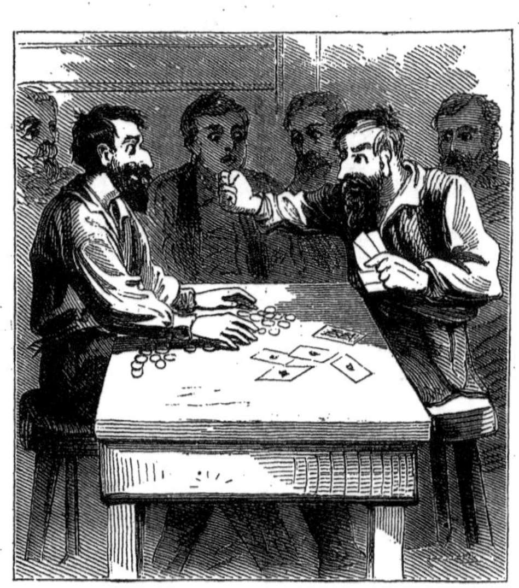

A FAMILY RESEMBLANCE.

So they went on, drinking and complimenting each other on their mutual good looks and family resemblance, and by a curious fatality, winning, between them, all the money from the other parties around the board. The losing members of the distinguished company bore this until it became considerable of a bore, and it grew evident that if the game went on in that way all night, most of them would be ruined past the hope of redemption. It is beautiful to see brethren dwelling together in unity, but when you have to stand the expense, and make them happy out of your own pocket, the spectacle loses much of its attraction; at least, so thought the others present that night. At length, Joe Ackerson got the deal, and there were some heavy hands out, apparently, judging from the way different parties invested their beans. Downton had gone a "blind;" and Gerry saw it and raised it. Downton made the blind good and raised *him*; then Gerry saw it and raised *him*; and so it went on until each had his entire pile on the table, and all the other players had drawn out, and were looking on, except Joe Ackerson, who had announced himself as having had chicken-pie enough, and retired to his luxurious bunk, drawn the drapery of his couch—San Francisco eight pound woolen blankets—around him, and to appearance, at least, laid down to pleasant dreams.

They came to a call at last, and showed their hands. Gerry threw down four kings triumphantly, and reached forward to rake down the coin; but Downton gently repulsed him, and laying four aces before his astonished eyes, pulled it all over to his side of the table, and commenced counting it into twenty dollar heaps, preparatory to stowing it in his pockets and handkerchief. It was perfectly astonishing how quickly these two affectionate and gushing brothers forgot their probable relationship, on which they had doated so much a few minutes before, and went into criminations and recriminations, and from that to belligerent demonstrations.

Business reverses will sour any man's disposition, and I have known the peace of many a happy and devoted family irretrievably wrecked by an unfortunate commercial venture, or an investment in stocks on a falling market.

Luckily, neither of them had their revolvers within reach at the moment, but they made a general average on the chairs and furniture—all the property of others as it happened—and when the company separated them, we—the owners of the property destroyed—were temporarily ruined, and they went their way, vowing undying hatred of each other to the end of their days.

Since that moment I have had a horror of meeting people who resemble each other, and it was an infinite relief to me when I found that this man whom I met on the road, and my friend in White Pine, were of different nationalities, and not likely to greet each other as natural brothers, should they ever come together.

Ten miles ride in the valley took us out from among the broken hills, and the view became magnificent. The mountains along the eastern horizon, beyond the lakes of Mexico, lay like great purple clouds against the deep blue sky. Popocatapetl, monarch of them all, lifted his head, white with the snows of ages, majestic and awful in its grand proportions, far into the unclouded heavens in the distance. Truly, the beauty of the Valley of Mexico has not been overrated.

Ten miles from the City of Mexico, Señor Lerdo de Tejada, and Matias Romero, two of the most noted men of the Cabinet of President Juarez, and the United States Minister to Mexico, Mr. Nelson, were waiting with carriages and an escort of brilliantly uniformed cavalry, and the party left the coach in which we had traveled from Guadalajara, for the more luxurious method of conveyance. We passed to the left of Chapultepec and the Molino del Rey, and directly by the famous tree under which Hernando Cortez found shelter on the memorable *Noche Triste*, when his forces cut their way by night through the hosts of the infuriated Aztecs, piled up the dead to make a causeway on which to escape across the shallow laguna, and at last, sorely pressed, disheartened, and almost annihilated, escaped from the city. Then the glorious panorama of the great City of Mexico unrolled itself before us.

At the Garita de San Cosme, the stern, old champion of Republicanism, the man of many adventures and the most wonderful history and most varied fortunes, the man of the iron will and indomitable resolution which stand out on every feature, the man with the charmed life, who has escaped unscathed from more plots, conspiracies, and accidents, than any other man now living; the man who will live in history as one of the wonders of our age, the man sent by Providence to repel foreign invasion, crush and destroy the despotism of the church, free the peon, establish schools, suppress insurrections, deal the last blow at imperialism in America, and rule a turbulent nation with a rod of iron, the Citizen President, Benito Juarez, stood waiting to receive the nation's guest. He was dressed in plain black, and had not even a liveried servant in attendance; his wife and daughter accompanied him. The brief, friendly greeting over, and the other members of our party having been introduced by Señor Bossero, the cavalcade resumed its way and entered the Capital City of the Republic.

Driving past the old Alameda de Montezuma, where

the last great King of the Aztecs used to walk beneath the trees at morning and evening, and the famous, gigantic equestrian statue of Charles the Fourth, in bronze, we went, directly, to the palace-like residence at the corner of the Castle de Alfaro and Arco de San Augustin, which had been expressly fitted up for the

INTERIOR OE MR. SEWARD'S HOUSE IN MEXICO.

reception of Mr. Seward and party. President Juarez, who had driven ahead—emerged from the gateway, bareheaded, and said to Mr. Seward:—"will it please you sir, to enter your house? This is your home, sir!" He then waited upon him to his apartments, bade him a kindly "good-evening!" and immediately drove away, and we were at home in Mexico.

CHAPTER XI.

MEXICO AND ITS SURROUNDINGS.

I CANNOT imagine a place which has more of interest to the traveler, than the city of Mexico, both within its walls and in its immediate surroundings. Paintings and statuary, fine old buildings, beautiful flowers, objects and points of historic interest, and women whose lovliness is proverbial, attract the attention of the traveler, go where he may. When I had been a week there, it seemed but a day, and with all the longing for home and its associations—to none dearer than to myself—I could but look forward with regret to the hour of our departure, two weeks later. If one could with safety, ride out unarmed and unaccompanied by guards, through the environs of Mexico, I know of no place where he could spend a whole year with more complete satisfaction. Mexico ought to be the Paradise of the earth, and the day is coming when it will be so considered. Even now, it presents almost irresistible attractions to the traveler, and the more one sees of it, the more one admires it, despite all its drawbacks.

We plunged at once into the enjoyment of life in the Capital and its vicinity, paying particular attention to the beautiful and historic surroundings, and suburban resorts. On the Sunday after our arrival, Mr. Seward's party, accompanied by Señor Romero and his accomplished American wife, and his sister Señorita Luz Ro-

LADIES OF MEXICO.

(1) Señora Doña Rosa Mancillas. (2) Señorita Dolores Mora. (3) Señora Adela Mexia de Hammeken. (4) Señorita Soledad Juarez. (5) Señorita Malcovia Hill.

mero, his mother-in-law Mrs. Allen, Gen. Mejia the Minister of War, and his daughter,—a magnificent blonde, one of the acknowledged belles of Mexico,—attended by a strong guard, rode out to Tacubuya, and from thence, via the old battle fields of Contreras and Churubusco, to La Cañada, a hacienda situated in a deep gorge in the mountains, fifteen miles from the city.

This is one of the most noted places of resort in the vicinity of Mexico, and one of the most beautiful in the world. The views of the snowy peaks of Popocatapetl and the grand amphitheatre of Mexico are magnificent, and beyond description. The hacienda itself is equally beautiful, and it is not to be wondered at that Maximilian, who desired to purchase or appropriate every beautiful spot in the country, desired very much to acquire La Cañada, and probably would have succeeded had the Empire and his funds held out. The party lunched there and returned to the City delighted with the excursion.

For myself, I stopped at Tacubuya, to call upon some friends temporarily residing there, and spent a most delightful evening. There I met Mrs. Gibbon, a Mexican lady, whose husband—a member of the family which produced the great historian—is a wealthy mine-owner of Pachucha; Mrs. Adele Mexia de Hammekin, the beautiful and accomplished wife of an American gentleman long a resident of Mexico, and daughter of the Republican General Mexia, who was shot in 1836, after his defeat by Santa Anna; Señor Acosta, a thorough scholar and accomplished civil engineer, and his daughter Señorita Luz Acosta, one of the most accomplished young women, and most devoted and loving daughters I have ever met, who, subsequently, visited the United

States to study English in our schools; Señorita Olivia Boulay, a fair young Californian, who in three years residence in Mexico, had almost lost the faculty of speaking English, though born in San Francisco; Mr. Brennan, of the projected Tuxpan railroad, and his wife, and others.

From the windows of the residence of Mr. Gibbon at Tacubuya, there is a magnificent view of the Castle or Palace of Chapultepec, and the Molino del Rey, and from the roof, Mrs. Gibbon watched the progress of the battles of Contreras, Churubusco, Molino del Rey, Chapultepec, and the running fight down the line of the aqueduct to the Garita del Belan, and the surrender of Mexico. There, too, she often saw Maximilian walking in the gardens of Chapultepec, and all the incidents of the siege of the city by the Republicans under Porfiero Diaz, were familiar to her, as his head-quarters were at Chapultepec.

Mrs. Hammekin speaks English, French, Spanish, German, and Italian, with almost equal fluency, and has an inexhaustible fund of anecdotes relating to the different personages that have figured in Mexico since 1830. Mr. Hammekin is an American by birth, and one of those who achieved the independence of Texas, and was taken prisoner in the unfortunate "Mier Expedition." They live in one part of the extensive house formerly owned and occupied by Gen. Urega, whose complicity in the Empire caused the confiscation of all his property. The grounds are very extensive and have been very fine, but are now neglected and going to decay. Grottoes of lava, a subterranean cave with a well at the bottom *said* to have been excavated by Montezuma—I wonder what old Monte did not do in Mexico!—immense baths in the open air shut out from the gaze of curious and prying eyes by thick foliaged overhanging trees, broad avenues, beautiful shrubbery, and countless flowers—such as grow only in the tropic climes—a billiard saloon, bowling alley, and other places of amusement and recreation, are among the attractions of this delightful resort. In such company, and amid such surroundings, the hours went quickly by, and it may well be believed I was in no haste to return to the city.

On our way back, we passed the American and English Cemeteries. Over the gate-way of the American cemetery was lately to be seen this startling inscription:

"Here lies the bodies of seven hundred, buried under an Act of Congress."

I am glad to be able to add that the stone bearing this astounding inscription, was stolen just before our visit, but sorry to say, also, that the thieves broke into the cemetery and carried off many of the tomb-stones, to be worked over and made into furniture, and sold. The Imperialists, during the latter days of the Empire, did all the damage in their power to the cemetery, demolishing a part of the fences in the erection of batteries and earth-works, and it has long been a scandal and a reproach to the United States. We owe it to the memory of the brave men who laid down their lives in a war—right or wrong—to carry our flag into distant lands, that their graves should not be left in the present disgraceful condition.

The Republic of Mexico, to its credit be it said, after the return of Juarez to the Capital and the expulsion of the Imperialists, spent a considerable sum in repairing the damage inflicted by the invaders, and re-erecting over the graves of their gallant enemies who had fallen in the attack on their own beloved city, the monuments commemorative of their names and deeds. Had the Government of Mexico possessed sufficient funds for its own immediate necessities, it would have completed the work. As it is, what they did is a standing reproach to us, and we should see that the necessary funds are provided at once.

On the following morning, Major Hoyt of San Francisco, Col. Geo. M. Green of the Republican Army of Mexico, Señor Antonio Mancillas, Member of Congress from Durango, Señor Ribera, Judge of the Court of the Federal District of Mexico, and myself, started out for a ride through the suburbs of the city. We drove first to the Grand Canal which connects Lakes Chalco and Tezcoco, by way of which a large part of the fruit, vegetables, and other provisions enter Mexico. This canal has a rapid current towards the city, and is navigated by almost innumerable boats, of small size, propelled by poles in men's hands after the old Mississippi "broadhorn" style. Everything entering the city must pay a duty, as in Paris, and there is an arched gate-way at one point thrown across the canal, where the customs collectors and their deputies are on duty night and day. The assistants have long spears with which they probe and run through a cargo in a few minutes, or seconds, and it is seldom that any contraband article escapes their vigilance. This station is called "*La Garita de la Vija*"—or "the Gate of the Beam." It is said that the customs collected from the boats loaded only with farm produce, at this garita, average twelve hundred dollars per day.

When General Porfiero Diaz was besieging this city

after the fall of Queretaro, Colonel Green, with the American Legion of Honor, had his head-quarters on Piñon Island in Lake Tezcoco, about a mile off shore, in front of the city on the east. They stopped all the boats on the canal, and with sixteen hundred of them, built a pontoon bridge from the main land to the island. This island is evidently of volcanic origin. At this time a deep rumbling sound is to be heard beneath it, and the matter is attracting the attention of scientific men, who think it worthy of careful investigation.

The famous "Floating Gardens of Mexico," lie along the shore of this lake, for miles, and on both sides of the Grand Canal. They were, all, sections of a great "float" or "raft," composed of the roots and stalks of water plants, originally, and thickened into a thin sheet of rich soil, in time, by alluvial deposits, such as may be seen in various parts of the Western States, and along the borders of the sluggish rivers of the far south-west. This float, originally, rested on the surface of the water; but most of that nearest the solid land has, already, become attached to the bottom, and in course of years all will become so. The old descriptions of these gardens will, in the main, hold good to day, allowing only for the gradual change in their condition. Between each is a narrow strip of open water, or canal, and most of them are highly cultivated and covered with garden vegetables. The flat-bottomed boats with awnings to keep off the sun, looking not unlike the Chinese "Sampans," run down the canal through these gardens, a long distance, and you can hire one to carry you twelve miles and back for less than a dollar; human muscle is cheaper here than steam.

In one of the outlets of the canal, opposite Piñon Island, we saw the wreck of the little stern-wheel steamer Guatamozin, which had exploded on her trial trip on the lake some months before. President Juarez and cabinet were on board, and the party just sitting down to dinner when the explosion took place. The little cabin was blown to atoms, and the whole upper works smashed into kindling wood, but strange to say, the whole party escaped unharmed, though Señor Romero was blown overboard,and was in the water sometime before being rescued. It seems as if Juarez must, indeed, bear a charmed life, and that his good fortune attaches itself to all about him.

On Piñon Island there are large deposits of nitrous earth, and a great number of Indians are engaged in collecting it, and washing it in small excavations, where the pure saltpetre is separated and dried in the sun. It was near the Garita de la Vija that Guatamozin's warriors were at last defeated, and where his monument now stands.

The story of the long siege, and the innumerable battles fought by Cortez and his determined band of Christian robbers, as they advanced, day by day, along this canal, destroying the houses and filling up with the ruins the gaps made in the causeway every night by the Mexicans, is told with vivid impressiveness by Bernal Diaz, and should be read by every student of history. This story knocks half the poetry out of the legends of old Mexico, and shows the besieged to have been ferocious cannibals and unmitigated savages, and the besiegers only a little worse, more savage, lawless, brutal and selfish, making the sign of the Cross with one hand, while they cut throats and robbed unoffending people with the other.

From this neighborhood we drove back through the southern part of the city, to the Garita de San Cosme, and along the great San Cosme aqueduct, which was constructed by the forced labor of the Indians under the Spaniards over three hundred years ago.

TERMINATION OF THE AQUEDUCT.

It is seven miles long, and still supplies the city with water; but the Mexican Railway Company is laying down pipes to take its place, and it will soon pass away.

Near the *garita* stands the famous, old cypress tree under which, or as some say, in the branches of which, Fernando Cortez and his subordinate officers were hidden on the "*Noche Triste*," while his troops and Indian allies were cutting their way out of the city, and across the morass which they had bridged with the bodies of their dead. The gnarled and twisted trunk of the old cypress is over sixty feet in circumference, and its age may be anywhere from one to four thousand years. In height it does not compare with the Big Trees of California, but it has a certain beauty of itself, and its history makes it one of the objects of interest in the vicinity of this wonderful old Capital.

There is an old church, half in ruins, near the old historical cypress-tree, which was erected in commemoration of the Noche Triste, and, singularly enough, the worshipers are all Indians—in fact, the Indians built it, and have always occupied it. In a niche in the church we saw an ancient Aztec idol, where a saint would be found in other churches. It appeared singular enough, among the images of Saints, Martyrs, and the Holy Family, but it is held in much reverence by the Indian worshipers, and the white priests do not offer to object to it on account of old associations.

In another part of the church we saw a sarcophagus, which the Indian boy who acted as a guide for us—in consideration of a rial—told us contained the body of the Savior of the world. I think that he must have been misinformed, as his story disagrees, in some important particulars, with the commonly accepted history of the crucifixion and resurrection; but as there was no possible good to be attained by a discussion with him, we did not stop to dispute it.

From the old church, we went to a beautiful pleasure-garden called the "Garden of San Cosme," where we found shady walks, trees, flowers, and many conveniences for amusement. It is true that the "Happy Family" consisted of a deer and a poodle-dog, only, but the other appurtenances of the place were perfect. They charge one dollar an hour for the use of a bowling alley, and we proceeded to rent the establishment and run it. We had champagne, and "the Judiciary of

Mexico," then ten-pins; then champagne and "the Bar of the United States," then ten-pins; then champagne and "the Press of the United States," then ten-pins; and then champagne and "the National Guard of California," then ten-pins; then champagne and "the two Republics, and death to all their enemies!" and then we went on having champagne and things until night; and we got home at last, all right, and satisfied that there were but two nations on earth worthy of mention, viz: the Republic of Mexico, and California; and we were right.

Coming home through the city past the house of a friend, I witnessed a scene which gives one a good idea of how police matters are managed in Mexico.

Workmen were engaged in erecting a new door at the entrance to the place, and the passage, otherwise kept carefully closed and guarded, was left open for the moment. One of the servants coming in, met a street loafer going out with a huge bundle of clothing which he had gathered up in the servants' quarters on the ground or main floor, and was about making off with them. She raised an outcry, at once, and the fellow was seized by one of the masons, while another closed the passage and prevented his escaping. A policeman was sent for, and meantime, the fellow pleaded earnestly for his liberty. He asseverated that he had only gathered up such articles as he had supposed were of no value, and thought that he was doing them a favor by carrying off the old rubbish which was in their way.

The story did not go down, and he was detained until the police arrived. The force consisted of two men, one on foot, and one, who appeared highest in rank, on horseback. The mounted man rode into the *patio* and asked for a statement of the facts. Several witnesses detailed them, and he then ordered the policeman to tie the prisoner. The scamp declared at first that he would not go a step, but the sight of a lariat on the saddle of the officer caused him to suddenly change his mind.

The policeman then tied a small cord tightly around his left thigh, apparently, to hamper him so that he could not run if he attempted to escape. At this the prisoner remarked:

"I was never arrested before in my life, and am an honest man; but if you are determined to tie me, do it this way."

Suiting the action to the word he crossed his hands upon his breast, in a manner so thoroughly professional and artistic, as to show that he was well accustomed to the tying process, and bring a loud laugh from the bystanders.

The policeman then started to untie the cord from his thigh and put it upon his wrists, when the fellow turned to the lady of the house and coolly remarked:

Señora: I am innocent; but will go with the officers just out of compliment to you!"

This freak of extraordinary politeness on the part of a thief, caught in the act, enraged the officer on the horse, and jumping down, he took hold of the cord and commenced to tie the culprit by the elbows behind his back, ejaculating at each jerk, as he brought the elbows nearer and nearer together:

"You will go with me out of compliment to a lady, will you? You must be a high-toned thief, you are so infernally polite! Out of compliment to a lady, eh?"

All the squirming and grunting of the thief failed to relax the cord a fraction, and he was soon in a condition

A STREET SCENE IN THE CITY OF MEXICO.

which would have defied the guardian spirits of the Davenport Brothers to release him.

The officer then told the woman to roll the clothing in a bundle and tie it up, which was done; then he ordered the thief to take it in his hand and carry it, which he refused to do. Thereupon he made a loop in the cord, and passing it over the neck of the thief, compelled him to carry it upon his back. As he mounted his horse, his attendant attached the lariat on his saddle to the cord with which the elbows of the culprit were tied, and told him to *vamos*! instanter. The officer rode off on horseback, with the thief at the end of his lariat carrying the bundle on his back, and walking by the side of the horse, the woman who owned the clothing and those who were wanted for witnesses following him, and the policeman on foot bringing up the rear. That evening the woman returned with the clothing, and brought word that the thief had been tried, convicted, and sentenced to six months in the chain-gang.

The great volcano of Popocatapetl is the grandest and most striking feature of the glorious panorama of Mexico. As seen from the Castle of Chapultepec, or the residences of the Barons or Escandons, at Tacubuya, it is so far beyond the power of language to describe, that only the veriest tyro would make the attempt. Only those who have sat for hours on hours, absorbed in the surpassing beauty and grandeur of the scene, can approach towards an appreciation of it.

It is related by some historians, that Cortez, having exhausted his supply of gunpowder in the siege of Mexico, scaled the height of Popocatapetl, and descending into the crater obtained therefrom a quantity of sulphur, with which he manufactured sufficient of the best quality of powder to enable him to carry on the siege to a triumphant close. But Bernal Diaz de Castillo, who was with him every day from the hour of his landing in Yucatan, until the final conquest of the country down to the Isthmus of Tehuantepec was effected, makes no mention of this fact; and as his history is the only one extant not made up from vague traditions, hearsay, or absolute, unqualified lies. the story may well be doubted

I have met men, in years gone by, who professed to have stood upon the edge of the crater of Popocatapetl; but since I have seen the mountain, and conversed with General Gasper Sanchez Ochoa—a thoroughly competent engineer, who owns the vast estate on which it is situated, and made the only actual survey of this stupendous work of the Almighty hand, which has ever been accomplished—I know that some were only liars and vain boasters.

Mr. Seward was extremely anxious to ascend the mountain, but General Ochoa, though offering to place every facility at his disposal, frankly told him, that the effort was one which a man of his years and infirmities had no right to make, and he could not anticipate fortunate results in case he attempted it. On this, the proposed expedition was abandoned.

The editor of the *Revista Litetaria* of Mexico, prepared and published a very interesting and valuable article on the subject, a portion of which has been translated, and will be read in the United States with interest sufficient to warrant its insertion here:

This immense snow-covered peak ascends from the center of the table-land of *Anàhuac*, and its base is several leagues in circumference: its slopes commence at a height of from eight thousand to nine thousand feet above the level of the sea, and form the mountainous ridges all around, among which is the *Iztlasihuatl*, (meaning *White Woman*, or 'Woman in White,' in the old Aztec language,) of fourteen thousand four hundred feet above the level of the sea.

"Perpetual snow covers this giant of a mountain, and its slopes are mostly composed of volcanic matter, (petrified streams of *lava* may yet be seen) forming an entirely broken ground, generally known under the vulgar denomination of '*Mal Paìs.*' The sand near the snow-region shows no sign of vegetation whatever, and immense rocks of basalt and calcareous formations may be encountered.

"In the language of the Aztecs the name of Popocatapetl meant: *smoking mountain*, or *hill producing smoke*, and in fact, the quantity of smoke, issuing constantly from its crater, forms a dark column, visible at a great distance, and especially so during a clear and pure atmosphere.

"The Popocatepetl may be compared to an immense silver-pyramid, rising from a great basin, whose surfaces are covered with all possible kinds of shrubs and trees; but the vegetation of these regions, so full of mystery and solitude, and so intimately connected with historical events, grows thinner and thinner, the nearer it approaches the eternal snows. The shrubs, in place of the beautiful cedars and oyameles, and the pale looking flowers growing out of the sandy ground or appearing in the crevices of rocks, indicate clearly, the great elevation and the thinness of the air unfavorable to vegetation.

"The few, who ever made the ascension of this *fuming height*, have admired, and very justly too, the imposing grandness, in which nature clothes itself in these regions. The exploring parties of the old Aztecs never penetrated any farther than to the commencement of the snows, and looked upon the Popocatepetl with great veneration and also fear, believing that a malignant spirit had taken up his abode in the interior of the mountain. The Spaniards, when short of powder during the times of the conquest, ascended the highest summit, but never penetrated any distance down the crater, having been enabled to gather sulphur on its edges, deposited there by the hot fumes. (Doubted as above. E.)

"Baron Von Humboldt was the first, who came as far as the mouth of the crater, but he did not descend into the latter; he contented himself with making some astronomical observations and like Baron Von Gros, who was there considerably later, afterwards published a geological analysis of the volcano.

"In the year 1856, a scientific expedition was undertaken, headed by the engineer Gen. Gaspar Sanchez Ochoa. Until then an exact description of the Popocatepetl had never been made and it was only through this expedition, that plans of the interior of the mountain were obtained, as well as a description of the horizontal projection of the crater, and the crater itself, its deposits of sulphur, etc., which were published soon afterwards, including a chemical, geological and botanical analysis.

"By the labors of this expedition it was ascertained, that the Popocatepetl rises to nineteen thousand four hundred and forty-three feet above the level of the sea, according to Gaylusac's barometer, which, in fact, differs but slightly from Von Humboldt's statement of nineteen thousand four hundred and forty feet above sea-level.

"The snow-fields of the volcano cover a surface of more than three thousand metres, stretching from its maimed summit away down to the sandy regions of its slopes, where may be seen and noticed the effects and devastations produced by its former fearful eruptions of lava and inflammable matter, as well as many rocks of black and gray basalt, all kinds of *tezontles*, valuable stones of various colors, and red, yellow and black clay.

"The excavations, which have been carried on in the slopes, where vegetation exists, have revealed many remnants of vegetable coal in an advanced state of petrification, which clearly testifies, that immense numbers of trees must have become carbonized by the hot lava, flowing at such a great distance.

"It would be very difficult, to designate with any exactness the time of the first outbreak of the Popocatepetl, but it may be as remote as four thousand years, judging from the result of geological investigations, and also from the opinion of Baron Von Sontang.

"The temperature of this enormous maimed cone, during the summer season, is about twenty-two degrees below zero, Fahrenheith. The edges around the mouth of its crater are more than five thousand metres in circumference.—Those parts which allow descending into the crater, have a surface of about twenty metres, are covered with snow, and are known as '*Interior edges;*' after this come various basalt and porphyry rocks, hanging out over the abyss, one of which is especially worth mentioning on account of its enormous dimensions; on its surface was located the *malacate* or windlass, holding a cable, by means of which a person was enabled to descend to a projecting acclivity, and from there to the *Plaza orizontal* of the crater.

"The height from the *malacate* to the aforementioned acclivity is some one hundred and fifty metres, and its entire depth about three hundred; the surface of the *Plaza* is about two hundred metres in circumference and the length of the acclivity some six hundred; the interior temperature changes, according to the proximity of the *respiraderos* or *sulfataras.*

"The *Plaza orizontal* of the crater contains rich and numerous layers of sulphur; from all parts more or less dense columns of smoke and deadly fumes are issuing forth, rising up towards the great opening, spouting out the sulphuric vapors. Among the principal *sulfataras*, some sixty are especially worth mentioning, but principally there are twenty-two, whose yellow outskirts of gold color denote the abundance of sulphur they contain; one of these *sulfataras* alone is about eighteen metres in circumference, and has several *respiraderos* in its center, from which a hissing sound is escaping, very much like that of a half-opened locomotive valve: of course, an immense quantity of sulphuric fume is ejected by these beautiful *sulfataras*, which may be counted as among the finest of the world.

"Complete day-light reigns at the bottom of the crater, as the rays of the sun penetrate down into it, and on account of this circumstance, a more picturesque or imposing scene can certainly not be imagined; but all this changes very quickly when a storm or a *borrasca* is coming on: then the air becomes completely darkened and the snow is drifting down in profusion, (only to melt as soon as it settles,) the *respiraderos* are roaring continually, the heat increases to such an extent, as to become insupportable, the centers of the *sulfataras*, from time to time, spout out flames and burning matters, whilst the wind is howling around the immense rocks at the summit, hanging over the edges, and threatening to uproot them and precipitate them into the abyss.

"Experiments, made in the crater of the Popocatepetl, have confirmed the belief, that by *comarcas movibles*, condensing the hot fume by refrigeration, pure and crystallized sulphur may be very easily obtained at little cost; on separating the oxygenated part from the hot vapor, sulphuric acid would be the result.

"The extensive and scientific descriptions, which have been at different times published by the engineer, Mr. Gasper Sanchez Ochoa, have since sufficiently posted the geological societies, both of Europe and the United States, as to this point, as formerly, but very scarce and inexact descriptions of those regions could be obtained."

The official and most noticeable demonstrations in honor of Mr. Seward in Mexico, were inaugurated by a dinner at the San Carlos Hotel, given by United States Minister Nelson to the distinguished American, the members of his party, and a few invited guests, including the members of the Cabinet of President Juarez, and Baron Schlozer, the Minister of the North German Confederation. This took place on the 18th of November. The speeches and sentiments were all eminently American, but as the demonstration was not one of national importance, and their insertion would necessarily crowd out other matter of more general and lasting interest, I am compelled to omit them.

On the 21st of November, Señor Don Matias Romero, Minister of Finance—a most onerous, thankless, and unprofitable office—and formerly Minister Plenipotentiary to Washington, gave a delightful private dinner to Mr. Seward and the members of his party, with a few friends. Among the ladies present were Mrs. Romero—formerly Miss Lulu B. Allen of Washington—her mother—Mrs. Allen—Señorita Luz Romero, Señorita Dolores Mejia, the beautiful and accomplished daughter of General Mejia, Minister of War and Marine, who was also present. The reunion was social, and of the most intimately friendly character.

MATIAS ROMERO.

Mr. Seward paid a high and well-deserved tribute to Señor Romero, for the services rendered by him to the cause of liberty and Mexico during his residence at Washington, and the latter replied in feeling and affecting terms, acknowledging that the policy marked out by Mr. Seward, though strongly opposed by himself and General Grant—both of whom were at the time in favor of armed intervention by the United States, and the expulsion of the French from Mexican soil by force—was the best in the end, and accomplished its object without entailing on Mexico the curse which usually falls on nations who call in a more powerful neighbor to relieve them from a present danger, creating thereby a danger still greater, and harder to meet and overcome.

This speech contained a revelation of some diplomatic secrets, the chief of which was, that at that time, Mr. Romero and prominent military men, were so determined to bring about an armed intervention, that they coalesced, with the object of securing Mr. Seward's removal from the Cabinet, but failed.

On the 24th of November, the party accompanied Mr. Seward to Chapultepec, to dine with the family of President Juarez. This dinner was a most sumptuous and elegant affair. Nothing that money could procure, and good taste suggest was lacking, and the decorations of the grand dining-hall, reception-rooms, and parlors were beautiful and tasteful in all their details. Señor "Don Benito,"—as his friends love to call him—and his amiable wife, did the honors of the house in a manner which put all the guests—fifty in number—perfectly at their ease, and they were assisted by all the sons-in-law and daughters, Miss Soledad, and Don Benito Juarez, jr. As the dinner was strictly a private one, and the toasts and sentiments such as would be given only at a family reunion of old and dear friends, I shall say no more about it.

The table was spread in the grand saloon in which the "Feast of Belshazzar"—as it has been not inaptly termed—took place, on Maximilian's return from Orizaba, just previous to his departure for Queretaro on the fatal expedition which resulted in the collapse of his mushroom empire, and the erection of a little mound of stones and three black crosses, at the foot of the Cerro de Las Campanas, as a monument and a warning to unscrupulous and ambitious adventurers for all coming time; the table, too, was the same.

We went up on the roof, and looked down on the

fair Valley of Mexico—the fairest, it seemed to us, on which our eyes had ever gazed. The grand, old forest with its huge trees covered with long, grey moss, hanging down like a funeral pall, and the winding road leading up to the castle, was at our feet. Up the slope to the rear of the castle, charged the victorious American troops, on the memorable day when the last bulwark of the unfortunate republic fell. All around the palace, or castle, were the beautiful gardens, filled with blooming flowers which Maximilian and Carlotta—I never heard her called "poor Carlotta" in Mexico—had planted.

CHAPULTEPEC.

Out by the gate-way stands the scarred and blackened tree, at whose foot—so tradition says, and probably tells the truth—Guatamozin, "heroic in the defence of his empire and sublime in his martyrdom," (as the legend on the monument just raised to the honor of his memory, on the banks of the grand canal where his final defeat took place, by the order of the Aguntemento of Mexico, tells us,) was put to cruel torture by the ruthless Spaniards, in the vain effort to make him reveal the hiding place of the treasures for which they are digging in the ancient city, to-day. In front of us was the fair Capital of the Republic, with its many towers and steeples, and white-walled palaces, and the beautiful lakes beyond, glistening in the bright autumn sun of the tropics.

To the north-east, beyond the city, was Guadaloupe, and the villages along the shores of Lake Tezcoco. Nearer by, off a little to the left, not far from the great aqueduct of San Cosme,—which, oh Vandalic outrage! is now being demolished to give place to a railroad track—is the Church of the *Noche Triste*, and the great tree in which Cortez hid on the night of his disastrous retreat from Mexico. To the right, Tacubuya, with its monument to the honor of the brave men who fell in the defense of Mexico against the American Army under General Scott, and the scene of many a fearful deed of blood and outrage. Behind the castle, the red-walled and flat-roofed "Molino del Rey," where so many gallant American soldiers laid down their lives; and further south, the battle-fields of Contreras and Churubusco.

The valley of Mexico, with its surrounding mountains, forms a perfect amphitheater, of which Chapultepec is the "dress-circle." Popocatapetl, the white-headed old monarch of all the mountains of North America, towers in everlasting grandeur high into the blue heavens, in the south-east, and "the Woman in White"—his glorious spouse—stands beside him like a royal bride at the altar. Every foot of the ground within the limit of our vision is historic, and around it clings nearly the entire romance of the New World.

Inexpressibly lovely, is the prospect from the verandahs of Chapultepec, turn which way you will, and I do not wonder, that Maximilian lavished such sums upon the spot which he fondly anticipated was to be the home of himself and his descendants, and the seat of power of a mighty empire, which he imagined he had founded on the ruins of liberty in America. The last official document signed by this infatuated dreamer, when he was surrounded at Queretaro, and captivity and a felon's death stared him in the face, was an order for the importation of two thousand German nightingales with which to stock the groves of Chapultepec.

The obscene statuary which he placed in the gardens and corridors of Chapultepec, though generally mutilated in no delicate manner, still stands there, and the walls are adorned with voluptuous representations of the Seasons, etc., after the style of an ancient Pompeian Villa, which he designed to imitate; but there are no pictures left in the palace, and most of the furniture, and all the costly plate and dinner-service was removed when General Diaz—who had his head-quarters here—reduced the city to a surrender and the last act in the ghastly farce was over.

We saw the bath room and chambers occupied by the royal couple, their beds and parlor furniture, or a portion of it, and a few other relics and souvenirs, but cared more for the attractions with which nature and art, combined, have invested the view from the verandah. The magnificent colonnade, which was being erected by Maximilian's orders along the whole front of the palace, next to Tacubuya, is still unfinished, and the stones lie just where they were left when the news came that Queretaro had fallen; and knowing that the end had come,

"The guests fled the hall and the vassals from labor,"

and the swift vengeance of the Almighty fell on all who had participated in the great crime against freedom and humanity.

We rode back at night-fall through the broad, straight avenue which Maximilian had cut from the old Alameda, under whose trees Montezuma once walked, and saw thousands of ladies and gentlemen riding up and down on the long *paseo*—a drive of a mile or more, the fashionable and only safe drive in the vicinity of Mexico—while the military band played in the plaza, and the cavalry of the Mexican army galloped, here and there, ensuring us and them against the attacks of the *bandidos* and *plagiaros*, with which even the suburbs of the capital swarm.

LERDO DE TEJADA.

CHAPTER XII.

FESTIVITIES IN MEXICO.

ON Thursday, November 30th, Señor Don Sebastian Lerdo de Tejada, Minister of Foreign Relations, (Secretary of State,) gave a bachelor dinner at his beautiful, and richly and tastefully furnished residence, in honor of Mr. Seward. The affair was strictly a private one, and only sixteen persons, all told, sat down to the banquet. The parties were: the host, Señor Lerdo, Mr. Seward, United States Minister Nelson, Minister Romero, Baron Schlozer, Minister of the North German Confederation, Minister Iglesias, Frederick Seward, General Savadera, General Mejia, Minister of War, Col. Albert S. Evans, Señor Bossero, George S. Skilton, United States Vice Consul, Minister Balcarcel, Mr. Fitch, Mr. Boal, Secretary of American Legation, and Mr. Foster.

Mr. Lerdo, of course, made the first after-dinner speech, cordially welcoming Mr. Seward, recounting his services in behalf of Mexico, and giving due credit to the Government and people of the United States, for their moral and physical aid and sympathy. He concluded with a toast in honor of the President of the United States, to which Mr. Nelson made a brief but effective reply, paying a high tribute to Señor Lerdo, and toasting President Juarez and Cabinet.

Mr. Seward then read the following address, which

was translated into Spanish and read, at once, by Mr. Bossero:

The year 1861 without calculation or effort, and almost without expectation on my own part, brought me to a position in which I had to confront a desperate, organized, and even armed resistance, to all the great political ideas which I had fondly cherished and peacefully promulgated through a period of many years. Slavery had taken up arms in alarm for its life, and had organized rebellion aiming at the dissolution of the Amercan Union. Spain, deriding what under the circumstances seemed the imbecile theory of the Monroe doctrine, through the treachery of President Santa Anna gained possession of the City of San Domingo, and re-established a Vice Royalty in that Island, and soon after seized the Chincha Islands from Peru; Great Britain, not yet cordially reconciled to the independence of her former colonies, the United States, struck hands with France, which had been their ancient ally, but was now laboring under a hallucination of imperial ambition, and with the concurrence, voluntary in some cases, and forced in others, of the other maritime powers of Western Europe, lifted the rebels of the United States to the rank and advantage of lawful belligerents. The statesmen of Europe, with its press almost unanimous, announced that the United States of America had ceased to exist as one whole sovereign and organized nation. The Emperor of France emboldened by the seeming prostration of the United States, landed invading armies at Vera Cruz and Acapulco, and overran the territories of Mexico, overthrowing all its Republican institutions and establishing upon their ruins an European Empire. With the United States in anarchy, St. Domingo re-established as a monarchy, and Mexico as an Empire, it was unavoidable that Republicanism must perish throughout the whole Continent, and that thereafter there would remain for those who had been its heroes, its friends, its advocates, and its martyrs, only the same sentiments of reverence and pity with which mankind are accustomed to contemplate the memories of Themistocles and Demosthenes, of Cato and of Cicero.

In that hour of supreme trial I thought I knew better than the enemies of our sacred cause, the resources, the energies and the virtues of the imperilled nation. In the name of the United States, I called upon the Republican rulers and statesmen of the Continent for moral aid, and conjured them by all the force of common sympathy, common danger and common ambition to be faithful and persevering in their own Republics. The universal answer was equal to the expectation. The United States became for the first time in sincerity and earnestness, the friend and ally of every other Republican State in America, and all the Republican States became from that hour the friends and allies of the United States. This alliance commanded respect and confidence in unexpected quarters. Switzerland, Italy, Russia, North Germany, Turkey, Egypt, Morocco, Siam, and China became the friends and moral allies of the American Republics, and their triumph at last was complete. The United States were restored, and Slavery abolished there. St. Domingo was evacuated, Peru was left independent, and Mexico resumed her noble Republican autonomy. For the heroes who led Republican forces in this great contest, Scott, Grant, Sherman, McClellan, Farragut, and so many others in the United States; Zaragoza, Diaz, Arteaga, Salazar, Escobedo and Corona in Mexico—for the statesmen who directed the councils of the nations who took part in it, Lincoln, Johnson, Stevens, Stanton, in the United States—Juarez, Lerdo, Iglesias and Romero in Mexico—Gortchacoff, Bright, Bismarck and Napoleon (Jerome) in Europe, I came to feel and acknowledge sentiments of gratitude, of respect and of affection, not inferior in force to those of fraternal confidence and affection.

This is the manner, Mr. Lerdo, by which you have won me to your side and secured my ardent wishes for your future prosperity and suceess as a man, a minister and a statesman. If I have not so expressed myself heretofore, since my arrival in Mexico, it was only because I was waiting for this most seasonable occasion.

The two great demonstrations in honor of Mr. Seward in Mexico, were the grand banquet at the *Palacio Nacional*, and the grand ball at the *Teatro Nacional*, which concluded the festivities.

The banquet took place on the night of Saturday, Dec. 27th, in the hall—four hundred feet in length—at the southern end of which Maximilian's throne once stood, and where the crimson canopy of rich silk brocade which surmounted it still stands, as if in mockery of the past, and a perpetual sermon on the vanity of human ambition. As if to add point to the lesson, the sword and sceptre of Iturbide, inclosed in a frame and covered with glass, were hanging against the wall, right above the chairs occupied by the Citizen President, Don Benito Juarez, and the Ex-Premier of the United State, Wm. H. Seward.

The invitations were issued by "*El Ministro de Relaciones Exteriores*," Señor Lerdo de Tejada, in the name of the President of the Republic, and in honor of the Hon. Wm. H. Seward.

The guests were received in the great drawing-rooms, hung with crimson satin tapestry, brought over and placed there by Maximilian; and the kind, amiable, and accomplished ladies of the family of the President,—though not participating in the dinner, as no ladies were invited—were in attendance to welcome them.

Four hundred guests, including all the prominent American gentlemen in the city, the sons-in-law and staff of the President, all the Cabinet, and the principal officers and heads of departments of the Government, with many members of Congress—among them some of the most distinguished leaders of the opposition—sat down at the table at 7 P. M.

The scene, when all the guests were seated at the table in the brilliantly lighted hall, was one such as is seldom witnessed on our continent, and never twice in a life-time. Juarez and Seward sat together, and the guests, Mexicans and Americans, were so distributed through the hall as to produce the most striking contrasts. Confederate officers, in exile, sat side by side and drank with veterans of the army of the Union, and next them, officers of the army of the Republic of Mexico, with their breasts covered with decorations commemorative of gallant deeds performed in the late war, or even as far back as the war between the United States and Mexico in 1846—7. Members of the Cabinet of President Juarez sat by the side of the most violent leaders of the opposition, and for the time, at least, all hostility and ill-feeling appeared to be laid aside, out of mutual good-will and respect for the guest of the nation.

Of the four hundred guests present, about three hundred appeared to have come charged with speeches and "*brindisis*," the military men forming the exceptional one hundred. Conspicuous in the vicinity of the President was General Mejia, Minister of War, in his gorgeous uniform of Commander-in-Chief, and directly opposite him I noticed Col. Geo. M. Green, late Commander of the American Legion of Honor, wearing the decoration for the highest order of merit for services rendered in the war against the Empire.

The hall, though of immense length, is quite disproportionately narrow, so that but one table was set through its entire length. This naturally made it impossible for the after-dinner speakers to be heard at either end of the table, and led to much confusion late in the evening.

The President, staff and Cabinet, with Mr. Seward and party, occupied the center. The northern end of the hall was occupied by a stage, on which the grand band was placed, and a company of some fifty professional and amateur vocalists rendered from time to time the national songs of Mexico and the United States, and choice selections from the most popular operas. The table was furnished sumptuously with French porcelain and plate: the great *epergne* in the center before President Juarez was a master-piece of art of immense value, being of pure silver, and all the figures and statuettes of solid metal—a relic of the defunct Empire.

When the speaking commenced at about 9 o'clock—it lasted until midnight—the center of attraction was, of course, at the middle of the table, but as all could not hear, another set of speakers were hard at work at each end of the hall, and the band (being unable to tell who was speaking and who was not,) chipped in from time to time with music at the most inappropriate moment, thus adding to the confusion, and making it almost impossible for any one speaker to be heard a dozen yards away. Nevertheless, the best possible feeling prevailed; all was excitement and enthusiasm, but there was no wilful disorder, and each seemed to be determined to do his utmost to honor the guest of the evening.

As most of the speeches were in Spanish, and the whole would fill a volume like this to the exclusion of all other matter, I can only give a few of the most important.

The citizen President Juarez was, of course, the first speaker. In a brief, but well considered and well delivered address, he welcomed Mr. Seward as the nation's guest, and paid a high and eloquent tribute to the American people and Government for their sympa thy and moral and material support, in the trying hours of the foreign invasion of Mexico, at the same time briefly recounting the services rendered by Mr. Seward himself.

After the band had played the "Star Spangled Banner," at the conclusion of the remarks of President Juarez, Minister Nelson made the following address:

Mr. President, Mr. Seward and Gentlemen: My greatest regret in attempting to respond to the sentiment just announced by His Excellency the President of the Republic, arises from the fact that I do not speak the Spanish language with facility, and that speaking my own language, I cannot be understood by a large number of the gentlemen present. I will therefore be brief. As the humble representative of the Government of the United States, I return my most cordial thanks for the toast in honor of that illustrious soldier and patriot who presides over the destinies of that Republic, and who, without previous experience as a statesman, is so discharging the duties of his great office as to command the confidence of a large majority of his countrymen and the respect of the civilized world. No man living more earnestly desires the peace, happiness, and prosperity of Mexico than the President of the United States. At the head of our armies he fought not only for the preservation of the American Union, but also for the American system of Government. Our victories were, therefore, your victories—our defeats your defeats. The success of the rebellion, would in my opinion, have resulted in the utter destruction of popular governments and republican institutions, there, here, and everywhere. No wonder then, that the patriots of Mexico and of all Spanish America—no wonder that people of every nation, kindred, and tongue, and representing every system of government—watched and waited with the most intense solicitude, the wavering fortunes of the conflict. The world comprehended the grandeur and magnitude of the issues involved. It was not, as was alleged by certain European statesmen, a contest for power on the one hand, and independence on the other; the war was not waged merely to crush a gigantic insurrection, or merely to destroy the curse of human slavery—but the Union armies were also fighting for those great principles which lie at the foundation of all free governments. The result of that contest, encouraged and strengthened republican governments, and the grandest problem that was ever submitted to human society, was solved—whether mankind could be trusted with a purely popular government. The victorious sword of Grant, and the earnest patriotism of the immortal Lincoln, aided by the wise statesmanship of Seward, settled these questions finally, and forever. The problem is solved. Republican governments can successfully resist the most powerful combinations, and do possess more energy, strength, and recuperative power, than any other system.

Another question was settled—a question which was the inevitable corollary of that war—I mean that of European intervention in American affairs; and it was decided, that European powers, cannot with impunity approach, too nearly, the ark of American liberties. The moral aid of our Government, conducted and directed by Mr. Seward, combined with the patriotism of your soldiers and statesmen, relieved this beautiful country from foreign domination. Many a time and oft, as Mr. Romero can testify, did General Grant manifest his warm sympathy for the struggling patriots of Mexico, during the intervention; and since his elevation to the Presidency, on the occasion of the official presentation of the distinguished Minister from this Republic, he used these memorable words: and what President Grant says I need hardly add he means:

"Your previous residence in the United States has made you familiar with its institutions and its people, and must have satisfied you that its Government shares the views of the Mexican statesmen who deem a Republic the form of government best suited to develop the resources of that country and to make its people happy. For myself, I may say, it is not necessary for me to proclaim, that my sympathies were always with those struggling to maintain the Republic, that I rejoiced when the evident will of the people prevailed in their success, and that they have now my best wishes in their labors to maintain the integrity of their country, and to develop its natural wealth. I am prepared to share in your efforts to continue and increase the cordial, social, industrial, and political relation, so happily existing between these two Republics."

It is the desire of the President of the United States that Mexico should be, and forever remain, free, sovereign, and independent; that she may wisely reap the fruits of her victories; that she may pass safely through every ordeal to which she may be subjected, and surmount every obstacle in the pathway of her prosperity, and that friendly relations between our respective Governments and people may be perpetual.

Gentlemen, I have the honor to propose the health of His Excellency, the President of Mexico, and the peace, happiness, and prosperity of the Republic.

Lerdo de Tejada, Minister of Foreign Relations, responded to Mr. Nelson in an eloquent and effective speech in Spanish. Mr. Lerdo's remarks were received with loud applause. The band played Yankee Doodle, and Mr. Seward then arose amid the acclamations of the entire company, and addressed the guests in a low but distinct and emphatic voice as follows:

President of the Republic of Mexico and Gentlemen: In an assembly where I am surrounded by four hundred American patriots and statesmen, the time which can be allowed to me to engage attention is very short, and the words which I may speak, however earnest, ought to be few and simple. The sentiments of a grateful nature no less than profound respect and loyal sympathies for this august assemblage, oblige me to express humble thanks from the depth of my heart for this hospitality and friendly welcome. Pardon me, gentlemen, for saying that these grateful emotions have brought up with them a somewhat painful apprehension that those who have bestowed this generous welcome upon me, may, to patriots of a less confiding disposition, seem to have incurred the fault of forgetting the interests of their own country, in extending their hospitality to a stranger. I have been accustomed to study and contemplate the commerce of the Atlantic and Pacific coasts of the United States, the teeming wealth of the Mississippi Valley and the golden treasures of the Rocky Mountains and the Sierra Nevada, and, I believe, without having awakened a suspicion of personal cupidity. I do not think it necessary, therefore, to disclaim that unworthy motive for my visit here, when, for the first time, standing among the mines of Guanajuato, Potosi, and Real del Monte, and contemplating with wonder and admiration the grains, and fruits, and flowers of temperate though tropical Mexico. As little, perhaps, need I disclaim common individual ambition as a motive of my visit to Mexico. Certainly, I ought to know now, if I have never known before, that the people of Mexico wisely reserve political places and honors not for foreign adventurers, but for their own loyal and patriotic citizens.

But what shall be said of the ambition of the United States, and of my supposed share in that ambition? Certainly, only this need be said, that while that ambition is always less than I would inspire my Government with, I am neither its agent nor in any sense its representative. But what shall be said of the ambition of the United States as a nation, and of my own complicity therewith? On this point I answer with a full and frank confession. The people of the United States, by an instinct which is a peculiar gift of Providence to nations, have comprehended better than even their government has ever yet done, the benignant destinies of the American Continent and their own responsibility in that important matter. They know and see clearly, that although the colonization, and initiation of civilization in all parts of this continent was assigned to European monarchical States, yet that in perfecting society and civilization here, every part of the continent must sooner or later be made entirely independent of all foreign control, and of every form of imperial or despotic power—the sooner the better. Universally imbued with this lofty and magnanimous sentiment, the people of the United States have opened their broad territories from ocean to ocean, and from the lakes to the gulf, freely to the downtrodden and oppressed of all nations, as a republican asylum. In their Constitution they have written with equal unanimity and zeal, the declaration that to all who shall come within that asylum they guarantee that they shall be forever governed only by republican institutions. This noble guarantee extends in spirit, in policy, and in effect to all other nations in the American Hemisphere, so far as may depend on moral influences, which in the cause of political truth are always more effective than arms. Some of those nations are communities near the United States, which, while they are animated like the American people, with a desire for republican institutions, and will not willingly submit to any other, are yet by reason of insufficient territory, imperfect development, colonial demoralization, or other causes, incapable of independently sustaining them. To these, as in the case of the ancient Louisiana, Florida, Alaska, St. Domingo and St. Thomas, the people of the United States offer incorporation into the United States, with their own free consent, without conquest, and when they are fully prepared for that important change. Other nations on the continent, liberally endowed with the elements and virtues of national independence, prosperity, and aggrandizement, more matured and self-reliant, cherishing the same enlightened and intense desire for republican institutions, have nobly assumed the position and exercised the powers of exclusive sovereignty. Of this class are Mexico —older as a nation, but newer as a republic than the United States—Venezuela, and Colombia, the Central American States, Peru, the Argentine Republic, and Chili. These republics have thus become, and are gladly recognized by the people of the United States with all their just claims and pretentions of separate sovereignty, fraternal republics and political allies. To the people of the United States the universal acceptance of republicanism is necessary, and happily it is no less necessary for every nation and people on the continent. Who will show me how republicanism can be extended over the continent upon any other principle or under any other system than these? If I forbear from dilating upon the influence which North America and South America with all their archipelagoes firmly established and fraternally living under republican institutions, must put forth and will put forth in advancing civilization throughout the world, it is because I have already said enough to show that loyalty and patriotism on the part of a citizen of one American Republic is, in my judgment, not only consistent but congenial with the best wishes for the welfare, prosperity and happiness of all other American Republics.

I give you, gentlemen, the health of President Benito Juarez—a name indissolubly associated with the names of Presidents Lincoln, Bolivar, and Washington, in the heroic history of Republicanism in America.

Mr. Seward's remarks were translated into Spanish, and reported by Señor Iglesias, Minister of Justice, and thus rendered, were loudly and emphatically applauded by Mexicans of all shades of political opinion present.

Señor Don Valentine Baz, Vice President of Congress, followed with a brief speech, closing with a toast, "To the Congress of the United States of North America." To this Mr. Seward responded as follows:

The distinguished Mexican speaker proposed a sentiment in honor of the Congress of the United States. Being the only person present who has been a member of that august body, I am expected to respond. Two things are necessary in every republic; one is a President, the other is a Congress. The safety of the State is the proper care of the President; the liberty of the people is the proper care of the Congress. May God now and always endow all Presidents and all Congresses with the wisdom necessary for the discharge of their supreme responsibilities.

Señor Savadera, Minister of Gubernacion, spoke next, and Deputado Rojo followed him, each giving, as did all the subsequent speakers, a sentiment in honor of Mr. Seward and the "moral alliance of the American Republics for the defence of republican institutions against foreign aggression."

Then came the great speech of the evening—that of the homeliest and cleverest orator in Mexico, the Indian scholar, radical republican, brave soldier, and anti-Church statesman, Ignacio M. Altamirano of Guerrero. This singular representative man of the aboriginal race of Mexico has nothing in his personal appearance to attract the attention of the casual observer, but the magical effect of his impassioned eloquence is beyond description, and one must see and listen to him to comprehend it.

IGNACIO M. ALTAMIRANO.

Born of Aztec parents in the State of Michoacan, and reared in the strict observance of the Catholic faith, this man has educated himself up to a standard seldom attained in the United States, or Europe, and learned to hate the priesthood who for centuries held in abject slavery the consciences and minds of millions of his race, with a hatred which finds expression in such language as that which he made use of a year or two since, when he shook his finger at the assembled dignitaries of the Church, and exclaimed with an emphasis and earnestness which had in it the spirit of prophecy:

"Look you, sirs! That henceforth you walk in the strait and narrow way, turning neither to the right nor to the left, as becomes the followers of the meek and lowly Jesus of Nazareth, or prepare for the inevitable day, in which the long suffering people of Mexico, shall arise in their might, level your proud temples to the dust, and scatter the fragments of your pagan idols to the winds!"

Of his speech on this occasion I give a very hasty translation, made by Señor Don Miguel Pedrorena, of San Francisco, premising however, that no translation however perfect, can give a clear idea of the torrent of fiery eloquence which flows from his lips when he warms to his subject. As he proceeded all the guests left their seats, and stood around the chair of the President to listen in silence only broken from time to time by enthusiastic applause, in which all joined.

GENTLEMEN:—The Minister of one of the republics of South America, perhaps the most flourishing, said, a few years ago, referring to the honors that had been tendered by his country to the illustrious Cameron and S. Martin, that "Those nations only that are grateful, deserve to be assisted."

A holy maxim, that has been stamped forever in the conscience of the people, the observance of which has raised them to the highest pinnacle of power, and the forgetfulness of which has dragged to degradation the most famous and powerful empires. The republics of this new Continent should always keep in their minds this maxim, that we may never forget it, if we wish to see America occupy that position that has been assigned to it by the laws of civilization, that is to say, the first in the world. Gentlemen, the motive that to-day unites us in this banquet, is one of friendship toward our venerable guest.

This banquet is not to the foreign monarch, who, leaving his throne for a few days to travel among us, is received with official ovations; nor to the fortunate conqueror, whom we see in our banquet, raising the cup to his lips with a bloody hand, a banquet offered through fear; but it is the apostle of human dignity and honor, the defender of the dignity of America, and one of the most venerable patriarchs of liberty, whom we welcome in our midst, and in honor of whom we decorate with flowers our Mexican homes, and tender to him our sympathies and admiration. See him! you see on his forehead no crown; but those venerable locks, those white locks which show his age—what an age! that shows us all that those years have been consecrated to the service of his country, consecrated for the good of all.

I forget, seeing Mr. Wm. H. Seward among us, the great statesman of the age, the premier of the United States. I see and only wish to see, in him, the friend of humanity, the enemy of slavery, and the liberator of the unhappy negro. Slavery! The infamous spot of the old world, the legacy left us by the past century, like a hereditary infirmity to modern civilization! That slavery which the Greek and Roman republics were not great enough to blot out from their codes of laws; that the barbarians of the middle ages took up with pleasure, as an auxiliary to their brute force; that slavery that even Christianity was unable to destroy; there was a time when the whole world seemed to believe that slavery was one of the precepts of Divine rights. That the Pagan world should have allowed and supported this servitude, was not strange, but that the Christian world should tolerate it was atrocious.

But the time came when this should have a change. The Democracy of the United States, that ought to have been the strongest party in existence, was born with this hereditary disease of slavery. The English Puritans and the Quaker Wm. Penn, had tried to form in this virgin country, (America) an evangelical society; but shortly after the arrival of the Puritans at the traditional rock, a ship from Holland put ashore on the borders of the James, the first group of slaves landed in the United States. From this on, the slave trade was carried on with force. Even Washington did not dare to interfere with this subject. And here let me say, for the honor of the fathers of Mexican independence, that they inscribed on their banners in 1810, the words "Abolition of Slavery."

But some few in the United States thought, and justly, that liberty was dishonored there by the existence of slavery. Among these could be found the Hon. Wm. H. Seward. Not satisfied with the idea, they set their shoulders to the gigantic task of washing away the dark cloud that obscured the stars and stripes of their noble flag. Gigantic task, I say, that threatened to annihilate those that should attempt it. John Brown raised the flag, and marched to martyrdom. Then two men appeared to whom power offered an opportunity to realize their wishes.

Abraham Lincoln and Wm. H. Seward were competitors for the Presidency of the Republic. The first being the choice of the people, he immediately called to Mr. Seward to stand by him in his work, and both together triumphed over their enemies.

The Emancipation decree was proclaimed on the twenty-second of September, 1862. You all know the rest. The most bloody civil war that has ever been witnessed, agitated that country with all its horrors, but Divine Providence—always just—put an end to it, giving the victory to the humane cause of the North. The thunderbolt fell, the heavens became serene, the dead were taken up from the battle-fields, the blood was washed away, and under the splendor of the rainbow appeared the slaves, with their chains broken asunder, and their foreheads illuminated with the sun of equality. The American flag now flies before the whole world free of stain, saying to the nations of the world, "The Liberty of America raises itself devoid of reproach." Such is the work done by these apostles of Fraternity, whom not even the crown of martyrdom has failed to visit! The venerable William H. Seward is one of these apostles. His heart, his thoughts, his whole life, have been consumed in the task that gave for a result, victory. How can we pay the homage due to his virtue? Gentlemen, in honor of avenged humanity, let us drink to the illustrious American, William H. Seward, who honors mankind!

Speeches and sentiments then followed thick and fast. Among the speakers were Señor Sierra, M. C., Señor Santa Cilia, son-in-law to President Juarez, Col. Alcerraca, Señor D. D. Alandrina, Señor Alcala, Deputy from Yucatan, Señor Arias, from the State Department, Señor Garcia Flores, Señor Urquida Branco, Deputy from Chihuahua, Gen. Zerega, one of the ablest speakers in the country, Señor Lafraga, Judge of the Supreme Court, Señor Rojo, and General Landman.

Señor Herrera, M. C. made an excellent speech in acknowledgment of the services rendered to the cause of liberty in both republics by the press of the United States. He paid the only just and comprehensive tribute to the power of the press, which I heard in Mexico, and gave as a sentiment: "The Press of the United States of America," calling on the writer to respond. My readers will, I trust, pardon me for the apparent egotism of reporting my own remarks on this occasion, as I was requested to do so,—for reasons which can hardly fail to be apparent,—by the party whose wish I would be most anxious under any circumstances to gratify:

"Señor President and Gentlemen: For perhaps the hundredth time in my life, probably more through the partiality of my friends than from any merit of my own, I find myself called upon to respond to the sentiment of 'the Press.'

Standing before men whose names and deeds have already passed into history and become indissolubly connected with the story of the progress of mankind, and amid scenes around which is gathered half the romance of the world's history, I cannot but be proud beyond measure, to be regarded as even the humblest representative of that mighty institution of civilization, which is not only 'the power behind the throne, but a power greater than the throne itself, a power before whose irresistible attacks all the thrones of the Earth are crumbling into dust to-day.

That the press of the United States of North America, and the press of the United States of Mexico may henceforth manifest the spirit of mutual forbearance and conciliation, and cultivate that spirit of fraternal kindness so necessary for the preservation of the peace, internal and external, of the two Republics, and ensure their progress, development and enlightenment, is, I believe, the sincere wish of every honorable journalist in America to-day; it certainly is my own.

Thus much for the press. And now a word on a subject still nearer and dearer to my heart.

Mexico! the valor of your sons has been proven on a hundred well fought battle fields and their patriotism there is now, thank God, none to gainsay. Happy indeed am I to see around me to night some of the brave sons of my own proud city by the Sunset Sea, who have fought gallantly side by side with the sons of Mexico, for the triumph of Republican institutions.

Mexico! The sun of your tropic clime is only less warm than the hearts of your children, and the flowers of your fields only less beautiful than the daughters of your land, whom I have known and loved and honored long and well.

But mightier far than the power of the press, grander than the courage of the soldier, nobler than the devotion of the patriot, more beautiful than all the flowers of the valley, are the memories, sweet and tender, and holy, which cluster around the sacred name of 'Mother.'

Gentlemen: the good son honors his mother; he who

honors his mother, will honor his country. For the honor of your country and of mine, let me ask you to drink with me to the health of 'the Mothers of Mexico,' so nobly represented in the person of the ever respected wife of your Citizen President Benito Juarez."

Mr. Iglesias having passed many high compliments upon the King of Prussia, and the North German Confederation, Mr. Schlozer responded; his speech being in French, was understood by most of his Mexican hearers, and was greatly applauded.

No Mexican banquet is complete without its poem, and on this occasion, Mr. Justo Sierra composed at the table, and immediately read, amid great applause, the following, which I give as a fair sample of what the *improvisadores*, who abound among all classes of the people, are capable of doing on the moment. It is impossible to translate it into English, without utterly spoiling it.

" Salud á la immortal, salud y gloria
Al arco de la alianza americana
Que esculpiera en el bronce de la historia
El credo de la fé republicana.
Salud á la que un dia
En el campo broto de la conciencia,
Y sacudiendo la Bretaña ropa
Anadió al diccionario de la Europa
Una palabra nueva: 'independencia,'
A la immortal que removiendo el seno
Del nuevo Continente,
Serena y sin encono
Descorrió sus immensos pabellones
Y allí sentó al trabajo sobre un trono
Y allí se hizo adorar de las naciones.

Hurra, salud á la divina madre
Que en su mente sublime engendró altiva
La gran locomotiva,
El Mesías de fierro, el gigantesco
Arado, en cuyo surco brota inmensa
La cosecha sagrada de los libres,
Y abandonando el fatigado suelo
Lanza espirales de humo, en donde pura
La oracion del trabajo sube al cielo.
En el zodiaco augusto de los tiempos
Mantendrá Dios con su mirada austera
La gran constelacion donde fulgura
La luz continental de su bandera;
Y el dia en que se escondan para siempre
Romas y reyes, dulce y apacible
Del hurra de los pueblos se desprenda
Rechazando el cortejo funerario
La libertad, lucero en el Calvario
Y sol en la conciencia de los siglos."

The banquet ended at midnight, the guests of the opposite nationalities taking the little flags of Mexico and the United States, which adorned the table, away with them as souvenirs.

CHAPTER XIII.

CONTINUATION OF THE FESTIVITIES.

ON Monday, the 6th of December, the Seward party, at the invitation of Francisco Foster, Miguel Pedroreno, Major Hoyt and Mr. Toler of California, started at 10 A. M., from the *Paseo de la Vija*, in company with the family of President Juarez, Mrs. Romero and Mrs. Allen, Mr. and Mrs. Skelton, Doctor Manfred and daughter, Col. Geo. M. Green, Gen. Slaughter, Major Clarke, Señor Antonio Mancillas and wife, Señorita Dolores Mejia, and others, on a boat excursion up the Grand Canal towards Lake Chalco.

The party occupied five boats, the musicians another, and the wines and provisions in charge of the servants, a seventh. Each boat was about twenty feet in length, six or seven broad, and flat-bottomed. Two stout boatmen in each boat poled the flotilla up the canal against the strong current, which comes down from Lake Chalco, into Lake Tezcoco, at the rate of four miles per hour.

We passed the newly finished monument to the memory of Guatamozin, on the spot where that monarch made his final stand against Cortez, was defeated, and made prisoner—the tree at the foot of which he was roasted by the Spaniards to make him reveal his treasures, still blackened by the fire, can be seen to-day, at Chapultepec—and for twelve miles through the famous "floating gardens of Mexico." These gardens are all stationary now, or at least, all those along the banks of the canal, having been anchored down by cotton-wood trees planted along their edges, which taking deep root, have fixed their hold firmly in the earth below the water. They rise, at most, but two or three feet above the surface of the water, and are in the form of oblong squares, and perfectly level. Every description of garden vegetables, corn, etc., etc., grow finely on these marsh gardens, many of which are fringed with tall cane, and most of them are highly cultivated. Hundreds of boats, loaded with "produce," were met coming down the canal, and others conveying passengers, or loaded with stable manure from the city, being carried out to the gardens, were seen at every point. There were also many little canoes, each about twelve feet long, and two feet wide, hollowed from the trunk of a single tree, in which stalwart Indians were poling their families up and down the canal.

A detachment of cavalry galloped along the banks as the flotilla moved up the canal, to guard it against a possible attack. It was a curious sight to see these bronze-hued soldiers of the Aztec blood guarding a party of another race, galloping across the bridge which Cortez seized and held as his first point of vantage against the city, which their ancestors defended with such desperate but fruitless valor against the Spanish invaders.

Disembarking for a few minutes, at the old, ruinous town of Santa Anita, we went on to an Indian village with an unpronounceable name, and a tumble-down, old church—in which the priest was hearing confessions from kneeling women, on both sides of his open box at the same time—and there disembarked for the final *picnic.*

All the way up the canal we had been indulging in Mexican music, French and Spanish wines, and the music of other days, alternately; the Hymn of Zaragoza, John Brown, the Danza, Home sweet Home, Star Spangled Banner, American cheers and the popping of champagne mingling in strange confusion.

A bountiful collation, picnic style, was spread beneath the trees and discussed with keen relish. We had not seen a single unpleasant day during the month that we had been in the City of Mexico, and on this occasion, the ladies, clad in thin stuffs and without shawls or capes, danced with the gentlemen of our party in the open air, for hours, as they might have done in New York in June, and felt no subsequent ill-effects from it.

After numerous toasts, and a very facetious speech by Major Hoyt in response to the sentiment of "the child, above all others of which I am proud—California,"—by Mr. Seward, the guard were called down to finish up the feast—abundance of everything being left for them, and a novel scene ensued. Colonel Green, between every speech and toast, called for *vivas* for every distinguished man he could remember, dead or alive, from Geo. Washington to Benito Juarez, Bonaparte to Grant, Hidalgo to General Mejia, and the defenders of Thermopolye to General Antonio Caravajal, all of which were given by the excited, swarthy soldiers with equal good will. An officer of the staff of the Governor of California addressed them for a moment, and offered a toast to peace and lasting friendship between the two republics, an enthusiastic soldier adding:

"Yes; and we will go out together as true brothers

and whip the whole old world into republicanism!" whereupon, the laughter and cheers were redoubled. Then Antonio Mancillas made a rousing, red Republican speech, going even to the extent of woman's suffrage, and was applauded to the echo at every sentence.

Then the party started down the canal on the return trip. We had hardly got under way when a contest among the boatmen as to who should get ahead, commenced, and the excursionists, from plying them with dollars to induce them to do their utmost, soon came to join in themselves, and a scene of indescribable confusion and excitement took place.

The moment that one boat attempted to pass another, it would be grappled by all on board the slower craft, and a dead lock would ensue. Major Hoyt, on the boat in which were Mr. Seward and Mrs. Juarez, clinched with a gentleman, whom modesty forbids me to name, on another, alongside, and both, falling, struggled for some minutes, the contest ending in the gallant Major being drawn, head-foremost, into our boat, and made prisoner. Dr. Manfred, holding like grim death to the Major's leg to prevent his being captured, was drawn overboard, and then pulled out of the water into our boat, and paroled as a prisoner of war. Then the Seward boat, getting a little ahead, was boarded by Mr. Foster, who pitched one of the boatmen headlong into the canal; whereupon, Col. Green went over and threw *both* of their boatmen, heels-over-head, into the chilly waters, and the flotilla came to a stand-still.

The uproarious laughter of the ladies as they cheered on their respective champions, testified to their intense enjoyment of the ludicrous scene. The boatmen who had been thrown over, were compensated—amply in their estimation—by a present of a dollar a piece, and quiet once more restored, we went rapidly back to the city which we reached at night-fall, after one of the pleasantest days we enjoyed in Mexico.

Among the minor demonstrations was the grand *funcion* by Bell & Buislay's Circus at the Circo de Charini in the old Convent of San Francisco. Great preparations had been made, specially, for the occasion, and the Government lent a military band and a regiment of its choicest troops, to add *eclat* to the affair. The grand court-yard of the convent is used for the circus, the ring covering the spot in which the dead of centuries lie buried, and the corridors rising one above the other, with their graceful pillars and costly ornamentation form the galleries, which are divided into boxes. What a change in the institutions and the religious sentiments of this once bigoted Catholic people this indicates, can be readily understood.

Noticing that the *mochos* did not appear to be there in great numbers, I asked the reason of a common mechanic or tradesman of some kind who chanced to be near me at the moment. His reply:

"Because they will not submit to see the burial ground of their ancestors desecrated by a circus," contains more of bitterness, satire, and hatred, than I have ever seen before in a single sentence, and is curiously illustrative of the state of feeling in the capital.

The vast audience arose and bowed, *en masse*, as Mr. Seward entered, and the troops presented arms, while the band played the national hymn. The performance, consisting of the usual ring exhibition, tableaux, including one representing the "Moral Alliance of the two Republics," etc., etc., passed off well.

There was also a "*grand funcion*," at—the "*Teatro Nacional*," at which an opera company gave the Spanish version of "*Crispino e la Comare*" in good shape, though the fairy was dressed in deep mourning; and a theatrical entertainment in which the "*Campania Zarazula*," gave us "Uncle Tom's Cabin" in Spanish, and a curious old cabin it was. They varied the plot so as to make the villain Legree get his deserts, being whipped to death by the slaves, to the great satisfaction of the populace, half of whom had been affected to tears by the imaginary sufferings of the slaves, though they had most of them seen bull-fights and kindred atrocities without a murmur of disapprobation, and probably, with yells of delight.

But the grand and closing feature of the demonstrations in honor of the nation's guest, was the ball at the *Teatro Nacional* on the night of Thursday, December 9th. Three thousand tickets, of which one thousand were to families, were issued, and more than three thousand persons were in attendance. The great theater—the largest on the continent of America—was decorated with flowers and the Mexican and American colors from floor to roof, and lighted within by three hundred and fifty chandeliers, each holding from twenty to fifty candles, which poured down a flood of mellow light and blistering stearine on all below. The stage was carried out so as to cover all the body of the vast house, the fine galleries or tiers of *palcos* rising one above the other to the roof, being reserved for the use of those not participating in the dance.

Outside, the scene was magnificent. The front of the *teatro*, from ground to roof, was covered with lanterns, the entire street, for a whole block, was arched over and illuminated, making a fairy arcade; and lines of cavalry and infantry, in superb uniform, kept the street clear and prevented the passing of carriages, either way. The Government paid twenty-two thousand dollars for the music, supper, and decorations for this ball, and it must have been honestly and economically spent. Its equal has, probably, never been seen on the American continent.

President Juarez and family, and the Seward party, occupied the double boxes, with crimson silk hangings and costly furniture, constructed for the sole use of Maximilian and his suite, and from thence looked down on one of the most magnificent scenes which the mind can imagine, or tongue describe. The costumes of the ladies in attendance were, generally, in excellent taste, and, not unfrequently, rich and elegant in the extreme. I noticed one lady who wore at least fifty thousand dollars worth of diamonds, and though this was a decided exception to the rule, there were many others whose toilets represented a fortune.

The men were all in black coats, black pants, white vests, gloves, and cravats, without a single exception. The youth, wealth, beauty, aristocracy and fashion of Mexico, were fairly represented, though some of the most strict and haughty of the *mochos* staid away.

At 10 P. M., Mr. Seward was received by President Juarez and family, and at 11 the dancing commenced. There was a lack of that animation which usually characterizes an American ball-room, but in its place, there was an amount of politeness and courtesy exhibited on all sides which would put us to shame.

The dinner was spread in the corridors and grand saloon of the Hotel Iturbide—once the palace of the Iturbide family—and plates were laid for three thousand persons. There was no convenient place for speech-making, except in the saloon where President Juarez and Cabinet and Mr. Seward were seated. There, in the late hours before day-break, considerable talking was done. During this speaking an incident, which may have some significance, took place.

Señor Valasquez of Monterey, the President of Congress for that month, had made a most enthusiastic speech in honor of Mr. Seward, and in response, the latter called his attention to two facts in the history of Europe and America within the last ten years, viz: that the Emperor of France had a well-marked and distinctive foreign policy, and a domestic policy, both of which were imperial and European. The first showed itself in the form of an intervention in the affairs of America, and an attempt to establish as a preliminary an Empire in Mexico; and the second in the furtherance of the project for the completion of the Suez Canal through the Egyptian peninsula which separates the Mediterranean from the Red Sea. On the other hand, the United States have a policy in regard to Mexico, and a foreign policy as distinctly marked, and altogether American, which shows itself in maintaining the independence of the sister Republic, and the construction of a ship canal across the isthmus of Darien which separates the Atlantic and Pacific oceans. Mr. Seward said "the Colombian Congress hesitates and stumbles. Secure for us Mr. President, a resolution of the Congress of Mexico, recommending the Colombian Congress to ratify the treaty for the construction of a ship canal across the Isthmus of Darien, which has already been negotiated between the two Governments, and I am sure that the

Congress of Colombia could not resist the friendly appeal."

Señor Valasquez replied, that he could not answer for the Mexican Congress as a body; it must speak for itself in its free and sovereign capacity; but he would cheerfully pledge his own personal support of such a measure.

President Juarez then arose, and in a brief speech set forth the merits of the project, pronouncing it the great work of Republican America and of modern civilization. For his own part he would give the project all the support and assistance in his power, and he trusted that Mr. Seward, as well as himself, might live to see the noble work accomplished. Thereupon all the guests at the table, a large number of whom were members of the Mexican Congress, stood up, and made the hall ring with enthusiastic *vivas* for the Darien Ship Canal.

The banquet and ball terminated together at sunrise, and the official ovations to Mr. Seward in the city of Mexico were over.

The more one sees of President Juarez, the more he is impressed with the conviction of his being a great man, in the fullest acceptation of the word. In person, he is below the average height of men of the Anglo-Saxon race, and he is stout built without tending to corpulency. In his dress he is exceedingly plain, but fastidiously neat. No one ever sees him without a full suit of black broadcloth, dress coat, black hat of fashionable Parisian pattern, and neatly polished boots. The only variation is on important social occasions like this, when he dons a white cravat and white gloves, in place of the customary black ones.

He rides in a common plain coach—no better than a first-class hack in New York—and will allow no servants in livery about him. His manner is always quiet, and his demeanor toward strangers courteous and affable, without in the least tending towards familiarity. His complexion is quite dark, with the reddish tinge indicative of Aztec Indian blood, eyes small and black, features strongly Indian, and the expression of his smooth-shaven face indicative of great self-possession, quiet self-reliance, decision and indomitable resolution. There is nothing quick, nervous, or "fidgety" in his manner. I doubt if any man living can say he ever saw Benito Juarez scared, excited, or irresolute for a moment.

He impresses you as one who moves slowly but with irresistible force, and is capable of any sacrifice and any expenditure of time, money, or blood to carry out his plans when once adopted. Whether entertaining the Nation's guest, as we saw him on this night, when thousands of eyes were upon him; sitting in his bare-walled room at El Paso del Norte, with a price upon his head, and but two hundred Indian troops to support him and the Republic, against the mercenary hordes of Europe, and domestic traitors; or walking in the garden of Chapultepec, smoking his cigarrito, and meditating on plans for putting down pronunciamentos, crushing the power of the Church, or establishing schools and providing for the education and improvement of his people, he is ever the same taciturn, self-reliant, hopeful, unexcitable man, believing in himself, and confident of the final triumph of Republicanism, over all trial and opposition. A horse-fancying friend described him once to me as "not a three-minute trotter, but a mighty good all-day horse, and safe for a long journey." The idea is sound, though expressed in a homely manner. He is never accused of forgetting his friends, and his triumph over all enemies and difficulties the most gigantic, stamp him as a man of no ordinary mould; one destined to fill a remarkable page in the history of the world.

There is a curious coincidence connected with this man's history. When the Spaniards conquered Mexico an old chief, or priest, at the Pueblo of Taos in New

THE PUEBLO OF TAOS.

Mexico, kindled a fire upon the altar on the walls of the Aztec temple there, and planting a tree in front, told his followers that when the tree died, a new white race would come from the East and conquer the land,

20

and when the fire went out, a new Montezuma would establish his power in Mexico. *The tree died in 1846, when the Americans conquered New Mexico, and the fire went out when the last of the Aztec priests of Taos died at his post, in the year that Benito Juarez became President of Mexico!*

I have no faith in miracles, ancient or modern, prophecies, saints, or "old wives' fables," but the coincidences above related are well authenticated, and sufficiently curious to be worth reading.

Time has dealt lightly with "the Don Benito;" his black hair is only slightly tinged with grey, his figure is erect, and his step firm and elastic as that of an American at thirty; his teeth are white and perfect, and his face shows few of the wrinkles. If I did not know his age I should —if he were an American —call him about forty years old and well preserved, and no one on seeing him any number of times would suspect him of having seen nearly sixty summers. He comes of a long-lived, enduring race, and in the ordinary course of nature has yet many years of life and the full enjoyment of mental and physical powers before him.

BENITO JUAREZ.

After the grand ball at the *Teatro Nacional*, there was a momentary lull in the demonstrations in honor of Mr. Seward. Private parties and dinners were given from time to time by citizens and officials, and we continued seeing the curious and wonderful things to be found in the Capital, from day to day, in a quiet way, avoiding public attention as far as possible. The houses of the most refined and elegant families of Mexico were opened to the party, and we had an opportunity to see the best as well as the worst phases of Mexican life.

Many of these families and persons engaged in showing these attentions, desired to be regarded as merely warm, personal friends, and therefore would not willingly allow their names to be paraded before the public in this connection.

The most noticable of these private demonstrations, took place on the 16th of December, at the residence of the resident representative of the great house of Barron & Co., at Tacubuya, when some fifty ladies and gentlemen representing the wealth, beauty, fashion, and aristocratic blood of Mexico, met to breakfast with the party. The truly palatial residence of Mr. Barron, contains five times as many treasures of fine art, as are to be found in any private residence in the United States, and more really valuable and meritorious old pictures, than we have ever been able to gather into any single public gallery. The magnificent residence of Señor Escandon, said to be the finest and most tasteful on the continent, adjoins that of Mr. Barron, and is even richer in art treasures, several superb pictures by Salvator Rosa, Murillo, and other famous old artists being among them. After the breakfast, which lasted from 12 M. to 3 P. M., the guests walked through both houses and the magnificent grounds around them, filled even at this season with fresh roses and many other lovely flowers, and every species of tree and shrub which can be grown in this prolific climate, played *boliche*, or danced in the grand saloon until night-fall, and then separated with regret, after one of the most delightful days ever experienced.

The view of the City of Mexico and the Valley, Popocatapetl and "The Woman in White," and all the lovely surroundings of this old, historic city, commanded by both houses, is only second to that from Chapultepec, in any respect, and superior to it in many particulars. Seen through the soft, blue haze in the warm, mellow light of the winter sun of Mexico, the landscape is beautiful as a vision of the fabled Acadia, and looking upon it but once, one cannot but appreciate the affection which the people of Mexico manifest for their country in all her misfortunes and calamities. It is a country to be proud of, to honor, and to love, and—American though I am—I must give it the palm over mine; had I been born there, I would live there and die there, nor wish for any better land to love, and hope and labor, and suffer for.

CHAPTER XIV.

AMID THE RUINS OF EMPIRES.

DID you ever go behind the scenes in a theatre after the play was over, the audience dismissed, and the actors had disrobed and gone? I did that, in Mexico. The theatre was an empire, and the actors played each a part in one of the mightiest dramas of our age and time. I went to the *Palacio Nacional* of Mexico, and saw in the garish light of day, the "scenic effects," "stage accessories," and tawdry "costumes," which dazzled the eyes of the outside world who witnessed the representation of "The Empire of Mexico," only three years ago.

In the long hall—made by throwing three rooms into one, by order of Maximilian—in which the grand dinner was given to Mr. Seward but a few nights before, I saw the full length portraits of Hidalgo and Guerrero, and other gallant men who sealed their faith in liberty with their blood, and laid down their lives for the independence of Mexico. With them, I saw the sword and cane of Iturbide, which he, under the influence of the Church, exchanged for a crown and a traitors death; and only a few yards off, the crimson canopy, which overhung the throne on which Maximilian sat. From the windows of this hall I looked out on the great Cathedral of Mexico, with its millions of dollars worth of tawdry ornaments, going slowly but surely into decay, and the palace which Hernando Cortez built and occupied, now a national pawnbroker's shop.

Then we went into the chapel which Maximilian caused to be arranged for the coronation which never took place, and saw the cushioned seats on which he and his Empress were to sit while the services progressed. Then into another and smaller chapel, and from thence, to the great store-rooms in which is piled like so much useless rubbish, the costly trappings which adorned the persons of the actors and the stage on which they strutted their little hour, in the last grand imperial farce of our time—of all time I trust!

In one room there are numerous paintings, and wooden, marble, and gilded plaster of Paris decorations from the palace of Chapultepec. There are two full length portraits of Maximilian in his imperial robes, one painted in Munich, the other in Mexico. In each, the artist has given an almost feminine beauty to his forehead and eyes, and the blonde English whiskers are the same; but the coarse, weak mouth defied all efforts at toning down and softening, and both artists wisely represented it in all its disgusting deformity.

MAXIMILIAN.

There is also a full length portrait of Carlotta, which so closely resembles the fancy pictures of Eugenie, current some twenty years ago, as to lead to the suspicion of a common model having served for each.

On a pedestal near by, are marble busts of Maximilian and Carlotta, doubtless sculptured in actual mathematical proportions, which are as much unlike the painted portraits as possible; the features of each being coarser, and more distinctly marked and characteristic. Mexico is filled with representations of Maximilian, painted, engraved, sculptured, and printed, and it almost seems as if he had done nothing else, but to sit for his portrait during his whole residence in the country. His vanity induced him to stamp his likeness on every conceivable object within his reach, and you see it everywhere.

CARLOTTA.

In a case in the same room, there is a miscellaneous collection of court costumes, which remind one of the wardrobe room in a theatre. There are gold and silver lace-embroidered coats and hats for the royal flunkies, gorgeous diamond buckles for the belts of gentlemen of the household, jockey caps for the outriders of the royal coach, silver and gold-mounted swords, and gold and silver buttons, for senators, representatives, cabinet officers, generals, judges, and every other member or officer of the imperial government. Great, gilt monograms of the Emperor and Empress, torn down from over windows and doorways, lay scattered about, and indecent statues in bronze, more indecently mutilated in some cases, were shown us.

In one room there is a pile of boxes filled with patents of nobility, diplomas of orders of military merit, and certificates, conferring the order of Guadaloupe of Mexico, on hundreds of persons, already signed and sealed by Maximilian and his ministers. I was permitted to carry away some of these, as curiosities, and the whole will doubtless be eventually scattered over the world in the same manner. Who wants an imperial decoration cheap as dirt?

In another room I counted eighty-five large, brass-bound, oaken chests, some of them of immense size, all of which bore the imperial arms and cypher, and now contain, or once contained, the silver and golden plate which was manufactured in Europe for the imperial table. In the scenes of wild confusion which followed the downfall of the empire, much of this plate was stolen by servants, or otherwise disappeared; but a great quantity still remains, and I cannot but wonder that the Government of the Republic does not, in its present exigencies, melt it all up at once, and make an end of it. Every piece of this plate bears the royal monogram, and much of it appears never to have been used.

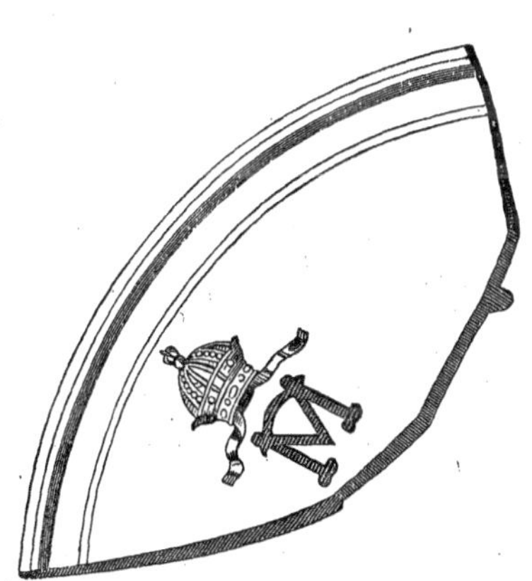
BROKEN PLATE FROM CHAPULTEPEC.

In another room I saw the English china dinner-service, in white and gold, which adorned the tables at Chapultepec and the palace in the city, each piece of which bears the monogram of

Maximilian. In the last grand banquet which took place at Chapultepec, before the fatal expedition to Queretaro—a banquet which proved a very Belshazzar-feast to the Empire—many pieces of this porcelain service were broken. I was presented with some of these curious mementoes of that ghostly festival.

If one-tenth of the furniture, etc., etc., said to have been imported by Maximilian really came over at his expense, I am not surprised at the imperial treasury having been bankrupted so soon. I saw more billiard-tables than would fill the largest hall in New York, each of which was "Max's private table;" every saloon in town has one or more, and most of the private houses indulge in the same costly luxury. I have made it a point to knock the balls around—I seldom make a point in doing so—on all of them, and so have possibly played upon his private table somewhere, though where it may have been, heaven knows. His carriages are equally numerous; everybody who can keep a carriage, at all, has one of them. But in a room in the old convent building where the Aztec relics are deposited, I saw the veritable carriage presented to Maximilian when he was on his way to Mexico, by the imperialists of Milan. It is a very large and cumbersome affair, a load for four horses, though it might be drawn on a very good road by two, and as rich with gold and silver plating, plate-glass, silk and embossed enameled leather as it would be possible to make it. Nevertheless, I confess to no envy for the couple who rode in it. At present it is nominally the property of the Republic, but I think that no one has ever ridden in it since the Empire went down in blood, and it is a useless piece of lumber. President Juarez, who is very plain in all his ways, and anxious to avoid all show and ostentation, would hardly venture to ride in it—probably could not be persuaded to do so—and it is now a chronic case, not of "what is it?" but "what shall we do with it?" It is said to have cost forty-seven thousand dollars.

And it was for these knick-nacks and gew-gaws, gilt buttons, gold and silver laces, florid pictures, marble, bronze, and silver statues, busts and medals, gold and silver plate and flashy porcelain table services, and tawdry tinsel and trappings, now fading away, growing discolored, moulding, and dust-laden, in the lumber rooms of the Palacio Nacional, that the royal wittol Maximilian of Hapsburg, bartered an empire, sacrificed the love and respect of all the friends he ever had in Mexico, drenched the land in blood, clad a nation in mourning, and finally signed a decree which proved his own death-warrant, closed the door of mercy against him, consigned him to a bloody grave, and covered his name with infamy for all time!

Maximilian had a court as complete in all its appointments as that of Napoleon III, but no empire beyond the reach of the bayonets of his foreign mercenaries, and all the money went in raree-shows, and such theatrical displays as could be gotten up with the court-trappings which I have been describing. The bankrupt Prince from Mirimar lost, completely, what little brains he had to lose, when he found himself before the footlights playing the role of Emperor. The millions wrung from a starving and terribly oppressed people, or cajoled from the humbugged and swindled subscribers to the Mexican loan in Europe, were wasted in such nonsense as this, while the people wanted bread; public improvements, which might have deferred, if not averted the evil day, could not go on for the want of funds, and the army—such as it was—subsisting on the plunder of helpless villages, perpetrated every conceivable atrocity, and, at last, drove the whole nation to forget private quarrels and unite, as one man, in a war of extermination against the invaders.

When money began to fail, and creditors to clamor, and it became evident, even to his dull senses, that a change must come, instead of reducing expenses, converting everything available into funds with which to pay the army and recruit followers from all ranks of society, then inaugurating a new and vigorous, but honorable campaign, he dallied and trifled, yielding to first one party, then the other, never being in the same mind two days in succession, and, finally, committed the fatal mistake of endeavoring to crush his enemies at a blow of the pen instead of the sword, and by compelling them to fight with the halter around their necks, increase the effectiveness of his own army, which wanted every element calculated to ensure success for his cause. When he signed the black flag decree, he reduced his followers to the level of common cut-throats and banditti, and drove his opponents to desperation.

I do not believe that the establishment of a permanent Empire in Mexico was ever practicable, but Maximilian might have won to himself a large and influential party, which would have sustained him for a long time, and in the end might have retired from the country without dishonor to himself, and with the respect, if not the sympathy of mankind, had he but possessed the smallest amount of practical common sense, and been less easily tickled with empty compliments, paid applause, and the gaudy feathers and tinsel with which he covered himself, and strutted his little hour upon the stage.

Probably it is better as it is, and Maximilian served the world better as material with which "to point a moral, and adorn a tale," than he could ever have done as a statesman and a ruler by "right Divine;" nevertheless, one cannot but feel a touch of regret, as he stands amid these ruins, and reflects upon the wide difference between the mournful fact, and the brighter possibility; what was, and what might have been.

The archives contain the decrees and other documents issued by each of the different governments and administrations of Mexico, from the Spanish conquest, down to the present day, with the single exception of those of Maximilian's Empire, which are ignored and treated as of no validity or importance whatever. All the documents emanating from that source are kept separate, as having no part in the legitimate history of Mexico. Among them is one which must stand as a full, complete, and irrefutable answer to all charges of cruelty and undue severity on the part of Mexico and the Juarez administration, in the matter of the execution of Maximilian. The act has been denounced in the most unmeasured terms by the sympathizers with monarchy, and the admirers of royalty in the United States and Europe, and even men whose education and natural instincts have led them, in all other matters, to take the side of the people against those who pretend to rule by "right Divine," have been so far misled by false statements and perversion of fact, as to characterize it as a murder.

Let us see the facts: Maximilian came into Mexico at the invitation of Napoleon III., backed by French bay-nets, and followed by an army of foreign mercenaries. A vote, taken only in places held by the French where the result was a foregone conclusion, and the entire movement a farce of the broadest description, as he well knew, proclaimed him the choice of the Mexican people, and he assumed the title and state of Emperor of Mexico. The defenders of the Republic were hunted down like wild beasts, and killed as fast as captured, until all hope seemed gone, and the Empire appeared so securely established that the professions of good will, mild intentions, and clemency, with which he entered the country, could be safely ignored, and the mask was thrown off, at once. The report was spread abroad in advance—as an excuse for the decree which was to follow—that President Juarez, who had been pursued with the most vindictive energy by the partizans and retainers of Maximilian, had been, at last, driven across the Rio Grande, at El Paso del Norte, into the United States; and thereupon the following proclamation, which lies before me as I write, was issued:

PROCLAMATION OF HIS MAJESTY, THE EMPEROR.

Mexicans: The cause which Don Benito Juarez defended with so much valor and constancy has already succumbed under the force, not only of the national will, but also of the very law which that officer invoked in support of his pretensions. To day even the faction, into which the said cause degenerated, is abandoned by the departure of its Chief from the native soil.

The national government for a long time was lenient, and exercised great clemency in order to give the chance to misled and misinformed men to rally to the majority of the nation, and to place themselves anew, in the path of duty. It has fulfilled its object; the honorable men have assembled under its banner, and have accepted the just and liberal principles which regulate its politics. The disorder is only maintained by some leaders, carried away by unpatriotic passions, and assisted by demoralized persons who cannot reach to the level of political principles, and by an unprincipled soldiery, the last sad remnants of the civil wars.

Hereafter, the contest will only be between the honorable men of the nation and the gangs of criminals and robbers. Clemency will cease now, for it would only profit the mob who burn villages, rob and murder peaceable citizens, poor old men and defenceless women.

The Government resting on its power, from this day will be inflexible in its punishments, since the laws of civilization, the rights of humanity, and the exigencies of morality demand it.

Mexico, October 2d, 1865. MAXIMILIAN.

In other words the French and mercenary troops had driven Juarez over the boundary—he never crossed it but the assertion was made for effect—and the Empire now felt strong enough to throw off the mask and hoist the black flag in form; it had done so, in fact and practice, from the very outset, but a show of clemency must be made, in order to conciliate public opinion and blind the eyes of the world at large, until a time arrived when it could with safety adopt a truly imperial policy, such as would be in keeping with the traditions of the house of Hapsburg-Lorraine.

On the next day after the publication of the above quoted decree, the famous and infamous "Black Flag Decree," which cost Maximilian his life two years later, was signed and issued. This most remarkable document of our times was as follows:

MAXIMILIAN, EMPEROR OF MEXICO.

Having heard our Ministers and our Council of State; we decree:

ARTICLE 1. All persons belonging to armed bands or corps, not legally authorized, *whether they proclaim or not any political principles*, and *whatever be the number of those who compose the said bands, their organization, character, and denomination*, shall be tried militarily by the Courts Martial, and *if found guilty, even of the fact of belonging to the band, they shall be condemned to capital punishment within the twenty-four hours following the sentence.*

ART. 2. Those, who belonging to the bands mentioned in the previous article, are captured with arms in their hands, shall be tried by the officer of the force which has captured them, *and he shall, within a delay never extending over twenty-four hours after the said capture*, make a verbal inquest of the offence, hearing the defence of the prisoner. Of this inquest he will draw an act, closing with the sentence, *which must be to capital punishment if the accused is found guilty even if only of the fact of belonging to the band. The officer shall have the sentence executed within the twenty-four hours aforesaid*, seeing that the criminal receive spiritual assistance. *The sentence having been executed*, the officer shall forward the act of inquest to the Minister of War.

ART. 3. From the penalty established in the preceding articles shall be only exempted those, who having done nothing more than being with the band, *will prove* that they were made to join it by force. or did not belong to it, but were found accidentally in it.

ART. 4. If, from the inquest mentioned in article two, facts are elicited which induce the officer holding it to believe that the prisoner was made to join the band by force, without having committed any other crime, or that he was found accidentally in it, without belonging to it, the said officer shall abstain from passing sentence, and he shall send the accused, with the respective act of inquest, to the proper court-martial, in order that the trial be proceeded with by the latter, in conformity with article one.

ART. 5. Shall be tried and sentenced conformably with article one of this law:—1st. All those who will voluntarily assist the *guerrilleros* with money or any other means whatever.

2d. Those who will give them advice, information or counsel. 3d. Those who voluntarily, and knowing that they are *guerrilleros*, will put within their reach, or sell them, arms, horses, ammunition, subsistence, or any article of war whatever.

ART. 6. Shall also be tried conformably with the said article 1st:—1. Those who will hold with the *guerrilleros* such relations as infer connivance with them. 2. Those who voluntarily and knowingly will conceal them in their houses or estates. 3. Those who, by word, or writing, will spread false or alarming reports, by which public order may be disturbed , or will make against it any kind of demonstration whatever. 4. All owners or administrators of rural estates who will not give prompt notice to the nearest authority of the passage of some band through the said estates. Those included in paragraphs 1st and 2d of this article, shall be punished by imprisonment from six months to two years, or by hard labor from one to three years, according to the gravity of the case. Those who, being included in paragraph 2d, were the ascendants, descendants, spouses, or brothers of the party concealed by them, shall not suffer the penalty aforesaid, but they shall remain subject to the vigilance of the authorities during the time the court-martial will fix. Those included in paragraph 3d of this article shall be punished by a fine of from twenty-five dollars to one thousand dollars, or by imprisonment from one month to one year, according to the gravity of the offence. Those included in paragraph 4th of this article shall be punished by a fine of from two hundred dollars to two thousand dollars.

ART. 7. The local authorities of the villages who will not give notice to their immediate superiors of the passage through their villages of armed men, will be ministerially punished by the said superiors, by a fine of from two hundred dollars to two thousand dollars, or by seclusion from three months to two years.

ART. 8. Whatever resident of a village who, having information of the proximity or passage of armed men by the village, will not give notice of it to the authorities, shall suffer a fine of from five dollars to five hundred dollars.

Art. 9. All residents of a village threatened by some gang, who are between the ages of eighteen and fifty-five years, and have no physical disability, are obliged to present themselves for the common defence as soon as called, and for failing to do so, they shall be punished by a fine of from five dollars to two hundred dollars, or by imprisonment of fifteen days to four months. If the authorities think it more proper to punish the village for not having defended itself, they may impose upon it a fine of from two hundred dollars to two thousand dollars, and the said fine shall be paid by all those together, who, being in the category prescribed by this article, did not present themselves for the common defence.

Art. 10. All owners or administrators of rural estates, who being able to defend themselves, will not prevent the entrance in the said estates of *guerrilleros* or other malefactors; or, after these have entered, will not give immediate information of it to the nearest military authority; or will receive on the estates the tired or wounded horses of the gangs, without notifying the said authority of the fact, shall be punished for it by a fine of from one hundred dollars to two thousand dollars, according to the importance of the case; and if it is of great gravity, they shall be put in prison and sent to the court-martial, to be tried by the latter conformably with the law. The fine shall be paid to the principal administrator of rents to which the estate belongs. The provision of the first part of this article is applicable to the populations.

Art. 11. Whatever authorities, whether political, military, or municipal, shall abstain from proceeding, in conformity with the provisions of this law, against parties suspected or known to have committed the offences provided for in said law, will be ministerially punished by a fine of from fifty dollars to one thousand dollars; and if it appear that the fault was of such a nature as to import complicity with the criminal, the said authorities will be submitted, by order of the government, to the court-martial, to be tried by the latter, and punished according to the gravity of the offense.

Art 12. Thieves shall be tried and sentenced in conformity

with article 1st of this law, whatever may be the nature and circumstances of the theft.

Art. 13. The sentence of death pronounced for offences provided for by this law shall be executed within the delays prescribed in it, *and it is prohibited that any demands for pardon be gone through.* If the sentence is not of death, and the criminal is a foreigner, even after its execution, the government may use towards him the faculty it has to expel from the territory of the nation all obnoxious strangers.

Art. 14. Amnesty is granted to all those who may have belonged, and may still belong, to armed bands, if they present themselves to the authorities before the 15th of November next, provided they have not committed any other offences subsequently to the date of the present law. The authorities will receive the arms of those who will present themselves to accept the amnesty.

Art. 15. The government reserves the faculty to declare when the provisions of this law will cease.

Each one of our ministers is charged with the execution of this law in the part which concerns him, and will give the necessary orders for its strict observance.

Given at the palace of Mexico on the 3d of October, 1865.

Maximilian.

The Minister of Foreign Affairs, charged with the ministry of state.

Jose F. Ramirez.

The Minister of War,

Juan de Dios Peza.

The Minister of Improvement,

Luis Robles Pezuela.

The Minister of the Interior,

Jose Maria Esteva.

The Minister of Justice,

Pedro Escudero y Echanova.

The Minister of Public Instruction and Religious Worship,

Manuel Siliceo.

The Sub-Secretary of the Treasury,

Francisco de P. Cesar.

The suborned apologists for Maximilian—the records of the Imperial treasury show that the sum of fifteen thousand dollars was remitted monthly to New York "for the press"—have asserted that this infamous proclamation was issued under the false impression that Juarez had fled from the territory of the Republic, and that Maximilian was deceived in this matter by the French. But it will be seen that this proclamation was issued October 3d, 1865, and Maximilian's surrender to, or capture by the victorious forces of the Republic, took place on the 17th of May, 1867,—*nearly two years* later. *During all this time the butchery of prisoners of war under this decree went on, without so much as a protest against it by Maximilian*, and *the decree itself* was *never modified, nor action under it suspended for a moment.* Surely, when he stood at bay at Queretaro, with the Republican army surrounding him at all points, he could not have been under the impression that the war had dwindled down to a mere guerrilla conflict; *and still the butchery of prisoners under this decree went on.* Only two or three days before the capture of Maximilian at Queretaro, a young man named Mercado, son of one of the best families of Mexico, was captured by the Imperial forces, and murdered within the twenty-four hours, as prescribed by this decree.

Again, it is alleged that the decree was only intended to beheld *in terrorem* over the heads of Republicans, and was never intended to be put in force. The falsity of this plea is evidenced by the decree itself, which in express terms forbids the reception of any petition for pardon by the officer, and directs him to report the capture of prisoners *after* they have been executed, and not before.

Then it was said that this was only aimed at the guerillas, and not at the regular Republican army. Articles one and two are drawn in terms which cannot be mistaken, and leave no possibility of a question on this point; and if any doubt existed after reading the decree, the records of the Empire itself prove beyond a question, what was meant and what was done.

Among these records, the first document relating to executions under this decree, is a report to the War Department from the State of Michoacan, signed by Colonel R. Mendez, and dated October 13th. In this report Col. Mendez details the particulars of the surprise of General Arteaga by his command, and adds:

"Among my prisoners is the commander-in-chief, *Arteaga*, General Salazar, Colonel Diaz Paracho, Villa Gomez, Perez Milicua, and Villanos, five lieutenant-colonels, eight commanders, and a large number of subordinate officers, a list of whose names I will send you."

Appended to this report is a note by the officer next in command, as follows:

"This achievement, one of the most glorious of the campaign, does the greatest honor to Colonel Mendez, and simplifies the task of pacificating Michoacan. Arteaga, without being a skillful general, is an honest and sincere man, who has distinguished himself more than once in his career by traits of humanity. Justice to the conquered." CH. D. BARRES.

All these officers, and many hundred captured subsequently, were murdered under this decree. Señor Romero writing to Mr. Seward on this subject, under date of Nov. 20th, 1865, says:

"This barbarous and bloody decree, the most cruel ever yet

seen, has already begun to be executed. I have information, of the truth of which unhappily, there is no doubt, that the two generals and four colonels were barbarously sacrificed in flagrant violation of the laws of war, and every principle of justice.

These generals and colonels belonged to the regular army of the Republic, were officers of education and profession, and had fought for the independence of their country from the time the French first landed in Mexico.

General Arteaga had reached the highest rank in the Mexican army, and had recently succeeded ex-General Uraga in command, in the army of the center. He was thoroughly loyal, a patriot without blemish, and enjoyed a high reputation for honesty and probity among his fellow-countrymen of all political shades. His constancy and suffering in the campaign against the French, Austrian and Belgian invaders in the State of Michoacan, for the last two years, would suffice to give him a great reputation, if he had not already possessed one. His humanity was proverbial, as the French, Belgian, and Austrian soldiers who were taken prisoners by his forces at different times can testify.

The other chiefs and officers who were made prisoners with General Arteaga, though they had not arrived at the high position of their leader, were not less respectable and worthy.

These distinguished Mexicans were executed in accordance with the above-mentioned bloody decree of the usurper of Mexico."

Nor has the worst and most damning fact in connection with this fearful crime been related. The officers named, fell into the hands of the traitor Mendez on the 13th of October, and he, being in doubt of the true purport of the decree, or willing, for his own credit, to appear to be so, kept them alive until the 21st of October, *and then shot them all in obedience to a peremptory mandate from the Imperial Minister of War, directing him, on this and all subsequent occasions, to execute the provisions of the decree to the very letter.* Can any honest man stand here with these damning records before him, and maintain that Maximilian did not deserve his fate? It does not seem to me to be possible, and I can only attribute the sympathy Maximilian has received in the United States, to gross ignorance of the facts of history, and his true character.

There is a positive relief in turning from the perusal of this infernal decree, and the record of the butcheries performed under it, to the letters of the loyal men who were the first sacrificed, written to their mothers during their last moments. These letters should be translated into all languages, and published, as the most effective answer to the charges of cruelty and unnecessary harshness in the matter of the treatment of Maximilian, made so freely against the Liberals of Mexico. Here they are:

"URUAPAN, *October* 20, 1865.

"MY ADORED MOTHER: I was taken prisoner on the 13th instant by the Imperial troops, and to-morrow I am to be shot. I pray you, mama, to pardon me for all the suffering I have caused you during the time I have followed the profession of arms, against your will.

"Mama, in spite of all my efforts to aid you, the only means I had I sent you in April last; but God is with you, and he will not suffer you to perish, nor my sister Trinidad, *the little Yankee.*

"I have not told you before of the death of my brother Luis, because I feared you would die of grief; he died at Tuxpan, in the State of Jalisco, about the first of January last.

"Mama, I leave nothing but a spotless name; for I have never taken anything that did not belong to me; and I trust God will pardon all my sins and take me into his glory.

"I die a Christian, and bid you all adieu—you, Dolores, and all the family, as your very obedient son,

"JOSE MARIA ARTEAGA.

"DONA APOLONIA MAGALLANES DE ARTEAGA, *Aguas Calientes*."

"URUAPAN, *October* 20, 1865.

"ADORED MOTHER: It is seven o'clock at night, and General Arteaga, Colonel Villa Gomez, with three other chiefs and myself, have just been condemned. My conscience is quiet; I go down to the tomb at thirty-three years of age, without a stain upon my military career or a blot upon my name. Weep not, but be comforted, for the only crime your son has committed is the defense of a holy cause—the independence of his country. For this I am to be shot. I have no money for I have saved nothing. I leave you without a fortune, but God will aid you and my children, who are proud to bear my name. * * *

"Direct my children and my brothers in the path of honor, for the scaffold cannot attaint loyal names.

"Adieu, dear mother. I will receive your blessings from the tomb. Embrace my good uncle Luis for me, and Tecla, Lupe and Isabel; also my namesake, as well as Carmelita, Cholita, and Manuelita; give them many kisses, and the adieu from my inmost soul. I leave the first my silver-gilt watch; to Manuel I leave four suits of clothes. Many blessings for my uncles, aunts, cousins and all loyal friends, and receive the last adieu of your obedient and faithful son, who loves you much.

"CARLOS SALAZAR.

"MRS. MERCEDES RUIZ DE CASTANEDA.

"POSTSCRIPT.—If affairs should change hereafter—and it is possible they may—I wish my ashes to repose by the side of my children, in your town."

Things did change indeed; and the remains of Arteaga and Salazar were removed to the Pantheon at Mexico, and entombed with great pomp among the Nation's Dead, a short time before the visit of Mr. Seward to the Republic.

To the honor of the Belgians in the employ of Maximilian, let it be said that they protested most emphatically against this decree, and the murders which were perpetrated under it.

Two hundred Belgians, who were at the time in the hands of the Liberal forces at Taçambaro, signed a formal remonstrance to Maximilian on the subject, and Colonel Breuer issued the following manifesto:

TACAMBARO, *October* 24, 1865.

To the Representatives of the Belgian Nation:

GENTLEMEN: The Mexican question has frequently been discussed by you, but the chief point has been the legality or illegality of recruiting for the Belgian legion. Now, however, an event of great gravity obliges us to call your attention to it anew. The lives of two hundred Belgian prisoners are involved. Considering the question some time back, the force was intended solely as a guard of honor voluntarily offered for the protection of a Belgian princess. The emperor, disregarding the special service for which the legion was destined and the neutrality of the Belgian nation, ordered us to take the field, and being Belgian soldiers, we obeyed, and marched to the front cheerfully, animated by the love of war. Although we achieved triumphs, we also, unfortunately, sustained reverses, and two hundred of us Belgians are prisoners. Without taking our position into consideration, the emperor recently issued a decree which may cause terrible results. It announces to the republicans that after the 15th of November, all persons caught with arms in their hands will be shot. At the commencement of this month an imperialist colonel, named Mendez—an ex-republican, who sold himself to the empire—a man hating the Belgians, took a large number of prisoners from the republican army in a fight, including two generals, and several officers of high rank, whom he caused to be shot, without regard to military law, and without waiting for the expiration of the period fixed by the decree, stating after the execution, to persons who remonstrated with him upon the enormity of the deed: "What matters it? They can only revenge themselves upon the Belgians." This alluded to the fact that all the other (French) prisoners had been exchanged.

We expected that all the Belgian prisoners would be put to death; but the republic of Mexico being great and generous, like all free nations, deferred to act until after learning the action of the administration of the empire toward this Colonel Mendez.

The emperor is very fond of this man. He has already sacrificed our brave colonel, and he may sacrifice the lives of all the Belgian prisoners.

Gentlemen, it is incumbent upon you to intervene. The Belgian legion desired long since to return to its native country. It did not wish to take part in this iniquitous war, or to serve longer under an empire wherein such deeds are allowed to be committed.

Representatives of the nation, your duty calls you to act wherever the Belgian name is at stake. This is not a question of party, but of nationality.

Representatives of Belgium, remember our motto, "Unity and Strength." It behooves you to speak. We call upon you in the name of Belgium, whose honest confidence has been abused. Representatives of Belgium, it behooves you to see that the blood of Belgians be not sacrificed. In the name of the country do your duty.

BREUER,

On behalf of the Belgian prisoners taken by the Republican army.

But "whom the Gods would destroy they first make mad." Maximilian never disowned the act, nor raised his finger to put a stop to the other butcheries which followed, and Mendez continued in his favor to the end. The tide turned at last, and Escobedo was compelled to shoot one hundred and sixty-three foreign mercenaries, taken prisoners by him in the battle with Miramon when the latter was defeated at Zacatacas. Then, the whole United States rung with lamentations and denunciations of "this act of barbarism," on his part. Maximilian was hunted down and brought to the Cerro de Las Campanas, to receive the punishment due to a fillibuster, robber, and murderer of prisoners of war, and the royal sufferer had all our sympathy. Is this impartial justice between man and man?

The business of "finding" Aztec relics, pottery, etc., etc., is carried on here and in the vicinity quite extensively, and there is good reason to suppose that many of the articles thus brought to light from time to time, are veritable relics of that ancient race. I am indebted to Señor Miron of Vera Cruz, for some recently dug up at Medalin, which are undoubtedly genuine. On the other hand, many articles of pottery in the form of hideous, half-human, half-brute monstrosities, which I have had offered me as relics recently exhumed from the ancient burial mounds and ruined temples, I am satisfied had not been buried a year, and I would not pay the freight on them to San Francisco if they were given to me.

All around the Lakes of Mexico there are traces of ancient potteries, and I noticed that the bits of broken red earthenware scattered about them, are identical, in composition and color, with those I have picked up in the valley of the Mississippi, and supposed to be relics of the ancient mound-builders.

Among the veritable relics of the Aztecs over the authenticity of which there can be no question, may be mentioned the great Aztec calendar, cut on the face of an irregular block of lava from Popocatapetl, some twelve feet in height by ten in breadth, which has been so often described by travelers and scientific men, from Cortez to Humboldt, and from Humboldt down. This is now built into the western wall of the great Cathedral of Mexico, and can be seen and inspected by everybody.

But more interesting than this, is the collection which I found, lying heaped carelessly together, and unguarded from Vandal hands, in the *patio* of one of the old Convents—now a school for young ladies—near the Palacio Nacional. If this collection was left thus unguarded, at the mercy of the relic hunters of the United States or Europe, there would not be a piece as large as a chestnut left in forty-eight hours. The people who cut into infinitesimal chips, the three last ties, and broke into fragments and carried off, within two hours, the last iron rail of the Pacific railroad, or those ladies(?) who rushed to the place at the table at which the Prince of Wales had been sitting in an English town a few months since, and quarreled and fought for the possession of the cherry stones which he had spit out of his mouth, would make short work of them.

The chief of these relics is the great sacrificial stone, a block of fine-grained lava, shaped like a mill-stone, ten feet in diameter, and over three feet in thickness, covered with boldly sculptured figures, and elaborately wrought on every part. In the center of this stone is a basin, holding about as much as an ordinary American wooden pail, into which the blood of the human victims ran, when the Priests of the Sun, cut open their bosoms with flint knives and tore out their living hearts. From this basin a channel cut in the face of the stone conducted the blood to the side, from whence it ran down into a large stone trough, which is now to be seen near the great stone itself. Thousands of victims perished on this stone; some say hundreds of thousands; and the blood so permeated the porous lava that the dark red stain can still be distinguished, after the lapse of more than three centuries.

The hideous idols, serpents, and other monstrosities —all rudely cut from great blocks of lava—which adorned the temple of Cholula, lie piled against the wall, neglected and covered with dust, in the vicinity of the great altar stone. I am told that this huge sacrificial stone—contrary to the common belief—is not that which adorned the great temple of Tenochtitlan which stood on the site of the great Cathedral of our day, but was brought from Cholula. It must have been a tremendous feat to move such a heavy weight so great a distance, over such roads, and without steam power. The veritable sacrificial stone of the great temple of Tenochtitlan, is said to lie buried under the Cathedral, where the great cross is now erected, and it is certain that the bones of many thousands of human beings supposed to have perished upon it, fill all the ground where the Cathedral stands.

It is believed by many, that nearly all the old city of Tenochtitlan—the Aztec name of Mexico—is buried under the present city, and some even assert that below that are to be found ruins of a still older city, built by a race before the Aztecs. However that may be, it is evident that Tenochtitlan was built on an unhealthy marsh much below the level of the streets of Mexico, and nearly surrounded by water. The foundations of buildings in the present city are laid very deep, and the walls are immensely thick. All over the city, wherever an excavation is made for building, old Aztec relics are thrown up. Probably no city in the world now inhabited, has so many relics of ancient days buried beneath it. The accumulation of centuries has gradually raised the surface of the whole city, and buildings erected a hundred or two hundred years since have lost the whole, or a portion of their lower stories, in many instances. At the residence of Mr. Hammekin, Calle Independencia, No. 1, which comprises a portion of the old Convent of San Francisco, I was shown a well twelve feet in depth, the bottom of which is what was formerly the surface of the ground in the *patio*, and the marks of old stair-cases, etc., etc., on the walls of the lower story, show that the filling in to bring it to the present level of the streets, could not be less than six to twelve feet.

Señor Altamirano, the best Aztec scholar living, claims that the proof is conclusive that the Aztecs did not come here from Asia, as has been almost universally believed, but were a race originated in America, and as old as the Chinese themselves, and that China may even have been peopled from America. He points out on their old maps and charts, various things which Humboldt misunderstood and by which he was led into error, and demonstrates that the Aztecs, indeed, occupied Arizona in the fifteenth century as Humboldt supposed, but only as a colony sent out from the Valley of Mexico—not as a people making a temporary halt on a long march in search of a new home. If he is correct—and I think he is—extensive excavations in the "made land" of Mexico, would result in interesting revelations.

I had often heard the great *Nacional Monte de Piedad* of Mexico, spoken of in terms of unqualified praise, before my coming to the country, and it was therefore, with not a little pleasure that I accepted the kind invitation of the director, Señor Don Francisco De P. Cendejas, to inspect it in all its details, and accompanied my kind friend Colonel Enrique A. Mejia, to the place.

This great establishment was founded, not as a matter of speculation, but as an act of practical Christian charity, by Pedro Romero de Torres Count de Regla, who on the 2d day of June 1774, gave three hundred thousand dollars in coin, for a perpetual fund for loans, and himself wrote out the rules and regulations under which, with some modifications, it is conducted to this day.

The object of the pious and philanthropic founder, was to provide the poor and temporarily needy, with a place where they could deposit whatever they might have of valuables in safety, and obtain upon them an advance in coin, at such a rate of interest as would not put it out of their power to reclaim them; thus protecting them, effectually, from the rapacity of the proprietors of the old-fashioned pawn-broker's shops; and how well he succeeded the present condition of the institution testifies.

The Spanish Vice Rey of Mexico, designated for the use of the institution, the great and magnificent house erected by Hernando Cortez for his own use, immediately after the conquest, and into which he built the great cedar beam found in possession of the Aztecs, which was regarded, for its immense size, as a curiosity in its day, comparable with the great trees of California in ours, with a certain amount of religious veneration thrown in. That beam nearly cost him his position, in spite of all he had done for the glory of God in the way of butchering Indians, and the honor and aggrandizement of the Kingdom of Spain, in acquiring by fraud and violence the mighty dominion of Mexico. It is still sound, and uninjured by time, though it has been removed to the Museum as a public curiosity, and no longer occupies its old place in the structure.

The building fronts upon the grand plaza, opposite the great cathedral of Mexico, and is almost in the exact condition to-day in which it was left, when its great founder died, more than three hundred years ago. The same cedar beams support the roofs of all the grand halls and corridors, and the hideous heads, sculptured by his command and placed in his presence over the doors and windows, still look down on the visitor with their derisive grin, as they did before the Pilgrims landed on Plymouth Rock. The very staircases, with steps cut from great blocks of fine-grained lava from Popocatepetl, which he ascended, are ascended by the visitor to-day; and in the great *patio* you walk over the flag-stones trod many a time, and oft, by the grandest fillibuster and most pious and heroic butcher of all time.

On the 25th of February 1775, this great establishment was solemnly dedicated to the honor of God and the good of mankind, and thrown open to the public. From that day to this it has never been closed, and its business has continued uninterruptedly, though earthquakes have shaken its walls, though men and kingdoms have passed away, and the whole political and social aspect of the world has changed. Revolution after revolution has culminated in the grand plaza in front, or the palace beyond; but within its thick and solid walls, all has been quiet; and silently and undisturbed, the work planned by its founder, has gone on day by day, as it will go on years on years after the writer, and the reader of to-day, shall have been forgotten.

I can conceive of no more perfect system for the protection of the interest of the borrower, than that upon which this institution is operated to-day; and I wish it were possible for us to establish such a bank in every city in the United States.

You—no my friend, some other man—must raise funds to meet a temporary—it is to be hoped—emergency. A watch, or diamond ring, or some other valuable is offered as security at the *Nacional Monte de Piedad.* Two valuators are called on to pass upon it. They make their estimates, separately, and then on comparison of the two, the medium is adopted. On diamonds and other precious stones, and similar articles of unchanging value, the bank will loan up to seven-eighths of the agreed valuation, and on articles of less determined and permanent value, a lesser sum, according to circumstances; the average being much more than could be obtained on the same articles in the United States, by a stranger, at an ordinary pawnbrokers.

The interest varies, according to the time on which the loan is made, and the amount. The lowest rate is about three per cent., and the average nine and three-quarter per cent. per annum, on all the transactions of the institution. You—no, our friends—borrow money for a year, and can pay interest on the loan and have it carried on for any number of years, if desired.

When interest is no longer paid, the article pawned is kept in the vaults for seven months, and then taken out and passed into the hands of the official valuator who estimates its market value, and places the figures upon the ticket. From his hands, it passes into the sales-room, where it is exposed for sale for one month, at the price fixed by the valuator. If not sold at that sum during the month, it is again re-valued, the price being reduced, and again placed on sale for a month. And so on for five months. If at the end of a year from its forfeiture, or five months from its first exposure for sale, it still remains unsold, it is offered at public auction, and if it fails to bring as much as the loan and interest, the public valuator must refund to the bank the amount of the deficit, from his own purse.

If, on the other hand,—as is generally the case—it brings more than the amount due the bank, then the surplus is placed on deposit to the credit of the party who obtained the loan, and it remains subject to his order, or the order of "his heirs, executors, administrators and assigns," for one hundred years. If it is not claimed within the century, it is reasonably supposed that the depositor has died intestate, or moved to some other locality, and the money belongs to the bank. The centenial anniversary of the foundation of the establishment is now near at hand, and after that there will be many such sums forfeited annually.

Three sets of books are kept, viz., those of the "*Contadurin*," "*Depositarin*," and "*Tesoreria*," and the ticket must exactly agree with, and the article be identified from each, before it can be given up or disposed of. The smallest sum loaned is one dollar, and the largest four thousand dollars; but it is now intended to change the law so as to admit of loans being made up to ten thousand dollars. No loans are made upon real estate or any kind of goods not deposited in the vaults. The

22

profits of the business were, for seventy-five years, devoted to paying for masses for the repose of the soul of the pious founder of the institution; but as a gentleman connected with the institution naively remarked to me, "it is fair to suppose that after seventy-five years of prayer, one's soul will be out of hot water if ever," and the masses are now discontinued, and the annual profits applied to the founding of branch establishments, of which there are three now in the city.

The original capital of three hundred thousand dollars is still intact, and in addition there are accumulations and deposits to the amount of four hundred thousand dollars, so that the capital actually now in use, is seven hundred thousand dollars. Last year the number of loans made at this parent bank was one hundred thousand in round numbers, and the aggregate of the amounts loaned, one million six hundred thousand dollars, or an average of sixteen dollars to each loan. The number of loans seldom falls below two hundred in a day, and often reaches two thousand. Of all the articles deposited in the bank as security for loans, about two thirds are ultimately redeemed. The bank, in any event, never loses. If after all precautions, an article is found to have been stolen before being pawned, the owner must repay the amount loaned.

Señor Cendejas, in order to accustom the Mexican people to the use of paper money in some shape, and to encourage them in accumulating and laying it up against future contingencies, has introduced the system of receiving "confidential deposits," for which the bank issues certificates payable to bearer at sight, which are now current for their face at any point in the Republic. The bank also receives jewelry, plate, diamonds, and other not bulky valuables on deposit for safe keeping, the owner being required to make only a nominal loan of one dollar upon them, in order to bring it into the books of the institution. It also takes on deposit, in trust, from the courts, all moneys in dispute, and the proceeds of unsettled estates, and receives one or two per cent. per annum for ensuring its safety. It is contemplated also to found a savings-bank feature of the institution, and by putting the money at interest, aid the depositors to increase their funds without risk.

There are three grand divisions; one devoted to clothing, another to miscellaneous goods, and the last and most important, to diamonds, plate, and costly jewelry. In this last named, I saw goods piled up in separate compartments in a single room, valued at two million dollars upon the books of the institution, and probably worth in the United States, at least four million dollars or five million dollars. The valuation of diamonds is at about the rate of sixty dollars per carat, for perfect stones of that weight,—say, at least thirty-three and one-third less than the value in our market; and I am told that the diamonds, pearls, rubies, and emeralds, which are sold, are largely purchased by people going to the United States and Europe who frequently realize large profits from their sale in those countries. One set, which sold that month at the public sale, for five hundred dollars, has since been sold at one thousand dollars to my knowledge, in New York, and will be sent to Europe to be sold again.

At this time, when there is an immense amount of suffering among the "middle classes," and the old families, who were once rich, but now deprived of all income with no hopeful future before them, at the same time that they must struggle to "keep up appearances" before the world, the deposits of diamonds, watches, and fine jewelry are something enormous, and constantly increasing. I was shown,—under cover of the promise of secrecy, of course—set after set of diamonds and pearls of great value, which had adorned the persons of the proudest and most haughty beauties of any land, many of whom are known to history. One set, of antique pattern, but great value, once adorned the brow of "Isabella the Catholic," who sold them to fit out Columbus for his voyage which gave to Castile and to Leon, a New World. I was allowed to draw from its solid gold and diamond incrusted scabbard, and inspect, the sword of one of the famous generals of the early part of this century, on which twenty-seven hundred dollars had been loaned.

Such a commentary on the vanity of human pride and ambition as may be read on each of the four walls of this great, cold, silent, vaulted chamber, I do not care to read again. All the forms which human vanity assumes are there. The jeweled order bestowed by Iturbide, or Santa Anna, or Maximilian, or some European monarch; the golden cup which figured at the baptism of some child of a noble house; the silver plate off which royal guests have dined; the saint in frame of solid gold; the saddle, one mass of burnished silver, on which the successful revolutionist rode in triumph; the watch-chain and trinkets of the courtezan, and the jeweled cross worn on the bosom of the pious and sainted mother of an honored family, lie there side by side, and will go out together, to be sold to strangers, and borne away to strange lands, to be regarded, henceforth as curious mementoes of travel and adventure, and nothing more.

THE CATHEDRAL OF MEXICO BY MOONLIGHT

It was with a feeling as of one coming forth from the tombs of the dead past, that I emerged from this cave of weird enchantment, and stood once more in the cheerful sunlight of day, while the great iron door closed with a clang, behind us.

In the sales department I noticed an article of some value, which I desired for a present to one of the dearest of friends, and offered to buy at the price fixed. The salesman gravely held it up, and asked if anybody present would pay more, explaining that the law required him to do so; and no one responding, it was wrapped up and handed to me. Then we went into the parlor, where Cortez received and entertained his guests, drank a glass of the bright, yellow wine of old Spain from Parisian glasses with the Director, Señor Cendejas, bade good bye to one of the most interesting localities I have ever visited in my life, and strolled out upon the Plaza to look on the richly-clad women of Mexico with prayer books in their hands, walking with grave, decorous silence towards the great Cathedral; and the thousands of ragged bare-footed Indians, from villages twenty-five, fifty, or a hundred miles away, bearing great burthens on their backs, as they trudged patiently along, on their annual pilgrimage to the shrine of their adored Saint and Holy Mother and protector of their race, the Virgin of Guadaloupe.

CHAPTER XV.

RELIGION AND ART.

THE story of the apparition,—or rather—numerous apparitions of the Virgin Mary, commonly known by the appellation of the "Virgin of Guadaloupe," in December, 1531, immediately after the conquest of Mexico, to the Indian convert, Juan Diego, and the subsequent erection of the church of that name on the spot, has been often told by historians and travelers, and I need not again relate it in detail.

Suffice it then to say, that on the 12th of December 1531, the pious Juan Diego, praying by night on the volcanic hill of Guadaloupe, about three miles outside the north-eastern gate of Mexico, and some five miles from the grand plaza, saw the Virgin, clad in robes of wonderous splendor, with a face dark as that of the Indians, but radiant with a light not of earth, standing above in the air. She told him that in order to save the Indians of Mexico, and prove to them that she was indeed their Mother, she had appeared in this complexion, and desired him to go to the Bishop of Mexico and tell him that it was her wish, that in her honor a church should be erected at that point. He was so astonished at the apparition that he dropped his *sombrero* from his hand,—you can see the same old hat there now just as he dropped it—nevertheless, he rallied his wits, and talked back until he was satisfied that he had the full purport of the message, and then hurried off to the

Bishop's Palace and told the illustrious Señor Don Fray Juan Zumarraga, first Bishop of Mexico, what he had seen and heard.

The Bishop listened, but doubted. In sore trouble Juan Diego went back to the hill, and at its foot the Virgin again appeared to him, and repeated, in substance, her first message, adding, that the Holy Mother Church would never be blessed in Mexico, until the church was erected in her honor at the point she had indicated. A great, flowing well or spring of mineral water, dark and turbid, but excellent for scrofula and other diseases of the body and the soul, burst out from the rock where she stood this time, and it is flowing yet; I drank some of the water just three hundred and thirty-eight years, to a day, thereafter, and it did not make me seriously sick. He went back to the Bishop, and still the worthy prelate doubted.

A third time she appeared to him, and told him to carry, as a proof of his story, to the Bishop, a bunch of full-blown roses, such as do not bloom, even in Mexico, in midwinter. He wrapped them in his blanket and hurried to the Bishop. When the latter unrolled the bundle and saw the roses, his unbelief was disturbed; but when the roses fell apart and disclosed a beautiful picture of the Holy Virgin, miraculously painted on the coarse cloth of the country, the dark face glowing with sacred light, he knew that the message was indeed of Heaven, and falling on his knees, he kissed the hem of her garment, and declared that the church should be erected as ordered.

When the Spaniards, under Cortez, escaped from Mexico on the Noche Triste, one of the soldiers dropped a rag-doll, or image, and on their return in triumph, they found it unharmed, and christened it "Our Lady of the Remedios." They built her a great church, and she was the patron saint of Mexico until the Guadaloupe arose to contest the devotion of the populace with her. The war was long and bitter, but the Indians outnumbered the Spaniards ten to one, though conquered, and they had not a single Indian saint in the calendar—they have not one to this day, though many saints have been canonized in Mexico—and a brown-skinned Virgin was something worth fighting for. The Guadaloupe triumphed, and to this day her shrine is sought annually by the Indians of all Central Mexico, while that of our Lady of the Remedios is almost deserted.

Subsequent to the third apparition, the Virgin of Guadaloupe appeared to others, and directed where each structure should be raised. On the top of the hill, where she first appeared to Juan Diego, they raised a magnificent chapel in her honor: at the foot of the hill where the spring burst out, they erected a chapel over the well, and a small but costly church in the rear; and where she delivered to him the roses inclosing the miraculous picture of herself, they built a church which, though despoiled of much of its former wealth of gold and silver, is still a mine of the precious metals, a marvel to visitors from all parts of the world, and in the eyes of the poor Indians of Mexico the holiest shrine on earth.

For two centuries, it was no uncommon thing for one hundred thousand people to be gathered in and around the church and chapels of Guadaloupe on the anniversary of her apparition to Juan Diego, and from the 1st to the 15th of December, the place was one of daily resort for thousands on thousands of devout worshipers. A raised roadway paved with lava, and furnished with fourteen turnouts, or wide stations, each with a chapel, commemorative of the fourteen chief incidents in the life of Our Savior, are constructed from the northern gate of the city, to the enclosure of the church of Guadaloupe, and along this a thousand penitents might be seen at once crawling on their knees the entire distance, stopping at each station to spend some time in prayer and meditation. Of late years the fanaticism of the devotees at the shrine of Guadaloupe has fallen away, and the attendance is less great,—though still, almost incredibly large.

FLAGELLANTES OF TWENTY YEARS AGO.

The Indians come from all their villages within a radius of one hundred miles at least, on foot, packing their luggage and loads of fruit and vegetables, to be sold to procure funds for offerings at the shrine, all the way on their backs. Men and women, boys and young girls, tramp along barefooted over the dusty and stony roads, sleeping by the roadside at night; and children too small to walk, are carried on their parents shoulders, all the way. Even the donkeys and dogs belonging to the family accompanying them, and it is no uncommon thing to see a comely young Indian girl, with a sufficient dash of Spanish blood in her veins to cause her cheek to bloom like the sunny side of a yellow apricot, trudging along with a pet puppy in her arms, carrying him to taste the holy waters of the miraculous spring of Guadaloupe.

A railroad now runs along the road of the Penitents, and pilgrims are seldom seen crawling along on their hands and knees, as of yore. I went out there on Sunday, December 12th, on the holy anniversary. The road all the way from the northern gate to Guadaloupe, was so blocked with ox-carts, mule-carts, saddle-horses, and carriages, all bearing visitors to the shrine, that we could hardly force our coach along; and the multitude on foot, raised such a dust as almost to stifle us. We saw but one person—a poor old woman—crawling along upon the knees, by the side of the road; all the rest marched, or rode, straight ahead. The cars went loaded. Most of the people in the better class of carriages, and in the cars, were wholly, or partially, of European blood; but all those on foot, or in carts, were Indians. The former generally appeared to go to see what was to be seen; the latter all went, unmistakably, to worship.

We got within a quarter of a mile of the church, and leaving the carriage, made our way with difficulty through the motly crowd into the plaza in front of the church. There were probably twenty-five thousand to thirty thousand people, of all ages, sexes, and conditions there, and they were going and coming all the time.

All the bells in the towers of the church—some twenty in number—began ringing at once, and the air was filled with their melody. Those old Spanish padres were wonderful bell-makers. With the very rudest appliances, and only charcoal for fuel, they managed to cast here in Mexico, three centuries and more ago, better, and sweeter-toned bells, than we in the United States or Europe are able to produce to-day, with "all the modern improvements" and unlimited means at our command.

At last, after infinite toil and jostling and pushing through the ragged and swarthy crowd, we reached the church door, and entered it. The whole worn and worm-eaten floor of the great edifice was covered with kneeling Indians, all devoutly repeating prayers, and many carrying lighted wax-candles in their hands. Quietly as was possible we worked our way through the crowd, and reached a central point upon the floor. The air was filled with the incense burning in golden censers around the great altar, and yellow with the dust which the ever-coming and going throng raised in clouds from their soiled garments and the dirty floor.

The wealth once held within these four walls was almost fabulous, and even now when silver and gold in many places have been replaced by baser metal, heavily gilded, it is still enormous. The choir and surroundings of the great organ are all of precious metal, and the gallery, leading down from the choir through the center of the church to the great altar on the north, has on either side a massive railing or balustrade of solid silver, sufficient in aggregate weight to load a first-class railroad car, at least. The altar is surrounded by burnished metal on every side, and all the altar ornaments, which are almost numberless, huge, and massive, are of solid gold and silver.

Wrapt devotion was on every face, but the intense

bigotry which once characterized the assemblages here, is fast passing away. We stood erect, though bareheaded and silent, amid the vast kneeling throng, and not a single reproachful look, so far as we could see, was cast upon us. Twenty years ago, had four heretics from a distant land thus dared profane this holiest of God's holiest temples with their accursed presence, their lives might have paid the forfeit; but while the faith survives, the fierce fanaticism is dead, and to-day we were only pitied, not hated. The confiscation of the Church property, and destruction of her temporal power in Mexico, has done much to bring about this state of things; and slowly, but surely, the light of a higher and nobler civilization is dawning on even the most benighted portion of the people of Mexico.

All around the walls of the church were tables at which sleek priests sold little books giving a full history of the Virgin of Guadaloupe, and ribbons, each about two feet in length, on which there was a black mark some six inches long, and the inscription "The true measure of the face of Our Lady of Guadaloupe of Mexico." These little ribbons are supposed to possess great virtues, guarding the wearer against many diseases and misfortunes, and every pious visitor, however humble his or her means, carries away at least one of them. Each ribbon is *said* to have been touched to the divinely painted picture of the Virgin, which, inclosed in a solid gold frame, hangs against the northern wall over the high altar. I saw a half bushel of them brought in at once and piled up on the table before one of the priests, who spreading out his hands blessed them in a hurried business-like manner, and then bow-ing politely to me said, just as a dry goods clerk in New York, might have said:

"Yes, Señor, one rial each, how many will you please to have?"

I took a couple to carry home as presents to some young Catholic friends, and with them got his blessing which I propose to keep for my own use.

On one side of the church I noticed a great number of rude pictures representing miracles in the way of cures of deadly diseases, or direct interposition to save the imperiled from instant death, performed by the Blessed Virgin of Guadaloupe. These were hung there by the pious recipients of such favors, and they appear to be regarded with much reverence by the simple worshipers. I noticed that the paint on the picture of the Virgin which came down from Heaven with the roses which Juan Diego delivered to the Bishop, had begun to crack and peel with time, but have no doubt but that it will be miraculously restored again, and it is likely to outlast many generations of mankind to come.

From the church a winding pathway leads up the steep face of the rocky hill to the chapel on the summit where the Virgin first appeared to Juan Diego. Half way up the hill is a curious structure of stone, plastered and whitewashed, which represents the sails, mast, and yard of a ship. In fact, the mast of a ship is said to be really built into the masonry. This was erected many years ago by a pious old Spanish rover, who in the hour of mortal peril on the Spanish Main vowed to the Virgin, that if she would enable him to tack, and prevent his galleon going on the rocks, he would do this in her honor; she did it; and he kept his word like a man and a christian.

In the chapel, which is richly ornamented like the church, is the original picture of Juan Diego after receiving his message hurrying to the Bishop to deliver it. I was pained to notice that the picture was that of a Spaniard with thin features and a slight curling beard —not that of an Indian at all. There must have been a mistake here somewhere. However, the old clothes which Juan Diego wore are still there, and as they prove the truth of the story in the main, why should we care for a few discrepancies in the minor details.

At the foot of the hill, just below the main church, we saw where some enthusiastic explorer had been boring for oil, with regular Pennsylvania machinery. The rock is purely volcanic, and pitches directly away from the point where he was boring; nevertheless, if he *had* found oil there in such a sacred place, it would beyond doubt have been unusually valuable for illuminating and other purposes.

We worked our way around to the chapel on the north-east of the church, which stands over the great flowing well of mineral water which opened at the touch of the Virgin's foot. There was a dense crowd around it, and all were drinking of its waters and filling jars and earthen jugs and bottles with it, to carry away to their homes to be used as medicine until their next annual visit. I noticed that the copper kettle with which the water is drawn up from the well, is chained fast; but that is the custom of the country, and must not be construed into a direct reflection on the honesty of the pilgrims. A Mexican lady who visited the well with me, tasting the water remarked, "It is very disagreeable!" when a woman standing by her rebuked her with:

"Yes, but you must remember that it is sent by the Holy Mother, and is good both for your body and your soul!"

Thousands come here from long distances to be healed of scrofula, etc., by the waters of this well, and *are* healed. But then I am compelled to add, that I know springs in Arizona, Nevada, and California, which yield equally healing waters, beside which no Virgin is known to have ever appeared by any sort of miracle.

The Indian-blooded crowd appeared to regard the festival as partaking, to some extent, of the character of a religious anniversary and a general holiday combined. Of the thousands who pushed and jostled each other in the plaza and the streets around the church, more than half were eating something as they went, and in all directions might be seen small family parties seated on the dusty ground, picnicing with evident hearty relish on the coarsest viands. Dried meat, mainly that of sheep and goats, particularly the latter, appeared to be the staple, and boiled or roasted *calabras*, or coarse pumpkin, stood next in order. Here you would see a whole family marching along, each munching quietly at some part of a dried goat, the hind leg, apparently having the preference, and there another, greedily devouring pieces of cold boiled pumpkin, without salt, pepper, or butter. One healthy young fellow, I noticed gnawing away at the head of an ancient billy-goat which he held by the horns, and evidently "as happy and content as Swimley's boarders, the best looking men in town," etc. etc.

Oranges, bananas, cheremoyas, aquacates, piñons, and other fruit and nuts were exposed on mats on the ground, for sale, all about, and the dealers in tortillas and cakes of all kinds drove a thriving trade. It is said that pocket-picking is one of the chief features of the annual festival of Guadaloupe, and many of my friends have been robbed there in the most adroit manner; but our party did not suffer from any such depredations, and one of us to my certain knowledge stood in no serious danger of heavy loss at that time.

The whole festival reminded me of the annual pilgrimage of the common people to the pagan shrines of India, in some of its features; nevertheless, there was an evident earnestness and religious conviction in the manner of all the worshipers, which must entitle them to the respect of even the greatest cavilers and scoffers at their form of faith. The great mass of the believers in every faith in the world, are honest and earnest in their convictions, and these simple worshipers at the shrine of the Virgin of Guadaloupe, are entitled to the foremost rank in that list. If simple faith shall justify and make men whole, they, surely, have less to fear, and more to hope for in the future life, than most of us who claim to hold more enlightened opinions on religious subjects.

Coming home, we passed the old palace of the Inquisition, an institution which flourished in all its purity and vigor in the Vice Royalty of Mexico in its earlier days. A grand, gloomy old pile of architecture, with reminiscences of untold horrors and cruelties, indescribable, clinging to every stone in its massive walls. It was confiscated and put to better uses long ago. Opposite it is the ruinous old church of San Domingo, and by its side, the little plaza in which the French under the Empire, used to murder their prisoners of war at daybreak; the wall is still pitted with the bullet marks as if it had the small-pox. Strange, is it not, that Mexico did not love the Empire?

The Protestant movement in Mexico is something which I cannot fully understand, and which particularly surprised, and I may say astonished me, more than anything else I witnessed. I am not a member of any church, and profess no special creed, but as an enemy of every form of slavery and oppression, I cannot but regard this Protestant movement with interest and sympathy. That it will accomplish all which is expected of it by its friends, I am not inclined to believe; but that it will be the means of reforming the Catholic Church of Mexico and removing the abuses which made it a by-word, reproach, and curse to the country, I regard as highly probable. I must bear testimony to the earnestness and devotion of these "Evangelical Christians" of Mexico, and their wonderful success. I am not inclined to meddle much with the religious affairs of any people, but as a matter of fact, and as illustrating the condition of the country, I append the statement of the leader in this great movement, without endorsing his conclusions. The mere facts, I know to be as he has stated them:

"The immense number of magnificent stone churches that are to be seen in the cities and villages of this republic, remind the traveler of the overwhelming power that Rome once exercised over this land. The convents, church buildings, jewelry, gold and silver, and real estate that she once owned, won for the Mexican Roman church the title of "the richest of churches." A vast part of the mineral wealth of Mexico passed into the hands of the satellites of Rome that swarmed here, and enabled them to fortify themselves till they imagined their position to be impregnable. Like a vessel becalmed in mid ocean, the Roman church seemed once to lazily float on an ocean of abject superstition, ignorance, and blind fanaticism, beneath Mexico's bright skies. But a hurricane struck her from the north, and the Mexican Roman church is now on her beam ends.

The example of the United States led to the formation of the liberal Mexican party, and has constantly inspired it with the love of liberty and progress. For more than fifty years has the Roman church in Mexico unscrupulously and murderously fought the liberal party, and with the sword in her hand, stained with the blood of Mexico's best sons, tried to destroy the hopes and influence of the Mexican liberals. The liberal party gradually gained strength, and won victory after victory, until by its constitution of 1857 and "laws of reform," it shattered the political power of the Roman church in Mexico. In vain did she bring about the French intervention to recover her lost position; that effort but branded her with the name of *traitor*. The constitution of 1857, and the "laws of reform," emptied all the convents and scattered their inmates to the four winds; separated church and state, gave entire liberty of worship, forbade religious processions, the wearing of ecclesiastical robes, and the carrying about of the "host," in the streets; declared ecclesiastics ineligible to hold offices in the government, established civil marriage, nationalized the church property, and in many other ways broke down the political power of Rome in Mexico. In vain did the Roman church excommunicate those who accepted the constitution of 1857 and the "laws of reform." They have become the laws of the land. The gigantic and protracted contest waged by the Roman church against the liberal party has convulsed the nation, impeded the education of the masses and left them poverty stricken. That contest has been condemned and opposed by a few liberal and patriotic presbyters in the Mexican Roman church. Several of these threw off the yoke of Rome in consequence, and tried to establish an independent and patriotic Mexican church, while others from deep evangelical convictions sympathized with this effort. The clergy that connected themselves openly with this movement were called "the constitutional clergy." Many in the liberal party sided enthusiastically with them. Some church buildings were put at the disposal of the "constitutional clergy," but they, after struggling against poverty, the novelty of their position, their ignorance of what steps they ought to take to establish a reformed church, and the many difficulties and persecutions that they encountered, concluded to await a more favorable opportunity to carry out their plan.

One of their number however determined to work on, and he succeeded in gathering a small congregation around him in the capital, mostly from the poor. I am told by an English gentleman, long a professor of English in this city, who knew him well, that he died from the debility brought on by want. Shortly before passing away he said to some friends who surrounded his dying bed—"in this solemn moment when there is no further possible earthly interest to bind me to falsehood, I want to testify before you all, that so long as I remained connected with the Roman church my soul was ill at ease, and full of self-reproach; since breaking away from it I have had peace of mind." To a friend he said that his trust, and all his trust was in Jesus. He felt very sadly about leaving his congregation, not knowing what they would do without him. He died with his Bible in his hand. They bore him to his grave with deepest sorrow. His congregation yet continue to meet, and have done much for the cause of the gospel in the republic.

During the French intervention many leading liberals, and among them some of the constitutional presbyters, visited the United States. I made the acquaintance of the latter and became interested in the cause they represented. Specially invited by Mexicans to come to this city and assist them to establish the gospel and gospel churches in this republic, I have spent nearly a year by their sides assisting them. Through the dark, threatening clouds that hang heavily in the night of Mexico's misery, some stars are shining that relieve the gloom and inspire hope. About forty Mexican evangelical congregations now meet weekly in this republic. Many leading men, editors, lawyers, and some former Roman Catholic presbyters take an active part in gospel work in this nation. With deep christian faith, purity of life, and with the open Bible in their hands, large numbers of evangelical native christians are now working with intense zeal for the evangelization of their native land. Statues, and pictures of saints are being frequently burnt and destroyed, and in their place, the ten commandments, printed on a large sheet, and framed, may be seen in many houses. A good church building has been leased us by the government in the capital. A private individual has given us a chapel building in Pueblo. An evangelical weekly called the "Evangelical Torchlight," is published with great ability in Cos, near Zacatecas. A very large number of christian tracts have been published in the capital and circulated throughout the nation. I believe that the evangelical congregations in Mexico might soon number a thousand if the gospel work in this neighboring republic were properly stood by and encouraged by the American evangelical church.

I have found multitudes who are earnestly desirous to learn gospel truth. I have preached to about seven hundred men at a time. New congregations are being formed very frequently. There are in the capital two evangelical congregations composed of lads, and conducted by themselves. One of these lads was recently locked up by his mother in a room for about twenty-four hours, with the hope of inducing him by this punishment to return to the Roman church. In the said room he found a chair, a table with a skull on it, a loaf of bread and a glass of water. While a prisoner he sang hymns and offered up prayers. His mother at last decided that he was incorrigible and set him free.

The Pueblo congregation, recently attacked by the mob, are working on bravely. A young man belonging to one of the leading families of the capital was locked up in his room by his mother to prevent his attending and taking part in an evangelical service, after having thrown herself at his feet, kissing them, and wailing and crying and begging him not to appear in public in the gospel work until after her death. This young man has an influential position in the post-office, and circulates Bibles and christian tracts throughout the republic with great effect. He sends them to governors of states, and many of the most influential men in the nation. Many young men are preparing for the gospel ministry. How great would be the evil if the Bible were taken away from the people in the United States; how great would be the gift and its blessings, were it given to the people in Mexico, widely and generally. Numbers are beginning to read, and love, and follow its teachings. Most of the great, advance, liberal movements in Mexico have commenced among the poor. Multitudes of the poor are now enthusiastically joining the gospel movement in Mexico, and are full of hope, expecting to gain glorious victories for Jesus and His truth, in this beautiful but benighted land. I hope that American christians may take an interest in this gospel work in Mexico. Funds in aid of it can be sent—stating the object for which they are sent, viz: the gospel work connected with *the Mission in the City of Mexico*—to Rev. Dr. Butler, American and Foreign Christian Union, 27 Bible House, New York.

The little effort already put forth in behalf of Mexico has obtained marvelous results, through God's blessing, and ought to encourage American christians to greater effort. A Mexican who has been connected with the army, purchased a Bible some time since at his wife's request. The latter determined to find the ten commandments, and by them decide whether or no the Roman clergy in their teaching were faithful to the Word of God. On reading several times the second commandment which the Roman church suppresses, dividing the tenth into two, she stood up and walked across the room to where she had a picture of the Virgin Mary, that she was specially fond of worshiping, took it down from the wall and put it into the fire. Her husband, Ponce de Leon by name, was the hero of the defence, during the recent attack made by the mob, led on by two curates dressed in citizen's dress, on some christians, when assembled on a Sunday in Pueblo. He has established many evangelical congregations and expects to gather a hundred more before the end of next year. More self-sacrificing, heroic, devoted, zealous and faithful christians than they are it would be difficult to meet. That one Bible that was purchased and read by them, has already been the means of great good. The Spanish publications of the American Tract Society, are intensely useful to us. Would that they might supply us with them more generously.

A Roman Catholic presbyter, from deep conviction abandoned the Roman church. His example deeply influenced his congregation. He was cruelly persecuted by the Roman clergy during the French intervention, on the pretext that he was a liberal, and after having, as they thought, "degraded him" by removing the skin from the crown of his head, and fingers, they had him shot. The instant before they fired on him he exclaimed:

"May Jesus reign!"

A father died and left his two sons, among other property, an image which they both specially valued. When they came to divide the property they got to quarreling about the image, furiously. A member of an evangelical congregation passing by at the time and ascertaining the origin of the quarrel, siezed a hatchet and split the image in two. The sons then turned on him, but he quieted them, inviting them to the evangelical congregation and advising them to seek Jesus. An aged father took his son who attended an evangelical congregation, to a Roman Catholic missionary, that the latter might argue with him, with the object of inducing him to return to the Roman church. The said missionary commenced to draw a comparison which the son turned against him very prettily. The missionary asked the young man what would be thought of a person who, on receiving a crown full of diamonds for safe keeping, while its royal owner was absent from his realms, should begin to remove the diamonds and substitute them with bits of glass. The son interrupted him, and said to him that that was what the Roman church had done with the teachings of the Bible; substituting many of its precepts with the doctrines of men, and then went on to prove his point. The father became convinced that the truth was on his son's side, and instead of his father winning him over to Rome, the son led him to the gospel.

I trust that some hearts may respond to these facts.

H. CHAUNCEY RILEY.

Among the many interesting institutions in Mexico, the National School of Art and Design is worthy of special mention. This establishment is on an immense plan like every other public institution, but is in many particulars imperfect, for want of sufficient funds to carry out all the ideas of its founders. The building, of cut stone, very costly, and substantially built, covers a great area, but is only partially furnished and occupied. Commenced in the last century, its style of art is still of the ancient order, though perfect in its way. Many really fine painters have graduated here, and their works cover the walls of the vast salons.

Among the recent graduates is Felipe Gutierrez, who two years since, attracted much attention in San Francisco, California, as a portrait painter, and after earning a respectable sum in that branch of his profession, went to Rome, and there recommenced his studies under the most favorable auspices. I heard of him a few weeks since, as one of the most promising artists of the art capital of the world. Among the pictures on the wall I saw and recognized several of his.

The Mexican people—I might say the Spanish American people—have a natural talent for music, painting, and the fine arts generally, far beyond that of our own countrymen or even of the Europeans; and the wealth of painting and sculpture, the former especially, to be found in Mexico, in public institutions and private residences, is almost beyond belief.

Nevertheless, I must confess to some disappointment on visiting the School of Art and Design. Hundreds of historical, scriptural, religious and classic pictures, elaborately, and, generally, well executed, adorn the walls; but there are not a dozen, illustrative or commemorative of the grand and romantic incidents of the Spanish conquest and subsequent history of Mexico; and, stranger still, the wonderful scenery of this glorious land has been almost wholly neglected. There are dying saints and martyrs by hundreds, Abrahams leading Isaacs to the sacrifice, Judiths and Holofernes, Sampsons and Delilahs, Susannahs and Elders, Kings and Queens of old Spain and old Europe, Monks and Bishops, and Hermits and Brigands, without end.

There are a number of pictures of undoubted authenticity, from the old Spanish Masters, and more Virgins of Guadaloupe and elsewhere, than would stock any reasonably-sized heaven; but one looks in vain for the scenery of the Sierra Madre, the Barrancas of Beltran and Atenquique, Popocatapetl, Orizaba, the Valley of Mexico, and a thousand other glorious subjects for the landscape painter which this country affords.

Of the new pictures, I saw one representing Virgil and Dante looking into hell, which is magnificent in the simplicity of its design and the savage force of its execution. Another—not quite finished—representing the Indian girl who first discovered the art of making pulque from the milk of the aloe plant, with her attendants, presenting the liquor and the plant itself to the King of Tula, is very beautiful and artistic in design, gives a perfect idea of the costumes and appearance of the ancient Aztecs, and is worth a square acre of fly-blown saints, musty martyrs, damp, old hermits in mouldy cells, and the heroes and heroines of classic literature, in costumes suggestive of rheumatism, diptheria, pneumonia, and early death.

The department devoted to painting is the largest and most complete. One of the four grand salons is surrounded by portraits of the old masters and classic authors in fresco, executed quite recently by Ramon Sagrado, an artist of Mexico, in excellent style. Among the art objects in all the public and private houses of Mexico, the portraits, statues, and busts of Humboldt invariably attest the regard for the memory of that great man, which prevails among all classes of society. The art galleries are now being renovated and put in good order once more. When I visited them it was during vacation and I did not have the pleasure of seeing the students at work. There are many empty frames in the salons, and we were told that the pictures which once filled them were borne away as spoils by the French, who appear to have laid their vandal hands on everything rich, beautiful, and desirable, in Mexico.

The department devoted to sculpture is also very extensive, and contains many objects of rare excellence in art; but the same lack of originality and nationality, and the same slavish devotion to European styles and models is visible everywhere. In the department devoted specially to engraving on copper and steel, crayon, and pencil drawing etc., there are many specimens of work of rare excellence, and a great number of very fine and curious old English, French, German Spanish, and Italian engravings, such as cannot be found elsewhere on the continent.

In the department of coins and medals, there is a collection embracing many thousand specimens. All the gold, silver, and copper coins and medals, struck in Mexico since the Spanish conquest, with their dies, all in perfect preservation are there, and thousands of old Roman coins, with most of the coins and medals issued in Europe within the last five centuries. There are many specimens of the coins and medals issued by Maximilian. Among the former is one in silver, representing the Virgin of Guadaloupe on one side, and Maximilian on the other, and another which represents Maximilian and Carlotta on the obverse, and the Virgin on the reverse. Maximilian was exceedingly vain of his repulsive face, and placed his likeness on every thing which could be made to bear it. With all its faults and short comings, the National school of Art and Design in Mexico is infinitely superior to anything similar on the continent; and it will be long before we shall equal it in the United States. Some years since the students planned and erected a magnificent structure for this School outside the San Cosme Gate in the direction of Chapultepec, near the Agricultural College, but during the siege by Porfirio Diaz, the Imperialists occupied it, and his cannon riddled it into a cullender, and it is now a complete ruin. I rode out there one day, and saw where the Californians under Col. Green crawled up in a ditch to within a hundred yards of the walls, and with their Henry rifles shot down the Imperialist gunners at their posts, silencing their cannon, while the batteries of the Republicans sent their shot crashing through and through the structure, until it became a perfect wreck and untenable.

The College of Mines or Mining College was one of the noblest educational institutions of Mexico in its design, and it had been famous for half a century, before, even an attempt at founding such a school had been made in the United States. The building—cut granite, commenced in 1780 and completed about the beginning of the present century—is one of the largest, and most beautiful and substantial structures on the continent. It is three stories in height and built on the general plan in Mexico, with capacious *patios* or court-yards surrounded by broad corridors, everything being of stone, even down to the floors. From the flat stone roof the view of the city is magnificent. The college was intended to give young men a complete practical education in all that pertains to mines and mining, engineering, etc., etc. Provision was made for an astronomical observatory, and the scientific apparatus was always of the latest, best, and most complete character. But the college has suffered sadly from war and violence, and it will take years of peace to fully restore it. In 1846—7, the American troops were quartered there. What damage they did I am of course unable to say, but it is certain that when the French evacuated Mexico, a vast number of the richest and most intrinsically valuable specimens in the collection of minerals and metals disappeared; and a great portion of the most costly scientific apparatus had been wantonly destroyed, or rendered useless when the Republicans re-entered the city. At present there are but about thirty students in the college which could easily accommodate five hundred, or even one thousand. Efforts are being made to repair the damage, and place the college once more in a perfect condition.

The collection of minerals, all neatly arranged in glass cases, and carefully catalogued and labeled, is very large; larger, I think, than any two in the United

States; and many of the specimens are of rare beauty, and of great interest to scientific men. I have seen collections made in California and Nevada, by private citizens, which contained more silver and gold, and had therefore more intrinsic value, but never any which approached this in variety and general excellence.

There is also a large but heterogeneous collection in Natural History, embracing some very rare and beautiful specimens; it is not, however, equal to that which was burned at the Smithsonian Institute at Washington a few years since, and the collection of stuffed birds is not equal in artistic merit to that of the Audubon Club at Chicago.

CHAPTER XVI.

SOCIAL CONDITION AND CUSTOMS.

THERE is something curious, and—to me at least—painful, in the peculiar aspect of social life in Mexico. Though the Republic has decreed the abolition of *peonage* throughout Mexico, and made all men equal, at least in theory, before the law, it is powerless to break down the barriers of caste and long continued custom, which makes the woman of Mexico, though theorectically free, practically a slave. Religion has much to answer for in this; and customs as old as a race are hard to eradicate, when religion stands behind them.

The girls of the capital enjoy little of the liberty accorded to the young women of the United States, and really see but little of society until after marriage, if they are so fortunate, or unfortunate, as to ever marry at all. They are generally—I am speaking of the daughters of the wealthy or middle class families—educated in schools under the actual, though not nominal, control of the church—convents in which they were formerly educated having been abolished by law—and the system of education is not, as a rule, what we would consider liberal. They have a natural taste for music, play and sing with great ability, and often show remarkable talent for fine embroidery, wax work, drawing and painting. At home they are models of devotion to their parents, brothers, and sisters. Nowhere else on earth, have I seen such affectionate treatment of parents by children and children, by parents, as in Mexico. As a rule, the influence and control of parents over their children never fully ceases save with death, and after death their memory is cherished, it seems to me, with more fondness than elsewhere in the world.

I am proud of the daughters of my own loved land, and here in this world of tropical beauty, still longed to walk once more among them, to hear the music of their voices, and mark the air of independent self-possession which freedom gives, the bold, free step and proud grace of carriage which characterizes the haughty daughters of our conquering race. But there is one thing in which the children of Mexico far excel those of the United States, and that is, filial devotion. "Honor thy Father and thy Mother that thy days may be long upon the land which the Lord thy God giveth thee," is a command which the daughters of Mexico obey with a whole-souled earnestness that is beautiful to witness. But freedom of action outside of the family circle, there is little of any for them. An unmarried lady cannot go out upon the street alone in broad daylight; nay, she cannot even go out for a single block, in company of a gentleman, though he be the oldest friend of the family, married, and known to every man and woman on the street, according to the strict idea of social propriety in the capital. A married woman, or at least an old one, must always accompany her.

I rode out one day to Tacubuya, with a married lady friend and a young unmarried lady. Returning, we came first to the residence of the married lady, and as the carriage stopped I sprang out to help her alight; but she drew back with the remark:

"But L—is too tired to walk home, and she had better be carried there!"

"Oh yes, but it is only two blocks, and I can take her directly there in the carriage!" I remarked in my Californian simplicity.

"That will never do in Mexico!" was her prompt reply.

So I took them both to the young lady's house, left her there, and returned in the carriage with the married lady to her residence. That this incessant watching, and implied want of all confidence in the honesty and virtue of the young, is subversive of virtue, and tends to the defeat of its own object, seems to me quite clear; nevertheless, it is the custom of the country, and must be complied with by all residents in the capital. In justice to the women of Mexico let me say, that in my opinion, the custom is as unnecessary, as it is oppressive and odious in our sight.

None of the fields for independent effort and self-sustaining labor, which are open to the women of the United States, can be entered by the women of Mexico, and the future of a poor young widow, or an orphan girl with no immediate relations to care for her, may well be considered a dark and doubtful one. The natural kind-heartedness of the people, induces the most distant relatives, in such cases, to come forward to the support of the widow and the fatherless; but a life of unceasing dependence—often upon those least able to grant even that boon—is something only to be accepted as an alternative to the one thing worse.

Mexico is full of young women, naturally gifted, accomplished, and fitted to become good, loving wives and mothers, who are unmarried and have no prospect of ever being sought in marriage. Years on years of war and revolution, have forced into the army and killed off, or unfitted for marriage, a large portion of the young men of Mexico, and it is calculated that there are now in the capital, from four to seven unmarried and marriageable young ladies, to every young man of marriageable age who has any disposition to marry, or is in circumstances to justify his doing so. In the United States, a young couple may safely marry without a dollar to begin with, for new fields of enterprise are always open, and the poor, young man of to-day may be the richest of the rich a few years hence. But not so in Mexico. As a rule—there are honorable exceptions to it—the son of a Mexican family, once rich but now impoverished, lives upon such resources, as are left to him; rides his horse on the *paseo* at morning and evening, pays attention to his female friends in society, and while he is idly waiting for something to turn up to better his condition, lets so much of life slip by, that he at last finds himself an old bachelor and unfit to marry. In such a condition of society, a rich, young girl will of course have no lack of suitors, but the portionless girl, though never so good, beautiful, and accomplished, has but a poor chance indeed. These truths will fall unpleasantly upon some ears, and their utterance will be resented; but they are truths, nevertheless, I am sorry to be compelled to say.

The American, or other foreigner, in good social standing, can always marry well, so far as youth, beauty, and accomplishment go, in Mexico; but the chance of his marrying into a wealthy family, and profiting by it, are not nearly so much in his favor as if he were native born. Knowing what I do of Mexico, I must say, that if I were a young American, unmarried, and "fancy free," I would prefer the wider field of enterprise open to me in the United States, to the narrower field in Mexico; but if I had been born in Mexico, I would marry among my own people, settle down, and labor with all my heart and soul for the regeneration of my country. Mexico is a country well worthy the love and self-sacrifice of all her sons.

The children in Mexico strike you with surprise and admiration. You see no idle, vicious, saucy boys running around on the streets, annoying decent people by their vile language and rude behavior. All the boys you see have earnest faces, and walk with a sedate and grave demeanor like grown up men. I never saw a badly behaved child in Mexico. In the family circle the people are models for the world. The young *always* treat the old with the deepest respect, and the affection displayed by parents for their children and children for their parents, is most admirable. The daughter of a good family in Mexico, though grown to womanhood, will kiss the hand of her father when she meets him on the street, and always kisses her parents, brothers, and sisters at morning and evening, and many times during the day, with the greatest warmth, and earnestness. When the children marry, they usually remain under the parental roof as long as the parents live, and the parents control the house.

The people of Mexico are, to-day, very poor. Among the very lowest classes there is less suffering than among the class who have once been rich, and are now laboring to keep up appearances after all actual prosperity has gone, and their available resources are exhausted. Beggars lounge around everywhere, and accost you upon every street and on every block, and you can only escape their importunities while in your own house or hotel, by giving the strictest orders to your servants to exclude them. Many of these beggars are really needy, sick, maimed and helpless; but many others are graceless impostors. There is no public provision for the helpless and deserving poor, and every year the beggars increase in numbers. The increase of late years has been very great. Only when you say "*pardone!*" will the street beggars bow and leave you. The numbers of horribly maimed wretches you see on the streets of Mexico is almost incredible.

"TENGO NADA SEÑOR!"

The absence of anything like the bustle and noise of a northern city, is noticed at once by a stranger in Mexico. Wholesale trade there is next to none at all, and the retail stores are small, and for the most part poorly patronized. You see no drays loaded with goods for the interior, going through the streets as with us, and the cry of the auctioneer is unheard. Mexico is in no sense a commercial or manufacturing city; its productive industries hardly equaling those of a town of a tenth part of its population in the New England States. You hear the voice of the "church going bell," from morning to night, but listen in vain for the note of the steam-whistle calling operatives to their work, or the hum of busy factories, and the clanking of the laboring engine. Church towers attract the eye on all sides, but you look in vain for the factory chimney.

EARTHENWARE SELLER.

Hawkers of all kinds of goods, *rebosas*, and *serapes*, bridles, saddlery, spurs, boots and shoes, jewelry, and in fact nearly everything usually kept in a country variety store, swarm about the plaza, and under the portals, on all the principal streets. Around the market, a large portion of the country produce and garden vegetables are sold by the men and women who bring it in upon their backs, in great crates or hampers. The chicken, orange, vegetable, and earthenware venders will be readily recognized by any visitor to Mexico. The protuberance of the eyes of all these people, caused by carrying such enormous back-loads from infancy, is their most marked feature.

The citizens of the capital are supplied with water, in a great measure, by licensed water carriers, who sell the contents of a three pail jar borne on their backs, and a smaller one carried in front, all for three cents, delivering it in the house. The water carrier generally finishes his work by noon, and by 2 P. M. is blind, but quietly drunk on pulque.

WATER CARRIER.

A curious but effective illustration of the character of the climate of Mexico, is found in the fact that comments on the weather—the staple subject of conversation with us—are seldom heard, and do not enter into or form a part of the regular topics of the day. I noticed many times during our stay in the capital, that when Mr. Seward would remark, "It is a delightful day!" or pass some other comment on the weather, the Mexicans present would respond politely in the affirmative, but with an air which plainly indicated that they were in doubt as to what was meant by the remark. One day, after a glorious ride out to Tacubuya and Chapultepec, in which I had most heartily enjoyed the pure air and warm, soft sunshine, I said to one of the younger daughters of the President, a frank-hearted, outspoken, and most amiable young lady, "This is a beautiful day!" She looked at me a moment with the old look of puzzled doubt on her face, and said, "I do not understand you!" I repeated the remark, and she then replied: "*Si Señor*

Como no?" (Yes sir; why not?") and then went on to say that all the days were beautiful as a general thing; only now and then a norther making it otherwise. The fact is, that the weather is so generally beautiful, and the exceptions so rare, that the words we use so often every week in our changeable climate, have no appreciable meaning to the dwellers in this favored clime.

The belief in the "evil eye," a superstition of purely Eastern origin, is quite common among the lower classes of the Mexican people. Many times I have seen a poor Mexican mother standing by the roadside, with her young infant in her arms, and on observing one of our party looking towards her, draw the end of her rebosa quickly over the face of the child, lest its fortunes should be blighted and its soul imperiled by the glance of the stranger. The superstition is confined solely to the lower class of the people, but it manifests itself exactly as it does in Arabia and the Barbary States to this day, and evidently came to America with the Spaniards.

ORANGE SELLER.

It is customary in all Spanish American countries to offer a guest everything which he may require for his comfort and convenience, and literally, to put the entire house, and every thing in it, at his disposal for the time being. This practice grows out of a genuine feeling of liberality, and hospitality, but the language used is such as to be quite readily misunderstood by a stranger who measures expressions by the cold matter-of-fact rule in use in colder countries, and attaches more weight to a mere formality than it is justly entitled to. When you enter the house of a friend, or even a person to whom you have a letter of introduction, in Spanish America, he at once tells you, that you are "in your own house," and that you are the master and he your guest, or something to that effect. He really expects you to make yourself at home in the broadest sense of the term, but on the other hand, pays you the compliment of supposing that you have, at least, an ordinary amount of common sense, and will know enough of what constitutes the rules and customs of society, not to abuse the offer, and outstay your welcome.

POULTRY SELLER.

If you particularly admire any picture, or article of jewelry or furniture, he will immediately tell you that it is at your disposal, and you are quite welcome to carry it away with you. He does not, in all probability, expect you to accept the offer; but if you are ignorant or ill-bred enough to do so, he will conceal his chagrin, if he feels any, and permit you to carry away anything you fancy, however inconvenient it may be for him to part with it.

Sometimes ludicrous, and even painful results follow this misapprehension of the true value of courteous expressions made by a host or hostess to a guest. I remember a case of an English lady who was on a visit to Mexico, and on making the acquaintance of a family of wealth and position, was one day offered a beautiful and valuable set of diamonds and emeralds, which had been in the family for generations. She was told, of course, that she was welcome to take them away with her, and in the innocence of her heart did so.

VEGETABLE SELLER.

The result was, that mutual friends learning the true state of the case, were compelled to go to her and explain how matters stood, much to her mortification. She at once returned the jewels with an explanation that they had proved, on trial, not to suit her complexion and style of dress, and offering in return for the courtesy shown her, to send a set of her own jewelry to the house, as a present to one of the daughters of the family. Of course her offer was declined, with many thanks, and renewed offers of service from the other side. Good common sense in this case, made up for the lack of familiarity with the social customs of the country, but I have known some of my own countrymen and countrywomen who were less fortunate.

For years, the residents of San Francisco were familiar with the face and form of an eccentric, and probably mildly insane old individual, who delighted in the sobriquet of Uncle Freddy, *alias* Washington the Second. What his real name was I never knew, but he was an Englishman by birth, I believe, and while he imagined, or affected to imagine himself the very counterpart of Washington, he really did resemble the portraits of Benjamin Franklin, in a remarkable degree.

Uncle Freddy could be seen parading Montgomery street any fine day, dressed in a full buckskin suit and cocked hat, regular "old Continental" style, or black velvet, similarly cut, and with knee-breeches, white stockings, and silver buckled shoes. Sometimes he carried a gorgeous banner, the legends on which commemorated his deeds of valor and humanity, and his claims upon the public crib as a benefactor of our country and race. Any contribution in acknowledgment of his eminent services was welcome, and the larger the donation the more profuse were his apologies and protestations of gratitude.

The sun of fortune seemed to shine lovingly upon Uncle Freddy, but he had a weakness like all other great men, and in an evil moment it proved his ruin. He imagined himself a woman-killer, and would indulge in the most ludicrous demonstrations of politeness towards every body on the street whose attention was drawn to his slightly obese figure, set off by the curiously antiquated costume which he affected.

San Francisco has still another speciality, in the shape of "Norton I., By the Grace of God and the Will of the people, Emperor of the United States, Protector of Mexico, and Sovereign Lord of the Guano Islands," as he styles himself in all his proclamations. You may see him to-day, dressed in a soiled and greasy uniform, cocked hat and feather, carrying a heavy cavalry sword and a huge knotty cane up and down Montgomery street, or peering curiously into the shop windows, examining every work of art, with a critical and appreciative eye.

The cares of state weigh heavily upon Norton the First, and in his advanced age he is becoming subject to certain slight ebulitions of wrath, on the slightest provocation. He daily sends off communications to the different crowned heads of Europe and Asia, commanding them to do this thing or that thing, immediately. His telegraphic dispatches would—and generally do—fill an ordinary waste-basket every week in the year, and the number of proclamations which he sends to the different newspaper offices, with command to publish at once, on penalty of instant death and confiscation of property, is beyond computation. He was a wealthy speculator in breadstuffs, in the early days of San Francisco, and probably receives more or less assistance from his old and more fortunate acquaintances, and possibly also, from a secret order of which he was once a member; but the full secret of his living and maintaining his royal state, is a mystery to most people.

When Maximilian arrived in Mexico, he received communication after communication from the Emperor Norton I., signed by His Majesty in person, and adorned with seals of the size of a small cheese, giving him much good advice, and offering many suggestions as to the method of conducting the affairs of the new Empire, which it was evidently supposed would receive due consideration, as coming from an old hand and successful operator in the business of Imperialism. These documents received much attention at first, and for a long time bothered the head of the son of the House of Hapsburg-Lorraine, and all his ministers, exceedingly.

One day, Uncle Freddy mentioned to a friend, in confidence, that he had written to Queen Victoria on some subject, and the treacherous friend at once related the circumstance to the Emperor, adding that he—Uncle Freddy—had denounced the Emperor as a humbug and a swindle. From that moment the Emperor Norton First, and Washington the Second, were mortal enemies, and every day added fuel to the flame of their animosity.

Washington opened a curiosity shop on Clay street, and the Emperor went up there and smashed it, and all its contents, into a cocked-hat. Washington appealed to the police, and was told, that the Emperor being the source of all power, no writ would hold against him. Then Washington met a Chinese woman of the better class on the street, gorgeously arrayed, and as she looked at him with curiosity, bowed to her. This incident was reported to the Emperor, with the addition that the young female Mongolion was a Chinese princess, sent over to America to be married to His Majesty, in order to bring about an alliance offensive and defensive between the two Empires, and that Uncle Freddy was endeavoring to get her prejudiced against royalty, and in favor of himself.

This last straw broke the Imperial Camel's back, and Norton the First, at once issued a peremptory order to General McDowell, for the arrest and execution of Uncle Freddy, adding, that if the order was disregarded as others had been, he would go out, sword in hand, and put down the rebellion summarily. The wags who had been carrying on the joke, seeing that matters had come to a dangerous pass, and bloodshed was not unlikely to follow, consulted together, and determined to induce Uncle Freddy to emigrate, at once, to New York. On the way down the coast, the steamer on which Uncle Freddy was a passenger, touched at Acapulco, and the venerable representative of the Father of His Country, asked Señor Mancillas, now of the Mexican Congress, who was also a passenger, to introduce him to General Juan Alvarez, then in command of the port of Acapulco, and Governor of the State of Guerrero. Mancillas thoughtlessly complied, and the old fellow at once made himself extremely familiar with the authorities on shore.

When the time for the steamer to depart arrived, Mancillas went to pay his respects and bid good-bye to General Alvarez, and was not a little surprised to find Uncle Freddy installed in the house in all the pomp of the Father of His Country, indeed, and a guest of national importance. He had informed the gallant old Republican General, that he had rendered distinguished service to Mexico during the war of 1846–7, which he had opposed with all his might, and final success. The General of course told him that he was welcome to the country, and that the house and everything in the house was his own. If he could make up his mind to spend the remainder of his days in so poor a country as Mexico, and so poor a city as Acapulco, he would feel only too happy, to have him for a guest for the rest of his life.

Uncle Freddy took a look at the premises, rather liked the way everything was arranged and proceeded to dine sumptuously. When Señor Mancillas, at his last call, reminded him that the steamer's gun had been fired, and it was time to go off in the boat, he stretched his legs comfortably in the cool verandah, and informed him that he had determined to accept the hospitable invitation which had been extended to him, make that his home, and consider himself the guest of General Alvarez and the Mexican Republic, for the remainder of his days. Mancillas argued and expostulated in vain; Uncle Freddy had struck too good a thing, and he meant to enjoy it.

At last, in a fit of very desperation, Mancillas sent a party to invite the healthy old shade of the father of his country outside the door, and then seize him, and hurry him down to the boat and off to the steamer by main strength.

When General Alvarez heard of the "outrage" he was in a great passion, and could only be appeased by hearing the whole story, and learning that the kidnapping had been done by the order of Señor Mancillas, in order to relieve him—the General—of the presence of a lunatic, whom he had thoughtlessly introduced into the house, and who proposed to take the General at his word, and stay there for life.

Uncle Freddy was borne away from the shores of Mexico sorely against his will, and when last seen, on

Broadway, New York, was still bitterly bewailing the lost opportunity, like the man who being asked to "excuse" a lady to whom he had popped the question, excused her, and as he informed his friends, regretted having done so, to the end of his existence.

Many strangers are inclined to look upon the profuse offers of hospitality on the part of the Spanish American people, as utterly insincere, and made with an expectation in advance that they would never be accepted. This view of the case is, however, far too broad and sweeping. As a rule, the people of Mexico are truly hospitable in the broadest acceptation of the term, and strangers are welcomed and entertained with pleasure; but it is, of course, expected that they will use reason, and show some sense of delicacy; and a mere arbitrary translation of the expressions used would be unjust, as putting language into the mouth of the host or hostess which they never intended to use.

It is quite the fashion for foreigners of all classes, to denounce the Mexicans as a set of thieves and scoundrels, false, treacherous, cowardly, unreliable, and without a single redeeming characteristic. I will not claim for the Mexicans that they are a nation of angels and saints; they have their virtues and their faults like all other nations. But that they are more dishonest, or more given to disgraceful peculation and swindling than many of the foreigners with whom they have had to deal, I cannot believe. There are some most notable exceptions among the foreign-born residents of Mexico, but it is nevertheless the fact, that far too many of them bore but an indifferent character in their own country, came to Mexico to get rich "by hook or by crook," and have no scruples worth mentioning as to how they make the money so that they make it and get away with it. I have heard a thousand stories illustrative of the practices of foreigners of this class in Mexico; a couple will be sufficient to convey a fair idea of the conduct of those who are accustomed to denounce the Mexicans, in the most unmeasured terms, for alleged dishonesty and unreliability.

During the French intervention, a large European importing house, doing business in Western Mexico, landed a large invoice of goods at Manzanillo, which port was then in possession of the Republicans. The city to which they desired to send the goods for sale, was in the possession of the Imperialists, and they must deal with both parties in order to have them passed through the lines of the opposing forces. They accordingly proposed to the Republican authorities to pay the duties, contingently. As they represented that the Imperialists would in all probability let the goods go through, but there was no certainty of their doing so, they proposed to give the Republic drafts on themselves, payable on the receipt of the acknowledgment that they had been passed. The Republicans being sorely in want of funds consented, and gave receipts to be exhibited to the Imperialists as evidence that the goods had already paid duty.

The goods went through all right, and were disposed of at swinging profits within the Imperialist lines, the Imperialist collector being convinced that a heavy duty had already been paid, and that it would be wrong to exact a second under the circumstances. Then, when the drafts were presented for payment, the drawers replied: "Oh! but you are not representative of the Government of Mexico! The Governments of Europe have acknowledged the Empire as the only legitimate Government in Mexico, and it will be necessary for you to have these drafts presented by the imperial authorities; we cannot recognize them in any other hands." The Mexican authorities were fairly outwitted, and both parties swindled out of the entire duties.

A friend of the house which perpetrated this neat little piece of thieving—for it is nothing less—told the story to me as an illustration of the shrewdness and business ability of the head of the concern, and really seemed to think it a very creditable transaction on the part of the importers, who pocketed a small fortune by the operation.

Another transaction, the parties to which were men occupying prominent positions in politics, took place at the City of Mexico. A revolutionary party was driven out of the capital by the legitimate authorities. As they —the revolutionists—were hurrying away, a gentleman of wealth, who was complicated and found it necessary or desirable to leave with them, in order to save his magnificent private residence from occupation and confiscation by the Government, made a lease of it at a nominal rent to the French minister, who immediately took possession. The owner soon made his peace with the Government, and according to the previous arrangement returned and demanded the restoration of his property. He was put off and refused on one pretext or another, until a new French minister came out to replace the first, and the property was then turned over to him, against the indignant and emphatic protest of the hapless owner. The new minister held the property until turned out of it by a decision of the last court of appeal, and then, when the owner was restored to the possession, he found that every article of furniture, all the rich and costly plate, etc., etc., was gone, and that in fact, only the four walls of the once magnificently furnished house remained. The plate was taken to the United States, and a part of it, at least, was sold at auction at Washington, and is now in the possession of a friend of mine who purchased it in good faith, little dreaming that men so high in office and authority could be guilty of having stolen it outright.

I suppress the names and dates for obvious reasons, in both cases, but the facts, especially in regard to the last transaction, are so well known in Mexico that any person can verify them who cares to do so. Such transactions are bad enough in all conscience, but they are not worthy of being mentioned in connection with such frauds as the "Jecker Claim," which was backed up—cooked up I ought to say perhaps—by the minister of a first-class European power, and in the hands of a cunning imperial schemer, served as one of the principal pretexts for the invasion of Mexico, and the attempt to establish a hostile Empire on our borders.

I ought to say on behalf of the women of Mexico, that all foreigners, even those who denounce the men in the most unjust and unmeasured terms, unite in praising their constancy, faithfulness and devotion. They are not only as wives and mothers devoted to their husbands and children, but they are ever ready to assist in every possible manner, the afflicted. The suffering of every nationality, even those who have come among them as enemies, always find them ready to sympathize, aid, and comfort to the utmost of their ability. From highest to lowest this is the rule. You have only to tell a Mexican woman that your life is in danger and that you throw yourself upon her protection, and you may be sure that she will risk her own life, honor, everything in fact, to protect you.

In this fact is found the ready explanation of the escape of so many revolutionists after their defeat by the Government. The most detested wretch on the earth can appeal to the women of Mexico for food and shelter, and it will be given him. To refuse either, would be in the eyes of a Mexican woman, an unpardonable sin against God and humanity, and thus it is that men like Marguez, who have committed murders and other crimes without number, almost invariably escape justice, and succeed in reaching a foreign shore. A prisoner sentenced for a long term, applied to me to say a good word for him to the authorities, and a Mexican lady, who accompanied me at the moment, urged me to comply.

"But he is a rascal and an enemy of your family!" I said.

"Oh Señor, that is true, but he is sick and in prison, *pobrecito!*" was the only reply.

She is a better Christian than I.

The Mexican servants in the City of Mexico are a peculiar class. They earn but a fraction of what we in the United States would call a salary—say from three to fifteen dollars per month, five or six dollars being a fair average. They often remain several years in a family, and many of them, in fact, are born, raised, and die in the same house, and in the family of their first master. With foreigners, they are generally a little less reliable than when serving native masters, probably, because they are less closely watched, and their employers, being less familiar with their habits and peculiarities, are less able to protect themselves from their eccentricities. They will generally leave a very valuable article or large sum of money untouched, but small articles of finery and small coins are very likely to get lost, if left around loose in their reach.

With us, it is the custom to pay the largest salaries to those of our employes who have the responsibility of handling the most money, but a lady in Mexico told me with charming naivette, that the rule was just the contrary there, as those who handled the most money had the least need of a salary. It is so common a thing for the cook or purveyor for a family to make a small percentage off the purchases, that it is looked upon as quite a matter of course, and nothing is thought of it.

One day Mr. Fitch, in passing along the street in Mexico, saw a pair of patent-leather gaiters, which being highly ornamented, pleased his fancy, and he forthwith ordered a pair built to fit him. When the servant brought them home, I asked him how much they cost. He answered promptly:

"Five dollars and a half!"

I said—as I could with impunity, since Mr. Fitch did not understand Spanish:

"You ought to add fifty cents for yourself!"

"I have done so, Señor!" said the fellow promptly, smiling knowingly, as if he understood the situation at once.

But you should have added a dollar instead of fifty cents; the padre is delighted with the boots and would stand it!"

The fellow, without a moment's hesitation, turned to Mr. Fitch and told him the bill was six dollars. The money was paid, and as he received it and turned to go, he dropped five dollars into his pantaloons pocket, and transferred one-half-dollar of the balance to his jacket pocket, and with the most amiable and knowing air imaginable, held the other fifty cent piece out in his open hand for me to take, as he passed me in the doorway. He meant to do business on the square, and come to a fair divide. From what I had said, he took me for the financial man of the party, and supposed, of course, that I was—pardon the Californianism—"on the make" as well as himself. My natural and unconquerable modesty, coupled with the fact that I wore a uniform which I felt bound to honor while in a foreign land, induced me to refuse the money, and whisper to him to keep it as a present. He kept it!

The servants furnished to Mr. Seward's party by the Mexican Government during our stay in Mexico, certainly would compare favorably with any I have ever seen, being attentive and efficient, and at least, as honest as they will average anywhere. From one side of the continent to the other, our clothing and other articles of baggage were at their mercy, and we lost nothing whatever. In fact, we found it impossible to lose some things which we would gladly have left behind us.

At one point on our journey, some inconsiderate friend presented Mr. Seward with a huge petrifaction from some stone quarry. This proved a perfect fossil elephant, and after the shins of the entire party had suffered fearfully, it was left behind us—by accident of course—at Puebla. The next day we were congratulating ourselves on the loss, when Pedro, one of the servants who had accompanied us across the continent, came smiling up to the coach door, with the monstrosity carefully done up in a rag—he had carried it this way the entire distance, and was proudly conscious of having, in so doing, deserved well of his country and mankind in general. He was duly thanked, of course, and we kicked it about from one side of the coach to the other, with many a secret blessing on the donor and the faithful servant who had returned it.

At Palmar, I placed it under my bed, and congratulated myself on having seen the last of it, as the coach rolled away next morning. Vain delusion! At Orizaba, next day, I went into the dilligence office to transact some business, when the agent said to me:

"Señor, you lost something at Palmar, but give yourself no uneasiness; it will be down here to night by the dilligence. They are honest people and would not take anything from you."

"Was it money that they found?" I asked, affecting a carelessness I was far from feeling.

"O no, Señor: a big rock; very curious indeed, and doubtless very valuable."

My heart was too full for words, and I could only bow my thanks and shake his hand in silence.

On leaving Orizaba I tried it on and failed more ignobly, for it was picked up and placed upon my hat-box, which it smashed down at once; and so in spite of every effort I could make, it clung to me like the nightmare, and turned up in due time at Vera Cruz.

But in that ancient city I was master of the situation. I occupied a room at a hotel, pending the arrival of Mr. Seward from Orizaba,—having gone down to the coast in advance of the remainder of the party from that point—and had no one to watch my actions, with a view of doing me a service on every occasion in spite of myself. I took it one night, carefully wrapped up in paper, and carrying it down to the city front, climbed upon some railroad material and hurled it over the wall into the shallow water outside.

I got back to the hotel unobserved, but going down to the mole next day, I observed a party of fishermen and idlers gathered about something which they had picked up and brought there in a boat; it was that accursed petrifaction again. I bought it from the happy finder for twenty-five cents, and carried it to where some men were overhauling a lot of goods in boxes. From them I borrowed a hatchet, and pretending to be deeply curious as to what was inside, proceeded with the wise look of a regular "rock-sharp," to smash it into a thousand pieces. I found no gold inside it, and in well simulated disappointment gathered up the pieces, and threw them, one after another, as far as I could send them, out into the deep water, taking good care that no two pieces, of any size, fell near together. I have not seen any of it since, thank Heaven!

The men servants are generally better posted than the female servants in the matter of foreigners. One female servant in the family of a friend who was going to the United States on a visit, was horrified at the thought of the fate that awaited her beloved mistress.

"Oh Señora for the love of God and the holy saints, don't go among those Yankees! They will eat you; they will *certainly* eat you!" was her constant cry when she saw the final preparations for departure being made. They left her in tears and despair, fully convinced that her dear mistress would be devoured as soon as she put her foot on American soil. She told her mistress that when the army of Gen. Scott entered Mexico, she fled to the mountains with her husband, and staid there until they left the country.

They never talk back, after the manner of the Italian servants in America, but reply to every epithet with a fresh offer of service.

"You d—d drunken loafer!" thundered a master to his servant who was endeavoring to back an unusually heavy load of *pulque.*

"Si Señor, at your service!" was the polite and prompt reply, as the *mozo* lifted his hat and bowed like an India rubber man.

It takes about four servants in Mexico, to do the work of one in the United States, and as you board them, the cost of labor for a family is considerable, after all. If you pay a servant his or her wages in advance, or day by day, the chances are, that you can keep them almost any length of time; but let them get a few dollars due them, and they are almost certain to come to you, and say:

"Please Señor or Señora, I want to have my wages settled up on Saturday, as I am going to the village where my family reside, to rest a few weeks. When I have had a good rest I will come back if you want me!"

The idea of allowing money to accumulate on their hands is exceedingly against their fancy, and they make it a point to get rid of it as soon as they lay their hands upon it. I thought before this trip, that servants in the United States were the worst in the world, but heard just as much complaint about them in Mexico as in California. In all fairness I must say, that I think the Mexican servant system better, or at least, less troublesome than ours.

The census takers in the United States sometimes complain of the annoyances and indignities which they are made to suffer; but they have a glorious time compared with their fellow-laborers in Mexico. It is said that the actual population of the country can only be approximated, it being impossible to get at the number of able-bodied men in any given town. The intelligent and educated families will answer at all times, correctly; but among the lower classes from which the army is mainly recruited, it is next to impossible to get correct returns. The appearance of a man with a book, or roll of paper and pencil, is the signal for all the men capable of doing military duty to skedaddle in double-quick time, and the women, fearing that it is a preliminary arrangement for a conscription, persistently declare that there is not an able-bodied man on the premises.

CHAPTER XVII.

THE ARMY, PRESS, AND POLITICAL SITUATION.

THE Mexican army is to-day, stronger in actual numbers than that of the United States, and in spite of the prevailing stringency in the treasury, tolerably well paid, and in a good state of discipline and efficiency. The army absorbs half the annual revenue of the Republic, but as it must not only garrison the towns and maintain peace, but do guard duty, patrol the road, fight *pronunciados* and *bandidos*, escort travelers, and specie and imported goods trains, and do a variety of other work not often required of an army in other countries, it would seem impossible, in the present condition of the country, to reduce its numbers. I doubt if it can be done safely for years to come.

The men are generally stout, compact, muscular, and active—though less in stature than American soldiers—very enduring, and capable of marching rapidly and on the smallest amount of food. They are, nearly all, of the dark, bronze hue, which indicates pure, or nearly pure Indian blood, but the commissioned officers are usually of lighter complexion. They are well drilled, mostly armed with American muskets or breech-loaders, and march with great precision. There are three battalions constantly on duty at and around the Palacio Nacional, and others are in various parts of the city.

One of these is the "Invalid Corps," composed of maimed veterans who are still able to do guard duty. This corps was founded by Maximilian, and on the capture of the city by General Diaz, after the fall of Queretero, they fought more savagely than any others, against their old comrades, the republicans. Nevertheless, the corps was not disbanded by Juarez, and in case of the attempt being made to carry the city by *pronunciados*, or foreign invaders, they would probably fight as stoutly on the side of the Republic, as they then did against it.

The students in the Military College—who are soon to return to their old quarters at Chapultepec—are nearly all, mere boys; but they are determined republicans, and during the French invasion, more than once, fought with the most desperate valor against the invaders.

One or more of the battalions stationed at the Palace, marched past our house on full dress parade every morning, and we could hear every footfall at exactly the same time, so that it seemed like the movement of a great machine. They have each a splendid band, and I noticed that they played something in compliment to Mr. Seward, nearly every time. One day they came down Alfaro street, playing

"Tramp, tramp, tramp, the boys are marching!"

in as good style as I have ever heard it played in the United States, and I suppose had we stayed longer, we might have heard the

"Battle cry of freedom!"

I saw only infantry and cavalry corps, but was told

that they had artillery as well. The lance is no longer used, and the cavalry, for desultory warfare at least appears to be fully equal to our own.

The press of Mexico is yet in its infancy, and falls far short of holding its proper position in the community. Though nominally free, it is hampered in many ways. The name of the "responsible editor" and proprietor must be given in every edition. The Government of the Republic and the different State governments have subsidized organs, which publish the laws, speak authoritatively, and reflect the views only of the party, at the moment, in power. This discourages enterprise, and intensifies and embitters party feeling; the few opposition papers being driven to pursue the most violent course, as the only means of living at all. Such a thing as a newspaper sustained wholly, or to any considerable extent, by its advertising patronage is unknown. The entire circulation of all the daily and weekly papers in the Republic combined, is not equal to that of a single one of the second class dailies of New York.

In the City of Mexico there is something like progress displayed by the press, but it is very little, after all. The dailies are specially deficient in the matter of local news; an event of startling importance—as it would be regarded in the United States—occurring within two blocks of the office, may find its way into a paper within a week, or it may never be alluded to. The political editorials are often very bitter and abusive, but generally well-written and forcible, and the literary department is usually good. Each paper publishes a serial novel in a division at the bottom, so arranged that it can be cut off and bound in pages into a volume complete, when the story is finished. The subscribers always cut these off the bottom of the paper, and save them for this purpose.

In the matter of foreign news, the press of Mexico is usually, very greatly behind the rest of the world, and a New York daily will spend—and by reason of its liberal patronage, is well able to spend—more in one day for telegraphic matter, than a Mexican daily will devote to the same purpose in a year.

There are many finely educated, literary men—men of extensive reading and rare accomplishment—in Mexico; and many books have been published at the capital, which would compare favorably with those from any country, on the same subject. Poetry is especially popular, and many volumes of purely native composition are to be found. The people of Mexico excel in music, and many of their native airs are of a high order of merit. "The Hymn of Zoragasa," in celebration of the victory of the Mexicans over the French at Puebla, on the "*Cinco de Mayo*," are equal to anything ever produced in the United States. Many of their love songs and patriotic ballads are very beautiful.

Probably the most complete and extensive printing establishment in Mexico is that of the "*Siglo Diez y Nueve*," owned by Cumplido & Son. The elder Cumplido was born in Guadalajara in 1811. At fifteen years of age he had read enough of the history of the United States to desire to see that country, and leaving home, he walked all the way to Mexico. There he worked until he obtained sufficient means to carry him to the United States. After mastering the printing trade in New York, he started back with a complete printing and engraving establishment. He arrived off Vera Cruz to find the port blockaded by the French—in the winter of 1838—9—and the vessel put back towards New Orleans. On the way back the vessel was lost, and everything on board went to the bottom. The passengers were saved, and reached New Orleans, and an American war-vessel—the sloop *Natchez*—carried Señor Cumplido to Tampico, from which point he walked to Mexico in nine days.

Again he set to work to retrieve his fortunes, and in three years was enabled to start once more for New York. There he again fitted out an office, and returning to Mexico with ten printers, engravers, and lithographers, established the first daily newspaper in Mexico. He has gone through all the changes of fortune incident to public life in Mexico; has been exiled, had his property confiscated, etc., etc., but has every time, by his energy and resolution, placed himself again on his feet. He has visited the United States ten times, and his love of republican institutions has increased with each visit. He has published several very creditable volumes of polite literature, and still takes an active interest in the business of the office. His summer residence at the suburban village of San Angel, beyond Tacubuya, is a model of elegance, beauty and good taste, and he is counted as a man of independent wealth. His son still carries on the business which the father commenced, and "*El Siglo XIX*" is the oldest and most flourishing paper in Mexico. Its old editor, Francisco Zarco, who died while Mr. Seward was in Mexico, was the ablest journalist among the Reform party in the Republic. His place is now ably filled by Señor Antonio Mancillas, formerly publisher of "*El Voz de Mejico*" in California, and now member of Congress from Zacatecas.

The Congress and people of Mexico are now discussing schemes for inducing immigration from Europe and the United States. There are some fanatics who oppose all immigration, and in order to keep the country and all its institutions *exclusively* Mexican, are willing to see the present state of things continue indefinitely; but these are few in number, and not very influential. The mass of the educated and thinking men admit the necessity of great changes in the condition of the country, and look to a liberal immigration as one of the most important, and, in fact, indispensable measures for the regeneration of Mexico. It seems to be the prevailing impression that the general system of internal improvements which has been projected and is now being slowly carried out, will result in the end, in drawing into the country a great immigration.

In this I fear that Mexico will be in some measure disappointed. My reasons are these: First, the incessant revolutions and wars of fifty years have created the impression that there is no stability in the institutions of Mexico, no guarantees for the safety of life or property, and no security for the future; and even now, when we see a tolerably strong government and a state of comparative peace, people abroad cannot believe that either will last. Secondly, that the inducements to common labor, unbacked by capital, are so much stronger in the United States, where there is yet an unlimited extent of virgin soil, that the tide will almost inevitably turn that way. Wages for common labor in the United States range from one dollar and a half per day in the East, to two dollars and a half, or even four or five dollars in California. In Mexico the average is from twenty-five to fifty cents at the utmost, and there is a surplus of labor in the market even at these rates. Then the laboring classes of Mexico live in a manner which no other population—the Chinese, perhaps, alone excepted—would willingly endure, and they can afford to work for a mere fraction of what would support a European or American laborer's family. For these and other reasons, I think that there is no immediate prospect of a large industrial immigration to Mexico from any part of the world.

But, on the other hand, does she need it? I do not think so. Mexico has to-day a population of eight million, five hundred thousand people—and that, too, after fifty years of wars and incessant revolutions, which have forced into the army the bulk of the able-bodied men of the nation, depopulated the rural districts, and reduced the great mass of the community to the most abject poverty. Its population equals that of the United States in proportion to its present area; and as fecundity is one of the most marked features of the native population, it must be evident that a few years of peace would very largely increase it. With peace will—or would—come railways and manufactories, and an influx of foreigners with more or less capital to invest in all kinds of enterprises, which would build up the country, and rapidly develop its almost illimitable resources. These foreigners would employ the native laborers, who are admitted by all to be patient, enduring, and anxious to work if paid and decently treated. As the condition of the laborers improved, and the agricultural population, now landless, began to become land-owners on a small scale, wages would rise, and foreign laborers would find it to their interest to come here and settle. Mexico has rich mines, wonderfully rich lands, and a climate which the world cannot excel; but she must have other inducements than these alone, to offer to immigration. The time is not far distant, if peace continues, when she will have such induce ments; but at present she must "learn to labor and to wait."

Now this may look like a discouraging view of the conditions and prospects of the Republic, but I do not so regard it. There are enough of willing laborers now unemployed, or but partially employed in the country, to develop a large trade along the line of any railroad yet projected, and ten or twenty years of peace would immensely increase the available laboring population of the country, without any addition from immigration. If the Government can hold its own against factions and disorganizers, and the people can learn to restrain their natural impatience, and refuse to listen to the appeal of demagogues and unprincipled political charlatans, for that time, all will be well with Mexico, and she will then care little whether immigration comes, or stays away. Her institutions, and the patriotism of her people are now being tried to the utmost, and a year or two more will tell the story, and decide the fate of the country for good or ill, for centuries to come.

Despite the poverty of the Mexican Treasury, the depression of trade and manufacturing interests, and the frequent abortive attempts at revolution in the various States, the administration is quietly and steadily carrying out an extended system of internal improvements which, when completed, will prove of immense benefit to the country, and the grand effects of which are already felt to some extent. The railroad from the City of Vera Cruz is now a fixed fact one hundred and twenty miles—to Puebla—being completed at this end of the route, and fifty from Vera Cruz westward, leaving a gap of only about one hundred and twenty miles. The Tehuantepec Inter-Oceanic Railroad may be built, the Tuxpan and Manzanillo or San Blas Railroad grant will soon pass Congress, and other roads are projected. The Valley of Mexico is to be drained and rendered healthy by improvements already well advanced, and soon to be completed.

Among the many improvements going on, I may mention as particularly promising, the projected line of communication between the City of Mexico and the port of Tampico.

Under the special decree of the 25th of May, 1868, the Mexican Congress made an appropriation of three thousand dollars per month, to open a wagon-road between Ometuzco and the river Panuco. The object is to connect the City of Mexico and the port of Tampico by the most direct route, and at the same time, give protection to one of the richest and most interesting portions of the Sierra and Huasteca country. A Commission of Engineers, headed by John C. C. Hill, was appointed by the Government of Mexico on the 10th of June, 1868, to explore the country, in order to select the best route, with the understanding that the road must, under any circumstances, touch at Zacualtipan and Huejutla, and terminate at the most suitable point on the Panuco river, where navigation is at all seasons of the year practicable, by small steamboats down to the Gulf. The point selected is Tanjuco, a small Indian town, conveniently situated on the east bank of the Panuco river, about fifty miles above Tampico.

Ometuzco is one of the stations of the Vera Cruz Railroad, forty-two miles from the City of Mexico; therefore the wagon-road from Ometuzco to Tanjuco will only be about two hundred miles in length when finished. The works on this road were commenced on the 15th of October, 1868, and have been progressing ever since, notwithstanding the reduced resources of the Government. The work is divided into three main divisions: first, from Ometuzco to Zacualtipan; second, from Zacualtipan to Huejutla, and third, from Huejutla to Tanjuco. The works on the first division are pretty well advanced; the first section, comprising about thirty miles from Ometuzco to the City of Tulancingo, has been open to the public for the last eight months, and will soon be completed to Zacualtipan, ninety miles from Ometuzco.

If the resources of the Government will permit the work to progress as it has during the present year, through communication may be opened within two years, when this portion of the country, which contains so many undeveloped elements of wealth, and a population as large in proportion to its extent as any other part of the Republic, will commence a development, which, with peace, will exceed the brightest anticipations of the friends of the enterprise.

The projected line of railroad known as the "Tuxpan," which is to run—if built—from the Gulf of Mexico to the Pacific, is a most important enterprise. It will run through a beautiful and highly productive country, and the local trade ought to be sufficient to support it, in its full length.

Benito Juarez has now been ten years in power in Mexico, and with such a premier as Lerdo de Tejada, he could hold his own for life, and reduce all the factious elements in the Republic to order, if he had a treasury even moderately well supplied, so as to enable him to pay the army regularly, and keep the civil employes of the government beyond the reach of want and constant temptation.

But there is the great trouble. Señor Don Matias Romero, the Minister of Hacienda, (i. e. Secretary of the Treasury,) is probably more obnoxious to the violent opposition faction in Congress than any other man in the cabinet, and Congress, with a stupid blindness to the good of the country, obstinately persists in defeating all his *iniciatives*, utterly crippling the Government, and paving the way for endless disorder, misery, and confusion, by depriving the treasury of all its sources of supply. Whether any improvement in the condition of things would result from a change of ministry is doubtful. Romero seems to have done all that any man can do, to repair the finances. and bring order out of disorder.

Meantime, the Government has on its hands any amount of work in putting down brigandage, and suppressing the pronunciamentos, which though thus far detached and disconnected, are constantly breaking out in all parts of the Republic. No sooner is one put down than another—generally originating in local causes but none the less dangerous on that account—breaks out at some distant locality. So long as the troops are paid they will support the Government, faithfully, and they have certainly shown great efficiency, and accomplished much within the past two years. But when the point is reached—if it ever is reached—that the administration cannot provide means to pay the troops, then successful revolution will become, not only possible, but certain.

A few more general revolutions would render all hope of the establishment of a permanent government in Mexico, by the Mexicans themselves, out of the question, and the United States would be driven, against the will of our people, to consider, seriously, the question of intervention in some form, for the protection of the common interests of America against Europeans, and Republicanism against Monarchy. Try to disguise it as we may, the United States stand in the position of God-father to Mexico, and we are morally responsible for her future.

It is our interest not to absorb Mexico, nor to cripple her, but to aid her in establishing an independent and stable government, and developing her almost incalculable resources. We have territory enough, and need not covet the fair fields of Mexico. But there must be an end to violence and disorder some time, and if all our hopes should be blasted—God grant that they may not be—and Juarez is compelled to give way to a series of irresponsible military chiefs—who will follow each other in quick succession and each leave the country more impoverished and helpless—the end is inevitable, and we must prepare to look the question fairly in the face.

I know from personal observation—and am sorry to say it—that there is a large party among the educated and intelligent native-born population of Mexico, who look without a particle of confidence, or ray of hope, on the present and future, and regard absorption by the United States as the least of the evils which threaten them, and, in fact, something inevitable. The foreign creditors of Mexico, and many of the European-born residents, would hail with delight the annexation of Mexico, peaceably or forcibly, to the United States, as it would give them assurance of the ultimate liquidation of their claims, and the restoration of order to the country. But while Mexico *might* be benefitted—I have my doubts whether she would be immediately, to the extent people in the United States generally suppose—we should be compelled to increase very largely our standing army, add immensely to our debt, and add an unhomogeneous element—numbering more than eight millions of people—endowed with all the rights of citizenship, to the population of the United States of America. Can we afford to do this? Ought we to do it?

With all the drawbacks in Mexico, one cannot but admit that there has been substantial progress made since the Liberal Party, with Benito Juarez at its head, came into power. Notable things have been accomplished. 1st. The sequestration of the vast landed estate of the Church, and the destruction of its temporal power. 2d. The establishment of complete religious toleration and protection of all in the right to worship God according to their own consciences. 3d. The establishment of Public Schools and the inauguration of a system of free public instruction yet in its infancy, but destined to work the greatest benefit to future generations. 4th. The liberation and enfranchisement of all *peons*, and the destruction of the last form of legalized slavery. 5th. The freedom of the press, not yet complete, but nearly so, and soon to be perfect.

Few nations have been able to do as much in so few years, and, that too, in the face of the most violent opposition from a bigoted and intolerant anti-progressive church party, and amidst domestic war, and a merciless and murderous foreign invasion, backed up by the strongest empire, and employing as tools and mercenaries, the scum of all Europe.

Shall not a nation which has fought so long and well for its independence, and accomplished so much in the face of such obstacles, have a helping hand from its more favored and prosperous neighbor if it needs it? Shall Mexico not be allowed the fullest grace, and most ample opportunity to conquer the elements of discord yet remaining within her borders, and advance to the place God intended her to occupy in the family of nations?

CHAPTER XVIII.

PUEBLA, TLAXCALA AND CHOLULA.

ON the 18th of December, the Seward party were, at last, in readiness for departure from the Capital, and at 10 o'clock A. M., were all on board the special train, including Maximilian's—now President Juarez's—private car, which had been placed at Mr. Seward's disposal by Joseph H. Gibbs Esq., resident director of the Vera Cruz and Mexican Railway.

The house on Alfaro and Arco de San Agustine streets, had been crowded with friends until a late hour on the night previous, and our leave-takings were therefore mainly over. Only a few of the most intimate acquaintances of the different members of the party, accompanied us to the depot, to say "good-bye" again. A small detachment of the crack regiment of Mexico, the Zapadores, under command of a war-scarred veteran, Captain Ramirez, whose coat was covered with decorations for meritorious services, was sent along as an escort of honor, by the Government.

General Mejia, Minister of War, Señor Don Sebastian Lerdo de Tejada, Minister of State, and Señor Don Matias Romero, Minister of Hacienda, accompanied the party to the first station out of the city. Some of the ladies of the families of Señor Romero and President Juarez, went along to the Ometusco station where we met the return train, and Colonel Geo. M. Green, and

Señor Don Antonio Mancillas, Deputy to Congress from the State of Zacatecas, with his beautiful young wife, accompanied the party all the way to Puebla.

The railway from Mexico to Puebla—about one hundred and sixteen miles, English,—is a first class one in every respect, and a part of the route was made at the rate of forty-five miles per hour. In the "Chief of Traffic," Mr. Geo. Gliddon, who has control of the running of all the trains, and accompanied the party, I recognized an old friend, whom I had known in the south before the late "little onpleasantness" sent one of us to the other side of the continent, and the other into the ranks of the rebel army. The engineers were also Americans, and know their business. The engine and cars were of American manufacture, though the road was built, and is owned and run by an English company.

The road runs out from the city in a north-eastern direction, past the famous old church of Guadaloupe, and along the shores of Lake Tezcoco; then makes a long detour, and runs south-eastwardly to Puebla, through an open valley country skirted by high mountains all the way. The distance by wagon-road is only twenty-four or twenty-seven Spanish leagues, but the railway, in order to avoid the heavy grades, takes the longer circuitous route. For the first fifty miles the country is comparatively dry and poor, and the road runs through an almost uninterrupted aloe or maguey field, that plant requiring no cultivation, and paying better than any other crop on such ground. Though the plant yields material for rope, cordage, cloth, thatch for houses, etc., etc., it is used, almost exclusively, for the manufacture of the mildly inebriating swill called *pulque*, which forms a staple drink of the lower classes of the people. When the blossom stalk starts out, it is cut off, and the center of the plant is hollowed out so as to form a deep cup. In this reservoir the sap collects, and once in twenty-four hours the Indians, with long calabashes, with holes in each end, go around to gather it. They thrust one end of the calabash into the sap, and applying the other to the mouth, suck the sweet fluid up until the calabash is filled, then let it run into the pig-skins, in which it is carried to market. A little of the old *pulque*, already fermented, is added to the fresh juice, and the skins being exposed in the sun for a few days the fluid is ready for drinking. None for me, thank you! We saw them gathering the sap all along the road. The amount of *pulque* consumed in Mexico is almost beyond belief.

"Wall stranger, what's a bar'l o' whiskey in a fam'ly o' eleven children, an' no cow?" was the indignant reply of the Wabash Valley Hoosier, to an inquirer after useless knowledge, named Fitch, some years since. The same idea prevails with regard to *pulque*, among the poorer Mexicans. Special trains are run over the road to carry *pulque*. to the capital, and still, by far the greater portion is brought in upon the backs of men, mules and donkeys.

Some twenty or twenty-five miles from the city we passed the first pyramids, known as those of San Juan Tehuacan, which stand about a fourth of a mile from the railway, up towards the hills. There are two large ones, each apparently three hundred to four hundred feet in height, and well defined in their angles after the lapse of so many centuries. They were built from *adobes*, and then covered over with earth, and sodded, to protect them from the rains and sun. A zigzag path leads up to the summit of the finest one, on which there is a cross. The fine old church of San Juan Tehuacan stands near the pyramids, and there are little villages and hamlets all around. There are several smaller pyramids in the plain, but they appear to have been only begun and never finished. It is said that the largest of the pyramids of Tehuacan was opened by orders of Maximilian, and found to contain abundant evidences of great antiquity and many Aztec relics, but nothing of much intrinsic value. Soon after passing the pyramids, we went through the great battle field of Otumba, where Cortez, with his regular Spanish soldiers, and Tlaxcalan allies fought, and, after the most desperate struggle, routed, one hundred thousand Mexicans. There is a current tradition, to the effect that Otumba owes its name to an exclamation of Cortez after the battle. As he looked at the piles of the dead on the field, and bitterly counted the thinned ranks of his army, he exclaimed:

"O tumba de mi soldados!" (O tomb of my soldiers!)

The story may be safely regarded as on a par, in point of reliability, with those which pretend to give the origin of the names of Ohio, Iowa, Alabama, etc.

There are only adobe-walled hamlets, patches of corn, and wide fields of aloe plants, to-day, on the ground where the fate of Mexico was decided nearly three centuries and-a-half ago. Not even a monument marks the spot, and if there were no railway station there, the traveler would pass it without being aware that he was upon grandly historic ground.

At Ometusco, eighteen leagues from Mexico, we met the up-train bound for the capital, and took leave of the families of the President, Señor Romero, and Mr. Nelson. At Apam, half-way between Mexico and Puebla, we breakfasted as well as we could have done at any railroad station in the United States.

At this point the country begins to change. Between Mexico and Apam the country resembles Lower California to a considerable degree; but from Apam to Puebla it has more the appearance of the foot-hills of the Sierra Nevada, in the gold belt of California, though the red soil of the latter is lacking. The aloe fields now begin to give place to corn fields, and the country is productive, and densely populated.

We were now in the ancient State of Tlaxcala, in a plain situated among the grandest mountains of our continent. On one side Popocatapetl lifts his grand head, white with the snow of countless ages, and turbaned with white, fleecy vapors which cling, lovingly, around it, far into the deep, blue, cloudless sky. Next him stands his royal sister, "*La Muger en Blanco*," ("The woman in white,") and opposite stands the "Malinchi," named after Cortez's Indian mistress, a mighty mountain, but not snow-crowned, covered with deep green pine forests, up to within four or five thousand feet of its summit, and surrounded with almost numberless villages, each with its white church, and rich, wide corn-fields.

The number of these hamlets, with large churches, is astonishing. It is said that there are no less than fifty-eight of them in the district known as the Malinchi, in the immediate vicinity of the mountain, and the entire country for hundreds of miles around is equally blessed. In spite of all this, the region has a villainous reputation as the favorite haunt of robbers and kidnappers.

and the population was supposed, by many, to be in that dissatisfied condition which would make it readily available for carrying out a *pronunciamento*, by any ambitious and unscrupulous chief who has the money or influence to fairly start it.

Right before us, standing out bold and clear, and sharp in all its outlines, against the sunlit sky of Mexico, white and cold and peerlessly beautiful, stood the monarch of the land of the Aztecs—Orizaba. I have looked at the picture in wonder and delight for hours, but yet can find no words with which to describe the scene, and the emotions which follow the realization of the dream of a life-time.

Twenty-one miles from Puebla, after passing the iron smelting works, we stopped a moment at the old Indian town of Santa Anna, the station at which passengers disembark for the old city of Tlaxcala, and then went on with accelerated speed over the descending grade to Puebla.

We entered this old city of wealth, fashion, bigotry and revolutions, at 5 o'clock P. M., and the Governor and suite having met and congratulated Mr. Seward, the party went directly to the palace of the Bishop of Puebla, a structure almost as solid and massive as the pyramids, covering an entire block or square, and superbly furnished and decorated with gems of art. Each room is a house in itself, so grand are its proportions, and the palace is, altogether, equal to a small town. It faces the great cathedral of Puebla, the largest and richest religious edifice on the American continent, infinitely superior to even the great cathedral of Mexico, and, in fact, one of the wonders of the world.

After dinner I went out with some friends to walk

in the Plaza, and saw the full, round moon rise up from behind the mountains, flooding the whole grand landscape with such a light as can only be seen, in perfection in the pure, dry atmosphere of Mexico, and throwing over the city of Puebla, with its ninety-seven churches, its ruined walls, its beautiful plazas, its green alamedas, and its hundred objects of historic interest, a beauty and a glory indescribable. Such a moonlight scene one witnesses nowhere outside the tropics, and rarely even there.

We entered Puebla on Saturday evening, and not caring to intrude upon the worshipers in the great cathedral on Sunday morning, concluded to defer our visit to that leading object of interest until another time. We therefore accepted the invitation of Mr. Adolfo Blumenkorn, an American citizen long resident here, to ride out through the suburbs, and see the ruin and desolation wrought by the late terrible war of which Puebla was the center. We went first to the old church of San Zavier, which was fortified by the Mexicans on the arrival of the French, and withstood the first attack. The streets leading to it all show evidences of the desperate struggle which here took place. All the buildings, for many blocks, are in ruins, or pitted with cannon-ball and bullet marks, and earth-works and temporary defenses, now in ruins, are seen in all directions.

After the defeat of the French by the Mexicans under General Zaragoza, on the *Cinco de Mayo* outside the city, they received re-enforcements, and having learned caution from sad experience, advanced on a different line, and in a more guarded manner, on the city. The new state-prison, which was almost finished when the war commenced, stands adjoining the great, old church of San Zavier, on the side fartherest from the city, and of course in direct range of the batteries of the French, which were mounted upon a small hill some half mile further out. The state prison and church were held by the Mexicans until the walls were perforated everywhere by balls, and the flying stones, knocked down at every volley from the French batteries, made the position no longer tenable. They then retreated into the plaza, nearer the heart of the city, where they threw up entrenchments. The French immediately took up their position in the church and state-prison, but that night the Mexicans opened upon them, and sent four hundred cannon balls through the two structures before morning, and the French, after a loss of some five hundred men, found the buildings too hot to hold them. Both buildings are now so riddled and shattered as to be untenable and worthless, and it is the general opinion that it will be cheaper to pull down the walls of the state-prison and rebuild from the foundation, than to attempt to repair it.

When the Mexicans saw that the fall of Puebla was unavoidable, they blew up and wholly, or partially, destroyed a large number of churches around the outskirts of the city, to prevent their being used as defences by the French, when it should be their turn to be come the besiegers, and that of the French to be the besieged. The wisdom of this action was demonstrated when General Porfiero Diaz, who had made the brilliant campaign of Tehuantepec and Oaxaca, sweeping everything before him like a hurricane, arrived before Puebla while Maximilian was being besieged at Queretaro, by Escobedo. Marquez, with the imperial troops, had advanced from the city of Mexico to Apizaco, only one day's march from Puebla, to relieve the garrison and meet Diaz, when the latter determined on the desperate but brilliant movement which decided the contest at a blow. At three o'clock in the morning he ordered a general assault by all his forces upon the city, which had not been besieged for an hour, and his victorious, but almost exhausted and worn out army responding with enthusiasm, one of the most determined and desperate conflicts of our time followed.

Dividing his force into thirteen columns, and charging directly into the city from all points at once against a murderous fire from every house-top, earth-work and commanding position, he carried the place at the first assault with a loss of eleven hundred and seventy-six men, killing or capturing the entire Imperialist force with all its supplies, artillery, and munitions of war, and compelling Marquez to fall back on the capital in all haste, and put it in a condition to withstand a siege by the Republican forces, until the fall of Queretaro, the Empire and Maximilian rendered further resistance hopeless.

From the church of San Zavier we rode out to see the battle field of the *Cinco de Mayo*, already famous in song and story. It has been so often described that I will not go into details. Coming back we saw more of ruin resulting from war, than we had previously noticed in Mexico. The destruction of life and property by this infamous war must have been enormous, and I doubt if Puebla will ever fully recover from it. The population of the city cannot now exceed eighty thousand; it is doubtful if there is more than sixty thousand or seventy thousand, and after all the destruction, there is still one great church for every one thousand men, women, and children in the city. There are various manufactories in and around the city, and the country in the vicinity being very productive, there is considerable trade, especially since the completion of the railroad to Mexico in September last, but the city cannot be said to be in a very prosperous condition, nevertheless.

We heard less here than in the city of Mexico concerning the pronunciamento against the Government in the Sierra, in the State of Puebla. The general opinion at Puebla was that the movement had not any head, and that the various bands were small in numbers, and acting without concert or definite plan. But on the other hand, it was said that a deputation had been sent to Oaxaca to consult with the famous military chieftain, Porfiero Diaz, and ask him to take command, promising him the support of the disaffected in every part of the country, and a general and preconcerted rising against the Juarez Government. Their success wonld be a greater disaster to Mexico than the French invasion. If Mexico is to exist, as an independent nation, *she must have peace*, and the inauguration of another general civil war would be the death knell of the Republic.

We saw troops marched through the streets, and found General Alatorre absent in the mountains with some three thousand men, operating against the bands of guerillas which were making all the trouble, but could learn nothing more definite. There had been no fighting since the Sixth Battalion was surprised and routed at Xochipulco, on the 29th of November, for the reason that the guerillas were too active and cautious to be caught, or risk an engagement without great advantages on their side, and the character of the mountain country is such, as to make a successful campaign against them almost impossible. About sixty of the men of the battalion, wounded at Xochipulco, were there in the hospital under surgical treatment.

We made good use of our time while at Puebla, and in its vicinity. No part of our trip was more replete with interest, and we enjoyed it to the utmost. On the 19th we left Puebla, by railway, to visit the capital of the ancient Republic of Tlaxcala, renowned in the history of Spanish conquest for the part its people took in fixing the chain of the conquerors, upon the neck of Mexico. How the Mexicans, hearing of the arrival of Cortez at Vera Cruz, asked permission of their hereditary enemies, the Tlaxcalans, to be allowed to send commissioners through their territory, to see Cortez and find out what called him to the country; how the crafty Tlaxcalans consented, and then agreed to pilot them on their way, but secretly dispatched emissaries in advance to make a treaty with Cortez—which they did—and joined hands with the invaders against the Mexicans, whose costly presents to Cortez had excited his cupidity, and confirmed his determination to conquer their country, has all been told by historians, over and over, and I will therefore confine myself to what I saw and heard, on this old historic ground, in the last, bright, sunny days of the good year 1869.

From Puebla to the station of Santa Anna, by railway, is only twenty-one miles, English, and with a special train we made it in less than forty minutes; in Cortez' time it must have taken considerably longer. The old Indian town of Santa Anna, is half in ruins, but there is still a little life left there. We saw an immense enclosure of timber, in the form of an amphitheater, which they were erecting for a "*plaza de toros*," where thousands of people doubtless flocked from all the surrounding country, about New Years, to indulge in and gloat over the brutalities of the bull-fight.

Entering carriages, sent for us by the Governor of Tlaxcala, to ride some three or four miles down to the ancient city, we met, a little distance down the road, a train of pack-Indians, coming in from the mountains with lumber, with which to complete the amphitheater. Each Indian carried on his back, suspended from his head by a leathern strap across his forehead, a pitch-pine beam, twenty feet long, ten inches wide, and six inches thick. The weight of each of these beams, according to the lowest estimate made by members of our party, was four hundred pounds—I think it more probable that they would weigh five hundred pounds—and the load for a mule is only three hundred pounds; yet these sturdy fellows carried them off at a dog-trot, talking good-naturedly as they went, and had probably brought them fifteen or twenty miles that day. Could our gymnasts do this?

Half an hour's ride over a dusty and heavy road, all out of repair, brought us to the ancient city, which, in its prime, occupied the heights on both sides of a narrow valley for many miles; at least, so Cortez said. There were four great chiefs of the Republic of Tlaxcala, and each dwelt in a grand palace on these heights. The Spaniards built churches on the site of each; and we have now only the ruinous old churches, and the doubtful statements of fishy, old historians, in evidence of their once having existed. The old town along the heights at the base of the Cerro Blanco, or

White Hills, has nearly all disappeared, and the loose and gravelly soil has been so washed by the rains of centuries, as to make it impossible to trace with any certainty, its original outlines. There are still, any number of old churches, scattered here and there all over the wide landscape; but where the one hundred thousand people, who inhabit the little State of Tlaxcala, live, is more than I could see.

The present town, which is mostly Spanish-built, is situated on the flat between the heights, and may contain five thousand people, I should say at a venture. It has many buildings unquestionably dating back to the days of Cortez, and is a place no intelligent traveler in Mexico can afford to omit visiting.

The Governor of Tlaxcala, an intelligent gentleman, apparently of pure Indian blood, with his staff of officials, welcomed Mr. Seward, and escorted the party to the State Palace, an unpretending old building, in which the Congress or Legislature meets. This building, poor and plain as it is, contains priceless treasures for the antiquarian and student of history.

In the hall of Congress, I noticed portraits, rudely painted in oil, of the four Chiefs of the Republic of Tlaxcala after they had been converted to Christianity. Each has the prefix "Señor Don" before his name, and a Christian name before his unpronunciable Indian surname. They are in full, Indian costume, and by the side of each is his coat of arms. From the mouth of each issues the words he pronounced at his baptism. One says "*Viva Jesus!*" another *Viva Maria!*" another "*Viva Jose!*" and the last "*Viva Joachin!*" In costume and general appearance they would pass for Navajo or Mojave chiefs of the present day, and I have no doubt, that they were about on par with them in intelligence and civilization.

In the next room we saw the identical royal banner of Spain, which Cortez unfolded before the eyes of the astonished and delighted Tlaxcalan emissaries at San Juan de Ulloa, and which, after the conquest of Mexico, he presented to the city of Tlaxcala in acknowledgement of the eminent services rendered by the Tlaxcalans, in overthrowing the old Aztec Empire. Though three hundred and forty years have passed away since it was unfurled on the shore of Mexico, it is almost perfect to-day. It is some nine or ten feet long, and six broad "and swallow tailed" in pattern. The material is rich, heavy, silk brocade, originally of a light "maroon" or possibly "ashes of roses" color, and not badly faded. The cords and tassels and the points of the banner are a little frayed and worn, but not badly so. The Shield with the royal coat of arms, the two castles, and two lions rampant, is embroidered in red, on yellow silk, and sewed upon the upper right hand corner of the banner. The iron open-work spear-head with the monogram of the sovereigns of Spain in the center, once gilded, and the broken staff on which the banner was carried, are still with it. Vast sums have been offered for this old banner to be carried back to Spain, but the city of Tlaxcala has steadily refused to part with it at any price.

Then we were shown numerous old banners, including those of the ancient city and Republic of Tlaxcala before the Spanish conquest, very rude and very curious, and numberless manuscripts of great age and interest. One of these old illuminated manuscripts, is an authenticated translation of the original Indian document, ordering, on behalf of the Republic of Tlaxcala, eighty thousand picked men, to march with Cortez against Mexico. This was translated by the order of Cortez himself. Other documents beautifully illuminated, signed " *Yo el Rey*" (I the King,) and of the time of the Conquest, are there in abundance, with hundreds of later date, hardly less interesting. We could have spent days in looking over these curious old records of the dead and now almost forgotten past, but had only an hour or two at our command.

Among the curiosities in this room, is the war-drum of the Tlaxcalans, a curiously carved and hollowed log of dark, hard wood, like rose-wood, some thirty inches in length and six or eight in thickness, of which a full description and good illustration is given by Prescott. Two lips left on the upper surface, have play enough to give off sharp musical notes when struck by the hand, or with a stick, and the instrument, in the hand of a first-class professor of Tlaxcalan music, would doubtless be made to produce as inspiring strains as the old Scotch bagpipes, though I think one of our modern military bands in full play would discourage him.

One old document is particularly illustrative of the character of the pious people who spread religion and desolation through the land of the Aztecs. It recites, that after the conquest, a sub-tribe of the Tlaxcalans used to bring in large quanties of gold-dust from some placer in the vicinity, the locality of which they refused to disclose. They gave enough of this gold to the Church to make and pay for the crown of the Virgin of Guadaloupe at Mexico, which cost eighty thousand dollars. The Spaniards, excited by the sight of this wealth, took some of the Indians, tied them up in the plaza in front of the hall in which we read the records, and whipped them most unmercifully to compel them to reveal the locality of the mine. The Indians bore the torture in grim silence, and next day twenty thousand of them, including all who knew the secret, left for Guatamala, and the locality of the *placer* remains undiscovered to this day.

The same thing is now going on in a district between Puebla and Tuxpan. The Indians are bringing in, from time to time, quantities of gold dust, for sale, at a small town near which has been recently discovered the ruins of an ancient city. They also brought in a box of stones which have been pronounced diamonds of the first water, by the jewelers of Mexico, but refused to tell where the gold and stones came from. It is suspected that they came from the ruins, and a party of my personal friends are now being fitted out in the city of Mexico, to go and make a thorough exploration of the locality.

The Virgin of Guadaloupe has a rival in this locality, in the Virgin who has a church on the hill above the city of Tlaxcala. It is said that the Bishop of Tlaxcala being pursued at night, by his enemies and the enemies of the Faith, saw the Virgin among the limbs of a pine-tree, and just at the moment of his direst extremity, the trunk of the tree flew open, and shutting again like the trap-door in a pantomime, enclosed him within it. The enemy ran past without discovering his whereabouts, or, what is more singular, noticing the luminous Virgin roosting in the tree overhead, and the tree, opening again, let him out in safety. Of course this miracle could not be kept secret, and the church which was erected on the spot, rivals that of Guadaloupe in sanctity and attraction for the Indians of Tlaxcala and its vicinity. I think it is but right that it should do so under all the circumstances.

We went with the Governor to the ancient church of Tlaxcala, which was commenced in 1529, and is, unquestionably, the oldest structure devoted to the worship of God on the North American continent. It is in excellent preservation, but was never very rich in ornamentation, falling far behind many others we had seen in obscure parts of the country. The paintings too are poor and if it were not for its history there would be little to attract a visitor. But there we saw the pulpit which bears an inscription showing that it was the first erected in "New Spain," and from whence the gospel of the Cross was first preached to the natives of the New World.

Then we saw the great baptismal font, hollowed from a single block of lava, in which were baptised the four Chiefs of the Republic of Tlaxcala, and the General in command of the armies before the advance upon the City of Mexico. There are many old paintings of no artistic merit, representing martyrdoms and persecutions of the saints in all forms. Those old saints must have had a very rough time of it from all accounts and after seeing what they had to suffer, I am thankful enough that an all-wise Providence never designed me for one. I don't think I could fill the position with any degree of credit to all parties concerned. One picture represents the Pope in a triumphal car drawn by four fat and healthy horses, each led by a fat and healthy angel, riding over the bodies of the "Reformers," and dragging behind him in chains and disgrace, Luther and Calvin. Rather rough, this on the reformers, but it is their business, not mine, and if they can stand it, I can. The ceiling under the roof of this old church is a marvel of beauty. It is of cedar colored by time to the hue of mahogany, wrought with exquisite skill, gilded in places, and varnished. Tradition says that this work was done by the angels in the night, and that when the Bishop came at morning to begin it, he found to his astonishment that they had completed the church and left him nothing more to do. All over the country the same or similar work was done on the churches, the angels in most cases doing as much at night as the workmen did during the day, and so the structure was half mortal and half immortal in its origin. In this case they did the ceiling entire, and it stands unharmed by time in all its perfect beauty to this hour. If I were a doubter or scoffer—which I am not—I might be tempted to suggest that the miracle would have been more conclusive and effective, if the angels had come down in broad daylight, and performed the work in sight of the people; but my faith enables me to see that their doing it after dark, in silence, and without even a candle or lantern to attract the attention of the public, makes the miracle all the more wonderful, and the work more glorious. The job was done, that is certain, for there is the delicate fretted ceiling, as perfect to-day as it was three hundred and forty years ago, and I for one, find it cheaper and easier to believe at once, than to waste time in raising doubts and discussing questions which profit a man nothing.

After we left the church, a party of irreverent people from California, who came down by a train from Mexico, visited it, and carrying a basket of champagne up to the belfrey, proceeded to drink it and ring the bells in our honor, as we dróve off for Santa Anna again.

Among the decorations of this primitive church, are several effigies and pictures of Christ, of a character so utterly revolting as to fairly make one sick. It is alleged in explanation, that the Indians required very vivid illustrations, to excite their imagination and fix religious impressions in their minds. These ought to fetch them. In one chapel there is a full-sized effigy of Christ upon the cross. His head is covered with an enormous shock wig of brown-red hair, the eyes, mouth, and nose discharging blood, wounds and bruises on every limb and feature, and the agony and pallor of the dying struggle so fearfully counterfeited as to produce, in my mind at least, a sense of loathing and nausea almost uncontrollable. I would as soon think of going to a slaughter-house to worship the All-Merciful God who created the Heaven and the Earth, and made man in his own image and a little lower than the Angels, as to that chamber of horrors, in the first Christian church erected on the American Continent.

There are some old skulls lying about the church, and the Californians put two of them into the shawl which Mr. Gliddon was carrying. He did not discover the trick for some time, and when he did so he restored them to their place with the quiet remark, that as the superintendent of trains on the railway, he had been carrying so many "dead-heads" of late, that he did not notice the presence of one or two, more or less, unless his attention was specialy drawn to them. We got back to Santa Anna at 6 P. M., and returned to Puebla to dinner.

On the 20th of December, our party re-enforced by a number of friends from the capital, started in carriages for Cholula, to visit the pyramid of which nearly every school-boy has seen a picture in his geography. A ride of two leagues over a rough and dusty road, through an open country, brought us to the ancient city, said to have once contained four hundred thousand people. It is situated in an open plain, with the grand circle of great mountains, Popocatapetl, El Muger en Blanco, Malinchi, Orizaba and the lesser peaks in the distance. It must have suffered fearfully from the Spanish conquerors, and has been steadily declining in importance to the present day, being now but a mere fragment of its former self.

The people are nearly all of unmixed Indian blood, hardy, industrious, and peculiarly respectful and well-behaved. They cultivate a wide area of fertile valley land, in a manner reminding one of the Chinese, and supply the City of Puebla, almost exclusively, with market vegetables.

After the party entered the Valley of Mexico, the appearance of Mr. Seward seldom produced any remarkable demonstrations of enthusiasm among the common people, and we had no reason to expect any different reception at Cholula, in view of the apathy manifested at Puebla, so near at hand. But we were destined to witness a display, as novel and curious as it was unexpected.

The whole country abounds with old churches, all of which have chimes of fine-toned bells still remaining in their towers, though the greater portion of them have but a limited number of worshipers within their walls at any time in these latter and degenerate days. As we neared Cholula the people were seen running through the fields towards the town, and the bells commenced ringing from every tower in the city and its suburbs. The number of bells which thus at once sent forth their voices in welcome to the stranger, could hardly have been less than one hundred, and the ringers worked as if life and death depended on their exertions.

When the procession reached the Plaza, two fine brass-bands—all the musicians being natives of Cholula—struck up their liveliest airs, the *Prefecto Politico* and the *Ayuntemento* of the town came forward to welcome Mr. Seward, and the party, dismounting from the carriages, marched to the town-hall, the entire population, men, women, and children, with eager curiosity depicted on their features, following, or running by their side. In the hall, behind the desk of the *Prefecto*, was a full-length portrait of the Virgin of Guadaloupe, and on the desk lay two silver maces with globes at the end surmounted with the eagle and nopal of Mexico. These emblems of authority are not unlike in appearance to the mace represented in the picture of Cromwell disbanding the Long Parliament, when he exclaims, "take away that fool's bauble!"

The Prefecto made a warm and sensible speech in behalf of the people and *Ayuntemento* of Cholula, welcoming Mr. Seward and his friends to the hospitalities of the ancient city, and alluding in warm terms to the services rendered to the cause of Mexican independence, through him, by the Government and people of the United States; to which Mr. Seward replied:

SIR: The attendance of the civil authorities of the District, the complete array of the municipality of Cholula, more than both, the grave procession and thoughtful assemblage of citizens, leave me no room to doubt the sincerity of your generous words of welcome. The scene seems to me like one of those which awaken momentary inspiration. I am on the steps of the Aztec Pyramid, which is one of the most stupendous altars of human sacrifice that was ever erected to propitiate the Deity, in the ages when he was universally understood to be a God of Vengeance. Around me lies that magnificent plain where an imperial savage throne was brought down to the dust, by the just revenge of an oppressed aboriginal Republic. I am surrounded by Christian churches and altars which tell how foreign civilized states exacted eternal subjugation, and the civil bondage of a rude people, in return for conveying to them the Gospel of "Peace on earth and good will toward man."

The serious Republican aspect and deportment of the children of the Aztecs to whom I am speaking, remind me that after a long contest with ecclesiastical, monarchial, and imperial ambitions, the independence of the ancient Aztec race has been reconquered without the loss of the Christian Religion, and consolidated in a Representative Federal Republic. Witnesses of towering majesty and impressive silence, are looking down upon me; La Malinchi, bewildering because she is indistinct, and the volcanoes Popocatapetl, Ixtacihuatl and Orizaba, clad in their eternal vestments of snow, attest that nature remains unchangable, and only men, nations, and races, are subject to moral revolution.

Gentlemen and Citizens: the circumstance that I am here, not as an enemy, but as a friend; a friend of the town of Cholula, a friend of the State of Puebla, a friend of the Republic of Mexico, enables me to study Mexico, her country and people, more carefully, and I trust to understand them better. From this place at once so sacred and so imposing, I must take leave to say to all states and nations, that Mexico neither needs, nor desires foreign protection, that she is capable of independence and self government, and susceptible of friendship; but that in her case as in all others, those who would enjoy her friendship must offer her on their part a friendship, which, though it may not be benevolent, must at least be sincere and disinterested.

The party, on the conclusion of Mr. Seward's remarks, were escorted to the house of the Prefecto for a brief rest. At 2 P. M., the bands drew up in front of the house, and the party, escorted as before by the whole population, started for the fine old parochial church of Cholula, the second in age in Mexico. This church, though of enormous size and surrounded by an immense flagged court or plaza, is not to be compared to many others in the country for magnificence. In style it is purely Moorish and quite unique. There are fifty-six low Moorish arches, supported by sixty-four columns painted in brilliant lime colors, and the altar and other appurtenances are all curiously antique in style and character. There are, of course, many old pictures, but none of them struck me as particularly fine. The church was commenced in 1530, and stands to-day exactly as it was finished more than three and a quarter centuries ago.

The scene on the entry of the party to the church, was worthy the pencil of a painter, and curiously illustrative of time's revenges. Where Cortez and his companions had bowed the knee, and knelt with uncovered heads when the Host was raised above the multitude, came an old grey-headed statesman, from a land then unknown, who had slept in Maximilian's bed the previous night, walking by the side of a descendant of those who crucified the Savior on Mount Calvary, and escorted by the authorities of this ancient strong-hold of the Faith, while an American—Col. Green—with pale, sharp-cut, representative face, and, tall, slender figure, clad in the uniform of the Mexican Army, led on the band of swarthy Aztecs, who were playing with a will, the "March of Zaragoza," an air as obnoxious to

CHOLULA, AND THE ANCIENT PYRAMID.

the strict high church party, as is the *Marseillaise* to Napoleon III. The tall form of Mr. Nelson, the United States Minister, towered above the crowd behind; by his side walked General Slaughter—late of the Confederate army—or of the late Confederate army—and after them came a crowd of Californians whose devotion to thc cause of liberty is undoubted, but whose religious convictions of any kind, never deprived them of their capacity for imbibing champagne, nor kept them awake at night. A thousand curious natives followed, and seemed to heartily enjoy the entertainment.

After a half-hour spent in viewing the old church, the party started to ascend the great pyramid, which stands on the outskirts of the town, but five minutes' walk from the church. All the world knows at this day all that anybody knows, of the history of this pyramid. That it dates back to the days when the people of Egypt were erecting the pyramids which still form the land-marks in the Valley of the Nile, cannot be doubted, and that it upheld a heathen temple, and was drenched with the blood of thousands on thousands of the human race, offered up as sacrifices to savage gods, is, unfortunately, too well authenticated. The pictures I have seen of the pyramid give no clear idea of it, as they represent the sides and angles of the terraces, as too sharp and well defined. I think, that at no time since the conquest has the pyramid presented an appearance much different from what it does at present.

One of the gentlemen in attendance on the Governor told me that the pyramid covered a space equal to a little more than forty-three acres at the base, and that its height was one hundred and seventy-nine feet, English, or thereabouts. I should, at a venture, have estimated the size of the base at less than half that stated, and the height at nearly double the figures given, but presume that accurate measurements must have been made at some time, and its real dimensions are probably known. The lower terrace is quite perfect, but the upper ones have become so washed by the rains and disturbed by the great trees which have taken root in the soil, that they are traceable, with certainty, only in a few places. A winding or zig-zag pathway, some thirty feet in width, and paved with lava, leads up to the summit of the pyramid. The old Spanish Zealots erected a Christian Church on the ruins of the ancient heathen temple, and that, too, becoming dilapidated and untenable with the lapse of years, was pulled down, and a new and very tasteful chapel, erected altogether by the labor of native Indian craftsmen, is now being finished, and will soon be dedicated to the service of the Christian's God. With the vanity of the human race, this pyramid has been selected, also, for a burial place, and we saw several new graves on the upper terrace, in the soil which has been soaked, time and time again, with the blood of human sacrifices.

Two immense cedar trees, which must have been standing on the summit in the days of Cortez, were cut down, or hopelessly mutilated by the workmen engaged in erecting the new chapel, and our party carried off numerous samples of the wood as souvenirs of their visit.

It has been the commonly accepted theory of the origin of the Pyramid of Cholula, that it was built as a temple and place for human sacrifice, altogether by the hand of man; but while standing on its summit, and looking on the grand landscape which surrounds it, a new theory suggested itself to me. The pyramids in the Valley of the Nile stand out bold and grand, the great central figures in the scene,—undwarfed by comparison with any great mountains in the vicinity. We can understand how men could seek to erect in such a locality, an enduring monument to their power and greatness. But here, in full view of Orizaba and Popocatapetl, the mightiest work of man is but a mole-hill hardly worthy of a moments notice, and even the egotism of the most barbaric nature must stand rebuked in the presence of these perfect works of the Almighty hand. I do not believe that there was ever a race on earth so vain as to erect such a monument in such a locality; and furthermore, there was no necessity for such an expenditure of time and labor as the erection of such a pile of adobe, in the Plain of Cholula, as this pyramid, if wholly artificial, would have called for. Scattered through all the valleys of Central Mexico, are detached hills, composed of washed gravel and earth, equal or superior in size to this pyramid. You can see a number of them from the point where we stood.

It seems to me quite probable that one of these hills stood here where the Cholulans built their city; and that in order to fit it for use as a temple, they merely cut away the sides, and terraced it into its pyramidal form. The angles and faces of the terraces thus formed, must be protected from the effects of the storms, which would soon wash down the entire mound, and so they faced it over with *adobes*, laid up with care and intermixed with lava, which soon became a solid, concrete mass, as we see it to day. The adobes and layers of lava are perfect at many points, but in other places, where the storms of thousands of years have told most strongly, they seem to have disappeared, and I thought I could recognize the original formation of the hill beneath.

A little way off from the main pyramid is a smaller one, less regular in its outline, which is supposed by many—without any good reason that I can discover—to have been originally a part of the greatest structure; and a little farther away, an oblong pile of earth, with perfectly precipitous sides, resembling in shape a wagon load of hay or straw. Both these are evidently artificial. There are no excavations in any direction for many miles around the great pyramid, from whence the vast amount of material for building it could have been taken, and the finely cultivated fields which, cut by regular streets, radiate from the pyramid in all directions, indicate that the soil and surface of the ground in the vicinity, have never been disturbed. May it not be that the Cholulans, simply cut away the sides of the original hill as I have suggested, and with the earth thus removed, formed the smaller pyramid and lesser irregular pile near by? I do not care enough for any theory on any subject, to defend this one if it is ever attacked; but it seems to me to be a rational one under all the circumstances.

Members of the *Ayuntamento* accompanied us to the pyramid, a servant carrying before them the silver-headed canes which serve as badges of their office. After seeing all there was to be seen on the pyramid we descended, and returning to the Prefect's house partook of an elegant collation. Toasts were given and responded to freely, and in the midst of the festivities, in marched a band, of the ancient Aztec class.

The music produced by the three pieces, an Indian flute, kettle-drum, and a drum shaped like a flour barrel, and made like it of thin pieces of wood, hooped, with one end resting on the ground, bore a startling resemblance to that which you may hear any night in the Chinese theatres in San Francisco, being pitched at the same high key, and the air being almost identical with the "Song of the Jasmin Flower," which is the favorite, through all the central Flowery Empire.

The dark-hued, sandaled, and white-robed musicians played on through all stages of the entertainments, with faces as impassive as those of so many bronze statues. Only once did I see a look of startled interest for a moment steal over their faces. It was when the *Prefecto* gave the health of the President of the United States, and the health of President Juarez being given in response, the Americans gave three rousing cheers, and the Californians, springing to their feet, made the air of the sleepy, old town, ring with the wild yell of "the tiger." The look I had noticed faded from their faces as it came in an instant, and the music, so wild, and strange and weird, went on as before. When Colonel Green plied them with champagne, and whistled to them "Jordon am a hard road to travel," they took up the air, and played it with the same cold, quiet manner as they had played those of their native land; and when paid and dismissed, they marched away in grave, respectful silence, without a word or action to indicate whether they were pleased or displeased with the days—to them—novel proceedings.

Mr. Seward was presented with a certificate of honorary membership of the *Ayuntamento*, or Common Council of Cholula, and with wishes of success and a pleasant reunion with old friends among the home scenes of our native land, the kind people of Cholula bid us good-bye, and in the gloaming of the evening we rode back to Puebla.

OUR AZTEC MUSICIANS AT CHOLULA.

I shall attempt no elaborate description of the Cathedral of Puebla, for several good and sufficient reasons. One is, that no description could give the reader any adequate idea of the vast proportions, great wealth, and exceeding beauty and grandeur of this wonderful temple of the Christian faith, and another is, that so many descriptions have been attempted and resulted in failures, that I have no ambition to follow in the old, beaten track, knowing that I cannot command the language adequate for success.

The Seward party visited the cathedral, and saw all its wonders, from the grand choir, which outside is one mass of gilding and burnished precious metal, and inside a curious mosaic of beautiful woods inlaid with wonderful skill, the great altar, which is built of variegated marbles, alabaster, and other beautiful stones from the State of Puebla, and gold and silver by the cart-load, the great pillars of bluish-grey granite, supporting arches of the same material which uphold the immense weight of the solid stone roof, and the fourteen stations of the cross—each a marvel in itself—to the skeletons of the saints and martyrs, covered with wax and so artistically wrought into the semblance of fresh human forms as to cheat the eye completely, dressed in robes of great richness, and shodden with golden sandals set with gems, which lie in state, each in its own great casket, all around the building. Even the tomb of the Bishops was thrown open and inspected.

The mighty pillars were covered from their capitals down to the pavement, with crimson silk plush, edged and embroidered with gold, in preparation for the grand Christmas festivities, and the whole church was being cleaned and prepared for the occasion. The last time the metal work—then nearly all gold and silver—in this cathedral was cleaned, the work cost four thousand dollars in coin, though done at the least possible expense.

Much of the riches of this old cathedral have disappeared within a few years, it is said, but the eye of the stranger looks in vain for any trace of the hand of the despoiler, save where once hung near the main entrance, the great chandelier, which Miramon took down and melted up, to pay his troops for fighting the battles of the church against the Republicans. He got forty thousand dollars out of this chandelier, and the curses of all the pious Catholics of Mexico, who were quite willing he should fight for the church, but wished him to make the enemy—not the church—pay the cost, and denounced the act as one of sacrilege, sure to bring down destruction on its author.

What the value of the gold, silver, and precious stones in the cathedral at present may be, I have no idea, and no one can do more than make a random guess at it. I was greatly disappointed in the cathedral of Mexico, which is much dilapidated, dusty, and tarnished throughout, and fell far short of my ideal, formed from descriptions I had read of it; but the cathedral of Puebla far surpassed my expectations.

We visited many other churches, the old college of the Jesuits, and the library—now secularized and thrown open to the public—which contains twenty-four thousand four hundred volumes, mostly of great age, and valuable only to the antiquarian; the school of design; the Glass Factory of Puebla, which is among the most extensive and complete works of the kind on the continent; the hills and fortifications of Loreto and Guadaloupe, from which the French army, forty thousand strong, was repulsed in the attack of the Cinco de Mayo, and many other objects of interest in and around Puebla.

Among the places visited was the Public Hospital of San Pedro, an excellent institution, clean, neat, and admirably managed, containing one hundred and sixty-three patients, of which fifty were women. While there, a printed slip was handed around with the following inscription:

"The American and Mexican Union are Sisters. Therefore the Asylums of the sick of Puebla, present their respects to the Hon. Mr. Seward as one of their Brothers. Hospital gral de San Pedro Diciembre 21 de 1869."

The manifestations in honor of Mr. Seward closed with a dinner to forty gentlemen, mostly Mexicans, given by His Excellency, the Governor of Puebla, Señor Don Ignacio Romero y Vargas. At the banquet Mr. Seward excused himself from making any lengthy speech in answer to the toasts in his honor, on the ground that he had already said enough to fully convey his ideas of matters and things in Mexico since he landed at Manzanillo, and did not care to impress his own countrymen with the idea that he was becoming unduly garrulous and loquacious. He said of Mexico:

"The season of her calamities is ended; Mexico is still youthful, ambitious, hopeful. She possesses all the material and moral elements of national greatness. All that her people want is rest and peace, for five years, ten years, twenty years or fifty years; the longer the better; and she may now assume the way that leads to prosperity and power among the nations. For this reason, when at Vera Cruz I shall be bidding adieu to Mexico, I shall wrest the inscription, "*Requiescat in pace*," from its customary application to the dead, and use it with all the inspiration of hope, affection, and gratitude, as an invocation of a blessing upon the living, "Mexico Requiescat in Pace!"

The stupid ignorance of the numerous seekers after the treasure supposed to have been buried in the United States by that famous Captain, whose "name was Robert Kidd, when I sailed, when I sailed," and the Californian expeditionists in search of the pirate treasure buried on Cocos Island, has its parallel in that of the buried treasure hunters of Mexico to-day. All over the country the impression prevails, that the Jesuits, when suddenly expelled from Mexico by the Spanish Government, buried, or otherwise concealed millions of dollars worth of treasure, gold and silver statues, church plate, jewels, etc., etc., and millions have been expended and are still being expended, in search of the precious deposits.

Mr. Adolpho Blumenkron is one of the most inveterate of these treasure seekers. As we rode out of the city, we were shown several old convent and church structures of great extent, now secularized, which he has purchased, and mined under and burrowed about, like a ferret, in search of the treasure of the Fathers, but always with the same total want of success. He told us, how on one occasion he found the vault in which were buried some of the old church dignitaries of Cortez's time, and looking down into it, was gladdened by the sight of two mummies each with a golden crown upon his head. He was into that vault in no time, with the help of Providence and a crowbar, and bore the glittering crowns out to the light of day. Fancy his feelings, when with trembling hands he applied a file to the gaudy baubles, and found them to be a base cheat, a sham, bilk, delusion, fraud, and rascally imposition! Would you believe it? those crowns were made of tin or some other base metal, and gilded, and if the holy fathers ever had any others—save the final crown of glory—they were not buried in them, for reasons best known to themselves or their servants.

It is believed that there were twelve statues of the Apostles of life size, made wholly from silver and gold, in the Jesuit College, and that the fathers—having received a secret intimation of the intention of the Government—buried them somewhere thereabouts, and the search for them is not yet abandoned.

In the City of Mexico, an apparently better founded

search is going on. It is well known that when Guatamozin was finally defeated by the Spaniards, the immense treasures which he was supposed to possess could not be found; and that the pious conquerors roasted him at a tree still standing at Chapultepec, to make him reveal their place of concealment.

"This is not a bed of roses," is said to have been his quiet remark as they grilled him, but he never let up, and the secret—if there was any—died with him. Now, they have what purports to be the will of Guatamozin, in the Aztec language, setting forth the secret of the deposit, alleging that it was in the ground near where the last fight took place on the outskirts of the City of Mexico, and providing that his descendants should never reveal it nor search for the treasure until the power of the Spanish should be broken, and even then, that no Spaniard should ever be allowed to profit by it. Now, when the power of Spain on the continent of America is broken, and the Church she founded in Mexico, in blood and outrage, has lost, or is fast losing its hold on the people, a descendant of Guatamozin produces the will, and directs the search for the long buried treasure. I found that Col. Enrique Mejia and other ripe scholars in whose judgment I would implicitly rely, believed the will to be genuine, and that the treasure was really buried in the vicinity of the spot where the search is now being made, though they think the chances of the search being successful, after the lapse of centuries and the changes which have taken place in the locality, as extremely problematical, to say the least, and they do not take stock in the enterprise.

We had heard much of the religious bigotry and fanatical hatred of foreigners—especially Americans—manifested by the Pueblanos, before our arrival, and the late religious riot had led us to believe many of the statements to be true. But to whatever extent this feeling may exist among the lower and more ignorant class, it was never manifested by word or deed, toward Mr. Seward or any member of his party. We were lodged and sumptuously fed during our stay, in the "*Obispado*," or Palace of the Bishop of Puebla, and nothing could be more kind and respectful than the demeanor of all classes toward Mr. Seward and his friends. I was all over the city by day and night, alone, wearing the undress uniform of an officer of the American National Guard, which left no chance for my nationality being mistaken, and always met the most kindly treatment. I was informed that the Government had given orders to General Alatorre and Governor Romero, to protect the Protestant congregation in Puebla in their right of public worship of God according to their own conscience, at any cost and under any circumstances, and that the Catholic clergy, though naturally opposed to the innovation on their customs, exercised through more than three centuries without dispute, were heard to rebuke, strongly, any disposition to resort to force and violence in opposing the spread of the—as they must of course regard them—heretical doctrines and practices.

When we left, all was quiet in Puebla, and unless the Government troops meet with some severe reverse in the campaign against the guerilla bands in the Sierra, the Protestant element in Puebla is not likely to be again disturbed, or in any way maltreated, unless itself guilty of some act of wholly unjustifiable imprudence.

CHAPTER XIX.

FROM PUEBLA TO ORIZABA.

HAVING hurried through Puebla as rapidly as possible, giving ourselves but half the time we should have taken earlier in the trip to inspect that old, historic city, its churches and its ruins, and the interesting country surrounding it, we left on the 23d of December for Orizaba. Mr. Fitch was placed under the care of Col. Geo. M. Green as a military and moral precaution, and sent off in advance by the regular diligence which left at 2 A. M., and the rest of the party, accompanied by Señor Bossero, the commissioner sent out to Guadalajara by the Mexican Government to escort Mr. Seward through the entire Republic, left at sunrise in a special coach. Miss Parkman, daughter of an American thirty-two years resident in Guanajuato and married to a Mexican lady, had joined the party at the City of Mexico to go home with Mr. Seward, to remain a year and learn the English language, of which she was, up to the time of our arrival, entirely ignorant.

The morning air was chilly and raw when we left Puebla, and for the first time since leaving Manzanillo, we saw a fog hanging over the landscape. This fog came from the Gulf of Mexico, and was, we were told, the effect of a Norther blowing down the coast.

After a time it lifted, and rolled up the mountains in thin wreaths of snowy vapor, which softened the ragged outlines of the great volcanoes, made the naked, brown, lavatic peak of Malinchi appear to shoot upwards thousands of feet higher into the blue heavens, and as it took on the hues of the sea-shell and the rainbow, when lighted up by the rising sun, crowned with a turban of glory the white head of the monarch Orizaba.

Our first halting place was at Amozoc, an old Indian city, now principally famous for the skill of its workers in iron, and the shrewd impertinence of its venders of the articles. The coach had not fairly come to a stop, before the windows were blocked by peddlers of finger-rings, spurs, bridle-bits, toy flat-irons, etc., etc., of blue steel, inlaid with silver and handsomely engraved, which they thrust in our faces, and offered at the most fabulous prices, at the same time inviting a bid of any kind. We got about a quart of toy flat-irons, rings marked "M. L."—*Mexico Libre*—or Mexico is Free—etc., for a few dollars, and then a youth with a sinister countenance, tossed a pair of Spanish spurs—each of which would weigh fully a pound avordupois—into my lap, and insisted on my purchasing them.

"How much?"

"Nine dollars, Señor, and they are very cheap!"

"I will give you three dollars."

"Oh no, your Excellency, but you shall have them for eight."

"Not if the court knows herself; I will give you three."

"You shall have the spurs—and the silver is genuine, Señor—and this magnificent bridle-bit for seven dollars?"

"Do you want three for the spurs? I don't want

the bit as a gift; it is a thousand years out of date, and must have been stolen by your ancestors from Hernando Cortez or Alvarado!"

"Five dollars, Señor?"

"No!"

"Four?"

"No!"

"Well, here take them!" and I did take them, and found next day that he had offered them to Col. Green a few hours previous for two dollars, and asked him what he would give—indicating a willingness to accommodate by going lower. I shall never wear those spurs with any degree of satisfaction.

The iron is produced near the railway, some twenty miles from Puebla, and is converted into steel and wrought up with much skill by the native citizens, with the very rudest appliances.

The people in the vicinity have a reputation for eccentricity. When the first telegraph line was erected along the road from Orizaba to Puebla, miles of the wire disappeared from the poles in the vicinity of Amazoc every night, in the most mysterious manner. At length the company offered to compromise with the iron-workers by giving them, as a free present, a given quantity of wire annually, provided they would ensure the line remaining intact. The proposition was rejected with scorn, as an insinuation of a doubt upon the honesty and fair fame of the iron-workers; but the wire continued to go off, until the company adopted a different material which could not be made useful by the skillful workers in blue steel and silver, and now everything is lovely, and the line hangs high and undisturbed.

When the railway company, at the collapse of the Empire, found it necessary to suspend work a few months, more or less, on account of the condition of the country, it is said that they sent an English sub-superintendent down to Amozoc, to take charge of the material on hand in that vicinity. With perfectly Anglican simplicity, he housed all the iron rails, and left the chairs and spikes out-of-doors. It is hardly necessary to say that on the resumption of work not a chair or spike was to be found, and I may add that the price of steel goods manufactured at Amozoc had mean time fallen to exactly the cost of the workmanship, no charge for material being reckoned by the enterprising Amozocians in their estimates of the expenses of carrying on the business.

The leaving of the chairs and spikes out of doors was of course an absurdity, but that it was quite necessary to house the rails is demonstrated by the fact that they used to disappear every night, when left out of doors and not fastened down. One day an officer of the company was riding some twelve miles distant from the track, when he saw a countryman driving an ox team, with one of the full length T rails, weighing sixty pounds to the foot, dragging on the ground behind them. Demanding to know what he was doing with the rail the fellow replied, with a shrug of the shoulders:

"Oh, just going to build a *puntacita*," (i. e., a little bridge.)

"But that rail belongs to the railway company; don't you know that?"

"Oh, no, Señor, I did not know who it belonged to. Do you represent the company?"

"Of course I do, and I want that rail?"

"Very well; if the rail belongs to you, I don't want it. Take it and welcome, Señor. *Buenos tarde* Señor!" and coolly unhitching the oxen from the rail, he politely lifted his hat and walked off with his animals, leaving the rail lying there, twelve miles from the track, for the owners to get it back as best they could; it did not appear to worry him a bit.

There are no silver mines in the vicinity, but the diligences were formerly stopped pretty regularly, and the supply of silver for ornamenting the steel work, appears to be still sufficient to meet the demand of the trade.

His Excellency, Governor Romero, and staff, accompanied us in his private coach from Puebla as far as Tepeaca, an old Aztec city nine leagues from Puebla. Here we stopped for breakfast, and parted with the Governor and his aids with mutual expressions of regret. The Governor had done all that any man could possibly do, to show Mr. Seward attention and respect, and made the stay of the party in the State of Puebla a pleasant one, and he will long be remembered with gratitude.

Tepeaca has a history, if we had had time to stop and look it up. We breakfasted in a fonda opposite the grand plaza. In this plaza, in front of the church, stands a tall, square tower of brick or adobe, painted white, with a red tile roof, arched port-hole-like openings near the top, and a sun-dial painted on the side perpendicularly, according to the Aztec custom, instead of horizontally as ours used to be. On the dial is an inscription to this effect: "Here I am, and there is no mistake about me." This was a fortress of the Aztecs, and being very curious, the Spaniards did not destroy it, but preserved it as it now stands in perfection; thank them for so much at any rate! It was doubtless a good thing in the days of bows and arrows, but a common six-pounder field-piece would have knocked it into a cocked hat in no time.

The Spaniards, in advancing up into the country from Vera Cruz, had a mare which they valued highly. Near Tepeaca the mare got loose, and ran away to the Aztec camp. The Indians determined to catch her alive, regarding her as the next thing to the God of the Spaniards, and one of the greatest contributors to their success. So they chased her on foot until many of them—so tradition says—dropped down dead from heat and fatigue, but their efforts were unavailing, for the Spaniards corralled her after all.

In the late war between France and Mexico, the noted guerrilla chieftain, General Caravajal—who accompanied us from Mexico to Puebla, Tlaxcala and Cholula—fought many minor battles along the road with the invaders, and always cleaned out his opponents. He is the very impersonation of the quick, adroit, brave, and withal patriotic guerrilla commander, and for such warfare has probably no equal on the continent. When the French were encamped at Tepeaca, he made a bet of five hundred dollars a side with Rojas, that he would with his small band of guerrillas, cut his way into the plaza and kill some of the French, before he (Rojas) could do the same with his force. The first party to kill a Frenchman in the plaza was to take the money. General Caravajal actually rode at full gallop directly into the plaza at day-break, killed several French officers in front of the commander's quarters, and rode off again unscathed, winning the money. He looks like a good, plain, honest American farmer of forty-five years of age, and is the last man in the world you would take for the hero of so many daring and recklessly brave exploits.

We were now in the maguey or aloe district of Mexico. This plant does not thrive well in the *tierre caliente*, but at the elevation of six to ten thousand feet above the sea, in this latitude is seen in its greatest perfection. Its home is the great valley and central plains of Mexico, though it is found as far north as Arizona. The whole country is covered with it in this vicinity. The houses are thatched with its leaves; ropes, matting, and cloth of a coarse texture are made from it; in fact, the common people are born, live, and get drunk and die on it in some form. Along here it is less used for making *pulque* than between Mexico and Puebla, and we saw thousands on thousands of plants with the center or flower stalk shooting up ready to burst into blossom. Each stalk is about the size of a common telegraph pole—perhaps three or four feet less in average height—and resembles—before the blossoms, have put forth—a gigantic asparagus shoot, in color and form.

The palm, of the stumpy, worthless variety known in Texas and Arizona as the "Spanish bayonet," is found here, covering all the hill-sides, and scattered along the roads. The mountains begin to lose their appearance of utter barrenness, and are clothed in dense chaparal or fair-sized juniper, cedar, oak, pine, and cypress trees; we were coming within the influence of the moist air of the Gulf of Mexico.

John Butler, Mr. Seward's dark servant, never had any patience with the Mexican servants with whom he came in contact, and each day's experience in the country confirmed his prejudices and deepened his convictions. As a rule he insisted that they were bound to understand English, and did understand it in spite of all their protestations. "Here blast you, set this trunk right down *there* I tell you, and I want you to *understand* it!" he would exclaim. The servants would of course comprehend from his gestures what he desired to have done, and comply with his command; whereupon he would turn to some of the party and remark triumphantly:

THE NEEDLE PALM.

"There, cuss their yellow hides, didn't I tell you they could understand English if they only had a mind to?"

But occasionally he would get hold of a customer who would persist in not understanding him, and after a little trifling his Christian meekness would give way, and his wrath find vent in words, forcible and to the point. At a little village where we stopped to lunch, Mr. Seward told him to go and buy a hundred cigars for the guard. He started off and soon after, hearing high words going on in a wayside shop, I looked in to learn the cause of the row.

"Here Colonel, come in here please, and tell this stupid thing that I want 'em *all!*" he exclaimed as he caught sight of me.

"*Todos* Señor? *Todos?*" replied the woman at the counter, with an expression of anxiety and doubt on her face, as she turned appealingly to me.

"No, cuss you no! I said *all*, didn't I? Don't try to run no *todos* on me; I want 'em *all!*" shouted John, seizing the box and pulling it from her reluctant hand. "Blast her, she is trying to retail them to me by the *todos*, when I told her more than forty times over, that I wanted 'em *all!*"

I explained to the irate descendant of Ham, that *todos* and all, were synonymous terms in the two languages.

"Then why did'nt *she* say so at once, and not keep me here fooling all day?" was his emphatic rejoinder as he threw down the two dollars demanded and left the shop, shaking his head wrathfully, and evidently more disgusted with the country and everything in it than ever before.

We staid over night at Palmar, an old Indian town twenty leagues from Puebla, and lodged at a fonda. There is nothing at Palmar worth describing—at least I saw nothing.

The splendidly uniformed commander of the Rural Guard of Puebla, mounted on a fleet little bay horse, all life and fire, with saddle, bridle, stirrups, holsters, etc., etc., one mass of beautifully wrought silver, accompanied us from Puebla to Orizaba. At intervals of about twenty miles, the guard of twenty-five to fifty men, all similarly mounted and presenting a magnificent appearance as they dashed along at full speed by the side of the coach, were changed; but this officer rode with us all the way, his fiery, little steed never flagging or halting to rest for a moment from morning to night. The road was fearfully dusty, and the coach mules, coach-wheels, and the horses of the guard, kept us in such a cloud of the sacred soil all the way, that no single individual was recognizable after we had gone a mile or two.

I wish I could present my readers with a picture of that peculiar and characteristic cortege, as we swept along the road from Puebla to Orizaba. Every color of the rainbow flashed in the costumes of the guard or the trappings of the horses. The men were wrapped to the eyes in scarfs and *serapes* to guard their faces and throats from the—to them—extreme cold, though we found it too warm to wear overcoats when sitting still, in the open coach. All the natives of this country thus protect themselves against the air, even in the warmest seasons, and the women you meet on the road have their faces, in most cases, all covered except the eyes, with their blue or black *rebosas*.

We left Palmar at 8 A. M., December 24th, for Orizaba, having only sixteen Spanish leagues to go. For the first six leagues the country was dusty, dry as the Californias during the dry season, and uninteresting. Then all in an instant the scene changed as if by mágic. At a sharp turn in the road we came upon the brink of a great cañon, like that of the American River above Colfax on the Central Pacific Railway in California. The sides of the cañon were wooded and green, and very precipitous. Down at the bottom of this cañon, from twelve hundred to eighteen hundred feet below us, we could see many great cotton-laden wagons drawn by twenty to thirty mules each, coming up from Vera

Cruz, the weary animals straining every nerve to pull the heavy loads up the zigzag road which winds like a serpent up the almost perpendicular face of the mountain.

We stood at last, at the dividing line between the great Central Plateau or elevated Table Land of Mexico, and the Tierra Caliente of the Gulf coast. The gay cavalcade of horsemen who formed our escort, dashed down the steep declivity at a gallop, and the coach, with breaks hard set, went down with a speed like that of a railway train, turning the sharp angles of the road without an instant's slackening up, and rocking and swaying like a ship in a storm until we were at the bottom. We congratulated ourselves on the experience, and all agreed that we had never seen anything finer, or enjoyed a more exhilarating ride in our lives.

A few minute's pause to rest our panting animals, and then we ascended a little hill, and instead of finding ourselves in an open plain as we had anticipated, looked down on another and greater cañon, which by its size made the first seem a mere bagatelle, dwarfed the great Barranca of Beltran by comparison, and would even challenge and win admiration, side by side with the Great Yosemite, the wonder of the world in our day and generation.

Slope back the walls of rock which form the sides of the Yosemite, so as to make them a little less than perpendicular, clothe them with low, green chaparral to hide the blue-grey stone, plant a little village with an old white church like that in the "Heart of the Andes," in the center of the narrow, green valley where Hutchings' house stands, and look down on the picture from Inspiration Point, and you have the greater of *Las Cumbres*, as we looked down into it on that bright, sunny afternoon of the 24th of December, 1869. By Heaven! it was a sight worth coming all these thousands of miles by sea and land, to look upon!

Away we went again, down, down, down, as the eagle fixes his wings and glides swiftly from his airy height in the mountains into the valley below. In half an hour more all had changed around us, and we stood again amid the scenes and surrounded by the rankly luxuriant vegetation of the tropics. We had descended six thousand feet within ten miles, and the land of the aloe and maize was behind us. Around us was the banana, the orange, sugar-cane and coffee, and the thousand glorious flowers of the tropics, high mountains—green-clad and glorious—on either hand, and before us, Orizaba in all his unspeakable majesty.

Through the green valley, skirted with Indian villages of low cone-thatched and open-sided huts, we drove at full speed for an hour, and then halted at a village a league only from the quaint old city of Orizaba, where we found carriages in waiting, and the authorities standing ready to receive Mr. Seward and escort him to our lodgings in the town, as the guest of the State of Vera Cruz within whose boundaries we had just entered.

CHAPTER XX.

ORIZABA—THE GREAT CONDUCTA.

ORIZABA is one of the most curious old towns which we visited in Mexico. It more resembles Colima in its surroundings than any other, but the growth of tropical vegetation in the immediate vicinity, is not to be compared with that which gives such an air of oriental luxuriance and magnificence to the City of the Sun, out by the Western Ocean, through which we made our entrance into Mexico. The heavy, flat or arched stone roofs of the central table lands and elevated plains of Mexico, disappear at the Cumbres, and at Orizaba we saw only low-walled buildings, for the most part but one story in height, with wide projecting eaves, and pitching roofs covered with the same old fashioned red tiles which the Spaniards placed there three hundred and forty years ago.

Mr. Seward's party were quartered in the most comfortable manner, in one of the few two-story houses in the city, which was owned by a young physician, Dr. Talivera, and from our windows we looked down upon the streets of the greater portion of the town. The streets are wide, and tolerably straight, and paved with lava. The gutters are in the middle of the street, and the sidewalks are mere *banquettes*, about three feet—rarely four feet—in width, hardly wide enough for two persons to walk abreast. Grass fresh and green—

though not tall I must admit—grows, more or less, in all the streets, and water-cresses are found along the margins of the little streams of fresh water which flow through the gutters in the center.

Off the main street, through which the *diligencia* passes twice or thrice a day, plying between the railway station at Paso del Macho, the present western terminus of the Eastern section, and Puebla, the present eastern terminus of the Western section which comes down from Mexico, one hardly ever sees a carriage of any kind, unless it be a heavy mule wagon, loaded with cotton, or a wooden-wheeled ox-cart lumbering slowly and painfully along. We found one street which appeared to be considerably traveled, so much so that Mr. Frederick Seward started off in an enthusiastic manner, to see where it led to, and ascertain the cause of its unusually lively character: it led to the cemetery, and nowhere else, as I am an honest and conscientious man.

The prospect of the railway being finished from Vera Cruz to Orizaba—the name of the city is always pronounced as if spelled Orizava, (i. e. O-re-zah-vah) with the accent on the last syllable but one—during the Empire, infused a little life into the town, and a very good sized "*Hotel de la Diligencias*" was erected and opened; but the work was suspended when the Empire went down, and for a long time all life appeared to be dying out. The work has been resumed with some energy, and the grading of the sixteen leagues between Orizaba and *Paso del Macho*, and up the mountain side around the Cumbres to the great plain above on which Puebla is situated, was so well advanced as to ensure its completion at an early day, and the people were again looking forward with hope to the future. Nevertheless, we found the town as quiet as a well-regulated cemetery, and saw no sign of life, such as would be found in an American city.

The mists from the Gulf of Mexico come up here almost daily, and it rains, more or less, nearly every week in the year. The atmosphere is of course very damp, and fevers are quite prevalent and severe.

Most of the freight between the end of the two sections of the railway, is packed through the *Cumbres*, and over the dusty plains to Puebla, or vice versa, upon mule backs; but all the vegetables, charcoal, country produce, earthenware, etc., etc., is still packed into this, as other towns, on the backs of stalwart male and female Indians.

It is wonderful how much these Indians will carry on their backs at a dog-trot, and how cheaply they will carry it. If they have to transport a given amount of freight for twenty miles, even right alongside the railway all the way, they never think of putting it upon the cars, but divide it up into three or four hundred pound packages, get it upon their backs, and go off at a pace equal to the average speed of a fast-walking horse.

If they start for a town, with a load of fruit or vegetables to be sold in the market, they will not dispose of it on the way, even if offered double the price at which they propose to sell it on the plaza. Like the negro, who when fishing for catfish, was seen to catch a fine, large pickerel, deliberately take him off the hook, and throw him out into the stream as far as his strength would enable him to hurl him, and who, in answer to an inquiry as to his reason for so doing, replied:

"I'se fishin' for catfish I is, an' when I fishes for cats I wants cats, an' dont want no pickerel to come foolin' aroun' my hook!" they will do just what they started out for, or die on the way. They are in no hurry to get back, any way; and the scene in the plaza varies, not unpleasantly for them, the dull monotony of the daily round of their quiet, uneventful lives.

Jokes are played off by travelers, on the habits and customs of all people, and all countries. I had often heard an assertion made in regard to these Indian packers returning from market, which I regarded as one of these traveler's jokes; but an American citizen, who has been engaged in Mexico as a railway builder, and has brought all the energies of a giant mind to bear upon the subject, told me at Orizaba that it is an absolute fact, that they are so accustomed to carrying heavy loads, that the moment the weight is off their shoulders they lose their traction, so to speak, cannot get a good hold upon the ground with their toes, and are as thoroughly "at sea," as a sailor on horseback. If they cannot find anything in the city to pack back to their homes, they will put a few chunks of lava, or boulders into their baskets, to ballast them and give them a traction, and start off, dissatisfied, but proudly conscious of having done the best that could be done under the disadvantageous circumstances of the case. A less speculative and more matter-of-fact people I never saw in my life.

There is a fine, large cotton mill with two thousand spindles, and a large paper mill with American machinery—brought out and erected by Mr. Richard G. Ashby, from Massachusetts—located near the city. The water-power is abundant, and labor cheap, but the high price of raw cotton, the depressed state of trade, and an overstocked market, render all hope of profit from the working of the cotton factory out of the question, at present. The cotton mill was not running, but it was proposed to start it up again as an experiment, soon, and run it for a short time at least. The paper mill is kept running at a moderate profit.

The city stands in a narrow, but beautiful and very fertile valley, with towering, green, forest-clad mountains all around, and Orizaba, snow-crowned and glorious, looks down upon it. There may be eighteen thousand to twenty thousand people in the city, all told, of whom a large number are engaged in trade or in waiting for trade to come to them; I saw plenty of shops and stores, but few buyers for the wares exposed.

On the hill above the city, the French and Mexicans had a fight by night, the latter being surprised, panic-stricken, and routed, almost in a moment; they did better later in the war. My window faced a fine old church, in the front wall of which I counted a dozen cannon balls, and the tower appeared to have been occupied by sharp-shooters who were receiving like attentions from the opposing party, as it was pitted all over with marks of musket-balls, as if it had the small pox. I asked a man who stood in front of it, when and how the ball and bullet marks came there. He said, with a grim humor, that he did not remember; it was *el costumbre del pais*, (the custom of the country) and might have been done at any time within the last fifty years. God grant that it may be the custom of the country no longer, and that Orizaba and all Mexico may have seen the last of such scenes!

The French and mercenary troops in the employ of

Maximilian, committed the most terrible outrages in the State of Vera Cruz in the vicinity of Orizaba. Whole villages were depopulated, or nearly so, and peaceable, unoffending citizens, shot down in cold blood from mere devilishness, by the Turcos and other troops. One Colonel Dupin was among the worst of the leaders who were concerned in the perpetration of these wholesale massacres. His motto was, "kill every man who wears leather breeches." As four-fifths of the common people of Mexico, wear leather breeches, when they wear any at all, it is evident that the proclamation of such a policy was equivalent to inaugurating a reign of terror, and a war of utter extermination.

No man was safe who attempted to pass over the roads of the state, unless he was in the uniform of the imperial army, and the residents of the most retired hamlets knew not at what moment a force of the imported cut-throats might be turned loose upon them, to kill, ravish, burn, and destroy at will. In the city of Orizaba, women were brought into the French camp and so maltreated by the Turcos that they died on the spot. Language is powerless to depict the horrors of that time. Dupin was, with all his infernal brutality, a man of courage, and repeatedly cut his way through the enemy when surrounded by a numerically superior force; but he was corralled and killed at last.

A similar character, a French colonel, met his fate in Durango during the occupation of that State. His troops caught a Mexican officer, and by his direction, shot him down in front of his own door, before the eyes of his young and lovely wife. To his astonishment the bereaved wife made no outcry, and did not reproach him for the murder. A few days later he met the beautiful woman at a party and was introduced. She took the matter so coolly that he inquired how it could be, and she replied that her husband was a brute; that she had never loved nor cared for him, and that she was glad when justice overtook him at last. An intimacy sprang up between them, and after some weeks the French colonel who had made her a widow, obtained her reluctant consent to visit her on a certain evening at her own apartments.

The meeting was tender and affectionate on both sides, and the Frenchman was delighted beyond words. The lady urged him to join with her in a glass of wine, and he, nothing loth, consented. After he had drank she stepped out of the room, and closing the heavy door between them, locked it in an instant and then called out to him:

"Colonel: you murdered my husband before my eyes! Your time has come now. That wine was poisoned, and in five minutes you will be a dead man! I have waited long for this; how do you like it?"

He fell, striving vainly to escape from the room, and expired in horrible agony. But her words had been overheard by a servant, who betrayed her, and she was condemned to death for the murder. She went to her execution with a smile of satisfaction on her face, and died glorying in what she had done.

It was Christmas Eve when we entered Orizaba, and all the bells were ringing, and they rung nearly all the time we were there. I rather liked it after I got used to it, but it was a little rough at first. The Christmas festivities are kept up in Orizaba for something like a month, and are mainly of two kinds. Those within the churches should take precedence of course.

A part of our party attended the midnight mass on the "Buena Noche," or night before Christmas, and saw the procession of the wise men of the East enter in search of the new-born Christ, while kneeling thousands looked on in admiration, and repeated the prayers for the occasion. The music was fine, the singing good, and the spectacle altogether a beautiful and imposing one.

On Sunday I went to the cathedral with two lady friends, one who went to pray with a simple, child-like faith, for the loved parents, sisters, brothers and friends she was leaving behind her in the home of her youth; and one of another faith, a happy young wife, who went with her, only to watch over her as is the custom of the country. I stopped at the door while they went in. My married friend wore a fashionable hat upon her head, and did not conform to the usages of the place, but stood erect, by the wall. These facts drew the attention of some of the worshipers, and one of them approaching her said reproachfully, but not exactly threateningly, and apparently more in sorrow than in anger, "I see that you are a devil!" whereupon, she came out at once, and waited by the door, until the young girl, with a face radiant with the pleasure which comes from the consciousness of duty well performed, arose from her knees and came forth to meet us.

A few years since it would not have been safe for a Protestant woman, with her head covered with a hat, to have been seen in that place, but now the case is different. There is some trace of the old bigotry to be seen among the lower classes still, but its fire is fast dying out in every part of Mexico.

On Sunday night we went to the theater, where

a grand sacred drama was being performed by a native company. The subject was the birth of Our Savior, and the scenes were laid in Heaven, on Earth, and in Hell. The play opened with a vivid representation of the commotion in the latter place, on the announcement being made that the Savior of mankind was about to be born. They could not raise the devil in better shape in the City Hall in New York, and they played hell, throughout, with a very strong caste. The scenes on earth were not so well done, and Heaven did not strike me as particularly attractive. It was all worth seeing once in a life-time. They have been some twenty years building a new theatre here opposite the cathedral, and the walls and roof are now nearly completed. The Dutch custom of giving presents to children and friends on Christmas, now so general in the United States, appears to be but little observed in any part of Mexico.

But the great feature of the Christmas festivities in Orizaba is the gambling. The whole plaza in front of the Cathedral is given up to it, and all who desire to open business, are licensed by the city. Thitherward the greatest crowds were tending on Christmas Eve, and I went with the majority. Along one entire side of the plaza is a row of booths devoted to *roulette*, played with French machines, and, apparently, "on the square." Crowds of all ages, colors, and conditions, were around the tables, and business appeared to be brisk. The banks generally had a goodly sum in silver dollars, halves, quarters, *rials* and *medios* in sight, but no gold. The bets were mostly small—few exceeding a dollar—and many being but one *rial* or a *medio* each. When I placed a dollar on the red as an experiment, won, and doubled it and won again, the crowd in front fell back respectfully, and I had the game all to myself until I was a dozen dollars ahead, and concluding the game too uncertain, bid the dealer good-night, received a courteous good-night in turn, and moved on. The poor people appear to play right on, as long as they have a dime left, and of course the bank comes out ahead in the long run.

Farther up there is a large booth in which *quino* is played, for fancy articles, china ware, etc., etc., the cost of a card being six and one-fourth cents, or four for twenty-five cents. I did not know the game, but Col. Green acted as my padrino, and in half an hour I was the happy possessor of seven sets of fancy china cups and saucers, with two servers to match, all at an outlay of only one dollar and a quarter. I regret to be compelled to add that I offered them for one dollar—they were valued at seven—and got no bidder among my companions; but I made a family of little children happy with them, and felt that I had got more than the worth of my money, after all.

Chuck-a-luck games ran down the center of the plaza; *monte*, *faro*, etc., etc., were scattered about—in the minority, and not well patronized—and the side opposite the *roulette* booths, is covered with a great shed capable of seating one thousand or fifteen hundred people, which is devoted exclusively to *quino*, played for money. The cards or tickets, are pasted down upon the tables and must number at least one thousand all told. Each player is provided with a handful of corn with which to keep the game as the numbers, drawn ont by the dealer are called, and as tast as one game is finished—it takes about three minutes—the collectors go around and collect in the *rials* for a new one. Each game costs each player a *rial*, or two *rials* if it is a "double up," and the bank gets nothing but a percentage on the amount paid in, for doing the business. This place is filled every night, and much of the day, by people of all classes; ladies and gentlemen of the best families making little parties at the tables, and enjoying the sport as heartily as anybody. I went there with a party of ladies and gentlemen, played half a dozen games without winning one, then went to a *roulette* table, bet twice on the red and twice on the black, won all four bets, and quit gambling. It is not a first-rate business to follow, even in Mexico, where it is regarded, generally, as quite legitimate, and in a very different light from that in which we see it in the United States.

The most singular thing about this wholesale gambling is the perfect good order which prevails in the crowd. I did not see a drunken man, nor hear an angry word or an oath among all the thousands of players. When you remember, that to four-fifths of these players the loss of a single dollar is of greater moment than the loss of one hundred to the average American patron of the gaming table, you can readily understand what an event it is in their lives. Yet courtesy and forbearance are displayed upon all sides, and the losers never give vent to audible grumbling, while the winners—what there are of them—pocket their gains without a sign of exultation. Men who have lost their last *medio* will sit down by your side, and keep the account of the game for you, condoling with you when you lose, and congratulating you when you win, with as much earnestness as if they had known you for years.

In many cities of Mexico gambling is now prohibited, and, as with us, can only be carried on by stealth; but in the smaller towns throughout the country, it is not exactly the vice but the prevailing misfortune of the people.

Procuring saddle-horses in Orizaba, a number of our party with several gentlemen from the city, rode out through fine fields of sugar-cane and orange and banana plantations, a distance of three miles to the Falls of the Rincon Grande. The Rio de Agua Blanco, a deep, swift-running, pure, fresh-water stream, comes rushing, like the Truckee in Nevada, down from the mountains on the eastward of the city, running most of the distance through a deep and very picturesque cañon.

At the point where the falls commence, the stream divides, one half running on down the cañon, and the other running out on the top of the mesa, or table-rock of lava, which forms one side of the ravine, then turning, and falling in many smaller streams over the precipitous face of the cliff into the bottom of the cañon, and in a cloud of spray, mingling with the waters of the main stream below.

The perpendicular fall, itself, cannot exceed fifty feet at this point, but in outline it is a miniature Niagara, and the wealth of tropical verdure and flowers which surround it, as the gold and enamel surround the diamond when it leaves the cunning hand of the jeweler, makes it a gem of exquisite beauty, such as can never be seen in colder climes than this. The trees all around are covered with long, grey moss, and numberless parasites, all of which bear gorgeous-colored flowers. Some of these flowers are in shape like an ear of corn, six to eight inches in length, of the most brilliant scarlet, and set in a cup of bright green leaves, the whole looking more like skillful wax-work, than the work of nature.

All around the falls the foliage and shrubbery is so dense as to preclude walking, except in narrow foot-paths cut for the purpose, and at the end of the year, when everything in the far North is buried in the snows of winter, all is as green, and red, and gay-colored and beautiful as in midsummer. In this tropical paradise, only man and his works pass away; the glory of Nature is eternal and unchanging: "In Summer and in Winter shall it be."

The rushing waters come down to the edge of the precipice through a rank growth of great canes, which swing and sway with the pressure of the current, like willows by our northern rivers when swept by the winds of summer. Clinging to the jagged lava rocks which divide the stream above the falls, wherever there is a handful of earth to nourish them, are great banana trees, with broad leaves like the banners of an army of giants, waving in the soft breeze of the South. All the face of the rock between the streams of falling water is covered with clinging plants and flowering shrubs, and one rock, shaped like a cross, which projected from the center out into the falling spray, was enwreathed with flowers like an artificial garland, as if they had been hung there by some dear woman's hand, to mark the last resting place of the loved and lost.

We went down by a winding pathway to the bottom of the cañon, opposite the fall, and sitting beneath the broad-spreading trees, gazed upon the scene until its beauty was indelibly impressed upon our minds, to be treasured up in memory forever; then gathered some sweet wild-flowers, to be pressed and carried away as souvenirs for our friends in the North, and re-mounting our horses, galloped towards the city.

On our way back we turned off from our road, and visited the great sugar ranch of San Antonio. The *hacienda* stands in a narrow cañon through which runs a small stream of pure water, and is surrounded by wide fields of luxuriant and rich-juiced cane, running up to the suburbs of the city. The sugar works are run by water-power, and though the crusher is of American make, all the other machinery and appliances are of the rudest and most primitive character.

The cane-juice is boiled in great, open, copper kettles set in brick-work, and is bailed from one to another until the last is reached, by naked-footed men, whose skin appears to be so indurated as to resist the action of the scalding fluid as thoroughly as the metal itself. The sugar, in its crude state, is placed in very large earthen moulds, wide at the top, and running to a point at the bottom, and covered with a peculiar clay made into a thin paste, which filtering through it, bleaches the mass to a pale brown color.

The sugar is sweet, and for coffee, fully equal to the article of a pale yellow hue called "coffee sugar" in the United States. This is the common product of the sugar haciendas of Mexico, and the process is that in general use all over the Republic from the Pacific to the Atlantic. With railways, a good and liberal system of revenue laws, and a few years of uninterrupted peace, Mexico could supply the United States, Canada, and much of Europe, with all the sugar required, and control the market of the world.

The coffee tree flourishes in the vicinity of Orizaba

in all possible luxuriance, and the product of the but indifferently tilled plantations between this point and Paso del Macho, is sufficient to supply the demand for a considerable extent of country. Mexico produces nearly, or quite, enough coffee for home consumption, and under more favorable conditions of society could furnish in a short time, an almost unlimited quantity for export. To sum up in a word, the Republic of Mexico has within her limits resources of wealth and comfort unbounded, and the day will come—I trust it may not be far distant—when she will be regarded, with reason, as the Paradise of the world.

In Mexico, there are no great Express Companies to transport specie cheaply and quickly through the country, as in the United States; and as the roads swarm with bands of robbers, from one end of the Republic to the other, when there is a chance for plunder offered, it follows, that the safety of the silver and gold from the mines of the interior, on its way to the coast, becomes a matter of such importance that the Government is compelled to assume the responsibility of providing for it. Accordingly, the troops are always held ready to escort it from point to point, and protect it, at any risk, from attack and plunder.

Notice is given, of the time a "*conducta*" will leave Guanajuato, San Luis Potosi, or other point for Mexico, and from Mexico for Vera Cruz, and shippers avail themselves of the opportunity offered, to forward the millions of hard dollars which accumulate in a few weeks or months at the center of one of the great mining districts, willingly paying the tax imposed in order to secure the protection of the Government troops; this protection is not *always* effectual, as recent events demonstrate that the escort itself, is, sometimes, not wholly trustworthy and incorruptible. When we were journeying towards the coast, the state of affairs along the route gave additional interest to the movements of the *conductas.*

For some weeks, the departure of the *conducta* from Mexico with treasure for Europe and the United States, had been the theme of much conversation all along the road. It was known that the *pronunciados* in the State of Puebla had their eyes upon this conducta, and would certainly attack it if they found themselves strong enough, or the guard weak enough, to warrant them in the attempt. Then it was further known, that Gen. Negrete had been in Mexico in disguise, and it was feared that his clandestine visit had some connection with a project to attack this conducta; and therefore the Government had made extraordinary arrangements for its protection.

From the hour of its starting from the Capital, down to the end of the trip, the bulletin-board at the *Lonja* at Vera Cruz, had shown the daily progress of the conducta, adding "all safe" at each new announcement. The precautions taken had proved all-sufficient, and the most dangerous portion of the road was passed or would be passed in a day or two. The silver was expected to reach Vera Cruz in season for the American steamer *Cleopatra* on the 10th of January.

On Monday, January 3d, the long looked for conducta came filing into the City of Orizaba, and the whole of the irregular, wide, main street of the town was filled with it. There were two million seven hundred thousand dollars in this conducta, and the entire train resembled a division of a grand army in appearance. There were forty-six carts, each drawn by fourteen to eighteen mules and loaded with over sixty thousand dollars in specie, and pack-animals and carts for the baggage of the escort, and the escort itself consisted of eight hundred men of all arms, viz: five hundred picked infantry, including two companies of *Zapodores* from the capital, under the immediate command of Major Rocha, nearly three hundred cavalry, and a detachment of artillery with two field-pieces, all under the command of Colonel Lerya of the regular army of Mexico.

The conducta did not take the railway, but marched down the old stage road, *via* Puebla, and came on, direct, toward Vera Cruz. Their encampment in the streets of Orizaba presented one of the most novel and interesting spectacles imaginable. Each cart had its separate guard, and the whole a general one, which was changed from hour to hour, day and night, with military precision; and whether on the march or in camp, on the wild mountains or in a quiet city like Orizaba, the care and watchfulness was never for a moment relaxed. I have already described the manner of the marching of a detachment of Mexican troops as we saw it between Colima and Guadalajara; but this was a repetition of that scene on a grander and more extended scale.

Of course the *conducta* was the grand feature of the day, and caused a great excitement, and an unwonted appearance of life in the streets of Orizaba. At night the spectacle, when the troops were preparing their suppers and making ready for the night, was more wild and picturesque than during the day.

In the morning, the long train of treasure-laden carts,

with its advance-guard, rear-guard, and immediate escort was in motion at an early hour, the trumpets and kettle-drums of the different corps filling the air with the harsh, discordant music, even before day-break, and making sleep at our quarters impossible.

Mr. Seward's party were to have been off for Paso del Macho, at 5 o'clock A. M., to meet the special train formerly kept for the special use of Maximilian and his family, and still known as "the Imperial Train," sent up from Vera Cruz, for the occasion; but owing to bungling mismanagement they were delayed until after 7 o'clock, and, of course, compelled to crowd on all speed to make up for lost time. The long train of the *conducta* was in motion, taking up all the highway, but when word was sent that Mr. Seward was at the rear, it halted and made room for the coach to pass, and the officers and men of each corps presented arms as he went by.

I went down to Vera Cruz ahead of the conducta, passing it on the way, and so had an opportunity of seeing it arrive at its destination and witnessing the final scene. The dangerous Pass of the Chiquihuite having been made successfully, on arriving at *Paso del Macho*—the western end of the Vera Cruz section of the railway—the cavalry and artillery were dismissed, and the specie transferred to the cars—a special having been provided—and thence went on to Vera Cruz under escort of the infantry only. The two million seven hundred thousand dollars in specie was all packed in coarse sacks of maguey fibre, each sack holding three thousand dollars, and it required twelve closed box, freight-cars to transport it.

When the special train arrived at Vera Cruz the cars

were run down to the Custom House Plaza in front of the entrance to the mole, and there they remained until all the money was shipped on board the steamers for New York and Europe. The American steamer *Cleopatra* carried about one million on the 10th of January, and the French steamer of the 13th,—owing to a quarrel about charges between the owners of the American steam line and the shippers, I believe—the remainder. Our American steamers ought, in fact, to monopolize the specie-carrying trade of Mexico, and could probably do so with a little effort.

While the cars remained in the plaza the troops were quartered under a *portal* in front of the train. A guard patrolled on each side of the cars day and night, and a soldier with a loaded musket stood on the roof of each car all the time. The point is further commanded by the guns of San Juan de Ulloa, and the treasure was therefore as safe as gunpowder, balls, and bayonets could make it.

It was, of course, not absolutely necessary to take such extraordinary precautions for the protection of this special conducta in Vera Cruz where all was then quiet; but it is the custom of the Government to require the officers in charge of the escort to see that discipline is never relaxed for a moment, and that all the regulations are carried out to the letter, until the treasure is delivered to consignees in the city, or safely on board the steamers, and then responsibility ceases. The Government gets eight per cent. on every dollar—amounting to two hundred and sixteen thousand dollars on this conducta alone—when it passes through the Custom-House gateway, as export duty, and is bound to afford full protection to the owners.

Much of the silver is delivered to the consignees at their counting houses in the city, and there recounted, and repacked in smaller bags containing but one thousand dollars each. I saw in the house of Schliden & Co., one day, a party of natives at work counting and repacking a half million of these bright new dollars. They get twelve and a half cents for each one thousand dollars which they count and sew up in the new bags, and are very expert in detecting defective or base coin. It is said that when they pour a bag of these dollars upon the table, they will decide in an instant whether they are of the coinage of Zacatecas, Guanajuato, or Mexico, by the difference in the ring of each, though it is wholly imperceptible to the ear of the uninitiated. If the bags are found short the deficit is charged to the shippers at Mexico or Guanajuato; if in excess—and this is not uncommon—the overplus is credited to the shippers.

I have never seen any specie-counters or experts, who, could beat these uneducated Indian-blooded Veracruzanos, save the Chinese experts, who do the same business for the banks in San Francisco, and who can discount the world beyond a doubt.

The scene reminded me of an incident which occurred at the city of Mexico when Gen. Scott entered the capital in triumph. A detachment of Harney's dragoons were quartered in the *Palacio Nacional*, and before order was fully restored they broke open a room in the Treasury department in which they found a large number of Mexican dollars—fourteen or sixteen large sacks, if memory serves me.

In an instant they went for the coin, and a general scramble took place. One would get a sack upon his shoulder, when another would slash it open with a bowie-knife or sword, and the precious *pesos* would pour down in a shower upon the floor. Another would fill a haversack with them, only to meet with the same treatment. At last they got the doors closed and came to an understanding. All the coin was piled down on the floor, and a fair division made. Then each took his share of the plunder and concealed it around his quarters as best he might. Harney was unable to understand for the time, how it was that this party kept so remarkably quiet and appeared so well satisfied, but after a while the secret leaked out.

A dragoon bought something on the streets, and offered a dollar in payment. The seller—a Mexican of course—touched the coin to his teeth, and returned it respectfully, with the single remark, "Cobre Señor!" Another was offered, and "Cobre Señor!" was still the cry. Another, and another, and still no change. The dragoon smelled a rat, and returned, a sadder and a wiser man, to his quarters. Each of the fortune-finders by himself, tried to buy something, sooner or later, and met with the same discouraging remark.

It turned out that the coin was the plunder of an unauthorized private mint—in fact a bogus-money factory—which had been pounced upon by the Government, and there was not a single dollars worth of genuine silver in the entire pile. A cheaper looking lot of disappointed speculators never congregated in a "played out" Western town, or skedaddled from a base metal camp in one of the Pacific Coast mining districts, than was seen that night among Uncle Sam's boys in the "Palace of the Montezumas."

CHAPTER XXI.

VERA CRUZ.

MR. SEWARD, worn out by the fatigues of the long journey from Manzanillo to the Gulf Coast, remained resting at Orizaba until Tuesday, January 4th, being for the first time in three months in a position to enjoy a little undisturbed quiet.

During his stay he ascended the famous *Sierra de Borregas*—or mountains of the Sheep—which overlook the city. The ascent of from eight hundred to one thousand feet perpendicularly, was made on foot, and was accomplished by the ex-premier with, apparently, as little fatigue as was experienced by any of the party.

On Sunday, the 2d of Jauuary, the party visited the Indian village of Jalapena, in a deep and romantic gorge or cañon in the mountains near the source of the Rio Blanco, the stream on which are situated the Falls of Rincon Grande, described in the last chapter. The inhabitants paid Mr. Seward every possible attention, and the visit, though devoid of startling incident, was a very pleasant one to the party.

On the Monday following, a deputation of the simple Indians came down to Orizaba, to present Mr. Seward with a curiously carved and stained cane, of a peculiar wood growing by the banks of the Blanco. This cane is of a single piece of wood, and the handle represents an eagle's foot with extended talons, very artistically carved by a native and wholly untutored artist. Among the hundreds of presents, many of which are very valuable, received by Mr. Seward in California and Mexico, I doubt if any will give him more pleasure than this.

I have already described the road from Orizaba to Vera Cruz. The Seward party was overtaken a few miles below Orizaba, by Joseph Branniff, the railway contractor's superintendent, who was going down to Paso del Macho, with a light buggy drawn by two fast mules. Mr. Seward accepted a seat with Mr. Branniff in this carriage, and they went over the seventeen leagues at a pace, which, if it did not endanger the necks of the party, at least, gave Mr. Seward a shaking which he will remember to the end of his life.

The magnificent scenery of the Chiquihuite Pass delighted him more than anything which he had seen since the *Barranca de Beltran*, and so reminded him of the scenery of Africa as to cause him to remark, that it only wanted a lion or two by the road-side to complete the picture, and make the illusion perfect. There are plenty of tigers lurking in the chaparral along this road, and the number of way-side crosses ought to be good evidence that they have a very satisfactory substitute for lions.

The work of constructing the railway at this point is truly herculean and reminds one of that upon the Central Pacific Railroad, where it passes over the summit of the Sierra Nevada. It is described as follows, in a late number of the *Diario Oficial* of the City of Mexico:

"After leaving the station of Paso del Macho, the road passes, by means of a bridge three hundred feet long and one hundred feet high, that immense neck of land which separates the base of the first level portion of the Cordilleras from the plains of the *terra caliente*, or the hot country. This bridge, the mason-work of which is entirely finished, only lacks the iron floor in order to be open to the public. Having passed this great work, we arrive, by a series of curves as boldly as scientifically run, at the great bridge of San Alejo, which is not as high as that of Paso de Macho, but several feet longer. From San Alejo to Chiquihuite there is nothing but deep cuts through the solid rock, and enormous terrepleins, making the great inequalities of that broken ground entirely disappear. Chiquihuite Bridge, which is over three hundred feet long, is elevated more than one hundred and fifty feet above that abyss, where the foaming, cold stream that gives its name to this part of the mountain, forever leaps and boils. The boldest spirit would not suspect the real *tours de force* conceived in the running of this road accomplished by the skill of Mr. Buchanan, and completed under the direction of Mr. Branniff, chief of construction.

"On leaving the bridge, the road follows the main highway for some distance, by a terreplein of sixty feet high, supported by a wall ten feet thick, and suddenly, as in the shifting of scenes in a theatre, the road runs around the mountain, suspended on its sides. It was necessary to cut it through solid rock, of which the side of this mountain is composed. The laborers engaged in this unequal piece of work have to hold on to the rocks, and are held up by ropes, which makes them resemble, at a distance, bees in a honey-comb. The road continues for about one hundred metres along that track before it enters the first tunnel of one hundred and fifty feet in length; it again re-appears only to continue its aerial route, and again disappears in a tunnel of three hundred and fifty feet. From this tunnel the road passes over a small iron bridge, raised eight hundred feet above the bottom of the ravine."

At Paso del Macho, the special train was in waiting at 2 1-2 P. M., and at 6 P. M., the party was in Vera Cruz. The American Consul Mr. Trowbridge, Emilio B. Schliden, an American citizen, formerly of California, now at the head of a large mercantile house there, who had placed a beautiful, large house, ready furnished, at Mr. Seward's disposal, Mr. Joseph Brennon, and a number of other American citizens were at the depot, ready to receive him and escort him to his home in Vera Cruz.

The party were hardly settled in the house, when the Governor of the State of Vera Cruz, the commandant of the military forces, the Collector of the Port, the officers of the Custom-House and garrison, and other Federal and State officials in full uniform, called to present their respects, and offer the hospitalities of the city and their own services in any manner desired, as the hospitalities of Colima and the Republic of Mexico had been offered on our first landing on the soil of the country at Manzanillo, three months before. There were no formal speeches made, but the greeting was off-hand and cordial, and Mr. Seward, in a brief reply, returned thanks for the honor done him.

The more I saw of this odd, old, and fearfully unhealthy city of Vera Cruz at this season of the year, the more I was interested in it. Its curious old fortifications, dating back to the days of the *conquistadores*, and now as useless piles of stone, copper, iron, and coral as could by any possibility be got together; its mixed and mongrel population; its wide, straight streets, paved in the old Spanish style with the gutters in the centre; the old churches and public buildings, gray and worn with the storms of centuries and any number of sieges and bombardments; its swarms of *Zapilotes*, and its hideous and importunate beggars; everything, in fact, about the place is interesting.

At the corners of all the principal streets are hitching posts of a novel character: old Spanish, iron guns, set in the ground, breech down, and often rusted away to such an extent as to be hardly recognizable. I would hesitate some time before hitching my horse to such a post; suppose it should happen to go off with him?

Many of the buildings still bear the marks of the balls and shells thrown into the city by the American Army under General Scott; and I noticed one old church which was then partially unroofed, and has never been repaired. In walking about the streets I frequently saw balls or pieces of exploded shells, embedded in the pavement. Many of these were thrown into the city by Miramon, in the attempt to dislodge Juarez in the early part of 1860—an attempt which was frustrated by the direct interference of the American Minister and the American fleet.

The *Zapilotes* were my friends; but for them I should have had no amusement or occupation for hours at a time.

You should have seen the jolly row I managed to kick up, by throwing a handful of garbage to them from a restaurant, and then sending a small dog among them, to worry them and make the feathers fly.

Nobody knows where they breed, and although inquiry has been made on the subject for almost three centuries and a half, the matter is still a mystery. One day we bought three large sea-shells, each with the original inhabitant in it. To get the monster sea-snails to come out, it was necessary to suspend them on cords, with a good, stout, fish-hook through the head of each. Little by little the creature loses his grip, and in about forty-eight hours he lets go his hold entirely, and gives up the struggle.

The three lines with the three great pulpy sea-snails on the three hooks, got tied together, and fell into the street, by accident of course—it is unlawful to kill or injure the *Zapilotes*, and a heavy fine is inflicted for doing so—and soon the *Zapilotes* had a turn at them. Perhaps it was not fun to see three of the great, black, awkward fellows fast at once, each going it on his own hook as it were! They have very strong stomachs —and well they might considering what they feed upon—but the strain was more than even they could stand, and I am of the opinion, that in every case, at least two out of the three contestants got turned wrong side outwards in the struggle. But it did not seem to discourage the rest for a moment; and for aught I know, they are at it yet, each taking a turn at the tempting morsels, and getting swindled. They seem almost wholly lost to the force of example, and like men, must learn, each for himself, by personal experience.

Even our hotel—and it was far the best in the city—was interesting as a subject for study. The charges were moderate, three dollars and fifty cents per day in coin, with wine and early coffee extra—say about five dollars all told, if you are not too extravagant in your tastes.

Every style of business is carried on in the building. There is a store-house, and tailor shop with several sewing-machines on the lower floor. Up stairs, the office, bar, and billiard room are all one. The best rooms in the house extend out over the *portal*, and are light and well ventilated, but not luxuriously furnished. I had one of these rooms. The room next me was occupied by a party who were playing poker all night for big money.

I was kindly invited to take a hand in this friendly little poker game, but being a youth of modest and retiring turn of mind, reluctantly declined. I thought it would break my heart, if I were to go in there and win all the money from such gentlemanly, courteous, and considerate young men; at any rate, I never could forgive myself for doing it.

The room next on the other side, was infested by some game of which I have no personal knowledge. Beyond this, Mr. and Mrs. Brennon were quartered, and a young Mexican lady going to the United States occupied the next. Adjoining was a *faro* or *monte* bank, and beyond that two *roulette* tables running all night. In the billiard room they were playing *pool* for money, through nearly the entire twenty-four hours. Business, it will be seen, is not entirely dead in Vera Cruz. The partitions between the rooms are of rough boards, and do not come quite up to the ceiling; so that the occupant of each room gets the full benefit of whatever may be going on in the next.

The principal business on the streets seemed to be selling lottery tickets in behalf of various useful public enterprises. The tickets cost twenty-five to thirty-seven and one-half cents each, and the prizes range from five to five hundred dollars. I never heard any man complain that he had drawn a prize and did not get his money; I think he would run a risk of getting it promptly if he ever drew one. I patronized "a favor del Telegrafo de Jalacingo a Tampico," to the extent of about the cost of a quarter of a mile of the line, more or less, and am satisfied that it is indeed "a favor" of the company; it did not come out in my favor on a single occasion. They draw every week and it appears to pay—the company.

All the carting which is done in the city is effected by mule power. One little mule with a sore back is hitched in the shafts of a huge, clumsy, high-wheeled wooden cart, and the driver rides upon another, which is slung alongside outside the shafts, and pretends to help the load along, as he doubtless does when in a tight place and he cannot help it. The arrangement is first-rate when it comes to swinging around a corner, but on a direct pull it might be improved. All the baggage is carried from the wharf or depot to the hotels, and *vice versa*, on the backs or heads of men.

The chain-gang, not merely in name, but in the good, old, southern, European style—is one of the institutions of Vera Cruz as of most other Mexican cities, and is made quite useful, if not entirely ornamental. The gentlemen connected with this branch of the public service wear a leathern belt around the waist, and a broader band of thick leather around the left ankle. Between these points there is a heavy chain, with links each about six inches long. In case of one of them being run over by a railway train, or cut into by a falling timber, this arrangement prevents the different parts getting scattered about and lost. For convenience they travel two by two, a metallic connection enabling them to keep step with military precision.

I saw about twenty of them at work one day at the mole, carrying heavy beams of Spanish cedar—the wood from which we make Havana cigar boxes in the United States—up into the city. They were guarded by a squad of soldiers, with loaded muskets and fixed bayonets, who kept them to their work in lively style, their chains clinking musically, all the time. By accident the sharp edge of a heavy beam came down on the sandaled foot of one of the operatives, when his great toe-nail opened like an alligator's jaws, and snapped viciously at the wood. The owner of the toe, picked up his end of the beam, and went off with his three companions on a dog-trot, seeming oblivious of the fact that there had been any quarrel going on.

Vera Cruz is the most important sea-port of the Republic of Mexico, and it may be interesting to the outside world to know how its population is made up, and what is the mental and moral standing of the inhabitants. The following figures I take from the official census returns made in April, 1869. The returns copied are for the Municipality of Vera Cruz, consisting of the old city within the walls and the district in the immediate vicinity, comprising almost as much territory as is included in the Metropolitan District of New York. The population of the municipality is as follows:

Males living within the walls, - - -	5,164
" " outside " - - - -	920
Females " within " - - - - -	6,372

Females living outside the walls - - -	1,036
Males living in the country beyond the city,	1,255
Females " " " " "	1,103
Total population, - - - - - -	15,850

The ages of the inhabitants are stated as follows:

Males under ten years, - - - -	1,810
Females " " " - - - - - -	1,813
Males between ten and sixteen years, - -	938
Females " " " " - -	1,002
Males between sixteen and fifty, " - -	4,157
Females " " " " - - -	5,131
Males over fifty years, - - - - - -	434
Females " " " - - - - -	565

EDUCATION.

Single males able to read and write, - -	2,531
" " not able " " " - -	3,140
" females able to " " " - - -	1,143
" " not " " " " " - -	4,652
Married men who can read and write, - -	879
" " who cannot " " " - -	540
" women who can read and write, - -	561
" " " cannot read and write, -	887
Widowers who can " " " -	129
" " cannot " " " -	120
Widows who can " " " -	286
" " cannot " " " -	982
Total males able to read and write, - - -	3,539
" " not " " " " - -	3,800

Total Females able to read and write,	1,990
" " not " " " "	6,521

RELIGION.

Catholics,	15,777
Protestants, (all foreigners,)	71
Jews,	1
Mahomedans,	1

The nationality of the inhabitants is as follows:

Mexicans,	14,384
Spaniards,	736
Cubans, (nearly all political exiles,)	242
French,	218
Citizens of the United States,	108
Germans,	68
Italians,	37
English,	23
Peruvianos,	5
Africans,	5
Other or uncertain nationalities,	24

The number of persons of all ages who have any lucrative and self-sustaining employment is set down at 7,407, while those who have no such employment is stated at 8,443.

In making up this list, the soldiers of the garrison, the sick in the hospitals, and the civil and military prisoners are not included. If they were included the disproportion of females to males would be still greater. The number of widows and unmarried women between sixteen and fifty, tells its own eloquent story of the desolation which so many years of civil and foreign war have brought upon the land. The greater number of those set down as having no lucrative occupation are, of course, women and children, but there must be at least fifteen hundred to twenty-five hundred adult, able-bodied males included in that list. The mole—what the storms have left of that costly work of the old Spaniards—swarms with them whenever a steamer arrives, and when a train with a few passengers comes in they rush up by dozens and fifties, to carry your trunk to the hotel on their backs; hacks and baggage wagons there are none in Vera Cruz.

Marriage is evidently not a popular institution in Vera Cruz, and the Church—however much it may preach against the sin of adultery—certainly in practice must be somewhat responsible for it, as its exactions make it quite difficult for the poor to contract marriage. As out of the entire population of fifteen thousand eight hundred and fifty souls, all but seventy-three are professed Catholics, and as there is no Protestant or other church organization, save the Catholic, in the municipality, the honor or blame of the moral condition of society in Vera Cruz belongs, altogether, to the Mother Church. Vera Cruz has more commerce and more travel than any other port of Mexico, and her population ought to rank higher in the scale of enlightenment and prosperity than that of any other sea-port town. Though the city is annually scourged by the Yellow Fever, or "Vomito," and is unhealthy from miasmatic influences all the year around, many educated and influential families, native and foreign born, reside here, and the circle of really good society is much larger than would be supposed from the above figures. Among the merchants there is discouragement and gloom, and among the people at large, more of uncertainty as to the future, apathy, or actual discontent, than I saw anywhere else in the Republic.

I went down with the crowd one day, to see the arrival of a coasting steamer—everybody in Vera Cruz goes down to the mole to see a steamer, big or little, come in. The arrival was the little square-toed side-wheeler, *Eujenia*, from Tlacotalplam—and steamer and cargo reminded me, forcibly, of the description of the Yankee trading craft which Marryatt in one of his novels, describes so vividly. I mean the craft he met coming out of the West Indies, whose captain sold his spars to a French privateer, and then sent the English privateer into a trap, by telling him that there was but one French vessel instead of two, and the force so small and unprepared as to make it perfectly safe to attack them when they were lying at anchor repairing. The steamer might possibly be one hundred feet long and about half as broad, with a bow so like an old fashioned man-of-war's stern, as to make it a matter of doubt whether she would travel best "end foremost" or "broadside on."

A motley list of passengers and a mixed cargo had been picked up along the coast. The passengers were of all colors and nationalities, and from seventy-five to one hundred in number. About half, appeared to have complexions disastrously affected by coast-fevers and malarious diseases. As for the cargo, it comprised a little of everything. Crates of live chickens, great earthenware jars for holding drinking water, bunches of plantains and bananas, rolls of tiger skins, bales on bales of goat skins, salt fish, boxes and strings of dried sausages, rolls of "*tamals*," turkeys in groups all around the decks tied by the legs, parrots of every hue and size all talking and scolding at once, crates of small, long-legged ducks of a peculiar kind such as I have never seen outside of Mexico, sweet potatoes, garden vegetables of almost every variety, and fruits of which I can give no description; oranges, lemons, limes, wooden-ware, and a variety of utterly indescribable manufactured articles of the country. The passengers were required to handle their own baggage, and owners of freight had to do the same.

All the passengers, crew, and outsiders were talking at once, though in the best of humor, and altogether, they made more noise than would have been kicked up in New York over the arrival of a Spanish fleet of war steamers, charged with the trifling task of bombarding all the forts and capturing all the fleets and sea-ports of the United States. But I must say in justice to them all, that no such scenes of ruffianism and rowdyism as we are accustomed to witness in New York, on the arrival of even a ferry-boat, took place, or ever take place here.

My stay in Vera Cruz was prolonged far beyond the limit we had fixed when leaving Puebla. At that time, we intended to leave for Havana, by the British steamer *Tyne*, on the 1st of January; but Mr. Seward having changed his mind, and determined to wait for the American steamer Cleopatra, ten days later, and a heavy norther delaying that steamer a day or two longer, I had considerable time to kill—as it turned out, time and the malarious atmosphere of the Gulf Coast got the best of it, and came very near killing me.

Meantime, a French steamer, the *Francia*, and an English freight-steamer plying between New Orleans, Tobasco, Tampico, Vera Cruz, Havana and Liverpool, "promiscuous," as it were, arrived; and with three steamers in port at once, Vera Cruz presented an appearance of liveliness quite unusual.

I swore at Guadalajara that I would never attend another bull-fight, and I meant it. But I did not say I would not attend a bear-fight. One Sunday, the walls of the City of Vera Cruz were placarded with posters announcing a grand fight to come off at the *Plaza de Toros*, between the celebrated California grizzly bear Sampson—the same I believe which chawed up and mortally injured "Grizzly Adams,"—and a "*valiente toro*," at 4½ o'clock P. M. In the pictures on the posters Sampson had a little the worst of the fight, but I did not believe that the artist was fully acquainted with his subject, and in company with other Californians backed our *piasano*, the bear, for the fight, against all odds.

The old fellow was about one hundred years old, more or less, and had lost in other fights, and by age, nearly every sign of a tooth; nevertheless, he was a healthy specimen of the grizzly, weighing about one thousand pounds, and able to entertain any bull ever raised in Spanish America.

The bull selected was one of the vicious, long-horned, black, Spanish brutes, not very large, but active, and when he was brought in by the *vacqueros*, in the morning, made it very lively for all the horses and loose boys and things in the neighborhood.

At the appointed time some two thousand or twenty-five hundred people, of all ages, sizes, colors and sexes were within the enclosure, with soldiers posted all around the barriers, to keep order, and a special squad within the outer ring, with loaded muskets to shoot the bear if he should escape from the inner ring of heavy, upright timbers, thirty feet across, in which the fight was to take place. It would have been a good joke on them had they ever fired at him.

The first part of the performance—consisting of tumbling, and cross-bar and ring exercises by a party of native artists—was looked upon with impatience by the crowd, and at last, when the cries of "*el toro! el toro!*" were getting too loud to be longer disregarded, Señor Bueno Core came forward and opened the door of the pen in which the bull was confined. In rushed the bull, and made a pass at old Sampson, who was quietly walking back and forth, looking at the audience.

At the first touch of the bull's horns, old Sampson raised his immense, bulky carcass, took the poor bull lovingly in his brawny arms, and grasping him by the neck with his worn-out teeth proceeded to shake him, as a terrier dog shakes a rat. His teeth were so bad that he could not break the bull's neck, but he held him as a mother might hold her infant, and compressed his neck as if it had been a loaf of bread. This went on until the bull called for help, and the audience began to call out, "give the bull a chance!" when the Señor and his assistants dashed water by the hogshead upon the bear to make him break his hold, and at last succeeded.

Then old Sampson, in a rage, went to the side of the ring, and began to dig a deep hole in the ground. All efforts to drive him from his work were unavailing for half an hour, and, meantime, he had a hole dug in which he might have buried an elephant. This excited the audience, who shouted, to urge the bull on to give the foreign bear fits.

At last, the bull was induced by the exhibition of a red blanket pulled over the bear's side by a cord from above, and the apparent cowardice of old Sampson, to go up and give him a dig in the ribs. He darted back as soon as he had done it, but old Sampson was now downright mad. He had stood the pounding and poking with iron bars and clubs without a word of emphatic dissent, but to be insulted by the bull and set down as a coward, was more than he could or would submit to. At a bound he was at the bull's side, folding him once more in his loving embrace, and prepared to show how they "rock me to sleep mother," in California. He, without more ado, carried the bull to the hole which he had been digging, bore him down with his immense weight until his back gave way under the pressure, and then placing him affectionately in the hole, held him down with one fore paw, while with the other he commenced to cover him up with dirt. The bull roared with pain and terror, and once got partially upon his feet in the struggle, but only to go back with greater force, and receive numerous slaps in the side from the enraged bear, which appeared to knock the breath all out of his body.

The audience were now satisfied that the bull was done for, and no match for a California grizzly bear, even without teeth, and began to move out. The backers of the bull gave up the fight, and Señor Bueno Core and assistants entered the ring, and after a long struggle and any amount of water poured upon him, compelled Sampson to let go his hold and return to his

SUNDAY AMUSEMENTS IN VERA CRUZ.

cage. And so the entertainment ended. I regret to add that when the bull was raised to his feet it was found that his back was so injured that he could not stand and he must be killed. The buzzards had already gathered in clouds in the vicinity, as if conscious that a feast was being prepared. This is Sunday amusement in Vera Cruz. But it was death on the bull.

But the bull does not *always* get the worst of it, in encounters with man and beast, in Mexico and elsewhere. I remember a bull and bear fight in New Orleans, in which the Attakapas bull General Jackson, doubled up the bear like an old shoe at the first charge, and made him bellow for help in a few seconds. I regret to say, that on that occasion my sympathies were so strongly with the bear at the start, that I lost all the money that my boyish industry had gathered together in several months. After the lapse of many years I got even at Vera Cruz.

A distinguished Mexican gentleman—whose name I suppress for various reasons—told us, one day on the trip from Guanajuato to Mexico, of his experience in bull-fighting in one of the larger cities of the Republic. It is the custom in bull-fighting countries, for the young bloods of the first families, who wish to distinguish themselves, to appear in the Plaza de Toros as amateurs, and fight the bull on important occasions. When Maximilian arrived in Mexico, a special *gran funcion* was gotten up for his benefit, and the young men of some of the oldest and most aristocratic of the Mocho families of the capital, appeared in the ring as *picadors* and *matadors*, the royal couple presiding at the brutal entertainment and delivering the prizes to the heroes of the conflict.

On such occasions the amateur is usually allowed a companion, who is posted in the ways of the ring and is called a "*padrino*." The *padrino* directs the amateur how to carry on the fight, and, in fact, acts as his chaperon and next friend, throughout. Our acquaintance was crowded into the fight against his will; but I will let him tell it himself as he told it to us:

"I said, 'No, no, the bull has done me no insult; why should I fight with him? But they all said, 'you are a brave young man, and want to make your way in the world, and be popular with the ladies; it is better that you begin now that you have so good time, and fight the bull.' So I let them put my name on the bills. Well, I liked this matter not very much at all, but I could not get out of it, and so they kept me in. When the day comes, I went in with my *padrino*, and said to myself when I sees the bull, 'I will keep over on the other side and let the others do the fight.' But after a time the audience began to get excited, and to encourage me on, they commenced to throw oranges and such trifles at me pretty lively. Then my *padrino* comes up to me and he says:

'Look you; this will not do very well at all! If you do not fight the bull there will be a row, and it is better that you do not disgrace yourself!'

"So I told him, I will fight the bull sooner as to dodge my head all the times from the oranges and bananas which the audience throws at me. He looked at my saddle and said:

'The cinch is loose, and it is better that you get off and let me tighten it before you go into the fight.'

"So I got off and stood by the side of my horse looking at him to *cinch* him tighter. This time I was stooping over, and saw not the bull, which I was thinking was on the other side of the ring. As I so stood I feel myself lifted up into the air, and when I came down the bull was on my top, tramping me, and using his horns on me, so that when they got him away I could not stand, and was confined to my bed for six weeks.

"Then they told me, when I was well again, that the judges had awarded me the highest prize, because I had expose myself so bravely to the bull, and not try for to get out of the way when he come for me.

"I said, that is all very well; I was always a brave man and care not much for the bull." Then they said:

'But the judges let that bull out alive, and decided that when you should recover and the bull should recover, you should fight it over once more again together. You are well and the bull is very well indeed.'

"I said, no, I have no desire to hurt the bull. He was receive much aggravation, and I forgive him for what he did do to me!"

"They said that such language would not do for the judges, and if I did not like to fight the bull again I was disgrace for life, and it was better I should leave the city that evening. Now there was a young lady there which I thought of very much, and I concluded it was better to fight the bull than to lose the lady.

"When we went into the ring again, I see the bull looking very mad and ugly, and I concluded I would go over on the other side and wait a little while; probably he might get better-natured or afraid to come at me. But pretty soon, the people they commenced to encourage me with fruit and such things as I don't eat, and cry out to me to go in and fight the bull at once, or come out of the ring. So I told my *padrino* I would fight him a little but do not feel very well.

"He said: "It is better you should throw the *bandarillas* into the bull's neck. I will attract the attention of the bull, and when you are ready to throw, you call out and I will jump aside."

"I said I would do so, and my *padrino* went up to the bull, and begun to dance around before his nose. Then I ran up to throw the *bandarillas*, but I was so excited that I have forgotten to call out to him to get out of the way, and, when I let them go they strike him in the back instead of the bull. Then my *padrino* he bellow louder as ever the bull should do, and begin to dance like a tarantula and catch at the *bandarillas*. At last he got hold of them and tore the barbs out of his flesh. Then he runs over to me and pulls me down, and begin to beat me over the head and the back with the flat side of his sword, and his foot and he says:

"Look here you now! It is better before we go any further, that one thing shall be understood immediate. Are you the *padrino* of *me*, or the *padrino* of the *bull?*"

"He was so very angry that I could not say an explanation, and so I told him I would go home, for I like not the sport, and it might make us bad friends or something if we kept on. Some of the oranges and apples and things which they throwed at me as I went out were very solid, and I left the town that night. Since then I have had no quarrel with the bulls, and I like not to have any more."

While waiting at Vera Cruz for the arrival of Mr. Seward from Orizaba, and the departure of the good steamer *Cleopatra* which was to bear us away, at last, from the shores of Mexico, I sought for and obtained, through the kindness of my Mexican and American friends, a permit to visit, and inspect in all its details, the Castle of San Juan de Ulloa.

Accompanied by two ladies, Mr. Brennan, and some military friends, we embarked in a Custom-House boat, and were rowed over to the famous old fortress, on a warm bright morning, when the sea was calm, and the water so clear that we could see every object in it down to the bottom. The waters of this coast fairly swarm with sharks of the most savage description, and we saw several of the grey monsters disporting themselves near the surface and keeping a weather-eye open for a chance to take somebody in, as we rowed along.

The Spaniards lavished millions on millions upon the construction of this fortress, which was intended to serve as a complete protection to Vera Cruz and the shipping which might gather here, from the attacks of the dreaded English buccaneers who were desolating the whole Spanish Main, and practicing cruelties on their luckless captives as atrocious as those which the Spaniards had inflicted upon the unfortunate natives of tropical America. Enormous rings of pure copper were built into the solid wall, along the whole western front of the castle next the city, for the ships to fasten to, under the protection of the guns of the fortress. Those rings are still there, but now amount to but so many tons of old copper, as the water has shoaled to such an extent as to render it impossible for any vessel above the grade of a yawl-boat to lie there, if there was any longer a necessity for their doing so. The steamers now anchor inside the reef, on the North of the Castle, and sail-vessels to the South of it. The

American steamer *Cleopatra*, being of comparatively light draft, and not large and unwieldy, runs in between the castle and mole, and was then lying at anchor there.

An immense coral reef extends out to the north-west from the castle for several miles, and from this most of the material for building the fortress was taken. The size of this coral formation is astonishing. Many of the specimens are three feet in thickness—like the trunks of great trees, in fact. As we neared the castle we could see that a section of the entire wall some thirty feet long, the same in height, and twelve or fifteen feet in thickness , being undermined, had broken out, and now leans over towards the city, leaving a great gap, which no attempt has been made to fill. The boat-landing is in the interior of the castle, a crooked passage, evidently excavated in the coral for that purpose, leading up to that point. This passage was formerly flanked by substantial walls, which are now in ruins.

No description of the castle would give any clear idea of its character, without a ground plan or diagram to illustrate it. The immensely thick walls, all the way around, are backed by a range of barracks, dungeons, and offices, whose roof of solid stone, flat, thick, and paved on the top with cement, would support batteries of almost any weight. All the guns in the fortress were originally mounted *en barbette*, upon this roof. There is nothing like a casemate with protection for the gunners about the castle. The guns—mostly of iron, and ranging from thirty-two to sixty-four pounders, made in 1844–5—are all in bad condition, the carriages nearly valueless from decay, and many dismounted and lying useless on the roof. Inside there are court-yards, plazas or parade-grounds of sufficient extent for a large force, and quarters for a thousand men or more.

The Spaniards, in constructing this fortress, made all provision for defending it to the last extremity against assault. The moat passed and the outer wall scaled, the assailants would find the garrison retreating into several minor castles, each with its own moat and draw-bridge, and, in those days, "a hard nut to crack," in every sense of the expression. The moat is now so filled with sand and debris as to be fordable even at high-tide, and the old draw-bridges being no longer of any use, have been replaced by bridges which are fixed in their places and answer better the purposes of communication between the different sections of the castle. I should say at a rough guess, that the whole fortification covers eight to ten acres.

Outside the old main wall, on the eastern front and northern end, there is now an earth-work of sufficient height to screen the gunners, and mounted with about twenty pretty heavy guns. This battery if put in order, might be capable of doing some serious damage to a hostile fleet; but the value set upon it by the French may be inferred from the fact that they dumped an enormous pile of coal—some thousands of tons—right into it, covering several of the guns on the north end to a depth of many feet, and the coal lies there yet, just as they left it in the haste of their departure. I suppose that I break no law of hospitality in saying what everybody who has visited the castle within the last ten years knows, that, practically, this old fortress, once one of the strongest and most formidable in the world, is to day utterly worthless for defence against a hostile fleet of any strength. So well aware are the military men and Government of Mexico of this fact, that no attempt is now made to improve it, or even keep it in repair; and it is now considered merely as a fortified prison, rather than as a real castle of defense against invaders. A vigorous bombardment of a few hours by heavy artillery would reduce it to a pile of ruins, but there is no likelihood of any necessity for even that, as the experience of Gen. Scott and other commanders, shows that the city can be taken with little trouble by an attack from the land side, and the castle is then useless to either party.

Leaving our boat at the landing, we passed into the main square or parade-ground, and from thence to the *Salle des Armas*, where we were received most courteously by the commandant Colonel Carbo, Captain Fortunato Mendez the second in command, and their subordinates. Even at this time—the early part of January—the heat of the sun—reflected back from the cement pavement and the white walls surrounding—was oppressive in the plaza as we passed through it; what it must be in June, July, or August, I have no wish to know from experience. It must be perfectly fearful.

The commandant was a young man of slight statue, but said to be a good officer and a man of great bravery and determination of character. From his quarters we went through the interior of the castle. The garrison consisted of two hundred men, and within the gloomy dungeons of this fearful place there were eighty prisoners, civil and military, several of whom are under sentence of imprisonment for life.

These dungeons were constructed by the Spaniards, and all smell of the rack, torture, and inquisition. My

God! such a place to immure a human being in! It makes one shudder to think of it, after looking at those dark, noisome caverns; what must it be to enter there with the word "*perpetua*" entered on the books against one's name! Death at once, would be a mercy beside it.

The number of these low, vaulted cells, connecting one with another, is hardly less than sixty to eighty, all told, and the best of them is but a little less horrible than the worst. The roof is low, and arched in each, the walls, roof and floor of one piece, as it were, and in most of them the only ventilation is through a small opening in the top, so slight as to admit of the entrance of but a mere glimmer of light at midday. A few have small, narrow, port-holes, or slits, through the outer walls looking seaward, but they are so cunningly contrived, being bent or curved as they pass through the thick stone-work, that the poor wretches inside can never see through them and get even a glimpse of a sail or the sea outside.

What fearful tales of hopeless misery, despair, and lingering but welcome death, could those damp, dripping walls tell if they had tongues. The damp sea-air collects in the the roofs of all of them, and falls, year after year, with a steady, unceasing drip, drip, drip, to the paved floor. This water is charged heavily with lime, and stalactites, three and four feet in length, hang from the ceiling, like slender icicles, by thousands. On the cold stone floor the dropping water forms large buttons of fine lime deposits, which give it the appearance at a casual glance, of having been laid in fancy mosaic. Remember that Vera Cruz is worse cursed with yellow fever, or *vomito* and malarious diseases of all kinds, than any other place on earth, that the climate is fearfully hot and damp, that the harbor outside the castle swarms with sharks which make the attempt to swim from thence to the shore certain death, in case a prisoner should by any chance escape from his cell, and you can form some idea of what must be the condition, mental and physical, of the prisoners of the castle of San Juan de Ulloa. I was not surprised when I saw by the light of the flashing torches of our guides, high up on the ceiling of one of these dens of horrors, rudely scrawled with charcoal, evidently in the darkness and through the sense of feeling alone, by some prisoner mounted on the shoulders of his companions, the familiar quotation from Dante:

"Who enters here leaves hope behind."

The inscription is in Spanish and without date, but in an adjoining room I saw the lion of Spain drawn in the same manner on the wall, with the date beneath, 1835, and from comparison judged the first to be the oldest.

The cells or dungeons occupied by the prisoners at the present time, are the most comfortable—or rather the least noisome and horrible—of any in the fortress; but they are fearful, nevertheless. There was a report in the city that two prisoners had been shot in the castle just before our visit, but the commandant assured us that such was not the case, as no executions had taken place there for some months. I saw nothing to indicate that the prisoners were treated with any uncalled for severity or cruelty by those in command there now; and, on the contrary, I believe that all that the arrangement of the place will admit of, is done to mitigate the horrors of their situation. I was told that at certain hours, those not guilty of attempting to break their parole, are allowed to promenade on the roof for a specified time daily, and such other indulgences as are possible are granted them.

Among the prisoners is General Castillo, who was second in command under Miramon in the expedition sent out from Queretaro by Maximilian to capture President Juarez, at Zacatecas. This expedition came very near accomplishing its object, but the fortunate intervention of a few American sharp-shooters, who held the imperialist advance force in check until Escobedo arrived and routed them, saved the President, and turned the tide of war back towards Queretaro, where Miramon arrived with but a handful of men left, out of all the splendid force with which he had started out in the full flush of hope and confidence of victory.

Castillo gave the Republic much trouble, and when, at last captured and sentenced to ten years banishment to Yucatan, as an alternative for death, foolishly and wickedly broke his parole, and returned to Mexico a month afterwards, only to be re-captured and sent to serve out his ten years in San Juan de Ulloa. He had been there a year, and was fast succumbing to the deadly unhealthiness of the place and the hopelessness of his position.

While in the City of Mexico, I was approached by parties who desired me to say a word in his behalf to members of the Government, and to carry him a message when I visited San Juan de Ulloa; but as I was situated, I felt that it would be wholly out of place for me to do so, and would have nothing to do with it. I learned after our visit, however, that one of my companions, a young, kind-hearted and sympathetic girl, had promised the General's wife, that if she had an opportunity she would give him the message of love and hope—love warm and true indeed, but hope, I fear, only delusive and empty—from her.

While we were in the castle the young lady went past his window near enough to speak to him. He was standing by the bars, and looking out, but the moment he saw us he turned away and concealed himself from our sight. I caught but a momentary glimpse of his blanched and haggard face, but that was quite enough. When I learned all the facts I was quite glad that the message was not delivered, under the circumstances, but I could not fail to honor the young girl for her sympathy and kindness of heart, however much it might have been impolitic and misdirected.

From the inner castle, we walked out upon the beach outside the eastern wall, and there in a small patch of cane-brake, saw the monument erected in memory of "the French who fell in the expedition to Mexico, in 1838–9." The monument is still perfect, but I saw several skulls and other human bones scattered all around it, and presume that the invaders have not been permitted to rest in peace, even in the silence of their lonely graves on the shore of the land they came to conquer.

The French, in the invasion which culminated in the "Empire," brought a large number of small steam launches of iron, for use in the harbor of Vera Cruz and vicinity. These are lying wrecked, with their bottoms stove in and machinery removed or ruined, and rapidly wasting away, all around the eastern side of the castle. They have been used in some places to make a breakwater, with the reef in which the castle is built, and are all now utterly worthless save for old iron; they will soon be worthless even for that purpose. Many old Spanish guns of the finest metal, thrown into the sea years ago, are still lying in the shallow water around the castle, and might be converted into ploughshares and pruning-hooks to the benefit of the country, but probably never will be.

I have spoken more freely of the castle of San Juan de Ulloa, and what I saw there, from the fact that I visited it independent of Mr. Seward, who did not go over until some days later; but it is not a pleasant subject to me under any circumstances. I am heartily glad that I went there, and thankful for the attention and courtesy which enabled me to inspect it throughout, but I am glad that I shall not look upon it, nor on its like, again.

In every life there is a question unanswered, a doubt unsolved, a mystery unexplained, which becomes more and more a subject of irritation and annoyance as age progresses. A positive insult may be forgiven, and time cicatrizes the wound inflicted by the fang of slander, or the physical assassin's weapon. But the doubt is worse than the reality.

What old bachelor, tottering down the hill of life alone, would not feel a sense of inexpressible relief, could he but know, to a certainty, that Jane Smith, on whom he was so spooney at twenty-one, would have refused him, out and out, had he dared to ask her the momentous question? He did not ask the question, and to day is in doubt whether, after all, she might not have said yes, instead of no, and so changed the whole tenor of his life and hers. It is that which worries him worst of all, and which will kill him in the end.

Now-shall I confess it?—a double doubt, a duplicate question, a Siamese-twin mystery—as it were,—will haunt me like a double-team of nightmares, while memory lives within me. As I leave the shores of Mexico, I carry away with me many a pleasant recollection on which I shall dwell with satisfaction in after years; but there is a lurking bitter in my cup of bliss; a sharp set thorn—as it were,—close under the rose of my happiness. Here is where my doubts come in.

As we journeyed one day through the mountains of Jalisco, we saw a son of the soil,—in scanty raiment clad—with unkempt hair and dilapidated sombrero—setting off a face which still bore the stamp of the grand pride of the haughty race of conquering Castile, —earnestly engaged in the humble occupation of driving a pig to market. He had lassoed the pig by the hind leg, and was endeavoring to make him keep the track by jerking the *rieta* with his left hand, while he encouraged him to advance by the vigorous application of a cornstalk to his hinder parts with his right.

THE LINE OF BEAUTY.

The pig thus urged, persisted in traveling, mainly with the two legs on one side, which naturally caused him to move in a circle, instead of advancing in a direct line. As the circle grew neither larger nor smaller as the day wore on, it was evident that neither man nor beast got nearer home or nearer market. It never appeared to occur to the man that if he would change the *rieta* and the cornstalk from hand to hand occasionally, the pig might be induced to change his tactics also, and adopt the line of practical advance and progress, in place of the line of beauty, which leads us, practically, nowhere, after all. The chances are that hunger, or the desire for "sleep, tired nature's sweet restorer" etc., in the fullness of time induced a change of tactics on the part of one or the other; but *which?* Did the endurance of the man equal his attachment to "*el cosas del pais*" and prove too much for the pig? or did the pig's proverbial obstinacy wear out the man? or did each hold his own, and are they both destined to walk around and around on that lonely hillside as we left them, through the endless cycles of eternity? I ought to have staid and seen it out; but an aching void within me urged me on, and I did not; I wish I had let it ache!

The other doubt is sadder, and more painful still. As we went down by rail from Paso del Macho to Vera Cruz, we looked from the window of what had been Maximilian's imperial car, upon a scene by the roadside which struck me nearer to the heart, and filled my soul with sadness and doubt more utterly unfathomable.

A poor, old steed—who may have borne Santa Anna and his fortunes in his day, or better served the world by drawing a dump-cart for a grading party on the railroad track—had been turned out to die. The *zapilotes*

—which are among the institutions of the country,—watching from afar, saw death's signal in his glazing eye, and wheeling down from their airy heights, came trooping from all directions to the coming feast.

THE HORSE AND THE ZAPILOTES.

As each detachment arrived they settled on the ground in successive circles around the horse, gave one searching look to make sure that they had made no mistake as to the ultimate result, then drew in their heads, humped their shoulders, and went to sleep, satisfied that in Heaven's own time, grim death would do his perfect work, when they would pick the bones of the animal before them as clean as a squirrel picks the kernel out of a nut. They could have finished him there and then with a little effort; but that politeness which characterizes every inhabitant of tropical America, forbade such unseemly haste, and why work for what would come without labor if they but waited?

So murmuring "*Manana*," "*poco tiempo*," and "*Salle luego*," as is the custom of the country, they dropped off, one by one, to sleep and pleasant dreams. The moribund knew as well as we did what they came for, and read his fate in their skinny, expressionless faces, but he was game to the last, and no rule of politeness bade him to hurry up with his dying; so he took his time for it, and showed them, unmistakably, by his looks that he regarded their presence as—to some extent—ill-timed and indelicate, and partaking of the character of undue familiarity.

They were engaged in this nice little game of "freeze out," as we left the station and passed out of sight. But who won? Did the zapilotes and death beat the horse at last? or did he starve them all while they waited? or are they still waiting and watching, he living and hoping, and the game bound to go on to the end of time? Look upon this picture, and then on that, and tell me what are the sufferings of common humanity to mine!

Reader: I have told you the secret of my blighted life. You will now know why my forehead is prematurely wrinkled, my hair turned grey before my time, and a tendency to grow hump-shouldered is developing in my frame, when you meet me on Broadway or Montgomery street. A blighted being, harassed with doubts which may never be solved, I go forth from the land where Cortez fought and conquered, and Montezuma died.

Let the riddle of the Sphynx go unread, the story of the Lost Tribes untold, the problem of the squaring of the circle unsolved; they are but as vanity and vexation of spirit to me; but would you save my grey hairs from going down in sorrow to the grave, skip all the rest, and come down to the ranchero and the pig, the horse and the zapilotes,—tell me who whipped, and oh, tell me quickly!

CHAPTER XXII.

THE LAST WE SAW OF MEXICO.

THOUGH we had still to touch at a distant Mexican port—that of Sisal in Yucatan,—at Vera Cruz, our long trans-continental trip through tropical Mexico, was practically over. The story of that journey is told, but its results and consequences—serious or otherwise for the Republic of Mexico and the Juarez Administration—remain to be developed in the future. So much idle speculation as to the object and purport of this visit of Mr. Seward to the Republic of Mexico, has been indulged in by the people and press of both nations, and so many efforts made to give it a false political significance and importance, that I have thought it best to put on record all the speeches and letters made and written by Mr. Seward in Mexico, that the world might see for itself, just what actually passed between him and the citizens and officials of Mexico.

To complete the work, I asked permission to copy, verbatim, the farewell letters written by Mr. Seward as we were preparing to go on board the steamer at Vera Cruz, to the President and the leading members of his Cabinet, Mrs. Juarez, and the Commissioner, Señor Bossero, who was sent out to Guadalajara by the Mexican Government, to meet the party, and provide for our comfort and enjoyment on our journey through the Republic.

VERA CRUZ, January 8th., 1870.

MY DEAR SIR:—I have at last arrived at this port, after a very interesting journey from the Capital, which has afforded me opportunities to study the structure, resources and prospects of the States of Puebla, Tlaxcala, and Vera Cruz, not to speak of the antiquities of Cholulu, and the marvelous scenery of the Cumbres of Orizaba.

It is with the greatest satisfaction that I find that the only popular discontents existing in the Republic are merely local in their character, and have no connection with the general conduct of national affairs.

These local difficulties will find a solution in the states where they occur, if the Federal Administration shall be allowed to treat them with impartiality and moderation.

It remains for me, only, to thank the President once more for the distinguished consideration and hospitality which I have received at his hands and the hands of the Mexican People. Renewing at the same time the expression of my most fervent wishes for the prosperity and happiness of the Mexican Republic, I take leave of the President and his distinguished associates, with the most profound respect and affectionate esteem.

WILLIAM H. SEWARD.

SEÑOR DON S. LERDO DE TEJADA, &c., &c., &c. Mexico.

VERA CRUZ, January 8th., 1870.

MY DEAR MR. LERDO:—In leaving Mexico after the visit which you have done so much to distinguish, and to render pleasant and instructive, I shall not fail to cherish the hope that the course of political affairs in Mexico, may allow you, at no distant day, to come to the United States, and renew with me there the studies which will be so useful to you hereafter, in a career, which I foresee is to be equally honorable to yourself and important to the Republican cause in America. Accept my warmest and most sincere thanks for all the honors and kindness you have bestowed upon me, and remember me always as a faithful and confiding friend.

WILLIAM H. SEWARD.

SEÑOR LERDO DE TEJADA, &c., &c., &c. Mexico.

VERA CRUZ, January, 8th., 1870.

MY DEAR MRS. JUAREZ :—Providence is not altogether capricious even in the direction of political events. It was a great kindness to me, that permitted me to see you and know you in your exile to the United States. But it is a crowning felicity, that after having done so I have been allowed to be your guest, after your happy restoration to your family, friends, and exalted position in Mexico. It is almost too much to hope that I may be able to receive you, your husband and friends, at my own house in the United States; still I will not relinquish that fond expectation. Meantime, and in any event, I pray to be remembered as among the friends who can be faithful and grateful to you, as long as I live.

WILLIAM H. SEWARD.

LA SEÑORA JUAREZ, &c., &c., &c. Mexico.

VERA CRUZ, January 8th., 1870.

MY DEAR MR. ROMERO :—It is not to renew my grateful acknowledgments that I write this parting letter, so much as it is to assure you of my profound sympathy with you, in your arduous labors for the restoration of law, order, prosperity, and prestige in Mexico.

I feel quite hopeful that these labors will be appreciated by the people and Government of Mexico, soon ; but even if this should fail to be the case, talents, energy, and loyalty like yours will not be suppressed. You will in that case, only rise to higher usefulness and honors hereafter.

With most grateful and affectionate remembrance, to Mrs.

Romero, her mother, and your sister, and sincere regrets that I am not allowed their society with yours any longer, I am, my dear Mr. Romero, forever your faithful and devoted friend.

WILLIAM H. SEWARD.

SEÑOR DON MATIAS ROMERO, &c., &c., &c. Mexico.

VERA CRUZ, January 8th., 1870.

MY DEAR PRESIDENT:—I have thought it most becoming, to address my parting words to you through the office of the Minister of Relations. But I could not think of leaving the country without making a more direct and unstudied acknowledgment of my profound sense of obligation to you, for the exaggerated attentions and hospitality with which you have received myself and family during our delightful sojourn in Mexico. I feel sure, that I am safe in congratulating you upon the finality of peace and regeneration, in the great country which you have rescued from anarchy and foreign conquest.

Accept, my dear Mr. President, my fervent wishes, that you may enjoy fullness of years, and the choicest blessings of Providence.

Your most obliged and most obedient friend and servant.

WILLIAM H. SEWARD.

DON BENITO JUAREZ, President, &c., &c., &c. Mexico.

VERA CRUZ, January 10, 1870.

MY DEAR MR. BOSSERO:—The hour of my departure from Mexico is so entirely filled with recollections of kindnesses received during my stay there, as to exclude even the thought of the welcome that I may hope to receive from my family and friends in the United States. In everything that has concerned me, the Mexican Government has not only manifested an unexampled sentiment of national hospitality, but they have practised in all things, a delicacy which only generous minds can justly appreciate. I was not slow in perceiving that it was that delicacy which was the motive for your commission to meet me at Guadalajara, and attend me to the hour of embarkation. I am unable to express the deep sense I feel for cares and attentions, which have not merely saved me from every danger and discomfort, but which have made the journey of my family and friends, a constant instruction and continual pleasure. I pray you to accept my most grateful acknowledgments, with affectionate wishes for your continued welfare and the health and happiness of your children. You will hear from me, my dear Mr. Bossero, on my arrival at New York, and I shall hope on that occasion, that I am not forgotten by you. I am, my Dear Sir, very truly your friend.

WILLIAM H. SEWARD.

At 4 P. M. on Tuesday, January 11th., 1870, we were all on board the *Cleopatra*, and she was steaming out of the harbor of Vera Cruz, past the Castle of San Juan de Ulloa, and the great coral reefs beyond it, into the Gulf of Mexico. At sunset, all on board subject to seasickness, were down with it; the writer among the number, of course. All next day we were out of sight of land with a rough sea. The morning of the 13th dawning clear and beautiful, revealed to us the low sandy shores of Yucatan along the southern horizon, and at noon we came to anchor off Sisal, in the open roadstead which serves for a harbor, save in case of a norther blowing, when there is no harbor at all.

The sea being rough Mr. Seward decided not to go on shore, though he was strongly tempted to do so and spend the next twenty days in visiting the ancient Spanish city of Merida, the mysterious ruins of Palenque, the logwood forests of Campeche, and other points of interest on the peninsula.

Worn out with seasickness, and feverish from miasma breathed at Vera Cruz, I determined to go ashore, and put off in a small boat with Mr. and Mrs. Brennan and others, to spend the night on the land. We were no sooner on shore than a committee called to learn what Mr. Seward's intentions were, and tender him the hospitalities of Sisal and of Yucatan, if he would land and accept them. Being told that he had decided not to land, they telegraphed at once to Merida to inform the Governor, and tendered me the use of the house provided for him in Sisal, for the little party who had come with me.

Sisal has not much to see of special interest. The houses are all palm leaf-thatched, with thick stone walls, rude, old-fashioned wooden doors, and glassless windows. The authorities showed us every possible attention, and we inspected what there was to be seen, with interest. The old castle or "Castillo,"—erected three centuries ago by the Spaniards,—is garrisoned by a company of regular troops of the Army of Mexico.

Yucatan is not the most devotedly loyal State of the Republic, and the Government is obliged to keep a strong force there to protect its interests, and guard against pronunciamentoes and revolutions. The wild Indians of the interior are also troublesome, being supplied with arms and ammunition—as the inhabitants of Merida justly complain—by the English traders and authorities in Honduras, and the contemptible "Kingdom of Mosquitia," whose orang-outang king is "the very good friend and ally of Her Majesty the Queen of Great Britain, etc., etc." Then, more than half of the—so called—civilized Indians of Yucatan, do not submit to be governed by the Federal or State authorities: so that the peninsular can hardly be called a first class, quiet place to live in. Nevertheless, the roads are good, the country is improving, and the State has more to show in the way of exports—the product of her soil—than any other in the Republic.

The annual receipts of the Custom-House at Sisal, amount to four hundred thousand dollars, and the export of hemp—the best article of the kind now produced in the world—amounted in 1869 to eighteen thousand bales of four hundred pounds each. This hemp is mainly raised around Merida, and the industry—which is a new one—is fast extending, and bringing prosperity and happiness to the State. Sisal has a population of all colors, ages, sexes and conditions, of one thousand, all told. A great swamp and laguna extends miles up into the interior, in the rear of the town, and the place is not specially noted for its salubrity.

Mr. Brennan and my old San Francisco friend, Lever,—who was a captain in the Volunteers during our civil war, and afterwards a member of the famous "American Legion of Honor," and a Lieutenant Colonel in the Mexican Army,—now U. S. Mail Agent on the *Cleopatra*, went out on the laguna shooting ducks, ibises, flamingoes and—Heaven knows what not,—and had a glorious time, returning well laden with spoils,—all of which were spoiled by the heat of the weather, next morning.

Groves of tall, graceful cocoa-palms, and rank luxuriant cane-brakes, give a peculiar tropical charm to the place as seen from the harbor. We saw but one carriage in the place. It was a private coach, with wheels and bed as heavy as that of one of our great lumber wagons, and had a little inclosed cab-like structure, for two persons, perched high up on leathern springs in the centre. It was drawn by three little mules harnessed all abreast, one in the shafts, and one on each side; it will be long ere I shall look upon its like again.

That night we all went to the Sisal theatre. It is a funny affair. The stage was under a palm leaf-thatched shed, open on one side, and the scenery was permanently fixed, admitting of no changing. The audience sat in a large open yard, with the starry Heavens above them for a roof, and a grove of cocoa palm trees in full verdure for a back ground. It is doubtless the tallest theatre in the world at this time, the best ventilated, and the safest in case of a fire or an earthquake.

What the play was I could not find out. The company was composed of amateurs, and the performance for the benefit of some charity which I hope deserved it. The theatre was filled to repletion, the mosquitoes occupying all the space not required by the audience of some five hundred people. The principal actor was the Prefecto Politico of the town, a fine, fleshy, old gentleman, who, despite the loss of one eye, played his part right well. I made his acquaintance, and found him a true gentleman, and very pleasant company indeed. Admission *dos rials*, and *un rial* extra for a chair—total, thirty-seven and one half cents. The scene was novel and interesting, and I shall not soon forget that evening's entertainment at the theatre, by the side of the restless, moaning sea, on the wild, lone shore of Yucatan.

That evening a party of officials and leading citizens left Merida, on receipt of the telegram announcing Mr. Seward's arrival, and come down to the coast before midnight, having galloped their horses all the way.

At ten A. M. Friday, January 14th., I returned on board the *Cleopatra*, with the Collector of the Port of Sisal, the Captain of the Port, the 2nd Captain of the Port, the Prefecto Politico and other local officers, the American Consul at Merida, Señor Perucho, the Secretary of the Governor of Yucatan, Señor Rivos, an old and highly intelligent merchant of Merida, and others, and the last official presentation and reception of Mr. Seward in Mexico took place.

After an hours conversation on political subjects, the Secretary handed Mr. Seward a letter of which the following is a translation:

The Governor of the State of Yucatan,
To the illustrious American, William H. Seward.

Mr. Seward:—I trust that you have been pleased with the reception you have received in every part of the Republic which you have visited.

You remain but a short time on the shores of our State, which are distant from its capital, but I hasten in the name of its people to cordially welcome you, and to pray you to accept the assurance of that sympathy which all lovers of liberty must feel for men of genius and of heart.

You, Mr. Seward, are a man of eminent genius, for you have to conduct with glory and with skill, the public affairs of your country. You are a man of heart for you have liberated the slaves, uniting in that great work with your fellow countryman, Lincoln, whose martyr memory is blessed to-day by all mankind.

Regretting that we shall not have the honor of a visit from you at this capital, I tender you my best wishes for a safe and pleasant voyage to your native land.

M. CIREROL.

MERIDA, YUCATAN, January 13th., 1870.

The party then took leave of Mr. Seward in the most affectionate manner, and his visit to Mexico was ended.

That evening our steamer sailed away for Havana, and as the sun went down in the west I sat on the deck smoking my last cigarrito, wrapped in smoke and thought, and saw the palm-fringed shore of Mexico slowly sink down in the horizon and fade away from sight. From sight, but not from memory! Beautiful, unfortunate Mexico; in all my after years, what visions of thee and thine will haunt me day and night!

Again shall I see the gay flotilla moving up the Laguna de Cayutlan, the wooded hills and tropical valley of La Calera; Colima—the beloved of the sun—with her gardens, ruins, and palm groves, and her great smoking volcano for a back-ground, will be before me. Again shall I see the gallant cavalcade and the flashing arms of the Guard of Jalisco, filing through the great Barranca de Beltran, or moving by torchlight over the hills of San Marcos. I shall see the full, round moon rise over beautiful Guadalajara, and hear the soft love song and notes of the light guitar, or watch the beauties of Mexico's cities floating through the voluptuous mazes of the *danza*. Again I shall see the blaze, and listen to the roar of the fire-balls, as they come crashing down into the dark depths of the earth, in the mines of Guanajuato. Again shall I tread your blood-stained battle fields, on which the problem of free government in America was decided; again stand by the little mound of stones and the three black crosses which mark an epoch in the world's history, amid the waving corn-fields at the foot of the lone Cerro de Las Campanas. Again, and yet again, shall I tread the deserted halls of Chapultepec, and look down on the fair valley and city of Mexico, and up to mighty Popocatapetl, crowned with eternal snow. Again shall I stand where

Cortez fought and Guatamozin lost and died. Still shall I see brown Dolores at the casement standing, and Juanita with the flashing eyes, ride past in her stately carriage on the *paseo.* I shall listen to the wild music of the trumpet and the kettle-drum in Colima, and the wilder notes of the Aztec band at the foot of the pyramid of Cholula, or stand in breathless silence absorbed in the fiery eloquence which pours like a flood from the lips of Ignacio Altamarino in the Palace of Mexico.

Again shall I descend the defiles of the Cumbres and dash at full speed through the Pass of Chiquihuite, and walk through the damp and dismal dungeons of the Castle of San Juan de Ulloa. Your flower-embowered and blood-stained shores have faded from my sight, but all these things, and a thousand other memories—bright and beautiful in the main, though occasionally tinged with sorrow and with sadness—are mine, and only death can rob me of them.

Land of history, romance, flowers, poetry, and song; land of dark and fearful deeds, violence, wrong and a terrible past; land with a present mixed and clouded, in which

"Men must die, and women must weep,"

to atone for the sins of those who came before them; land with a bright and glorious future, in which all your people,—educated and disenthralled of prejudice and bigotry—shall in truth be "sovereign, free and independent," and white-winged peace and prosperity shall walk hand in hand through all your borders, God bless thee! Adios!

www.ingramcontent.com/pod-product-compliance
Lightning Source LLC
LaVergne TN
LVHW021304110826
845150LV00003B/480

* 9 7 8 1 4 2 5 5 5 9 4 4 1 *